listening
TO JAZZ

listening TO JAZZ

BENJAMIN BIERMAN

John Jay College, the City University of New York

New York   Oxford

OXFORD UNIVERSITY PRESS

Oxford University Press is a department of the University of Oxford.
It furthers the University's objective of excellence in research,
scholarship, and education by publishing worldwide.

Oxford   New York
Auckland   Cape Town   Dar es Salaam   Hong Kong   Karachi
Kuala Lumpur   Madrid   Melbourne   Mexico City   Nairobi
New Delhi   Shanghai   Taipei   Toronto

With offices in
Argentina   Austria   Brazil   Chile   Czech Republic   France   Greece
Guatemala   Hungary   Italy   Japan   Poland   Portugal   Singapore
South Korea   Switzerland   Thailand   Turkey   Ukraine   Vietnam

For titles covered by Section 112 of the US Higher Education
Opportunity Act, please visit www.oup.com/us/he for the
latest information about pricing and alternate formats.

Published by Oxford University Press
198 Madison Avenue, New York, NY 10016
http://www.oup.com

Library of Congress Cataloging-in-Publication Data
Bierman, Benjamin.
  Listening to jazz / Benjamin Bierman.
    pages cm
  ISBN 978-0-19-997561-7 (alk. paper)
  1. Jazz--Analysis, appreciation. 2. Jazz musicians. I. Title.
  ML3506.B435 2016
  781.65'117--dc23
                                        2014039242

Printing number: 9 8 7 6 5 4 3 2 1

Printed in the United States of America
on acid-free paper

TO JOHN COPPOLA

CONTENTS

Overview   FROM SWING TO BOP: 1930–1950

Overview   BUILDING THE MAINSTREAM: 1950–1975

Overview   **INTO THE PRESENT: 1975–TODAY**

PREFACE

To the Reader

Welcome to *Listening to Jazz*. I wrote this book to help you learn about the history of jazz by discussing many of its important players, bandleaders, and composers from the early days of jazz until today. Most importantly, however, through careful, guided listening, you will learn how to listen to jazz by gaining an understanding of the basic elements that go into the creation of this exciting music.

Many students today have not had the opportunity to hear jazz. If you have heard some, perhaps it seemed a little hard to understand or difficult to relate to—it is generally quite different from the popular music you are probably used to hearing. In fact, I have heard from many people I meet who say a book like this is something they would love to read as they have always been interested in jazz but have a hard time understanding it.

On some level jazz can be complicated music, and much of it is quite sophisticated; but it is also direct, highly personal, and very expressive. If you can find a way inside the music—and I hope this book helps you do that—it will open up a whole new exciting musical world that will add to your music listening experience for the rest of your life. It takes an open mind and some effort on your part, but it's worth it!

While *Listening to Jazz* presents a historical overview of jazz from its beginnings until today, I also concentrate on giving you ways inside the music: simple things to listen for that help you appreciate the skills, commitment, and passion that went into making these beautiful recordings. I believe people can gain a better understanding and appreciation of jazz through learning the basic nontechnical inner workings of music as well as more about musicians' lives. I have tried to present some of these perspectives in this book in a variety of ways.

First, and perhaps most importantly, all of our **Listening Guides** and **Listening Focuses** examine the musical elements surrounding the style of a piece, its melody and harmony, how the tune approaches rhythm, and the types of accompaniment used. The Listening Guides give a full analysis of a key work, including a timed guide that you can use while you study the piece; the Focuses are designed to highlight just one key element, so you can focus your attention on it. The key recordings highlighted in the book's Listening Guides are available to purchase separately as a downloadable MP3 file. Your textbook may have been packaged with an information card about this downloadable file; if not, visit the website at www.oup.com/us/bierman to find a link for more information about it. There is also a Spotify playlist available for these and other recordings discussed throughout the book, and most recordings can be found on various streaming online sources. By the end of the course, through an improved understanding of these elements, you will be able to listen more actively and knowledgeably, both of which will enhance your listening experience as well as your appreciation of jazz.

Through a number of other features I give you insight, much of it from my professional experience, into what these musicians went through, in terms of both the skills needed and various aspects of a jazz musician's lifestyle, to be able to create and perform this thrilling music.

- The **Jazz Lives** sections introduce us to the musicians by providing biographies, the variety of musical experiences they have had during their careers, and what types of influences they have had on musicians as well as on jazz in general.

- The **Questions and Controversies** sections examine important issues in jazz. For example, issues surrounding race and gender are crucial to an understanding and appreciation of jazz and its place in history and culture, and controversies surrounding various subgenres of jazz such as jazz fusion and the avant-garde are an important part of jazz history and its place in the larger scheme of the music scene.

- **In Performance** brings an insider's perspective to issues such as jazz composition and arranging, spontaneous interaction in jazz, what makes jazz harmony different, important music venues, what being a musician on the road is like, what are the roles of side musicians, the roles of rhythm section players, and the roles of certain key band members.

- **Compare** offers contrasting versions of songs we present, other important related artists, and recordings showing different musical approaches from the musicians and bands featured in the Listening Guides and Focuses.

- **Overviews** placed throughout the book offer students and instructors a starting place for discussions and further study regarding the socio-historical contextualization of jazz. For example, how "The Great Migration" of African Americans from the rural south to the industrial north and west transformed jazz and blues and helped these styles to spread throughout the country, what the effects of the Great Depression and World War II had on the music business and jazz in particular, how the political climate of the 1950s influenced the broadening of styles within the jazz field, and how the shifting of liberal and conservative values reflected in the various presidential administrations affected jazz musicians and their music. These Overviews also provide timelines of **Major Musical Styles**, **Musicians and Their Musical Works**, as well as **Major Social Developments**.

- Each chapter concludes with several features:
  - **Chapter Opening Questions** are posed to highlight the key issues we will explore in each chapter.
  - **Coda: Chapter Summary** features key questions regarding the chapter's most important material along with concise answers to these important questions.
  - **Talkin' Jazz** offers key terms and their definitions.
  - **Key People** lists the musicians most important to the chapter.
  - **Think About This** includes questions for further discussion and study.
  - **Look It Up** notes key resources that can be used for further study.

- **Read All About It** links to readings from Robert Walser's *Keeping Time: Readings in Jazz History*, augmenting the text through key writings about jazz by musicians, journalists, and scholars that further elaborate and build upon issues discussed throughout the book.

Finally, I wanted to share with you some personal information about how I came to study and teach jazz. I am a trumpet player, composer, arranger, and music professor. Like most musicians, I'm not a star and never was. I played as a side musician with many big names, however, and spent most of my adult professional life toiling in the trenches that most working musicians occupy, working in many types of bands and playing many types of music. While I was building my career in New York City I performed in nightclubs and concerts both in New York City and on the road nationally and internationally with small jazz groups and big bands, blues bands, and some of the greatest Latin bands in the world. I also played R&B, funk, and nearly every other kind of dance music for parties and during the day played in the studios and performed at such diverse events as parades, outdoor concerts, and even funerals. I have been a bandleader for years in many kinds of situations, and I also produce both jazz and classical recordings. My musical experience is broad and represents a fairly typical musician's career. I also bring to the book my work as a scholar and professor, and I have been contributing articles to various publications such as peer review journals and collections of essays while teaching in higher education for 14 years.

Through my own experiences, I can tell you musicians are hard-working people and frequently work under extremely difficult circumstances. One typical day when I was working with Johnny Pacheco, one of Latin music's greatest stars, we played an afternoon outdoor concert two hours out of town (during which my girlfriend and mother had to avoid the drunken knife fights), got back to New York City, played in a nightclub in Queens from 10:00 p.m. to midnight, went to another club in Manhattan where we played from 1:00 to 3:00 a.m., and then took the subway to uptown Manhattan where we played from 5:00 to 8:00 a.m. at an illegal after-hours club. After that I was on my way home on the rush-hour train with everyone else going to work, bleary-eyed, exhausted, and with swollen lips from playing so much.

When I was touring with the Johnny Copeland Blues Band (that at times included rock-blues guitarist Stevie Ray Vaughn and avant-garde jazz saxophonist Archie Shepp), we traveled around the entire country in a crowded van pulling a trailer with our equipment. We would drive all day, get to the next town in time to unload and set up the equipment, change our clothes, play three sets of music in a bar that smelled of smoke and stale beer, and hope we could find a place to eat before going to bed around 3:00 in the morning, only to get up early and drive to the next town to do it all over again.

I also toured with a territory big band on the mid- and southwest ballroom circuit. We played seven nights a week for months on end, traveling in a bus, arriving in time to set up and change, and hoping to find a place to eat. We would leave early the next morning, and some members would not bother to sleep at night, choosing to drink instead and then sleep all day on the bus. Some would overdo it and find themselves seriously hungover or sick the next day, only to begin the entire process again. While you may have a romantic idea of what life on the road as a working musician is, the reality is often that the hours are long, the pay can be poor, and the work is grueling; yet this is how we learn our craft, and many cherish this lifestyle as well as the music.

Along with this, jazz musicians have practiced their craft intensely, care deeply about what they do, and have often sacrificed simpler and more secure lives to pursue a career as musicians. They use their creative abilities to produce music to express themselves and to entertain and enlighten us through their emotional, personal, and dynamic music. This music comes in many forms and styles, which you will see throughout the book, as jazz has gone through many changes and continues to do so. That is part of its dynamism in fact. Jazz is alive and growing, and musicians continue to expand the notions of what jazz is and can be. I sincerely hope that you enjoy *Listening to Jazz*!

Acknowledgments

I would like to thank and acknowledge several people for their help along the way in my musical life. I would first like to thank trumpet player extraordinaire John Coppola, my earliest musical mentor. My life as a professional musician began when I walked through his front door and up the steps. John assumed I was there to become a professional musician before I even knew that was possible and taught me everything I needed to know to begin a career in music. Philip Rupprecht has served as a mentor in the academic world, and without him I never would have entered it. Once I ventured into academia, Joseph Straus served as a model of

JAZZ STYLES TIMELINE

CHAPTER	1870	1900	1910	1920	1930	1940
2	Country/Folk 1870s–present Ragtime c. 1880s–1915 Classic Blues 1920s–1940s					Urban Blues 1945–present
3	New Orleans Jazz c. 1880s–1920					
4			Chicago Jazz 1917–1930			
5			New York Jazz 1920–1930			
6			Kansas City Jazz 1920s–1940s			
7–9					Swing Era 1935–1945	
10						Bebop c. 1944–1952
11						
12						
13						
14						
15						

professionalism for me. Joe also introduced me to my editor at Oxford University Press, Richard Carlin, without a moment's hesitation when I spoke of my desire to write this book. Henry Martin, Lewis Porter, John Howland, Jeffrey Taylor, and John Graziano also helped to shepherd me into the world of professional scholarship.

At Oxford University Press, Richard Carlin, Executive Editor, has been invaluable at every stage and with every aspect of the development of this book. I can't imagine anyone better to have helped me through the writing of *Listening to Jazz*—he is a true Renaissance man. I would also like to thank Richard's editorial assistant Emily Schmid for all of her help; the marketing team of Clare Cashen and Jeffrey Yerger; my production editor Jane Lee; and the designer Bonni Leon-Berman.

Without peer reviewers we would all be lost, so for their time, expertise, and crucial input, I would like to thank David Adler, Queens College, Aaron Copland School of Music; Lynn Baker, University of Denver; James Balentine, University of Texas–San Antonio; Philippe Charles Baugh, Tarrant County College; T. Dennis Brown, University of Massachusetts; Jay C. Bulen, Truman State University; Charles Hines, University of North Florida; Tammy Kernodle, Miami University; Anthony Marasco, University of Scranton; Brian McCarthy, Johnson State College; Michael Morreale, the College of Staten Island–City University of New York; Bruce Raeburn, Tulane University; Teri Roiger, State University of New York–New Paltz;

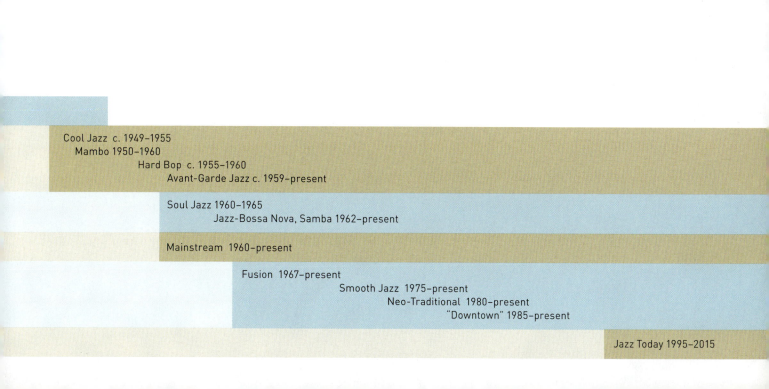

1950   1960   1970   1980   1990   2000+

Cool Jazz c. 1949–1955
Mambo 1950–1960
Hard Bop c. 1955–1960
Avant-Garde Jazz c. 1959–present

Soul Jazz 1960–1965
Jazz-Bossa Nova, Samba 1962–present

Mainstream 1960–present

Fusion 1967–present
Smooth Jazz 1975–present
Neo-Traditional 1980–present
"Downtown" 1985–present

Jazz Today 1995–2015

Jeffrey Taylor, Brooklyn College and the Graduate Center, City University of New York; Craig Thomas, University of Delaware; Gordon Vernick, Georgia State University; and Robert Walters, Seton Hall University. Special thanks also to John Wriggle, City University of New York, who served in this capacity as well as many others throughout the process.

Along the way I picked up the phone and called some friends when I needed help, and trumpeters Michael Morreale and Barry Bryson, pianists Adam E. Morrison and Lucy Galiher, drummer Terry Silverlight, bassist Kermit Driscoll, saxophonist Lou Caputo, and pianist-composer Whitney Ashe were there when needed. The insights of Peter Manuel, percussionist-bandleader Bobby Sanabria, and guitar and tres player, Benjamin Lapidus were crucial to my discussion of Latin jazz. Saxophonist-composer-arranger Bill Kirchner has also always been there for me in numerous ways.

Finally, I would like to thank my three sons, Emanuel, Leo, and Eli, who, more than anyone else, help me to believe in myself.

listening TO JAZZ

INTRODUCING JAZZ

1st Chorus What Is Jazz?

Imagine this scene. It's Saturday night at a dance club packed with people. They are all dressed in stylish, maybe even outlandish clothes. The music is vibrant, pulsing, and exciting, inspiring each dancer to outdance the next person. You can barely move on the dance floor, yet the dancers are almost acrobatic. The music drives on and on, taking the crowd to new heights. All of a sudden, the band breaks it down and plays a slow, sexy song, letting the energy in the club vibrate and sizzle, the dancers relaxing into a sensual groove, while also anticipating the next driving beat. The band lives up to the expectations, cranking it up and slamming the dancers with a driving and relentless tempo. The dancers drive the band on and the band drives the dancers on, and this amazing symbiotic energy builds and builds until the dancers and the band can hardly stand it. The set comes to a dynamic conclusion, and, exhausted and energized, the band and the dancers feel both disappointment and relief. While the dancers and the band both need a rest, and a trip to the bar or their tables is welcome, the dancers can't wait for the next set to begin.

This could be any Saturday night with any band during almost any era. But in this case, the band is a jazz big band and the year is 1938. Most of you, if you had been a young adult at this time, would have been a jazz fan and would have been at that club dancing to a music that is currently quite unfamiliar to you. You probably can't imagine why you would dance to jazz. Perhaps you have heard very little of it, or maybe you have never heard a jazz performance.

In this book, we will concentrate on how to listen to jazz as we discuss the history of the music and its musicians from the early days of jazz until today. Many people find jazz challenging and difficult to understand. I have heard many people say, "I like the beginning and end of the song when everyone plays together, but I get lost with the stuff in the middle." This is perhaps the most basic issue that we hope to address: what is "the stuff in the middle," and what's going on at the beginning and the end of the compositions?

Let's start, however, with a more basic question that is challenging to answer: what is jazz?

In this chapter, we will answer these questions:

- What Is Jazz?
- What Are the Elements of Jazz?
- What Is the Role of Composition and Arranging in Jazz?
- What Are the Different Types of Jazz Instrumentation?
- What Are the Various Types of Jazz Ensembles?

Photo by William P. Gottlieb. Courtesy William P. Gottlieb Collection and Library of Congress.

read all about it

"The Negro Artist and the Racial Mountain" by Langston Hughes

Walser, **Keeping Time,** *Chapter 14*

In this early essay, the famous Harlem Renaissance poet discusses the importance of jazz as an African American expression.

WHAT IS JAZZ?

Jazz seems to be impossible to define in a way that makes anyone very happy. Countless articles and books have made valiant, valid, and fascinating attempts to define it, yet none are wholly satisfactory. Most agree that jazz must **swing** and that **improvisation** is essential to the character of the music. (See "2nd Chorus: What Are the Elements of Jazz?" for further discussion of these key terms.) Not everyone agrees with either of these characterizations, suggesting, for example, that the notion of swing is subjective and comes in many forms, that some music in the jazz tradition can be fully notated and composed, and that other forms of music incorporate improvisation.

Even if we had a good definition, it would certainly be under a process of continual reevaluation. Jazz is always headed in unexpected and exciting directions. In addition, it is quite common for musicians to reject the label "jazz" entirely, insisting the term, in fact any term or label, is necessarily limiting, and instead simply refer to themselves as "musicians." Some things are certain however.

Jazz is an African American cultural and artistic contribution created in the United States, and it has been an important force in both the popular and artistic cultural life of the United States for the last 100 years. Though we cannot (or choose not to) define it, we can certainly learn to appreciate this magnificent and multifaceted music.

Jazz is primarily a blend of African American and European influences. But African Americans *created* jazz, and the vast majority of the important innovators in jazz have been black. There are, and have always been, many white and Latino/a jazz musicians, as well as jazz musicians from many cultures and countries; and many of these musicians have made extremely important contributions and innovations as well.

Jazz is one of America's most important artistic cultural contributions and one of its crucial cultural exports. Jazz has been embraced throughout the world and has wielded great influence over the music of different cultures around the globe. Latino and Latina musicians have expanded jazz, adding an entirely new and sophisticated approach to rhythm. Styles such as jazz fusion and smooth jazz that embrace rock, funk, pop, hip-hop, and other styles have been popular for many years; and the influences upon jazz continue to increase as musicians embrace different types of music from around the world and incorporate them into their musical styles.

Some refer to their seemingly jazz-oriented music simply as "improvised music" because the various influences they draw on make their music difficult to describe, yet the improvisation that generally characterizes jazz is central to their aesthetic. Other musicians and critics have a more narrow definition of jazz, perhaps limiting it to specific styles and approaches. This is an extremely complicated and contentious debate, and it is not this book's intent to solve these issues. Rather, we are interested in closely examining musicians generally associated with the jazz world and the music of great value that they have created and in expanding the reader's ability to understand and appreciate a broad spectrum of music in the jazz tradition.

The Roots of Jazz

Many of the earliest African influences arrived with the slave trade from West Africa. There are distinct differences in approach between traditional West African and European music makers. European/Western classical music tends to favor a fully developed melody, supported by a harmonic accompaniment in the form of a series of chords and performed in a fixed meter. The African aesthetic emphasizes multiple rhythms performed simultaneously, accompanying short, repeated melodic riffs. Further, while African music making tends to be communal, with music serving specific social functions, European concert music tends to be performed by individuals and is removed from specific functionality (other than for aesthetic enjoyment). While Western music is usually written down (or *notated*), African music was traditionally learned aurally and passed down from player to player. These are very broad generalizations, but they help to show how these cultures approach music making differently as well as how these different approaches complement each other.

The mixture of African and European elements in jazz has resulted in a music that is both harmonically and rhythmically sophisticated, employs improvisation and notated compositional practices, is a form of high art while also being a functional music (e.g., for dancing), and requires technical skill and precision (e.g., intonation, articulation, ensemble playing, and precise rhythmic control) while also highly valuing personal expression (e.g., the ability to manipulate pitch, the importance of the creation of a personal tone and vocabulary, and rhythmic control of various approaches to swing).

Jazz is often discussed as having a lineage—a natural progression from one style to the next. This is quite deceptive and questionable in some respects, though it makes sense in others. All timelines, of course, make the false assumption that when one period or musical style "ends," it is surpassed by the next and is never heard of again. In fact, musical styles have a tendency to repeat themselves in new circumstances, and the history of jazz (like that of all music) combines musicians' respect for past styles with their own need to innovate and build on them. When bebop was first heard, many fans of swing were appalled by the new music, while the boppers felt the swing fans were outdated. However, bebop did not replace swing, nor did it totally negate swing; in fact, many bebop compositions were based on the chord progressions of earlier swing-era hits.

There are also a number of political and cultural issues that are crucial to jazz and its place in society. Race is certainly primary in this regard, including issues such as appropriation of black music by white performers; but issues such as gender, class, and economics are also of vital interest. While these issues are acknowledged as crucially important here, it is not this book's intention to comprehensively cover the various controversies that surround them, as each instructor will take his or her own approach to these issues. They do, however, arise throughout the book as natural outgrowths of the history of jazz.

2nd Chorus What Are the Elements of Jazz?

Discussing the essential elements of jazz is the best way to initially become acquainted with this exciting genre of music.

Individual Expression

In jazz, emphasis is placed on **individual expression** beyond all else, and this is perhaps its most outstanding quality. While there is a shared repertoire and a basic musical language of jazz, each player strives for a personal tone and a unique vocabulary that distinguishes him or her from others. Therefore, the best jazz instrumentalists, composers, and arrangers are **stylists**; and the knowledgeable listener can generally immediately recognize their sound, playing style, and compositional approach.

There is no one standard for what is a good tone, for example. A trumpeter's tone can be dark and searching, like Miles Davis's (1926–1991, Chapter 13), while another's can be bright and playful, as is Clark Terry's (b. 1920). A saxophonist's tone can be solid and stately, almost unadorned, as was John Coltrane's (1926–1967, Chapter 13), or romantic and lush, like Dexter Gordon's (1923–1990). Even drummers have a tone. Elvin Jones (1927–2004, Chapter 13) and Jack DeJohnette (b. 1942, Chapter 14) could not be more different in their sounds, yet both are consummate jazz drummers. There is no single technical standard. In fact, that concept is anathema to jazz, a music that demands personality and individuality.

Melody, Harmony, and Rhythm

Melody, harmony, and rhythm are the building blocks of any musical structure. These are immense and complex subjects whose subtleties and nuances are beyond the scope of our discussion here. A few thoughts on them, particularly in relation to jazz, will be helpful however.

Melody is the combining of pitches and rhythm to create a musical line. The melody is generally the musical element of a composition that we most notice and remember. In jazz the melody is often called the **head** and is generally played at the beginning and end of a tune. When combined with harmony and rhythm, melodies have an endless variety of aesthetic and emotional qualities.

During their solos players are also creating melody, but since they are improvising they are essentially creating spontaneous compositions. To do this, all jazz players spend countless hours creating and expanding a unique musical vocabulary to use during their solos. They then combine the various elements of their vocabulary in innumerable ways to create continually shifting and varied solos. In some instances, for example, in the course of a long tour or in an ensemble with steady personnel, elements of solos, or even entire solos, can become routine, allowing the ensemble to hit supportive rhythmic figures behind the soloist or to create **breaks**, melodic and rhythmic figures that the entire ensemble plays together.

Soloists in different eras in jazz history have often tended to have different approaches to the creation of melody during their solos. For example, swing players leaned toward a simpler melodic style, more akin to the character of a tune's actual melody. Bebop players, while also creating beautiful melodies, tended toward busier and often more technically complicated solos while at times incorporating more sophisticated harmonies in their playing. In the late 1950s and 1960s, players such as saxophonist John Coltrane and pianist Cecil Taylor (b. 1929) introduced a soloing style that became so complicated and full of flurries of notes during the course of extended solos that to some there seems to be a lack of traditional melodic content. It is, however, just another style and form of personal expression, and this type of long and extremely complicated solo continues to be quite common in modern jazz. It is perhaps this style that is hardest for new jazz listeners to relate to and understand. When listened to with open minds and ears, all of these styles have the ability to be wildly expressive and beautiful and are well worth the effort to understand and appreciate.

Harmony is the combining of notes to create chords. For example, the notes C, E, and G are combined to create a C major chord and F, A, and C are combined to create an F major chord. When a series of chords are presented in sequence, they create a **chord progression**. A transition from a C major chord to an F major chord and back to a C major chord is an example of a chord progression.

The history of Western harmony goes back to ancient Greece and has a long and fascinating evolutionary history. Jazz harmony is a product of this tradition, and jazz musicians have added a high level of harmonic sophistication to it. Chords in jazz are particularly rich, full, and colorful. Also, jazz musicians have to have excellent harmonic skills because harmony is the basis of much of their improvisation (see "Improvisation"). As we will see in our listening examples throughout this book, harmony in jazz ranges from quite complex (for example, in the rich harmonic sensibility of pianist Art Tatum [1909–1956, Chapter 5]) to quite simple (as in the modal soloing of Miles Davis on his *Kind of Blue* album, Chapter 13).

Rhythm is central to all music but is very difficult to define. One way to speak of it is as a movement or pulse. Within this pulse is a pattern of strong and weak **beats** that creates **meter**.

Jazz was originally a dance music, and this tradition continues through a rhythmic dynamism that characterizes jazz. Traditionally in jazz the most common meter is 4/4. This contains 4 beats, with strong accents on beats 2 and 4 that create a **backbeat**. This immediately becomes more complicated, however, because these beats and their division are more flexibly interpreted in jazz than in, for example, Western classical music. In jazz, the rhythm is manipulated to create various types of swing, and we will hear many varieties of swing throughout the various jazz eras. Other meters commonly used in jazz are 3/4 and 6/8, and contemporary players are now regularly playing in an astonishing array of meters as rhythm in jazz continues to evolve.

Another crucial element in jazz is the use of **polyrhythm**, two or more simultaneous rhythmic patterns. For example, a jazz drummer will generally be playing four separate rhythmic patterns (two with the hands and two with the feet), while often suggesting at least two different meters, such as 4/4 and 6/8, simultaneously. This is a key feature of African music and plays a large role in African American music. Another crucial rhythmic feature in jazz is **syncopation**, the use of accents that go against the basic meter. Ragtime, one of the precursors to jazz, is rich in syncopation; listen to Scott Joplin's (ca. 1867–1917) "Maple Leaf Rag" to hear how the melody is syncopated against the regular oompah of the bass (Chapter 2).

Improvisation

The art of improvisation is essentially spontaneous composition, and it is a primary element in jazz. Almost the entire jazz repertoire relies upon improvisation as a central element. A common format in jazz is that the group plays the melody of the song, the members of the band then each improvise on the chord progression of the song, and the band plays the melody again to conclude (see "Form"). The art of improvisation is made to look easy by the greatest players, but it requires immense concentration and quick musical and physical reflexes. Each player has a rather specific role in this process (see "What Are the Different Types of Jazz Instrumentation?"). Jazz musicians constantly take in a huge amount of musical information from their bandmates, immediately process it, and then react with their fully formed musical statement. This is quite an amazing feat and is the essence of jazz.

A special type of improvisation known as **collective improvisation** was common in early New Orleans jazz ensembles. In the most common approach to this style the trumpet played the melody in a loose and improvised manner, the clarinet played arpeggios and fast runs, and the trombone provided support for the bass part, simple fills, and tailgate-style *counterlines* (melodic lines that complement the melody). Meanwhile the accompanying instruments (banjo or guitar, piano, bass, drums) would be more loosely synchronized than in bands that played from written arrangements. Because there were no written parts, the band was said to be collectively improvising an arrangement on the fly.

WHAT ARE THE ROLES OF COMPOSITION AND ARRANGING IN JAZZ?

Composition and arranging are essential elements in jazz. Using melody, harmony, rhythm, texture, timbre, and form, composers create compositions and musical frameworks. At times it takes a secondary role to improvisation, but improvisers base their performances on the formats created by composers and arrangers. The history of jazz composition and arranging is rich, and we shall explore it throughout the book.

Form

Musical **form** has numerous layers. The first level is the actual form of the tune itself, such as a 12-bar blues (see Chapter 2) or a 32-bar AABA Tin Pan Alley popular song (see Chapter 4). The next level is an overall form that involves the shaping of numerous choruses of these tunes. The creation of this overall form is called **composing** or **arranging** and is sometimes created by the group as a whole, sometimes by one person in the band, or, in the case of larger ensembles, perhaps by a separate arranger.

Form can take many shapes in jazz, but there are some traditional forms that characterize much of jazz. The type of instrumentation greatly affects the form that groups use. Smaller ensembles tend to have less complicated arrangements, while larger ensembles often have pieces with quite complex musical schemes. A typical small jazz group format is melody (head)—solos—melody. In other words, the melody is played, some or all of the band members play improvised solos, then the melody is played again. Possible additions to this form might be a composed ensemble passage for one *chorus* (one time through the form of a song) somewhere during the tune. This passage might occur somewhere in the middle of the tune but commonly will precede the final melody statement.

Frequently, the final chorus (or part of the final chorus) will be a climactic ensemble statement called a **shout chorus**, particularly in big-band writing, which embellishes the tune in some way. The dramatic ending of Count Basie's (1904–1984, Chapter 6) "One O'Clock Jump" is just one of many famous examples of the use of a shout chorus. Horn backgrounds are also common. For example, during a trumpet solo in a big-band setting, the saxes might play some kind of simple figure behind the soloist, encouraging the soloist to take the solo to new heights.

During extended big-band compositions, any or all of these techniques, as well as others, are often combined to make sophisticated compositions with many parts, often greatly stretching the song's form or perhaps going well beyond standard song forms. The notion of form is always changing, and today's players and composers are creating new and exciting forms that at times bear little resemblance to traditional jazz.

WHAT ARE THE DIFFERENT TYPES OF JAZZ INSTRUMENTATION?

Understanding the instruments in jazz is a great place to begin to develop your listening skills. Each of the instruments has unique qualities, and there is also a wide range of styles, tones, and approaches among players of a given instrument.

Because so much emphasis is placed upon individuality, understanding the instruments and being able to observe these various styles and approaches is crucial to the appreciation of jazz. For this reason, we will provide some examples of well-known players for each instrument and describe some characteristics of their styles. You may wonder why these lists are dominated by men; historically, women unfortunately had less opportunity to perform in jazz groups (until at least the 1970s) and were thus less often recorded and heard—with the exceptions of, for example, pianists such as Lillian Hardin Armstrong (1898–1971), Lovie Austin (1887–1972) (Chapter 4), and vocalists such as Billie Holiday (1915–1959) or Ella Fitzgerald (1917–1996) (Chapter 9).

Instruments in jazz are placed into two general categories, the **horns** and the **rhythm section**. In jazz parlance, the term "horn" refers to any wind instrument, whereas in classical music it refers to a specific instrument. The most common horns in jazz are the trumpet, saxophone, clarinet, and trombone. The rhythm section refers most commonly to some combination of piano, guitar, bass, and drum kit.

Louis Armstrong, ca. 1946. Armstrong was the first great master of jazz trumpet, elevating the instrument to a lead role in the music.

Photo by William P. Gottlieb. Courtesy William P. Gottlieb Collection and Library of Congress.

Trumpet

The **trumpet** is a member of the brass instrument family and is in the range of an alto or soprano voice—midrange to high in pitch. It is made of metal and has a mouthpiece in which the trumpet player's lips vibrate to create the sound (just as the vibration of the vocal chords creates our voices). A combination of tension of the lips, tongue placement, and the various ways that the three piston-like valves are depressed or opened create the notes. It is often thought of as having a bright tone, and it can be powerful and loud.

The trumpet player in a band often serves the function of a straw boss, acting as the lead instrument. In a big band (discussed in Chapter 7), the trumpet often sets the phrasing for the band and has a powerful influence on the swing and the feel of the music. The trumpet always stands out, and any mistakes trumpet players make are often the most noticeable. However, the trumpet is also capable of being soft, pretty, lyrical, and dark.

The trumpet family has some relations that are often found in jazz as well. The **flugelhorn** looks larger than a trumpet and is quite dark and mellow, with a full, rich tone. The **cornet**—often featured in early jazz before the trumpet gained greater popularity—is smaller than a trumpet and has a more veiled, warmer tone that does not have the trumpet's cutting quality.

Saxophone

The **saxophone** is a member of the woodwind family, but the instrument is made of metal. It comes in a variety of sizes, the most common, ranging from low to high, are baritone, tenor, alto, and soprano sax. Sax players can usually play several types of saxophones but generally specialize in one. Notice that the various saxophones correspond to the range of voice types.

The sax has a mouthpiece that holds a reed made of bamboo or other flexible material. The player places the mouthpiece and reed between the lips, and blowing across the reed creates the vibration that in turn creates the sound. Saxes have a very complicated collection of keys, and players use many key configurations to create the various notes. The most commonly played saxes in jazz are the alto and tenor.

Table 1.1 *Notable Trumpeters*

Name/Dates	Importance	Discussed in Chapter
Louis Armstrong (1901–1971)	An early jazz star as trumpeter and vocalist and one of the most important trumpeters in jazz	1
Bix Beiderbecke (1903–1931)	An early jazz star known for his lyrical playing and "bell-like" tone	2
Roy Eldridge (1911–1989)	An extroverted soloist from the swing era with a powerful and exciting upper register	5
Dizzy Gillespie (1917–1993)	Bebop innovator with a flashy, high-flying style	10
Miles Davis (1926–1991)	Trumpeter-bandleader who played with an extremely lyrical and sensitive sensibility	13
Lee Morgan (1938–1972), Freddie Hubbard (1938–2008)	Fearless, extroverted trumpet soloists known most for their small group playing	11 and 14
Jon Faddis (b. 1953), Snooky Young (1919–2011)	Powerful and confident lead trumpet players in a big-band setting	
Clark Terry (b. 1920), Art Farmer (1928–1999)	Mainstream soloists with distinctive styles	
Chet Baker (1929–1988)	Cool jazz soloist and vocalist with a lyrical melodic sensibility	11
Lester Bowie (1941–1999), Raphe Malik (1948–2006), Don Cherry (1934–1995), Bill Dixon (1925–2010), Leo Smith (b. 1941)	Avant-garde or "free jazz" trumpeters that frequently employ(ed) extended trumpet techniques	12
Woody Shaw (1944–1989)	Bold player with a modern harmonic approach borrowed more from saxophone players than is usual for trumpeters	14
Wynton Marsalis (b. 1961)	A stylist who reveres the jazz tradition while also creating a contemporary sound; perhaps the most visible spokesperson for jazz today	14
Tom Harrell (b. 1946), Brian Lynch (b. 1956), Terence Blanchard (b. 1962), Dave Douglas (b. 1963), Ingrid Jensen (b. 1966), Roy Hargrove (b. 1969), Nicholas Payton (b. 1973), Jeremy Pelt (b. 1976)	Trumpeters playing in the jazz tradition with contemporary sensibilities	15

The baritone is used in the big-band saxophone section, and there are also numerous soloists on the instrument, such as Harry Carney (1910–1974), Gerry Mulligan (1927–1996, Chapter 11), Cecil Payne (1922–2007), Pepper Adams (1930–1986), Nick Brignola (1936–2002), Hamiet Bluiett (b. 1940, Chapter 14), and Claire Daly (b. 1958). Fewer players specialize on the soprano sax, but most professional players play it in addition to their main horn (playing more than one instrument is referred to as a **double**, and the ability to play a variety of

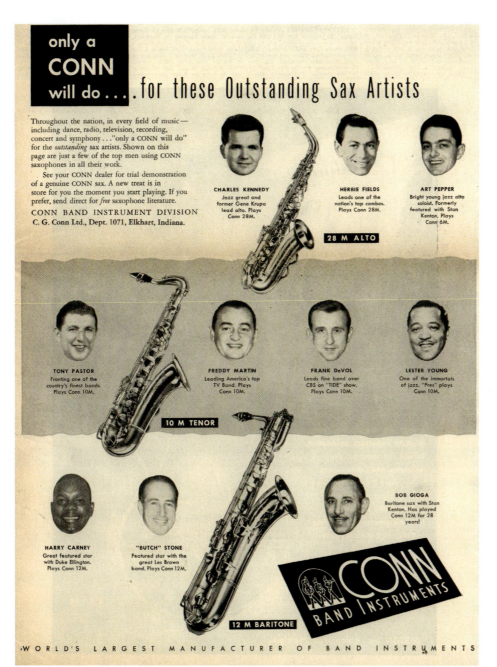

This 1950s advertisement for Conn saxophones shows the difference between alto, tenor, and baritone instruments. Jazz players like Art Pepper and Lester Young were so well known that their photos were used to help promote the instruments.
Courtesy BenCar Archives.

woodwinds, such as flute and clarinet, is a common professional requirement). Sidney Bechet (1897–1959, Chapter 3), an important early jazz instrumentalist, played the soprano sax and clarinet.

The sax player's role in certain types of bands is to be a "showstopper," creating exciting, charged solos that take advantage of the technical resources of the instrument, such as its ability to play fast throughout its range and to play shrieking high notes and honking low notes. This is not universally true, of course, and some players are more circumspect and introverted in their playing; but listening to John Coltrane and his "sheets of sound" or to a saxophone ensemble in a piece for big band by composer-cornetist Thad Jones (1923–1986) provides examples of saxophonists' abilities to play highly technical and note-filled solos and ensembles.

Table 1.2   *Notable Alto and Tenor Saxophone Players*

Name/Date	Importance	Discussed in Chapter
Alto Sax Players		
Benny Carter (1907–2003)	Alto sax and trumpet, and influential composer-arranger	5
Johnny Hodges (1906–1970)	Duke Ellington's (1899–1974) lead alto player for over 30 years who is known for his lyrical playing	8
Charlie Parker (1920–1955)	The brilliant bebop innovator	10
Ornette Coleman (b. 1930)	An influential avant-garde jazz player, composer, and bandleader	11
Cannonball Adderley (1928–1975)	Took Parker's melodic style in a new direction	12
Eric Dolphy (1928–1964)	An avant-garde stylist	14
Jimmy Lyons (1931–1986)	Lyrical avant-garde player	14
Anthony Braxton (b. 1945)	Avant-garde player and composer	14
Kenny Garrett (b. 1960)	Brings a modern mainstream approach to contemporary jazz	15
Miguel Zenón (b. 1976)	Brings a Latin influence and a complicated approach to meter to jazz	15
Tenor Sax Players		
Coleman Hawkins (1904–1969)	Brought the tenor sax to the fore as a main solo instrument in jazz	5
Lester "Prez" Young (1909–1959)	Prominent sax player with Count Basie; carried forward Hawkins' melodic innovations	6
Ben Webster (1909–1973)	Key sax player with Ellington; beginning in 1939, along with bassist Jimmy Blanton, introduced an exciting new era in Ellington's work	8
Dexter Gordon (1923–1990)	Carried forward a swing-oriented style well into the '70s and '80s	14
Sonny Rollins (b. 1930)	Known for high-powered, melodically inventive extended solos	14
John Coltrane (1926–1967)	The most influential modern stylist	10
Wayne Shorter (b. 1933)	Economical and lyrical player known for his work with Miles Davis, Weather Report, and his own groups; also one of jazz's major composers	14
Michael Brecker (1949–2007)	Modern stylist who was also a jazz fusion innovator	14
Joe Lovano (b. 1952)	Contemporary player who works in a number of different styles, ranging from traditional to avant-garde	15
Chris Potter (b. 1971)	Displays a technical ability that, mixed with his sensitive musicality, makes for a muscly, intense, and expressive style	15

Players, of course, have a wide variety of tones on the various saxes; and these can range from lyrical and gentle (as is the case with Dexter Gordon on tenor and Johnny Hodges [1906–1970] on alto) to brilliant and hard-edged (such as the playing of Michael Brecker [1949–2007] on tenor and Eric Dolphy [b. 1931] on alto).

Clarinet

The **clarinet** is generally made of hard wood, is part of the woodwind family, and is played with a reed attached to a mouthpiece in the same manner as the saxophone. It has a wide range, and in its lower register it has a dark, rich tone, while the upper register is powerful and bright. The clarinet played an important role in New Orleans–style jazz, and its popularity continued through the swing era with star players and bandleaders such as Benny Goodman (1909–1986) and Artie Shaw (1910–2004). Its popularity waned after the swing era, becoming more important as a "double"; but the instrument has made a comeback recently with numerous contemporary players concentrating on it as their primary instrument.

Trombone

The **trombone** is a member of the low brass family. In its upper register (the higher notes in its range) it can be quite bright, but generally it has a dark, full, and mellow sound. It is a lower-register instrument and can cover parts of the ranges of bass, baritone, and tenor vocalists.

Benny Goodman, ca. 1946. Goodman did much to popularize the clarinet as a lead instrument in jazz.
Photo by William P. Gottlieb. Courtesy William P. Gottlieb Collection and Library of Congress.

Table 1.3	*Notable Clarinetists*	
Name/Dates	**Importance**	**Discussed in Chapter**
Johnny Dodds (1892–1940)	Early New Orleans clarinetist that played with Louis Armstrong, "King" Oliver, and Jelly Roll Morton	3
Larry Shields (1893–1953)	Early New Orleans clarinetist, known for his work with the Original Dixieland Jazz Band	3
Leon Roppolo (1902–1943)	Early New Orleans style clarinetist from Chicago, known for his work with the New Orleans Rhythm Kings	3
Barney Bigard (1906–1980)	New Orleans clarinetist that performed with "King" Oliver in Chicago and is known for his work with Duke Ellington	
Benny Goodman (1909–1986), Artie Shaw (1910–2004), Woody Herman (1913–1987)	Clarinetists and star swing big-band leaders	7
Buddy De Franco (b. 1923)	Known for being one of the few bebop clarinetists	
Ken Peplowski (b. 1959)	Contemporary clarinetist known for playing in traditional New Orleans and swing styles	
Anat Cohen (b. 1975), Don Byron (b. 1958)	Contemporary clarinetists that bring other musical influences to their playing such as Brazilian and klezmer styles	15

A major distinguishing factor of the trombone is that a slide rather than valves (as with the trumpet) changes the pitch, along with the lips and the tongue. This gives the instrument a unique quality and creates advantages and challenges. Trombonists have great control over their pitch because of their ability to minutely adjust their slide, so bending notes and sliding into and out of notes is stylistically common. This can be seen in an early trombone style, **tailgating**, that involves the exaggerated sliding in and out of notes. At the same time, intonation is a challenge—knowing exactly where to place the slide is difficult for beginning players. Because of the inherent limitations of the instrument, trombonists tend to be more economical in their choices of notes; but they are also capable of technical brilliance.

Rhythm Section

The rhythm section of a band works together as a unit to provide a rhythmic and harmonic accompaniment for a tune's melodies and soloists. They also combine to create the swing (or groove). The piano and guitar provide harmonic support in a rhythmic fashion and are also important soloists in most ensembles. The drums and bass are the heartbeat of the band as they are central to creating the swing. The two instruments have a particularly close and intimate relationship to each other, and their ability to play together well ("lock in") is crucial to the success of any band.

Piano

The **piano** is perhaps the most versatile instrument in jazz as it can function in virtually any type of group as well as being a solo instrument. Since the advent of electric pianos and synthesizers, **keyboard** has sometimes become the word of choice as it refers to both electronic and acoustic keyboard instruments. However, while electronic instruments are commonplace in jazz now (even laptops and sampling are now becoming jazz "instruments"), some people still favor acoustic piano.

As a member of the rhythm section in all types of groups, the piano functions as an accompanist and as a soloist. As an accompanist, the pianist **comps** (short for accompanies), playing chords behind the horns as they play the melody and

Miff Mole playing the trombone at Nick's jazz club in New York City, ca. 1946. Mole was among a group of players reviving New Orleans–style jazz in the 1940s, using the popular "tailgating" style on the instrument.
Photo by William P. Gottlieb. Courtesy William P. Gottlieb Collection and Library of Congress.

Table 1.4	*Notable Trombonists*	
Name/Dates	**Importance**	**Discussed in Chapter**
Edward "Kid" Ory (1886–1973)	An early trombonist who played with King Oliver and recorded with Louis Armstrong's Hot Five and Seven groups. He used the slide to create the slurs, smears, and slides typical of the tailgate style. His big tone, and its rough, percussive edge set the standard for the trombone in early jazz	3
Joe "Tricky Sam" Nanton (1904–1946)	Made sensational use of the plunger mute and was featured with the Duke Ellington Orchestra. His uncanny ability to make the trombone sound like a human voice was featured in compositions such as Ellington's "Black and Tan Fantasy" (Chapter 8)	8
Jack Teagarden (1905–1964)	A smooth and lyrically oriented trombonist and a swing band leader	
Bill Harris (1916–1973)	A featured soloist with Woody Herman's (1913–1987) big band, Harris broadened the instrument's technical abilities and helped bring the trombone into the bebop era	
J. J. Johnson (1924–2001)	A soloist, composer, and arranger. His group with fellow trombonist Kai Winding (1922–1983) took the instrument's capabilities to a new level, both technically and musically	
Melba Liston (1926–1999)	Trombonist-composer-arranger, who was one of the rare women instrumentalists to play regularly in major swing bands; also involved in both bebop and post-bop movements	
Bob Brookmeyer (1929–2011)	A valve trombonist with a fluid, melodic style. His playing was based in the bebop tradition but with a contemporary sensibility. Also an innovative composer, particularly for big band	15
Slide Hampton (b. 1932)	An excellent soloist and composer-arranger in the big-band style	
Curtis Fuller (b. 1934)	Brought elements of the rough-hewn early trombone styles into the world of hard-bop while also creating a new contemporary approach to the instrument	
Julian Priester (b. 1935)	Brought a sophisticated and understated approach to both hard bop and more avant-garde musical settings	
Conrad Herwig (b. 1959)	A contemporary player who thrives in many musical environments	

solos. Chords (groups of three or more pitches) provide the harmonic structure for the songs. Pianists also provide rhythmic support for the melodies and solos as they comp, working closely with the rest of the rhythm section to provide a firm and swinging groove for the soloist. They also listen carefully to the soloist and react to what he or she is doing. Listeners often overlook the skill of an accompanist, but musicians revere these fine players, who are generally profound soloists yet spend much of their careers making others sound terrific (see the discussions of pianist Tommy Flanagan [1930–2001], bassist Milt Hinton [1910–2000], and drummer Jack DeJohnette in Chapter 14).

Pianists can also be talented soloists, and since they are using two hands and the entire keyboard, they are able to play chords and melody at the same time. This allows pianists to create both harmonically and melodically and gives them great creative

Table 1.5	*Notable Pianists*	
Name/Dates	**Importance**	**Discussed in Chapter**
"Jelly Roll" Morton (1890–1941)	One of jazz's earliest and most influential pianists and composers	3
Earl "Fatha" Hines (1903–1983), James P. Johnson (1894–1955), Art Tatum (1909–1956), Willie "The Lion" Smith (1893–1973), Thomas "Fats" Waller (1903–1940)	Stride piano specialists that expanded the harmonic palette of jazz	Hines: 4 Johnson: 2 Tatum, Smith, and Waller: 5
Teddy Wilson (1912–1986)	Swing stylist	
Mary Lou Williams (1910–1981)	Pianist-arranger-composer whose style progressed from Kansas City swing to early bebop	6
Thelonious Monk (1917–1982), Earl "Bud" Powell (1924–1966), Barry Harris (b. 1929)	Bebop innovators, each with a distinct style	Monk and Powell: 10
Dave Brubeck (1920–2012)	Helped to popularize a "West Coast" style and incorporated classical music resources in his work	11
Oscar Peterson (1925–2007)	Followed in the tradition of the stride pianists with immense technique and a rich harmonic vocabulary	
Bill Evans (1929–1980)	Influential stylist with a rich and personal harmonic vocabulary	13
Hank Jones (1918–2010), Red Garland (1923–1984), Tommy Flanagan (1930–2001), Wynton Kelly (1931–1971), Ronnie Matthews (1935–2008), Kenny Barron (b. 1943)	Known as important pianists in their own right, but also known as exceptional accompanists	Flanagan: 14
Cecil Taylor (b. 1929), Muhal Richard Abrams (b. 1930), Andrew Hill (1931–2007), Carla Bley (b. 1938)	Avant-garde pianists-composers-bandleaders	Taylor and Bley: 14 Abrams: 12
Marian McPartland (1918–2013), Erroll Garner (1923–1977), Ahmad Jamal (b. 1930)	Traditionalists who helped popularize jazz to a larger audience	
McCoy Tyner (b. 1938), Herbie Hancock (b. 1940), Chick Corea (b. 1941), Keith Jarrett (b. 1945)	Four of the most influential contemporary pianists	Tyner and Hancock: 13 Corea and Jarrett: 14
Joanne Brackeen (b. 1938), Marilyn Crispell (b. 1947), Michele Rosewoman (b. 1953), Renee Rosnes (b. 1962), Bill Charlap (b. 1966), Brad Mehldau (b. 1970), Vijay Iyer (b. 1971), Jason Moran (b. 1975)	Contemporary pianists, each with extremely different approaches and relationships with the jazz tradition	Moran, Mehldau and Rosnes: 15
Eddie Palmieri (b. 1936), Michel Camilo (b. 1954), Danilo Pérez (b. 1965)	Contemporary pianists who bring a Latin influence to jazz	Palmieri: 12 Pérez: 15

freedom. As with all other instruments in jazz, an individual approach is required, and there are many varied playing styles both from era to era and within eras.

Guitar

The **guitar** has long been an important instrument in jazz, but its role was originally rather basic. In early jazz bands, the guitarist would generally strum a steady beat, acting as both a harmonic instrument and a timekeeper. Today, the guitar functions in ensembles much like the piano. It accompanies the soloists and the ensemble and can also be a soloist. With the rise of guitar in popular music, guitarists have also increasingly become important bandleaders.

In contemporary jazz, the guitar has become even more prominent and one of the more popular instruments for young music students interested in jazz—as well as other musical genres—to take up (see Chapter 15). This has occurred for many reasons, including the fact that young jazz musicians have increasingly been interested in a variety of genres. Rock, funk, and R&B, originally greatly influenced by jazz, have now conversely become important influences on the jazz world.

Bass

The **bass** has both harmonic and timekeeping roles in the rhythm section. It plays the important beats in a steady fashion, constantly keeping the music pushing forward, while at the same time providing a solid harmonic foundation to the music.

Gypsy guitarist Django Reinhardt performing in New York City, ca. 1946. Reinhardt is playing an archtop guitar featuring a large body that gave the instrument enough volume to be heard in a larger group.
Photo by William P. Gottlieb. Courtesy William P. Gottlieb Collection and Library of Congress.

Table 1.6 *Notable Guitarists*		
Name/Dates	**Importance**	**Discussed in Chapter**
Lonnie Johnson (1899–1970), Eddie Lang (1902–1933)	Early and influential jazz guitarists	Johnson: 3 Lang: 4
Django Reinhardt (1910–1953), Freddie Green (1911–1987), Charlie Christian (1916–1942), Mary Osborne (1921–1992)	Swing-era guitarists; Christian generally credited with popularizing the electric guitar and single-note melody playing in jazz	Reinhardt: 12 Green: 6 Christian: 7
Wes Montgomery (1923–1968), Barney Kessel (1923–2004), Joe Pass (1929–1994), Jim Hall (1930–2013), Kenny Burrell (b. 1931), Grant Green (1935–1979), George Benson (b. 1943), Emily Remler (1957–1990)	Influential post-swing era mainstream guitarists and bandleaders	Montgomery: 12 Hall and Benson: 14
John McLaughlin (b. 1942), Larry Coryell (b. 1943), Pat Martino (b. 1944), Lee Ritenour (b. 1952), Mike Stern (b. 1953), Al Di Meola (b. 1954)	Fusion-oriented guitar players	McLaughlin and Coryell: 14
Bucky Pizzarelli (b. 1926), Gene Bertoncini (b. 1937), Howard Alden (b. 1958), Peter Bernstein (b. 1967)	Contemporary guitarists working in a traditional style	
Derek Bailey (1930–2005), Sonny Sharrock (1940–1994), James "Blood" Ulmer (b. 1942), Glenn Branca (b. 1948), Fred Frith (b. 1949), Elliot Sharp (b. 1951), Henry Kaiser (b. 1952), Eugene Chadbourne (b. 1954)	Avant-garde guitarists	Frith and Sharp: 14
John Abercrombie (b. 1944), Bill Frisell (b. 1951), John Scofield (b. 1951), Pat Metheny (b. 1954), Stanley Jordan (b. 1959), Ben Monder (b. 1962), Kurt Rosenwinkel (b. 1970)	Contemporary guitarists that bring a wide range of influences to their music, challenging what some feel are the established norms of jazz	Metheny: 14 Frisell, Scofield, Monder, and Rosenwinkel: 15

People tend to assume that the drums are responsible for keeping time in a band, but some believe it is actually the bass that has that responsibility in jazz, particularly since the bebop era when the drummer's bass drum was liberated from its role of playing every beat. In 4/4 meter (the most common meter in much of jazz), the bass keeps time (the steady beat or groove) either by playing beats 1, 2, 3, and 4 (called **walking** or **playing in 4**) or by playing beats 1 and 3 (called **playing in 2**). Bassist Walter Page (1900–1957), famous for his work in Count Basie's rhythm section, was one of the pioneers of the walking bass style.

Table 1.7	*Notable Bassists*	
Name/Dates	**Importance**	**Discussed in Chapter**
George Murphy "Pops" Foster (1892–1969)	One of jazz's earliest bassists, known for a "slap" bass style. Foster worked with such New Orleans artists as Sidney Bechet, "King" Oliver, Louis Armstrong, and "Kid" Ory	
Wellman Braud (1891–1966)	An early Duke Ellington bassist who helped develop the "walking bass" style, often using a percussive slap technique	
Jimmy Blanton (1918–1942)	Also gained fame with the Ellington orchestra and introduced a more melodic style and freed the bass a bit from its traditional role	8
Ray Brown (1926–2002), Paul Chambers (1935–1969), Percy Heath (1923–2005), Sam Jones (1924–1981)	Had big, broad sounds that solidly anchored most of the major players and bands in jazz while also having sophisticated solo styles	
Milt Hinton (1910–2000)	Played with most of the major players in jazz, and is one of the most recorded musicians in history	14
Oscar Pettiford (1922–1960)	An innovative player who ushered the bass into the bebop era	
Scott LaFaro (1936–1961)	Particularly in his work with the Bill Evans Trio, made the bass an equal partner in the group while also advancing the melodic and rhythmic possibilities for the instrument	13
Charles Mingus (1922–1979)	One of jazz's greatest composers and bandleaders, with an aggressive playing style	13
Ron Carter (b. 1937)	Has recorded with nearly all the major artists in jazz over the last 50 years while also working as a leader and featured soloist	13
Charlie Haden (1937–2014)	Specialized in more intimate and avant-garde settings, and known for a virtuosic, yet economic, highly personal, and expressive style	11
Jaco Pastorius (1951–1987)	Helped to bring the electric bass to prominence in jazz while also expanding its technical capabilities and its role in a band	14
Steve Swallow (b. 1940), Dave Holland (b. 1946), John Patitucci (b. 1959)	Ever-present in many contemporary jazz groups	
Christian McBride (b. 1972)	A first-call side musician and leads numerous ensembles of various sizes	15
Will Lee (b. 1952)	One of the most in-demand recording electric bass players in numerous styles, including jazz and jazz fusion	
Esperanza Spalding (b. 1984)	Has quickly made many waves with her relaxed and swinging bass playing and singing that incorporates numerous contemporary genres	15

Throughout the history of jazz, the acoustic bass has been prominent; but since the 1970s, the electric bass has assumed an important role as well. For practical reasons, most bass players play both instruments, and while some are equally adept on either instrument, most specialize on one or the other. While the two instruments have the same tuning and perform the same basic function in a band, they have many differences and suit different types of repertoire.

Drums

The **drums** are also responsible for keeping time, but while the bass supplies solidity, the drums provide the energy and excitement. Drummers are generally thought to be loud and flashy, and though they often are, there is great diversity in jazz drumming; and the approach a drummer takes is crucial to the "feel" of a band. They can be bombastic and drive a band unmercifully, yet they can also be quiet and subtle.

The **drum kit** (or drum set) evolved from the separate parade drums used in New Orleans. The basic components of the kit are bass drum (played with a foot pedal), a snare drum (played with drumsticks and used to accent important beats and rhythms), ride cymbal (played with sticks and used in jazz since the 1940s to keep time with a more or less steady pattern), and hi-hat (a double cymbal that is clapped together by a foot pedal and also played with sticks). Extra cymbals are added, as are extra, slightly deeper drums called tom-toms (they come in a wide variety of sizes). The drummer has at his or her disposal a variety of sticks—from bare wood sticks to mallets covered with felt to metal brushes—that he or she can use to greatly vary the sound and feeling of each percussion instrument. Jazz drumming has evolved from rather simple timekeeping to what can at times be incredibly complex and technical playing.

During the later 1910s through the mid-1920s, recording technology was still rather primitive. The sound of a full drum kit could not be properly balanced with the other instruments and would have overwhelmed the melody or lead players. For this reason, drummers often had to use simpler percussion instruments, such as woodblocks, in order to keep the basic beat. Later, often for novelty reasons, many drummers developed elaborate kits, such as Sonny Greer (1895–1982) of the Duke Ellington (1899–1974) band, who had at his disposal a full drum kit, woodblocks, chimes, gongs, and other novelty percussion instruments.

Vocalists

One issue that is often difficult for those who are not acquainted with jazz is the fact that jazz is largely an instrumental genre, but vocalists are also prominent and important throughout its history. Classic blues singers were important in early jazz, during the swing era male and female singers were important parts of the big bands, and singers working with their own small groups have also always been extremely popular.

Singers, of course, sing lyrics to popular jazz and pop tunes as well as original compositions; and their place in jazz continues to expand as the field itself expands, in both mainstream jazz and the avant-garde. Many singers, but not all by any means, **scat sing** by creating syllabic sounds for improvised solos, a style made popular by Louis Armstrong (1901–1971) and Ella Fitzgerald. Another important technique is **vocalese**, whereby singers write and perform lyrics to famous improvised solos by instrumentalists such as Charlie Parker (1920–1955, Chapter 10) and John Coltrane (Chapter 13).

WHAT ARE THE VARIOUS TYPES OF JAZZ ENSEMBLES?

Jazz bands come in a number of standard configurations. The most basic and common way to refer to them is by the number of players in the band, such as trio,

Table 1.8 *Notable Drummers*		
Name/Dates	Importance	Discussed in Chapter
Warren "Baby" Dodds (1898–1959), Arthur James "Zutty" Singleton (1898–1975)	New Orleans style drummers; Dodds played with several early bands led by King Oliver and Louis Armstrong	
Sid Catlett (1910–1951)	Drummer whose career spanned early jazz and bebop; helped evolve jazz drumming into a more flexible style with his solid and swinging playing	
Chick Webb (ca. 1909–1939)	Drummer and bandleader who influenced Buddy Rich (1917–1987) and Louie Bellson (1924–2009)	5
"Papa" Jo Jones (1911–1985), Kenny "Klook" Clarke (1914–1985)	Helped to move timekeeping from the bass drum to the cymbal, and Clarke was an innovator in the bebop style	Clarke: 10
Max Roach (1924–2007), Roy Haynes (b. 1925)	Early bebop innovators who freed the various parts of the drum set, such as the bass and snare drums as well as the cymbals	Roach: 10 and 11
Tony Williams (1945–1997), Jack DeJohnette (b. 1942)	Innovative modern drummers	Williams: 13 DeJohnette: 14
Elvin Jones (1927–2004)	Known for his work with John Coltrane and as a bandleader; had a powerful sound	13
Art Blakey (1919–1990)	Drummer and bandleader who launched the careers of generations of musicians	11
Al Foster (b. 1943), Billy Higgins (1936–2001), "Philly Joe" Jones (1923–1985), Billy Hart (b. 1940), Ben Riley (b. 1933)	Side musicians with quiet and understated styles	
Billy Cobham (b. 1944), Steve Gadd (b. 1945), Peter Erskine (b. 1954), Vinnie Colaiuta (b. 1956), Terry Silverlight (b. 1957), Steve Jordan (b. 1957)	Jazz fusion drummers	
Cindy Blackman (b. 1959), Sherrie Maricle (b. 1963), Terri Lyne Carrington (b. 1965)	Dynamic and powerful contemporary drummers who have proven that the drums are not a male-only instrument	

quartet, quintet, sextet, septet, all the way to the more open-ended term, "big band." Each format has unique qualities and characteristics.

Trio

The most common type of trio consists of piano, bass, and drums. In this case, the pianist is generally the leader, although the interaction between the three players is crucial to the success of the group. Some trios, such as the Ahmad Jamal

Table 1.9 *Notable Vocalists*		
Name/Dates	**Importance**	**Discussed in Chapter**
Bessie Smith (1894–1937), Ethel Waters (1896–1977), "Ma" Rainey (1886–1939)	Classic blues and jazz singers	2
Louis Armstrong (1901–1971)	Trumpeter crucial to the development of popular and jazz singing	3
Jimmy Rushing (1901–1972), Big Joe Turner (1911–1985)	Kansas City blues shouters	6
Billie Holiday (1915–1959), Ella Fitzgerald (1917–1996), Anita O'Day (1919–2006), Carmen McRae (1920–1994), Peggy Lee (1920–2002), Sarah Vaughan (1924–1990), Betty Carter (1929–1998), Abbey Lincoln (1930–2010)	Classic female jazz singers that performed with big bands and small groups	9
Billy Eckstine (1914–1993), Frank Sinatra (1915–1998), Joe Williams (1918–1999), Nat King Cole (1919–1965), Tony Bennett (b. 1926)	Classic male jazz singers with big bands and small groups	9
Louis Jordan (1908–1975), Louis Prima (1910–1978), Dinah Washington (1924–1963), Ray Charles (1930–2004)	R&B-jazz artists	9 and 12
Eddie Jefferson (1918–1979), King Pleasure (1922–1981), Lambert, Hendricks and Ross (Dave Lambert 1917–1966, Jon Hendricks b. 1921, and Annie Ross b. 1930), Mark Murphy (b. 1932)	Important vocalese performers	
Andy Bey (1939), Carmen Lundy (b. 1954), Cassandra Wilson (b. 1955), Diana Krall (b. 1964), Theo Bleckmann (b. 1966), Kurt Elling (b. 1967), Madeleine Peyroux (b. 1974), Gretchen Parlato (b. 1976)	Contemporary jazz vocalists	15

(b. 1930), Hampton Hawes (1928–1977), and Erroll Garner (1923–1977) trios, use carefully constructed arrangements, while others, such as the Bill Evans (1929–1980) Trio, have a looser format and greatly value extemporaneous interaction and equality among the members. Pianist and singer Nat "King" Cole (1919–1965) had an influential trio that consisted of piano, guitar, and bass and featured his vocals as well as his piano playing. Contemporary piano trio leaders such as Jason

Moran (who at times very creatively employs a DJ using samples), Cyrus Chestnut, Renee Rosnes, and Brad Mehldau are keeping this tradition alive.

There are many possibilities in a trio configuration however: guitar, bass, and drums; a front-line horn, piano, and bass; and a front-line horn, bass, and drums are a few of the possibilities.

Quartet

The jazz quartet is also a standard format. Most commonly, this includes a rhythm section (often piano, bass, and drums but guitar can replace the piano) and a featured horn player or vocalist. If fronted by a horn player, the group generally takes his or her name (for example, the John Coltrane Quartet), and the horn player is often the bandleader and sets the musical direction. If a vocalist is featured, the group takes on the name of the vocalist, and the rhythm section often gets separate billing, such as Ella Fitzgerald, featuring the Tommy Flanagan Trio (see Chapter 14). In the latter, the pianist (Flanagan in this case) usually serves as musical director.

Quintet

The jazz quintet is perhaps the most standard format and most commonly has two horns, piano, bass, and drums (again, guitar can replace piano). Most often the horns will be a trumpet and some kind of sax, but it could be anything, such as trombone and sax or trumpet and trombone. This format requires a more compositional approach to what the horns play than does a quartet as it has to have some kind of musical arrangement for the horns.

Sextet

By adding one more horn, a jazz sextet can be created. This creates an extra soloist, of course; but three horns (as opposed to two in a quintet) also greatly enhance the opportunities for a composer-arranger. For example, a common sextet instrumentation (trumpet, sax, trombone, piano or guitar, bass, and drums) allows various combinations of timbres. Three horns gives the arranger the opportunity to employ a block-chord style of writing, the most common writing style in jazz, which has the horns all playing together in harmony stacked upon each other.

Typically, the trumpet plays the melody, the sax a harmony just below the trumpet, and the trombone a harmony just below the sax. Different timbres and textures can be created as the sax or trombone can play the melody while the others either lay out (do not play) or accompany in some fashion. It is a very flexible format. Drummer Art Blakey (1919–1990) led a sextet for many years (with constantly changing personnel), and players in his band created a rich compositional and arranging repertoire that set the standard for this type of group from the 1950s through the 1980s.

Miscellaneous Small Groups

Other possibilities of relatively small instrumentation that are not as common but are frequently used are octets (four horns and four rhythm or five horns and three rhythm) and nonets (five horns and four rhythm or six horns and three rhythm).

Big Band

The term **big band** is a very flexible one and can indicate anywhere from approximately ten to forty players. A typical big band is seventeen pieces, with five saxes (two altos, two tenors, and one baritone), four trumpets, four trombones (three tenor trombones and one bass trombone), and four rhythm (piano, guitar, bass, and drums); but any combination is possible, such as three trumpets, two trombones, three saxes, and four rhythm or two trumpets, one trombone, three saxes, and four rhythm.

The big band was the standard ensemble in the swing era (Chapters 7–9) but has been around since early jazz and continues today as an important ensemble in jazz. For instrumentalists, playing in a big band requires the ability to be a strong ensemble player, perhaps more so than in a small group. Also, since it is a large band format, the solos are generally short and require a different type of discipline from the longer solos more typically found in smaller groups.

Big-band music is a format that relies heavily on composer-arrangers and is often the ensemble of choice for composers working in jazz as its large and varied instrumentation has an inexhaustible array of possibilities for **timbre** (the "color" or character of sound) and **texture** (the number of instrumental voices sounding simultaneously). Key big bands from various eras will be discussed throughout this book, but some contemporary ensembles include compositions and arrangements by ambitious composers such as Bob Brookmeyer (1929–2011), Jim McNeely (b. 1949), Maria Schneider (b. 1960), John Hollenbeck (b. 1968), and Darcy James Argue (b. 1975).

CODA Chapter Summary

What Is Jazz?

- Jazz as a musical genre defies easy definition, but most people agree that jazz must swing and that improvisation is essential to the character of the music.
- Jazz is an African American cultural and artistic contribution created in the United States, and it has been an important force in both the popular and artistic cultural life of the United States for the last 100 years.
- Jazz is originally the product of African and European musical traditions, but other races and cultures have made significant contributions to expanding the genre.

What Are the Elements of Jazz?

- Individual expression, melody, harmony, rhythm, improvisation, composition, and arranging are all key elements of jazz.

What Is the Role of Composition and Arranging in Jazz?

- Composition and arranging are essential elements in jazz. Using melody, harmony, rhythm, texture, timbre, and form, composers create compositions and musical frameworks.

What Are the Different Types of Jazz Instrumentation?

- Instruments in jazz are generally categorized into horns, which include the trumpet, saxophone, clarinet, and trombone, and rhythm section, which includes the piano, guitar, bass, and drums.

What Are the Various Types of Jazz Ensembles?

- Jazz ensembles come in a number of standard configurations and are commonly named for the number of musicians. Jazz bands typically range in size from a trio to a big band.

Talkin' Jazz (Key Terms)

Backbeat
Bass
Beat
Big band
Break
Chord progression
Clarinet
Collective improvisation
Comp
Composing (or Arranging)
Cornet
Double
Drum
Drum kit
Flugelhorn

Form
Guitar
Harmony
Head
Horn
Improvisation
Individual expression
Keyboard
Melody
Meter
Piano
Playing in 2
Polyrhythm
Rhythm
Rhythm section

Saxophone
Scat sing
Shout chorus
Stylist
Swing
Syncopation
Tailgating
Texture
Timbre
Trombone
Trumpet
Vocalese
Walking (or Playing in 4)

Think About This (For Further Discussion and Study)

1. Explain why jazz as a genre is difficult to define.
2. Describe how the horns and the rhythm sections in a jazz band function differently.
3. Listen to a jazz trio and then to a big band. Compare and contrast what you hear.
4. Explain how West African musical traditions influenced jazz, and provide examples.
5. Give examples of the prevalence of racism in the early history of jazz.

Look It Up (Key Resources)

Gennari, John. *Blowin' Hot and Cold: Jazz and Its Critics.* Chicago: University of Chicago Press, 2006.

Giddins, Gary. *Visions of Jazz: The First Century.* New York: Oxford University Press, 1998.

———. *Weather Bird: Jazz at the Dawn of Its Second Century.* New York: Oxford University Press, 2004.

Gioia, Ted. *The History of Jazz,* 2nd ed. New York: Oxford University Press, 2011.

Kernfeld, Barry, ed. *The New Grove Dictionary of Jazz.* New York: Oxford University Press, 2003.

Kirchner, Bill, ed. *The Oxford Companion to Jazz.* New York: Oxford University Press, 2000.

Roberts, John Storm. *Latin Jazz: The First of the Fusions, 1880s to Today.* New York: Schirmer Books, 1999.

———. *The Latin Tinge: The Impact of Latin American Music on the United States.* New York: Oxford University Press, 1979.

Walser, Robert, ed. *Keeping Time: Readings in Jazz History,* 2nd ed. New York: Oxford University Press, 2014.

Ward, Geoffrey C., and Ken Burns. *Jazz: A History of America's Music.* New York: Knopf, 2000.

Williams, Martin. *The Jazz Tradition,* 2nd rev. ed. New York: Oxford University Press, 1993.

PRE-JAZZ
1865–1910

MAJOR MUSICAL STYLES

Pre-1860	• Worksongs ("field hollers"), spirituals, dance music
1860–1880	• Minstrel songs • Early country blues
1890s	• Ragtime • Brass-band music
1895–1910	• Early New Orleans jazz and parade bands formed

The development of jazz coincided with a period of great changes in American culture and technology. The Civil War put an end to slavery, and in its immediate aftermath there were several important changes that occurred to integrate African Americans into American society. In 1866, the Civil Rights Act was passed by Congress that gave African Americans citizenship and granted them equal rights with whites. However, in a foreboding note of the tensions that still existed in American society, the same year saw the birth of the Ku Klux Klan, a white supremacist group, in Tennessee. The tension between those seeking racial equality and those fighting to preserve segregation would continue to grow over the coming decades. A decided setback for equal rights was the 1896 Supreme Court decision known as *Plessy v. Ferguson*, which legalized "separate-but-equal" facilities for blacks and whites.

In the aftermath of the Civil War, many of the freed African Americans remained living on large farms, transitioning from being slaves to being share-croppers. Under the new system, they would work a piece of land and pay the owner shares of the income received from selling the food or animals that they raised. Back-breaking work, abuse by landlords, low possibility for self-advancement, and dire poverty led many to move off the land and into the growing new urban centers, first in the South and eventually farther north and west. New musical styles would develop that reflected this change in lifestyle. Pre–Civil War African American music focused on work songs (so-called "field hollers"), religious songs (spirituals), and dance music (for recreation). With the move to urban areas, however, new musical styles arose such as the blues and dance-band music.

Beginning around 1870, a major influx of new immigrant groups came into the United States, including Italians, Germans, Irish, eastern European Jews, and Spanish-Caribbeans. All were seeking increased opportunities for work and many for less discrimination than they had faced in their home countries. While most of the European immigrants entered this country through the major eastern cities—primarily New York—the Spanish-Caribbean contingent often came in through southern ports of entry, like New Orleans. This rich mixture of immigrants from different cultures brought new musical styles, instruments, and ensembles with them. This led to new hybrid musical forms incorporating African, European, and Spanish-Caribbean elements.

Sheet Music, cover showing Christy's [sic] Minstrels. Note how the troupe is shown both in "normal" clothing and in their stage costumes, including blackface makeup.
Courtesy BenCar Archives.

Most of the immigrants ended up crowded into ghettos in the major cities, including New York, Chicago, and New Orleans. They formed a growing audience for new musical styles. Music halls sprang up that charged minimal admissions and became centers to experience the new music, along with fairs and expositions that drew wide crowds to experience the new wonders of late nineteenth-century life. Sheet music was equally inexpensive and widely sold. Ethnic songs were common both to celebrate and sometimes to satirize the different new immigrant groups; minstrelsy was widely popular; and ragtime—a showy new piano style—also swept the nation as a fad in the 1890s–1900s.

From the late 1800s to the early 1900s, a newly educated class of African Americans was struggling with continued racism and inequality in America. Various perspectives were brought forth to solve these inequities. Among the early and influential African American thinkers to tackle this entrenched discrimination were Frederick Douglass, an early supporter of education as a means of improving the lives of African Americans, and W. E. B. DuBois, who became a leading intellectual during the Harlem Renaissance of the 1920s. In 1909, DuBois was one of the moving forces behind the founding of the National Association for the Advancement of Colored People (NAACP), dedicated to gaining equal rights for blacks.

W. E. B. DuBois, c. 1910. DuBois was one of the leading thinkers of the period, who proposed that African Americans improve their lives through education.
Courtesy Library of Congress.

1865–1910

MUSICIANS/MUSICAL WORKS

1867	• Scott Joplin, ragtime pianist-composer, born
1873	• W. C. Handy, songwriter, born • Jack "Papa" Laine, New Orleans bandleader, born
1877	• Buddy Bolden, New Orleans cornet player, born
1880	• James Reese Europe, bandleader, born
1887	• Lovie Austin, pianist-bandleader, born
1890	• Jelly Roll Morton, pianist-composer, born • Freddie Keppard, cornet player, leader Creole Jazz Band, born • Paul Whiteman, bandleader, born

1893	• Willie "The Lion" Smith, pianist, born
1894	• Bessie Smith, blues vocalist, born • James P. Johnson, jazz pianist-composer, born
1895	• Joe "King" Oliver, New Orleans cornet player-bandleader, born • Buddy Bolden forms his first band in New Orleans, credited as among the first jazz ensembles
1897	• Sidney Bechet, New Orleans clarinet-saxophone player, born • Fletcher Henderson, bandleader-arranger, born
1898	• Lil Hardin [Armstrong], pianist-composer-bandleader, born

1899	• Publication of "Maple Leaf Rag" by Scott Joplin, first major ragtime success, selling over 1 million copies • Duke Ellington, pianist-composer-bandleader, born		• William "Count" Basie, pianist-bandleader, born • Glenn Miller, trombone player-bandleader, born
1901	• Louis Armstrong, cornet/trumpet player-bandleader-vocalist, born • Frank Trumbauer ("Tram"), Chicago-based saxophonist, born	ca. 1905	• Chick Webb, drummer-bandleader, born
1903	• Bix Beiderbecke, cornet player, born • Earl Hines, pianist-bandleader, born	1907	• Rex Stewart, cornet player, born • Benny Carter, alto saxophonist-bandleader, born
1904	• Coleman Hawkins, tenor saxophonist, born • Fats Waller, pianist-composer, born	1908	• Alberto Socarrás, flutist-bandleader, born
		1909	• Art Tatum, pianist, born • Lester Young, saxophonist, born • Benny Goodman, clarinetist-bandleader, born

1865–1910

MAJOR SOCIAL DEVELOPMENTS

1860–1865	• Civil War	1895	• First flat disc ("gramophone") record introduced • First successful radio transmission by Italian inventor Guglielmo Marconi • Leading African American speaker and author Frederick Douglass dies
1866	• Congress passes the Civil Rights Act, which gives African Americans citizenship and grants them equal protection under the law • The white supremacist group the Ku Klux Klan (KKK) holds its first meeting in Tennessee	1896	• In *Plessy v. Ferguson*, the Supreme Court allows for segregated, or "separate-but-equal," public facilities
1877	• Thomas Edison introduces the first working phonograph	1897	• Storyville established in New Orleans as a zone where prostitution was permitted; gave new opportunities for musicians to perform
ca. 1880s–ca. 1910s	• Major influx of eastern and southern European immigrants into major US cities	1906	• First AM radio station opens but broadcasts only speech, no music
1882	• Electric light introduced in New York City, mostly for the homes of the wealthy	1909	• The National Association for the Advancement of Colored People (NAACP) is founded to promote African American rights

PRECURSORS OF JAZZ | 1870s-1890s

1st Chorus The Blues

WHAT ARE THE BLUES?

When we say we have "the blues," usually we're referring to being sad or melancholy. And it is true that many **blues** songs express sad or angry feelings, whether related to love affairs gone wrong, bad working conditions, or illness. But not all blues songs are sad, and the feeling of being blue is only a part of how we define a blues song.

Exactly when the first blues song was composed or who was the first blues musician is unknown. Some trace the roots of the blues to earlier southern African American song styles, including work songs, religious songs, and particularly "field hollers." Workers picking tobacco or cotton would "sing" to each other, as a means of communication or simply to pass the time. For example, Louisiana-born singer-guitarist Lead Belly (Huddie Ledbetter, 1888–1949) recalled the holler "Bring Me Little Water, Silvie," in which the singer called out for the water boy to bring him a drink in the hot noontime sun. Lead Belly also recalled the holler "Go Down, Old Hannah," in which the singer begs the sun to set so that his hard workday will be over.

The Different Types of Blues

There are further complications when we try to define what is a blues song. The name "the blues" has been applied to a wide variety of musical performances beginning in the late nineteenth century through today. To simplify matters, many writers distinguish between three types of blues that developed in roughly chronological order:

1. **Country** or **folk blues** (late nineteenth century–1930s–today)
2. **Classic blues** (1920s–1940s)
3. **Urban** or **electric blues** (1940s–today)

Country blues is typically a solo performer playing guitar and singing. These artists played the blues and a variety of popular music for entertainment and dancing in informal settings. The Mississippi Delta region produced many important country blues artists, such as Robert Johnson (1911–1938),

In this chapter, we will answer these questions:

- What Are the Blues?
- What Is Ragtime?
- How Did Ragtime Influence the Birth of Jazz?

Photo: © Everett Collection Historical/Alamy.

Son House (Eddie James House, Jr.; 1902–1988), and Charlie Patton (ca. 1887–1934), though blues artists came from many areas of the South as well as the North. Some "country" blues singers, like Blind Blake (of Chicago; Arthur Blake, ca. 1896–ca. 1934) and Blind Willie McTell (from Atlanta; William Samuel McTier, ca. 1898–1959), spent most of their careers performing in cities.

The "classic" blues singers took country blues and popularized it through their performances, and the performance venues moved from bars, clubs, and more informal settings to theaters and other large spaces, such as vaudeville stages, as well as touring shows. While female performers are relatively rare in urban blues—the late Koko Taylor (1928–2009) and Shemekia Copeland (b. 1979), daughter of the late Texas blues artist Johnny Copeland, are exceptions to this rule—and even more so in country blues, classic blues singers are typically women. Bessie Smith (1894–1937), Gertrude "Ma" Rainey (1886–1939), and Mamie Smith (1883–1946) are all important classic blues singers; and they brought to the music a female aesthetic and emotional point of view that broadened the issues expressed in the blues.

Urban blues took the country blues aesthetic and urbanized it as African Americans from the South migrated north to industrial centers such as Chicago and Detroit from the mid-1930s through the postwar years. Many well-known urban blues artists were originally from the Delta area, including Muddy Waters (McKinley Morganfield, 1913–1983) and Howlin' Wolf (Chester Arthur Burnett, 1910–1976). The music was amplified (e.g., electric guitar and microphones for vocals and harmonica), and piano, drums, and bass were added. As the blues began to be performed by groups, as opposed to the solo country blues performers, the form became more standardized to allow bands to play together effectively.

There is a distinguishing format for many blues songs called the **12-bar blues**. The 12-bar form, at its most basic, is divided into three 4-measure phrases with the lyrics (or melody) repeating for the first two phrases and a third phrase that responds, creating a compact AAB form. The chord progression is also quite standardized, consisting of the I (first phrase), IV (second phrase), and V back to I (third phrase) chords of a major or minor key. Along with a standardized form, the blues sound is characterized by what are referred to as **blue notes**, primarily the third and fifth notes of a given scale or chord, that are slightly flattened to give a bluesy effect. Performers of the classic blues of the 1920s and the urban blues of the 1940s–today most closely follow the 12-bar blues form. Earlier country blues musicians were looser in their playing, often stretching the form in creative ways and sometimes ignoring it entirely. Creative musicians always push the boundaries of any form, so while the 12-bar blues style is a starting point, it is rarely exactly replicated.

The 12-bar blues is one of the more standard forms used in jazz, and the ability to play the blues effectively, while not an absolute requirement, is generally thought crucial to being a serious professional jazz artist. Blue notes are also a part of nearly all jazz musicians' vocabulary, though, of course, some employ them more effectively than others. The popular blues chord progression is also a staple of many jazz compositions, although in jazz this progression is generally elaborated on quite significantly while still managing to maintain its character.

While the blues and jazz are related and jazz is certainly deeply imbued with a blues aesthetic, the two types of music have evolved in more of a parallel fashion. It could be said that the blues influenced jazz more than the other way around, though some blues artists, such as the Texas guitarist T-Bone Walker (1910–1975), play in a sophisticated melodic fashion that is influenced by jazz. Though the forms remain tied today, early jazz was perhaps the time when the connection between blues and jazz was the strongest. This is apparent in the recordings of Bessie Smith, who was often accompanied by early jazz performers. One example is "Back Water Blues," on which she is accompanied by stride pianist James P. Johnson. We will see many other connections between jazz and blues throughout this book: the blues was central to the Kansas City sound in the 1920s and 1930s (see Chapter 6), saxophonist-vocalist Louis Jordan effectively combined the blues and swing in the 1940s (see Chapter 9, 3rd Chorus), and the blues was central to soul jazz of the 1950s and 1960s (see Chapter 12, 1st Chorus).

Bessie Smith

Bessie Smith, known at the height of her popularity as "The Empress of the Blues," was among the top "classic blues" singers of the 1920s. Though a blues singer, her work is also closely associated with jazz; and she was quite influential in the development of jazz singing. Smith's terrific vocal technique, her powerful and clear voice, and her emotional intensity combine to create dramatic and compelling vocal performances.

read all about it
"The Sexual Politics of Women's Blues" by Hazel B. Carby

Walser, **Keeping Time,** *Chapter 11*
A contemporary musicologist discusses the importance and impact of the female blues singers of the 1920s.

Smith grew up in abject poverty, partially the result of the early death of her parents. She began her career singing in the streets of her hometown, Chattanooga, Tennessee, by busking (performing for tips), eventually moving on to her first professional job in a touring troupe. Ma Rainey, known as "The Mother of the Blues," was also in the group. Rainey was an early blues artist who helped to take the male-oriented country blues style and develop it into the more female-centric classic blues genre.

As the recording industry realized the potential in the commercial marketplace for the blues, it began to produce so-called race records, recordings directed to the African American market. Smith, having gradually made her way up the professional ladder, was signed by Columbia Records and immediately had a hit with "Downhearted Blues," accompanied by pianist Clarence Williams (1893–1965). Eventually 2 million copies were sold, numerous other vocalists and groups performed the song, and it is considered to have influenced both jazz and rock music. Vocalist Alberta Hunter (1895–1984) and pianist-composer-arranger Lovie Austin (see Chapter 4, 3rd Chorus) composed the song.

Smith's career skyrocketed, and she became the highest-paid African American performer during this period. She went on to work with pianist-bandleader Fletcher Henderson, who we will encounter in Chapter 5, 1st Chorus. As was true for many artists, the depression derailed Smith's career; but she continued performing and recording into the early 1930s. Smith can be seen in a short film, *St. Louis Blues*, in which she performed the famous W. C. Handy song accompanied by an orchestra led by James P. Johnson.

Smith died from injuries sustained in a car crash in 1937, traveling late at night after performing at a small club. Her death is a tragic occurrence that is all too common for musicians as they have frequently relied upon touring for their livelihood.

Bessie Smith in the 1920s. Notice her elaborate dress and jewelry; Smith's stage outfits rivaled the costumes of today's biggest pop stars.
© Everett Collection Historical/Alamy.

JAZZ LIVES   JAMES P. JOHNSON

James P. Johnson (1894–1955) is a pianist and composer who was born in New Brunswick, New Jersey. His playing and composing were influential upon the stride piano style, sometimes referred to as "Harlem stride piano," an important East Coast solo piano style (discussed in Chapter 5, 4th Chorus) that absorbed ragtime, blues, popular music, and jazz styles, as well as compositional techniques and forms from Western classical music. Along with Jelly Roll Morton, Johnson's playing and composing helped bridge ragtime with jazz styles.

Although he is playing in a blues style in his accompaniment here, Johnson would become well known as one of the founding fathers of stride piano, along with pianist and composer Thomas "Fats" Waller (1904–1943) and Willie "the Lion" Smith (1897–1973). Johnson also composed songs for Broadway shows, including the popular dance hit "The Charleston" of the 1920s, as well as more complex concert pieces, including an extended piano work called *Yamekraw* (1928) and his orchestral work *Harlem Symphony* (ca. 1930s), which was performed at Carnegie Hall in 1945. To hear Johnson's stride piano playing, works such as "Carolina Shout" and "You've Got to Be Modernistic" are excellent examples. Johnson's influence on jazz has been powerful and continues to today as can be seen, for example, in contemporary pianist-composer Jason Moran's (Chapter 15, 1st Chorus) tribute to Johnson with his version of "You've Got to Be Modernistic."

James P. Johnson in the early 1920s. Johnson gained fame in 1923 thanks to his hit song "The Charleston."
© Pictorial Press Ltd./Alamy.

QUESTIONS AND CONTROVERSIES
Gender in the Blues

Another important element of the classic blues is gender. Classic blues singers brought a female perspective to the genre. The topic of love in its many forms and various degrees of satisfaction or unhappiness with one's partner were extremely common, as was the topic of female sexuality, often couched in double-entendre but generally quite easy to understand. You can hear this difference in two performances of "Careless Love," one of the best-known traditional blues songs. Bessie Smith made a powerful recording of the song in 1925 with a small ensemble including Louis Armstrong on cornet. Compare the recording by blues singer Blind Boy Fuller for a male take on the same song. While Smith expresses the agony of a woman wronged, Fuller is far more casual and carefree in his performance.

listening focus

"Back Water Blues" (1927) by Bessie Smith (vocal) with James P. Johnson (piano)

"Back Water Blues" consists of seven 12-bar blues choruses. Unlike popular songs, there is no contrasting melody (called a "bridge") or verse; the entire song consists of the same 12-bar melody repeated over and over.

LISTENING HIGHLIGHT, STYLE: Smith's powerful voice is intense, clear, and piercing yet full and round. Smith's intonation is excellent, and she expressively slides in and out of nearly all of her notes. Other than that, her delivery is quite straightforward with little embellishment. James P. Johnson, as was true of all the stride pianists, had remarkable technique. Johnson's left hand plays bass notes that outline a blues chord progression, while his right hand plays chords in various ways and melodically fills in the spaces between Smith's vocal lines. While the tune itself has little variation (this is often true with the blues), Johnson makes subtle but important changes in his accompaniment to keep things interesting by providing contrast. Choruses 1, 2, and 3 (0:05, 0:33, 1:01) all have the same rolling left-hand accompaniment. Chorus 4 (1:29) maintains the same rolling rhythm but employs more pitches. Choruses 5 and 6 and the final chorus 7 (1:55, 2:23, 2:50) create a sharper contrast and use a stiffer, march-like accompaniment with bass notes on each beat instead of the rolling feel of the previous choruses.

"Back Water Blues" is said to be inspired by an actual flood that took place in Nashville, Tennessee, in 1926 that foreshadowed floods in the Mississippi Delta that occurred over the next years, inspiring more songs. The lyrics give a straightforward account of the events as they affected ordinary people. Smith tells the story of a flooding river that chased her out of her home, comparing her individual plight with those of thousands more who suffered in its aftermath. Subjects that describe real-life hardships such as these are perhaps the most common for the blues.

2nd Chorus Ragtime

WHAT IS RAGTIME?

Ragtime is a musical style from the late 1800s that adopted the traditional multistrain form of marches of the nineteenth century. These, in turn, are closely related to much older Western classical forms such as the minuet and trio and the rondo. Like the blues, ragtime is a predecessor to jazz; but the lines of influence from ragtime to jazz are much clearer than those between the blues and jazz. Originally ragtime evolved as an African American dance music, but the style eventually became extremely popular with the general public during the first decade of the twentieth century.

Ragtime works began to be published as sheet music in 1897, and they became extremely popular. Scott Joplin's "Maple Leaf Rag," for example, is said to have sold over 1 million copies. Its popularity coincided with the accessibility of more affordable pianos as well as the mechanical player piano that enabled nonmusicians to hear music played at home.

The best ragtime compositions, such as "Maple Leaf Rag," consist of a series of attractive and catchy melodies that are heavily **syncopated** (rhythms that accent

JAZZ LIVES SCOTT JOPLIN

Born in Texarkana, Texas, Scott Joplin (ca. 1867–1917) was born into a musical family; and by the time he was a teenager he was already playing piano professionally. After moving to St. Louis in the 1880s, he was making his living with a variety of piano-playing jobs as well as beginning to arrange for ensembles. He also led his own band, in which he played cornet. In the 1890s he moved to Sedalia, Missouri, a state that was a hotbed for ragtime.

Joplin was a serious and ambitious composer. While he is most known for his ragtime compositions, he also wrote, among other works, two operas and a ballet. Consequently, Joplin's ragtime works, while easily appealing and catchy, are also compositionally rigorous and thoughtful, which helps to account for his longevity as a composer. A version of his 1902 rag "The Entertainer," used on the soundtrack for the movie *The Sting* (1973), was number three on the *Billboard* pop chart.

Joplin had tremendous success with "Maple Leaf Rag," but he never again attained that degree of commercial accomplishment. Beyond just the desire for commercial success, Joplin was musically ambitious and moved to New York City to market his more serious work, spending much of his later life attempting to get his opera *Treemonisha* (completed in 1910) produced. It was never performed in its entirety during his lifetime, and the complete work was not produced until 1972.

listening focus

"Maple Leaf Rag," Scott Joplin (composed 1897, published 1899; rec. 1916 on piano roll)

LISTENING HIGHLIGHT, FORM: AA (0:00) BB (0:43) A (1:25) CC (1:47) DD (2:34). This is a typical multistrain form in ragtime. Each phrase is 16 measures, divided into 8-measure phrases, which in turn can be divided into 4-measure phrases.

A multistrain format such as this gives us an excellent opportunity to begin to examine two of the most important elements of composition, repetition and contrast. Without repetition, we tend to get lost and not understand how various parts of the song are related; and without contrast, we get bored. Consequently, these elements are crucial to the success of a piece, as is the balance between the two. The most obvious repetition is that each section (A, B, C, and D) repeats twice. The A section also comes back after B, and the familiar melody makes us comfortable as we understand where we are in the song. It is similar to another typical form that exists within many types of American pop music, verse–chorus, which alternates between two sections allowing us to always know what to expect as well as to hear something familiar—the repetition of the chorus—and something different—such as the contrast between the verse and chorus.

traditionally weak beats of a measure). This type of syncopated playing is sometimes called "**ragging**," hence the name "**ragtime**," and is a key feature of the style. Primarily these are compositions for solo piano, with the pianist essentially imitating an entire band. The left hand plays the role of the bass by playing bass notes on beats 1 and 3 while playing the chords on beats 2 and 4. The right hand plays the melodies and fills in with chords. Rags can also be played on guitar and are written for larger ensembles as well.

The relationship of jazz to ragtime is difficult to exactly pinpoint, but the style was certainly influential on jazz and its development. The line between the two is at times clear and at times fuzzy. Comparing "Maple Leaf Rag" and Ferdinand "Jelly Roll" Morton's "King Porter Stomp" (which we hear in Chapter 3, 3rd Chorus), however, gives you an excellent picture of the difference between a classic ragtime piece and a ragtime-like piece that is more associated with jazz.

While ragtime's popularity faded around 1918, it has endured as a style and has continued to be regularly revived and brought to the public's attention, perhaps most notably in the early 1970s.

read all about it
"A Negro Explains Jazz" by James Reese Europe

Walser, **Keeping Time,** *Chapter 5*
An extensive interview with the bandleader on his return home from fighting in France conducted by a New York City reporter in 1919.

3rd Chorus Early Jazz

HOW DID RAGTIME INFLUENCE THE BIRTH OF JAZZ?

The line between ragtime and early jazz is essentially impossible to draw, but by the turn of the century the "ragging" of popular tunes had begun to come into its own. Orchestras such as James Reese Europe's played a large role in the transition from "ragging" to jazz in much the same way that individual players and bandleaders—such as Buddy Bolden and Jelly Roll Morton—did, as is discussed in Chapter 3 on New Orleans jazz. It is important to note that both musicians and audiences drove this shift. The musicians embraced the new swinging music, as did the dancing and partying audiences.

James Reese Europe

James Reese Europe (1880–1919) was an early twentieth-century bandleader with ties to many genres of music, including classical and popular music, as well as ragtime and jazz. Europe's relationship between the latter two positions him as an important figure in American music. His early band was not truly a jazz ensemble, but it featured many elements that would be developed further over the next decade and would lead to the formation of the mature jazz band.

Europe was born in Mobile, Alabama, 15 years after the end of the Civil War. His family was extremely musical, and along with his musical aptitude, Europe displayed leadership qualities and a knack for organization at a young age. Eventually moving to New York City, Europe began to build a career first as a

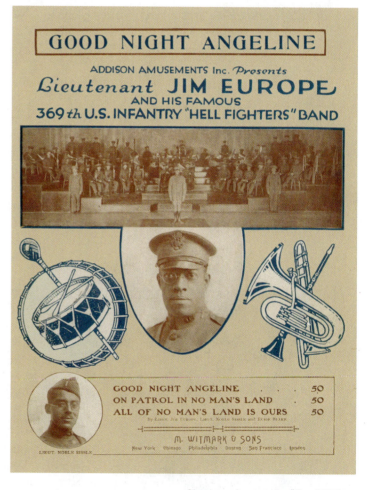

Sheet music cover for "Good Night Angeline" by James Reese Europe. Note how the cover makes a clear connection to Europe's service in World War I and the famous Hell Fighters regiment.

Courtesy Michael Ochs Collection/ Getty Images.

performer and then as a successful composer and bandleader-music director in black musical theater. Europe took his position as a prominent and successful African American musician seriously and spearheaded the formation of the Clef Club as a support network that functioned as both a union and a booking agency for black musicians in New York City. The Clef Club Orchestra was also formed under Europe's leadership and became the first orchestra to perform jazz-related music in Carnegie Hall in 1912. In fact, the orchestra featured only works by black composers. This 1912 concert was a huge and musically successful event. The success of this orchestra and the excitement it generated created excellent new

JAZZ LIVES W. C. HANDY

W. C. Handy (1873–1958) was an influential African American songwriter and composer. At times he is referred to as the "Father of the Blues," and while the title is certainly an exaggerated one, he is generally credited with popularizing the blues and bringing it to the attention of the general public. His interest in music began early, and he learned to play multiple instruments, becoming especially proficient on the cornet and trumpet. He went on to become a traveling performer, bandleader, and arranger for numerous types of groups such as brass bands, minstrel shows, and a vocal quartet.

Handy came into contact with the blues while leading his band in a performance in Clarksdale, Mississippi, a hotbed of the Delta blues style. He was impressed by the music itself as well as by its ability to appeal to a broad audience in the region that crossed racial boundaries. With his experience in a wide variety of styles such as marches, popular music, Tin Pan Alley tunes, African American folk traditions, and ragtime, he transformed the blues into a format that combined elements of all of these styles. He published "Memphis Blues" in 1912, and it became a hit. The piece, along with Europe's recording of it, brings together a swinging, bluesy style with elements of both ragtime and European concert music. After creating his own music publishing business, Handy went on to compose numerous popular works including many blues songs that became standards in the classic blues genre, including "St. Louis Blues," "Yellow Dog Blues," and "Beale Street Blues." He moved to New York City, broadened his scope as a composer and publisher, and recorded with his own band. Handy has been memorialized in film, he published an autobiography, and a US postage stamp honors him.

W. C. Handy, ca. 1900, shown in his band uniform holding a cornet (note its smaller size in relation to a trumpet). Handy had success as a bandleader before turning his attention to composing.

© Pictorial Press Ltd./Alamy.

listening focus

"Memphis Blues" by Lieut. Jim Europe's 369th US Infantry ("Hellfighters") Band (1919), composed by W. C. Handy (1912)

This is a jaunty arrangement and performance by James Reese Europe's 369th US Infantry Regiment "Hellfighters" Band of W. C. Handy's first blues hit. "Memphis Blues" is a multistrain composition that combines the 12-bar blues with a ragtime format and feel, effectively uniting two important musical forms that influenced and intersected with early jazz. Just how these intersections and influences occurred is difficult to assess and describe, but we hear it in this music.

LISTENING HIGHLIGHT, RHYTHM: Europe's group was known for bringing an African American rhythmic sensibility to rags, the blues, and popular tunes. Presenting this style of playing to the general public was a major contribution and helped to propel American music into the twentieth century. It played a swinging style that had been part of the African American experience for some time, and these musicians had already been playing it regularly in clubs and cabarets, as well as theaters and other venues.

The 16-measure trio, which is played twice, has a characteristically syncopated ragtime feel. It picks up in intensity, and notice that as the tune goes along it speeds up. In fact, by the second A it is already faster than it started. Speeding up is generally a natural tendency over the course of a song, but here this happens quite quickly. The band sounds like it is getting more and more excited, and the playing becomes continually more animated and raucous.

opportunities for its musicians and for New York City's black musicians in general and introduced to a wider audience a new swinging sound that crossed the stylistic borders of marches, popular, classical, ragtime, jazz, and society-style music, all with skill and swing.

Vernon and Irene Castle were leading performers of social dances, including the tango and foxtrot, creating a dance craze in the decade before World War I. After dancing to James Reese Europe's Society Orchestra at a private affair, they hired him as their bandleader, a bold move for these white performers at this time. They went on to form an extremely successful partnership. Europe's orchestra was in such great demand that he had to form several units to handle all of the work. The Castle–Europe team integrated Broadway's vaudeville theaters for the first time. This led to Europe and his orchestra receiving a groundbreaking recording contract with Victor Records.

Europe also held important positions in the 369th Infantry of the US Army, an all-black regiment known as the "Hellfighters" because of their valor in battle. Because of segregation within the US Army, the unit was temporarily assigned to the 16th Division of the French Army during World War I. Not only was Europe the bandmaster for the regiment, but he was also, as an officer of a machine gun company, the first African American officer to have led men in battle during World War I. Europe and the black troops made a triumphant return to New York City in 1919, complete with a parade that took them up Fifth Avenue to Harlem. Shortly after, he was stabbed and killed by one of his musicians in a dispute. Europe's legacy included several musicians whose careers he helped establish, including singer-lyricist Noble Sissle and ragtime pianist-composer Eubie Blake, who together scored the first all-black Broadway musical, *Shuffle Along*, in 1923.

CODA Chapter Summary

What Are the Blues?

- The name "the blues" has been applied to a wide variety of musical performances beginning in the late nineteenth century and continuing in the present.
- Three types of blues developed in roughly chronological order: (1) country or folk blues (late nineteenth century through the 1930s to today); (2) "classic" blues (1920s–1940s); and (3) urban or electric blues (post–World War II to today).
- The most common form is the 12-bar blues.
- Bessie Smith was one of the greatest of the classic blues singers, who was often accompanied on record by jazz musicians, including pianist James P. Johnson and trumpeter Louis Armstrong.

What Is Ragtime?

- Ragtime is a musical style from the late 1800s that adopted the traditional multistrain form of marches of the nineteenth century.
- It is noted for its syncopated rhythms.
- Scott Joplin was among the first and most important composers of "classic" rags.

How Did Ragtime Influence the Birth of Jazz?

- Bandleaders like James Reese Europe began incorporating syncopation into their playing, "ragging" popular tunes and marches.

Talkin' Jazz (Key Terms)

Blue note	"Ragging" (a melody)	12-bar blues
Blues	Ragtime	Urban or electric blues
Classic blues	Syncopated rhythms/	
Country or folk blues	Syncopation	

Key People

Bessie Smith	Scott Joplin	W. C. Handy
James P. Johnson	James Reese Europe	

Think About This (For Further Discussion and Study)

1. What are the primary differences between the various styles of the blues? Listen to an example of all three types, and describe the various instrumentations and approaches.

2. Discuss the importance of self-expression, as well as ways that you have found effective for expressing yourself. Can you relate your approaches to the blues in any way?

3. What are the various components of the ragtime piano style? How does the pianist simulate an entire band?

4. Experiment with syncopation, an important element of ragtime and jazz, by having one part of the class clap on all 4 beats of a bar while the other part claps on the offbeats in between their classmates' claps.

5. Discuss the relationship between ragtime and early jazz by comparing "Maple Leaf Rag" and Jelly Roll Morton's "King Porter Stomp" (which we will hear in Chapter 3, 3rd Chorus).

Look It Up (Key Resources)

Albertson, Chris. *Bessie*. New Haven, CT: Yale University Press, 2003.

Badger, Reid. *A Life in Ragtime: A Biography of James Reese Europe*. New York: Oxford University Press, 1995.

Berlin, Edward A. *King of Ragtime: Scott Joplin and His Era*. New York: Oxford University Press, 1994.

Gioia, Ted. *Delta Blues: The Life and Times of the Mississippi Masters Who Revolutionized American Music*. New York: Norton, 2008.

Handy, W. C. *Father of the Blues: An Autobiography*. New York: Macmillan, 1941.

Oliver, Paul, Tony Russell, Robert M. W. Dixon, John Godrich, and Howard Rye. *Yonder Come the Blues*. New York: Cambridge University Press, 2012.

Palmer, Robert. *Deep Blues: A Musical and Cultural History, from the Mississippi Delta to Chicago's South Side to the World*. New York: Penguin, 1981.

Wald, Elijah. *Escaping the Delta: Robert Johnson and the Invention of the Blues*. New York: Amistad, 2004.

NEW ORLEANS JAZZ | 1880s-1920

3

1st Chorus New Orleans: The Birthplace of Jazz

HOW DID THE MIXTURE OF DIFFERENT ETHNIC GROUPS IN NEW ORLEANS INFLUENCE THE DEVELOPMENT OF JAZZ?

The roots of New Orleans jazz are complex. Almost since the first jazz was performed, there have been conflicting accounts and theories about how the music began. Most everyone agrees, however, that jazz originated in New Orleans, with its African, French, and Spanish colonial heritage and its racially mixed and incredibly culturally diverse environment, including African American, European American, **Creole**, and Spanish-Caribbean influences, among others. In *New Orleans Style and the Writing of American Jazz History*, jazz historian Bruce Boyd Raeburn points out the importance of this heritage and its impact on New Orleans jazz:

> *Ethnic and racial diversity within working-class neighborhoods stimulated vernacular cultural development in the Crescent City. The prevalence of music in the streets via marching bands, wagon advertisements, and spasm bands meant that musical innovations coming out of the African American community were available to everyone within earshot, regardless of the strictures of segregation that sought to keep whites free from black cultural penetration. Tremé, the French Quarter, the Seventh Ward, Central City, the Irish Channel, and Algiers were "cultural wetlands" characterized by "crazy quilt" demographic configurations that predated implementation of segregation in the 1890s, interspersing Creoles, Latinos, Jews, blacks, and whites side by side within blocks (p. 8).*

New Orleans musicians were exposed to a wide variety of musical styles, such as popular tunes, marches, rags, light opera, hymns and spirituals, and brass-band music. Incorporating these influences, a style of playing came out of the black community. This music was performed in formal and informal settings such as dance halls, cabarets, speakeasies, houses of prostitution, picnics, and parades. The style had a unique and syncopated rhythmic approach that allowed for expressive embellishment of melodies that made the music new, vivid, exciting, and, perhaps most importantly, terrific dance and party music.

Photo: Courtesy of the Hogan Jazz Archive, Tulane University.

In this chapter, we'll answer these questions:

- How Did the Mixture of Different Ethnic Groups in New Orleans Influence the Development of Jazz?

- Who Were Some of the Key Early New Orleans Jazz Musicians?

- Why Was Jelly Roll Morton a Key Figure in the Development of Jazz?

- What Was the Influence of "King" Oliver on Early Jazz Music and Its Performers?

- Why Is Sidney Bechet Considered the First Virtuosic Soloist in Jazz?

- Why Is Louis Armstrong Among the Most Influential Musicians in the History of Jazz?

JAZZ LIVES BUDDY BOLDEN, FREDDIE KEPPARD, AND JACK "PAPA" LAINE

The African American cornetist Buddy Bolden (1877–1931) is one of early jazz's most mythical figures. He is often referred to as the first important jazz musician. This is problematic, of course, as many musicians are responsible for any type of music's development; but it speaks to his abilities and to the impact of his approach upon musicians, even though no recordings of Bolden have surfaced. Those who heard him, including Louis Armstrong, have spoken of his huge, powerful sound on the cornet. Additionally, one of the more important aspects of his playing seems to have been his individuality. The importance of an individual style to jazz cannot be overstated, and it is perhaps the most important element in the birth of jazz.

In order to make a living, players such as Bolden played numerous styles of popular music for many types of parties, parades, and dances. Yet they took the popular music of the day and put a stamp on it, distinguishing it from the European tradition of music making. Bolden's band stood in contrast to, for example, black Creole violinist John Robichaux's orchestra, which used written music and played popular dance music in the style that it was written. Bolden's band was said to be particularly exciting because it improvised on these popular melodies; introduced a swinging, danceable rhythm; and incorporated elements of the blues as part of its performances.

Another important early player was the Creole cornetist Freddie Keppard (1890–1933), who followed in Bolden's footsteps. He was featured with the Creole Jazz Band, a band that began as a New Orleans dance orchestra and became a nationally known vaudeville act. The band traveled widely and is credited with helping to bring the New Orleans style to other parts of the country. The band had an opportunity to record in 1916, before the all-white Original Dixieland Jazz Band's (ODJB) made its first jazz recordings (this chapter, 2nd Chorus); but Keppard is reputed to have convinced the band not to record. Why he insisted they decline the opportunity is unclear, but it was common at that time for musicians to concentrate on their live playing and touring, which is primarily how they made their living. Musicians could also be secretive and unwilling to make their recordings available in order to keep their live performances valuable while also preventing others from "stealing" their music.

Jack "Papa" Laine (1873–1966) was an important early white bandleader in New Orleans, and his bands were training grounds for many future jazz musicians. Laine's groups used the rehearsal process and improvisation to work out set arrangements for their "ragging" of popular material, a similar process that was used by Buddy Bolden and the early black jazz bands. While Laine's musicians were primarily white, he was also known to have hired light-skinned African Americans (who could pass for white) and Creoles. Among Laine's musicians were members of the ODJB (including cornetist Nick LaRocca), the first jazz group to record, as well as members of the New Orleans Rhythm Kings (including the clarinetist Leon Roppolo), a white group that went on to be successful in Chicago, including recording with Jelly Roll Morton (this chapter, 3rd Chorus). Laine's groups also played a variety of music that appealed to audiences for a wide range of functions.

Buddy Bolden (standing, second from left) with his jazz band. This is the only known picture (taken sometime before 1895) of Bolden. Band members in the photo include valve trombonist Willie Cornish (standing, third left) and clarinetist Frank Lewis (seated).
© Lebrecht Music & Arts.

Somewhat unique to New Orleans was the establishment in 1897 of an area of the city where prostitution was "not illegal." This 12-block area became known as "Storyville" and was established as an attempt by the city elders to limit prostitution to a controlled area. Large brothels were established, many run by women, which employed musicians as part of the "entertainment," giving steady work to pianists and bands. White customers were exposed to the developing jazz music when visiting the brothels; thus, the music crossed racial and social barriers that would normally have kept it within a single community.

Because of the public and outdoor nature of New Orleans life, this music enjoyed wide influence. In fact, one of the key, and perhaps underappreciated, aspects of New Orleans jazz was its broad and open outlook to the process of making music—musicians tended to use all of the musical resources at their disposal. When we examine contemporary jazz it will become clear that this tradition of openness and musical absorption still exists in much of the jazz world. It is important to remember that musicians, while enjoying what they do, play music for a living. It makes sense that the more successful New Orleans musicians, as well as contemporary players, would have many of the various musical styles that audiences hoped to hear at their fingertips. This was necessary for individual musicians to be hired by bandleaders or for bands to keep working.

The musical traditions born in New Orleans, such as collective improvisation, solo improvisation, rhythmic swing and intensity, and group **polyphony** (see Chapter 1), produced a style that eventually, through a series of developments, became jazz.

WHO WERE SOME OF THE KEY EARLY NEW ORLEANS JAZZ MUSICIANS?

Among the early musicians who contributed to the birth of jazz, some stand out as particularly important. These musicians had a breadth of musicality as well as a sharp business sense that helped them achieve their popularity. At this time, most of these musicians worked in segregated bands, an issue that continues to arise in jazz. The city of New Orleans, though diverse, also suffered from systemic racism.

All of these musicians' broad-based approach to music underscores the importance of individuality in jazz. Each group and each musician created a unique style within the larger jazz framework. For example, while the bands of important New Orleans musicians such as Jelly Roll Morton, King Oliver, and Louis Armstrong all were proponents of the New Orleans style, each group had a distinct approach to music making, which we will discuss as we hear the music. The music emanating from the black community in the unique cultural environment of New Orleans quickly mixed with Creole, European, Caribbean, and Hispanic influences and became New Orleans jazz. From there the music has evolved in an extraordinary number of different directions.

2nd Chorus The First Jazz Record

The Original Dixieland Jazz Band

While the all-white ODJB was certainly not *the* original jazz band, it was their 1917 hit recording of "Livery Stable Blues" that helped bring jazz to the attention of the public beyond those who played and heard the music in New Orleans. The recording essentially created a new market for jazz. Soon other performers wanted to capitalize on this music that people were excited and energized about.

Original Dixieland Jazz Band, ca. late 1910s. (Left to right) Tony Sbarbaro (drums), Eddie Edwards (trombone), Nick LaRocca (trumpet), Alcide Nunez (clarinet), and Henry Ragas (piano). The first jazz band to record, the Original Dixieland Jazz Band were a sensation when they performed in New York City in the late 1910s.
© *Pictorial Press Ltd./Alamy.*

The group was led by trumpeter Nick LaRocca, who had previously played with "Papa" Laine's band (see 1st Chorus). Going to Chicago in 1916, they were immediately successful and subsequently, a year later, were playing in New York, where they helped launch a craze for jazz. The New York lineup—LaRocca, clarinetist Larry Shields, trombonist Eddie Edwards, pianist Harry Ragas, and drummer Tony Sbarbaro—made the first true jazz records.

The success of the ODJB, as well as the fact that jazz originated in their city, resounded in New Orleans. At the same time, the monetary success of this all-white band, in comparison, for example, to Jelly Roll Morton, a mixed-race Creole, is an early example of economic disparity as a result of race. While early jazz found

QUESTIONS AND CONTROVERSIES
Listening to Early Jazz Recordings

Early jazz recordings were made when recording technology was young and can be a bit difficult to listen to. In the early days of recording, before the invention of electric microphones (ca. 1925), musicians had to play into large horns. Many studios were primitive; for example, Gennett Records, where Jelly Roll Morton and Bix Beiderbecke made their early recordings, had a studio overlooking a railroad track. When a train passed by, recording had to stop so as not to ruin a master. The studio was small, windowless, and uncomfortable. Rather than spending a lot of time perfecting a number, musicians were expected to get it right the first time, to save valuable recording discs.

But try and get past the thin sound quality and surface noise to appreciate the sound of these performers' enthusiasm for a new and developing music while also getting a chance to present themselves to a wider public.

listening focus

"Livery Stable Blues" (1917) by the Original Dixieland Jazz Band

Cornet: James "Nick" LaRocca; **Clarinet:** Larry Shields; **Trombone:** Edwin "Daddy" Edwards; **Piano:** Henry Ragas; **Drums:** Tony Spargo (née Sbarbaro).

LISTENING HIGHLIGHT, FORM: "Livery Stable Blues" is most noteworthy for its polyphonic character and its intensely syncopated rhythms. Everyone is playing together, yet each has his or her own part. They are independent but work together to make a complicated texture, like a woven rug with many strands that come together to make a complicated and satisfying design.

This music is clearly planned out and well-rehearsed. For example, listen to the clarinet part in the 1st and 2nd choruses, and notice how similar they are. There is more variation in some other parts but not much.

After a 4-bar intro (0:00), the 1st chorus (0:07) and 2nd chorus (0:25) are essentially the same. In the first 4 bars of the 3rd and 4th choruses (0:42 and 1:00) the trombone creates the feel of a series of breaks—even though the band continues to play—that temporarily suspend the forward motion. After these 4 bars, the pulse and the ensemble playing continue. The 5th and 6th choruses (1:18 and 1:36) bring in animal-like sound effects connected to the title of the tune. Each horn plays an effect in turn during the first measures and then, as in the previous 2 choruses, moves along in a full ensemble. The 7th chorus (1:53) continues with the full ensemble and a new cornet melody. The 8th chorus (2:11) repeats the breaks from the 3rd and 4th choruses, while the 9th and 10th (2:29 and 2:47) repeat the livery stable sounds from before as well. A short tag ends the tune in typical fashion.

its way from the black dance halls, clubs, marches, picnics, and parties, its adoption by a range of ethnicities and the monetary success of the ODJB reflected the economic disparity of not only the jazz field but American society in general.

3rd Chorus Ferdinand "Jelly Roll" Morton

WHY WAS JELLY ROLL MORTON A KEY FIGURE IN THE DEVELOPMENT OF JAZZ?

Born in New Orleans, Creole pianist-composer-bandleader Ferdinand "Jelly Roll" Morton (1890–1941) is one of the more important and colorful characters in early jazz. Born Ferdinand Lamothe, Morton was a huge self-promoter, to say the least; and some would even characterize him as an outrageous braggart. For example, he claimed to have "invented" jazz in 1902 (when he was 12!); and while this is, of course, a claim that no one can make, he certainly played a huge role in jazz's early development. With good reason, Morton is spoken of as one of the very first jazz composers; and his ability, in both his playing and his composing, to blend ragtime, the blues, and the latest New Orleans style of music was important to the development of jazz.

read all about it

"The 'Inventor of Jazz'" by Jelly Roll Morton

Walser, **Keeping Time,** *Chapter 7*

An excerpt from Alan Lomax's famous Library of Congress interviews with the pianist-composer in which Morton discusses his early life and musical influences.

Morton became a denizen of Storyville, the area of New Orleans that, from 1897 to 1917, was allowed to have houses of prostitution. Morton's middle-class family, whose heritage could be traced to Haiti, wasn't pleased to learn he was working in such a low-class, disreputable district. The music that was being created there, however, lured Morton to cross racial, social, and cultural lines to become part of the Storyville lifestyle. As a result, along with being a musician, he spent time as a pimp, a pool hustler, and a vaudeville entertainer. In his heyday he was also a flamboyant dresser swathed in diamond jewelry, including in his front tooth. This was all part and parcel of being a pianist in this period; there were certain expectations for entertainers, and Morton certainly lived up to these and more.

Storyville was Morton's education and starting point for a career that took him around the country, including as far away as California, before settling in Chicago, a leading center for jazz at that time, in 1922. Here he made some excellent recordings with the New Orleans Rhythm Kings, a white group from Chicago that included clarinetist Leon Roppolo, marking an early example of integration in jazz. He also created the Red Hot Peppers, a group that was created solely for recording in the studio, with whom he made numerous important records, including "Black Bottom Stomp."

Morton moved to New York City, but once the depression hit, as was true for so many, opportunities to perform became less plentiful. In addition, his style of music was being displaced by swing. While others were able to transition from one style to the next, he did not. Ironically, his "King Porter Stomp" would prove to be a hitmaker for numerous swing bands. Morton's subsequent move to Washington, DC, proved fortuitous as Alan Lomax, one of the most important folklorists in American music history, took an interest in him. Over the course of several weeks in 1938 Lomax interviewed and recorded Morton, who discussed not only his life and music but the history of jazz as he saw it, leaving a remarkable record of one of the most important early stars of jazz and jazz composition.

Jelly Roll Morton, ca. early 1920s. Morton is seated at a fairly fancy grand piano in this studio portrait made about the time he recorded a series of piano solos.
© Pictorial Press Ltd./Alamy.

4th Chorus Joseph "King" Oliver and Sidney Bechet

WHAT WAS THE INFLUENCE OF "KING" OLIVER ON EARLY JAZZ MUSIC AND ITS PERFORMERS?

Joseph "King" Oliver (1885–1938) was extremely influential upon early jazz, particularly in the driving swing that made his band famous. Some of Oliver's recordings were done even before those of Jelly Roll Morton's and along with his

"Black Bottom Stomp" (1926), Ferdinand "Jelly Roll" Morton and His Red Hot Peppers

INSTRUMENTATION: Piano-Composer: Jelly Roll Morton; **Trumpet:** George Mitchell; **Clarinet:** Omar Simeon; **Trombone:** Edward "Kid" Ory; **Banjo:** Johnny St. Cyr; **Bass:** John Lindsay.

In "Black Bottom Stomp," Morton employs the instrumental resources available to him to create a constantly changing texture throughout the piece. There is never a dull moment as different instruments are featured every time a section repeats so that, for example, even when the B section repeats seven times, each repetition is fresh and exciting. The B section itself gives life to the piece as it has a new rhythmic feel, kicking the piece into a higher gear. Also, various rhythmic techniques, such as breaks and stop time, are used throughout the piece, as we will see in the complete Listening Guide. While larger ensembles tend to use more composed or arranged material, some small groups, such as this one, also rely heavily on more involved compositions. We will see this in numerous eras, for example, during the 1950s with the hard-bop groups of Art Blakey, Horace Silver, and Clifford Brown and Max Roach (Chapter 11, 2nd Chorus).

FORM: At its most basic level, this composition has an AB form. The A section is 16 measures and consists of two 8-measure phrases, each of which can also be divided into two contrasting 4-measure phrases. The B section is 20 measures long and consists of an 8-measure phrase and a 12-measure phrase. After an 8-measure introduction, the A section repeats three times and the B section is played seven times. How Morton varies these repetitions to keep our interest is shown in the Listening Guide.

In pieces of this type, the B section is often referred to as the "trio," and most commonly the A section would have repeated after the trio, though in this case it does not. Each section could also be referred to as a "strain," another word for a section of music, often used when referring to ragtime pieces. This format ties this composition closely to ragtime and highlights the relationship between ragtime and early jazz. It is also related to classical forms such as the minuet and trio. The shift from jazz to ragtime is an important one, yet it is difficult to trace and explain; but comparing this work to Scott Joplin pieces is a good place to start. For example, ragtime compositions are multistrain works and generally have a trio but often have other strains as well. For example, Joplin's famous "Maple Leaf Rag" has four strains, with A, B, C (the trio), and D sections.

STYLE: This is an upbeat composition that exemplifies the best of the New Orleans tradition of dance music. This band, although put together strictly for recording, has the necessary skills and background in the New Orleans tradition, such as the all-important understanding of how to "rag" and swing a melody. They swing so hard that it had to be difficult to stay off of the dance floor.

MELODY AND HARMONY: The composed melodies of the various sections provide a terrific balance of repetition and contrast as Morton regularly alternates passages for the full ensemble and more solo-like passages. The alternation of ensemble melody and the solo-like passages also makes for a diverse and varied composition. The harmony of the composition is reminiscent of ragtime, again tying it to the earlier style.

continued

"BLACK BOTTOM STOMP" LISTENING GUIDE

TIME	FORM	STYLE	MELODY AND HARMONY	RHYTHM	ACCOMPANIMENT
0:00	Intro	The full ensemble plays a lively introduction.	The clarinet is featured in a peppy melody.	The introduction has a 2-beat feel as the bass plays only on beats 1 and 3. This is true for much of the piece.	The bass plays in 2, and the banjo helps to keep time. Because of the recording technology, it is hard to tell if the piano and drums are not playing or if it is just hard to hear them. Notice how all instruments play the last 3 notes of each phrase together.
0:07	A1	The full ensemble plays.	The first 4-measure phrase is long, held notes, while the second is more active. The melody moves from the trumpet to the clarinet.	During the first phrase the banjo keeps time, while the rest of the rhythm section plays only the first beat of each measure.	In the second phrase notice how coordinated the rhythm section is with the front line (trumpet, clarinet, and trombone).
0:22	A2	Trumpet solo	The trumpet plays a solo-like melody for the first phrase, and the full ensemble responds with the second phrase's melody from A1.		The rhythm section plays the same accompaniment as it does behind the full ensemble.
0:37	A3	Clarinet solo			The same accompaniment continues.
0:52	Transition	The trumpet leads the full ensemble to the trio.			The band members play a type of break where they play a rhythmic figure either behind or in response to the soloist.
0:56	B1 (Trio)	Full ensemble with a trumpet lead	While the trumpet plays the melody, the clarinet plays a busy counterline, and the trombone plays a simpler one. This is a classic New Orleans–style ensemble.	Trumpeter George Mitchell has a great lilt to his playing here and creates a light but swinging feel. The first phrase ends (1:01) with a break that is filled with a single trumpet note and then a tailgate trombone effect.	The bass player plays a huge role in driving the rhythm of the trio as he alternates between playing in 2 and 4. Lindsay also uses a slap technique, which increases its punch and helps propel the ensemble. Most of the second phrase is in 4.
1:15	B2	The clarinet plays a solo in its lower, or chalumeau, register; this is a deep, rich area for a clarinet's tone.	The clarinet solo consists largely of arpeggios. This is a common technique for all instruments, but some can play them more easily than others. For example, they are more difficult on the trombone. The clarinet is often played in this manner.	This strain ends with a type of rhythmic break—everyone plays exactly the same rhythm.	The bass stays in 2 during this clarinet solo. The banjo dominates the texture.

"Black Bottom Stomp" listening guide continued

TIME	FORM	STYLE	MELODY AND HARMONY	RHYTHM	ACCOMPANIMENT
1:33	B3	This is a Morton piano solo. It is a powerfully effective contrast, and it is the first time that the piano has a significant role that we can hear. It also exhibits Morton's skill as a pianist. His style has elements of stride piano (to be discussed in Chapter 5, 4th Chorus) and ragtime.			
1:51	B4	The entire strain is a stop-time solo for the trumpet. The ensemble plays a series of breaks as the trumpet solos through them.			This is the first time that we can hear some looseness in the ensemble playing as not everyone is hitting the rhythmic breaks at the same time. Remember, this is a band that only played in the recording studio, and the chances are good that they did not rehearse very much. The fact that the band is as tight as it is is a testament to these players' excellent abilities.
2:10	B5	Banjo solo	The banjo plays both chords and melody during this solo. This is a common technique for guitar as well, and we will hear it throughout the history of jazz.		Only the bass accompanies the banjo. Lindsay plays the same basic bass line from B1.
2:29	B6	The full ensemble plays a New Orleans–style ensemble.	The trumpet plays a lead melody, with the clarinet and trombone playing counterlines.		We hear the piano and drums clearly in the ensemble for the first time. The ensemble plays a break, and the drummer plays a rhythm on his cymbal. He hits it and grabs it just afterward to create a "choke" effect.
2:48	B7 plus a tag	The intensity is much greater as the full ensemble shouts the out-chorus (sometimes referred to as the "shout chorus"). The tune concludes with a classic New Orleans–style ending.	The trombone tailgates throughout the out-chorus and plays a powerful tailgating break between phrases.		The drums finally really kick in here to propel "Black Bottom Stomp" to a rousing finish.

continued

RHYTHM: This is a dynamic work and an excellent example of the use of rhythmic techniques in jazz. It includes numerous types of rhythmic devices, such as breaks and stop time, as well as playing in 2 (where the bass plays only on beats 1 and 3 of a 4-beat measure) and playing in 4 (the bass plays on all 4 beats).

ACCOMPANIMENT: A particularly noteworthy element of "Black Bottom Stomp" is how well integrated the rhythm section is into the composition. For example, the bass plays notes of the chords on its own as an accompanying technique with timekeeping and harmonic functions, but it also at times plays the same rhythmic figures that the rest of the ensemble plays. Careful attention to this type of detail is the key to giving this piece great ensemble cohesiveness.

Compare

Listen to these other recordings by Jelly Roll Morton:

- One of Morton's earliest works, "King Porter Stomp" was probably composed sometime between 1905 and 1910, a high point for ragtime. He recorded it throughout his career, and, just as importantly, it became a swing-era standard that was a hit, or the basis of a hit, for a number of the top swing bands, including Fletcher Henderson (we'll hear his version in Chapter 5, 1st Chorus) and Benny Goodman. Morton recorded this piece at his first recording session in 1923 as well as his last, placing it as an important work.

- "Winin' Boy Blues" was recorded as part of Jelly Roll's Library of Congress recordings made by folklorist Alan Lomax, revealing his talents as a vocalist and as a pianist. Compare this with Bessie Smith's "Back Water Blues" (Chapter 2, 1st Chorus).

influence on other musicians—including Armstrong, who stated that Oliver was his idol—place him as an early innovator. Like other New Orleans musicians, however, Oliver was well versed in various popular styles and able to tailor his playing and his band's repertoire to his audience. The "ragging" of popular tunes that was so crucial to the creation of jazz was a part of this musical flexibility.

Oliver's style was full of bluesy mannerisms, and his solos, as seen in "Dippermouth Blues," are simple and straightforward, yet emotionally charged, and well-planned. His Creole Jazz Band was extremely tight with highly organized arrangements, including the harmonized 2-cornet breaks played by Oliver and Armstrong that were astonishing for the day. How could Armstrong know what notes to play to accompany the main melody when Oliver was extemporaneously soloing? While Armstrong's harmonizing of Oliver's improvised breaks seemed mysterious, when playing a supportive part, such as 2nd cornet (supporting 1st cornet), working musicians must be able to create effective harmonies on the spot.

IN PERFORMANCE
Jazz Composition and Arranging

Morton's "Black Bottom Stomp" provides an excellent introduction to jazz composition and arranging as it is a fully composed, or at least a fully planned out, composition. This is in sharp contrast to pieces such as Louis Armstrong's recording of "Hotter Than That" (see this chapter, 5th Chorus) as well as many of the small group pieces we will hear, which provide a basic structure while leaving many musical choices up to the individual players. Morton essentially controls all aspects of this piece. Even the solo sections are planned out, and the fact that they sound improvised is a testament to Morton's imaginative writing and the excellent abilities of these players.

Some people believe that if there is no improvisation involved in a performance, it is not jazz. This is an extreme position, but certainly improvisation is a crucial element in jazz. Even the nature of improvisation is a murky area however. For example, in actual practice, performers playing with steadily performing groups frequently wind up creating something close to a set solo (sometimes repeated almost verbatim) for a given tune that works well for them and gets a good response from the audience. They are performers, after all, who are trying to appeal to their listeners. This is less true for situations where soloists are playing long solos, sometimes referred to as "stretching out." Also, while some claim that their work is always totally improvised, most improvisers create their solos from a series of set phrases and perfected melodic lines, as well as a wide range of other prepared musical elements that they spend their lives working on and learning to put together in different ways to create new solos. So an "improvised" solo may in fact occasionally be largely preplanned or at least

based on material that has been worked on to achieve maximal effect.

Improvisers need a good setting to play within, so the composed aspect of jazz is crucial. In contemporary jazz, in fact, composition is becoming more and more essential, though again this is a controversial topic. But since improvising styles have tended to stay relatively the same for some time now, players seem to be relying upon creating different types of environments within which to improvise as a means to stimulate new ideas, as well as to create interest for themselves and their audience. In addition, jazz composers have frequently looked to other forms of music for inspiration and compositional techniques, and this appears to be even truer today.

The difference between jazz **composing** and jazz **arranging** can be both very small and very large. The essential difference is that composers create all of the material in a piece, while an arranger takes already composed material and "arranges" it by deciding who plays what parts. An arranger generally adds composed material as well, such as introductions, backgrounds, interludes, transitions, and endings, as well as handling the composed material in an original manner. This is a high art that we will explore throughout this book. Jazz arrangers such as Fletcher Henderson (Chapter 5, 1st Chorus), Benny Carter (Chapter 5, 2nd Chorus), Neal Hefti (Chapter 6, 3rd Chorus), Quincy Jones (Chapter 6, 3rd Chorus), Gil Evans (Chapter 13, 1st Chorus), and Eddie Sauter (Chapter 7, 1st Chorus), to name just a few, are among the pantheon of important jazz artists. Jazz arrangers are most often also composers, but not always.

Lil Hardin, the pianist in Oliver's band and an important musician in her own right (discussed in Chapter 4, 3rd Chorus), was influential in Armstrong's career and soon became Armstrong's second wife (of four). While playing with Oliver, Armstrong, though a much stronger player than Oliver, took pains not to

JAZZ LIVES **KING OLIVER**

King Oliver was born in New Orleans and, as is typical, began his career playing a variety of jobs; but by 1920 he was leading his own band and touring with it as far away as San Francisco. He opened at Chicago's Lincoln Gardens, a South Side Chicago dance hall, and played there from 1922 to 1924. This group became known as King Oliver's Creole Jazz Band, which is the band heard here on "Dippermouth Blues." The band had an infectious and swinging feel that was perfect for dancing. His personnel were essentially all New Orleans musicians (pianist Lil Hardin, who was from Memphis, was an exception) including the important early clarinetists Johnny Dodds and Jimmy Noone. The band attracted many local fans, including up-and-coming jazz musicians from the Chicago area who became known as the Austin High Gang (see Chapter 4).

Players left Oliver's band one by one, and it gradually became the Dixie Syncopaters; but by the early 1930s Oliver's teeth and gums—so important to a trumpet player's *embouchure* (the positioning of a trumpet mouthpiece on the lips)—were deteriorating, leading to a decline in his playing. He continued to perform, and his musicality allowed him to do so effectively even as his playing became more difficult; but his career declined, and by 1936 he was working in a pool hall in Savannah, Georgia, where he died in 1938.

King Oliver's Creole Jazz Band, ca. 1923. (Left to right) Kid Ory (trombone), Baby Dodds (drums), King Oliver (cornet), Louis Armstrong (slide trumpet), Lil Hardin (piano), Bill Johnson (banjo), and Johnny Dodds (clarinet). Note the various mutes and the cornet on the floor in front of Armstrong.
© Pictorial Press Ltd./Alamy.

overshadow his leader; but with Lil's encouragement Armstrong moved on and eventually joined Fletcher Henderson's band in New York in 1924.

WHY IS SIDNEY BECHET CONSIDERED THE FIRST VIRTUOSIC SOLOIST IN JAZZ?

While Louis Armstrong is at times referred to as the first great jazz soloist, in fact clarinetist and soprano saxophonist Sidney Bechet (1897–1959) preceded him as a virtuosic soloist. Bechet transformed the clarinetist's traditional New Orleans jazz role from primarily playing fills in an ensemble to being a lead voice. His early shift from clarinet to soprano saxophone reflects this as the soprano is a louder, more forceful, and piercing instrument that can compete with the cornet or trumpet, as opposed to the more mellow clarinet.

Bechet's sound and improvisational approach were intense, exciting, and emotionally charged. Bechet and Armstrong are largely responsible for helping to stretch the concept of playing a solo. They gave more emphasis to improvisation in their soloing, as opposed to creating a set solo that would be repeated in each performance with slight variation.

"Dippermouth Blues" (1923) by King Oliver's Creole Jazz Band

DOWNLOAD
Track Number 3

1st cornet: Joe "King" Oliver; **2nd cornet:** Louis Armstrong; **Clarinet:** Johnny Dodds; **Trombone:** Honore Dutrey; **Piano:** Lil Hardin; **Banjo:** Bill Johnson; **Drums:** Baby Dodds.

LISTENING HIGHLIGHT, STYLE: "Dippermouth Blues" is a sensational example of the polyphonic, contrapuntal, collective improvisational New Orleans jazz style. Oliver leads the ensemble as the 1st cornet player, Armstrong generally supports him with a harmony or fills, and the clarinet and trombone fill, in a typical New Orleans jazz fashion. The ensemble is rhythmically driven by this collective improvisation. The most remarkable aspect of this recording, however, is the 3-chorus cornet solo by King Oliver, an unusually long solo for a recording of the period that helped to set the standard of the day. Here he shows his skill in using a mute (a device that gets placed into the bell of a brass instrument to provide a contrasting, and softer, sound), including the use of his hand or a plunger mute (often the rubber end of a toilet plunger) to create a "wah-wah" vocal-like effect that is popular in jazz. Notice that other instruments are playing along with him, yet he is clearly the featured soloist. His 1st chorus (chorus 6, 1:22) is filled with smearing blue notes and is a great example of a bluesy feel on the cornet. His 2nd chorus (chorus 7, 1:37) features blue notes as well but has a new melodic twist that gets repeated a little differently in each 4-bar phrase. His final chorus (chorus 8, 1:53) gets more intense as he plays a little higher and harder, before ending this terrific blues solo. The final chorus (chorus 9, 2:08) features a strong polyphonic ensemble and abrupt ending.

JAZZ LIVES SIDNEY BECHET

Sidney Bechet (1897–1959) was a Creole from New Orleans. His family was musical, and Bechet was deeply involved in the New Orleans musical tradition. He studied with Creole clarinetists, including George Baquet and Big Eye Louis Nelson, and took part in all levels of musical activity in New Orleans, from parades and dance bands to playing with top cornetists King Oliver and Bunk Johnson.

Bechet lived a typical touring musician's life, but his career took a major turn when he joined the African American composer and violinist Will Marion Cook's New York Syncopated Orchestra in 1919. Bechet was a featured soloist and brought a blues sensibility to the orchestra while also being able to contribute to a wide range of material, including classically oriented pieces. When the orchestra toured Europe, Bechet was a sensation. In London, Bechet purchased his straight soprano saxophone (as opposed to the curved version of the instrument), the horn that he was to favor. Appreciating the way he was treated, Bechet stayed in Europe briefly, paving the way for numerous jazz musicians who later moved to Europe to take advantage of a climate that to some seemed more appreciative of their music than American audiences.

When back in New York, Bechet recorded regularly with pianist and songwriter Clarence Williams, including "Cake Walking Babies (from Home)," a terrific example of the New Orleans jazz style that features Bechet and Armstrong, the two greatest and most dynamic soloists of the style. This particular recording is also important as an example of the

continued

JAZZ LIVES *continued*

incorporation of the New Orleans style into a popular song. It's interesting to note, though, that the New Orleans style and the pop vocal are kept quite separate.

As is true for most musicians, Bechet's career had its ups and downs. His recordings for Blue Note and Victor are highlights, including his version of "Summertime." Bechet continued to work steadily but did not achieve the kind of commercial success of Armstrong, at least in the United States. Bechet returned to Europe in 1951 and lived in France until his death in 1959. He was hugely popular there and even had a hit with his tune "Petite Fleur."

Sidney Bechet, ca. 1920s. Bechet was a pioneer of New Orleans–style clarinet who continued to perform into the 1950s.
Courtesy of the Hogan Jazz Archive, Tulane University.

read all about it

"Sidney Bechet's Musical Philosophy"

Walser, Keeping Time, *Chapter 1*
An excerpt from Bechet's 1960 autobiography *Treat It Gentle,* in which he discusses his musical roots.

5th Chorus Louis Armstrong

WHY IS LOUIS ARMSTRONG AMONG THE MOST INFLUENTIAL MUSICIANS IN THE HISTORY OF JAZZ?

Louis Armstrong (1901–1971) is among the most influential musicians in jazz and certainly one of the most important musicians of the twentieth century. His playing and singing have influenced performers of virtually all American styles of popular music. In both his trumpet playing and singing, Armstrong's approach to melodic lyricism and rhythmic phrasing has proven to be crucial to all who followed.

As a trumpet player, Armstrong had a physical and technical ability that stretched the limits of what was thought possible on the instrument. Among other qualities, his ability to play all over the horn (low notes and high notes), the power and consistency of his upper register, his physical endurance, his bright and individualistic tone, and a vibrato like none other set him apart and make him instantly recognizable. As a singer, it is hard to imagine how someone with a craggy, rough-hewn voice like his could be such an influence, yet his approach to shaping a melody set a new standard.

While many factors go into Armstrong's influence, two can be singled out as crucial. First is the elasticity of his rhythmic approach to phrasing. Melodies for popular tunes and jazz standards are generally written in a simple and straightforward

"Cake Walking Babies (from Home)" (1924) by Clarence Williams and the Blue Five

Cornet: Louis Armstrong; **Soprano saxophone:** Sidney Bechet; **Trombone:** Charlie Irvis; **Piano:** Lil Armstrong; **Banjo:** Buddy Christian; **Vocals:** Alberta Hunter and Clarence Todd.

LISTENING HIGHLIGHT, STYLE: The 1st chorus (0:00) features a very inventive and active example of the New Orleans collective improvisational style. Hearing Bechet's soprano sax almost overpower Armstrong's muted cornet makes his decision to play soprano sax instead of clarinet understandable as it can stand up to the normally dominant trumpet lead. Both players have distinctive vibratos and are very expressive. The 2nd chorus (0:59) is a vocal by Alberta Hunter (a blues singer and songwriter who went on to a long and important career) with harmony sung by Clarence Todd. These two were vaudeville partners under the name "Beatty and Todd." During the vocal they are accompanied only by banjo and piano. The last 2 choruses (1:40 and 2:23) are brilliant examples of the New Orleans style at its best, with two of the style's greatest players aggressively making their own powerful solo statements during the polyphonic ensembles. During each player's solo, the other player continues to play strongly and inventively, just barely managing not to overshadow the soloist. In the 3rd chorus Armstrong plays a stop-time solo (2:06), and in the 4th Bechet does as well (2:49). Bechet's stop-time solo is particularly vibrant and powerful, and we hear his quick vibrato intensify as the song comes to a sharp and quick, almost surprising conclusion.

fashion. If they were played as they are written on sheet music, everyone would sound the same and they would all sound rhythmically uninteresting. This is because we are now used to vocalists and instrumentalists taking those simple melodies and moving the placement of the notes slightly, maybe singing or playing them a little sooner or a little later, or perhaps stretching or compressing the phrase. This is something that Armstrong particularly excelled at.

Second, while shaping the phrases rhythmically, Armstrong also adorned them melodically. This has become the standard way for jazz players to approach the playing of a melody—almost never is it played as originally written—and every jazz-oriented player will play a melody at least a bit differently. Armstrong was able to make a melody his own by adding little bits of melody, connecting notes with others of his choosing, and perhaps even changing the original melody slightly, while always keeping it completely recognizable. Armstrong did this with impeccable taste. Jazz has a rich harmonic tradition that employs what are often referred to as "color notes"—parts of the chord that add color as opposed to establishing chord quality such as major or minor. Armstrong's melodic and harmonic embellishments do this in a completely natural, subtle manner. His playing and singing are incredibly sophisticated yet completely down-to-earth. This is a major part of his great appeal.

Another aspect of Armstrong's popularity was his contagiously joyful demeanor along with a generous, open spirit. This all comes shining through in his playing. Not all musicians give off that kind of feeling. Certainly Armstrong comes from a different generation, born out of the tradition of music as entertainment; and that was a guiding principle for him always—to make the people happy. Later, beginning in the 1940s, when jazz started to be treated by some musicians as listening music as opposed to music to dance to or as entertainment, many musicians downplayed their role as entertainers. They often talked as little as is possible on stage, perhaps just to announce the tunes and the band's personnel. But Armstrong was an unabashed entertainer.

Louis Armstrong was born in New Orleans on August 4, 1901, though he liked to say his birthday was July 4, 1900. He was raised by his mother and grandmother in the roughest of New Orleans neighborhoods under oppressively difficult financial conditions, but this area was also an early hotbed of New Orleans jazz. Armstrong lived near an important jazz club and marched ("second-lined") behind bands in parades, and even as a youngster he was paying attention to the important artists of the day, such as Buddy Bolden and King Oliver.

Armstrong had to work from a young age to support himself and his family. At times, he worked as a coal delivery boy, assisted a junkman who scrounged for discarded items to resell, and sang in a vocal quartet on street corners for change. In 1913, as a result of being caught shooting blanks from a pistol on New Year's Eve, he was placed in the Colored Waif's Home, an institution for "wayward boys" (as orphans, abandoned children, and runaways were called at the time). There, he received basic musical instruction, began to learn the cornet, and eventually became the 1st cornet player of the home's band. This was a life-changing period for Armstrong, and the support and discipline that he found at the home after a very chaotic and difficult childhood shaped much of who Armstrong was to become as a person. Along with this, a Jewish family, the Karnofskys, for whom he worked, was also extremely supportive and influential in his life, as was the example that his mother, Mayann, set for him by persevering through incredibly difficult circumstances with pride and integrity.

After this, Armstrong worked numerous jobs to help support the family including running errands for his idol, King Oliver, receiving lessons, in some form, in exchange. He also had his first professional jobs as a musician, including playing the blues in a brothel. When Oliver went to Chicago in 1917, he recommended Armstrong for his vacated position in trombonist Kid Ory's popular band; and Armstrong made a quick and powerful impression with his bold playing that was modeled upon what he had learned from King Oliver. He moved from Ory's band to the riverboats, where his musicianship continued to improve under the demanding African American dance-band leader Fate Marable. To play with Marable's band, Armstrong had to be able to apply his New Orleans "ragging" approach to a variety of musical styles, setting the stage for a long career during which he played many types of popular music while always playing them in his own jazzy style.

After returning briefly to New Orleans, Armstrong was off quickly to take advantage of his biggest break so far after receiving a telegram from King Oliver offering him a job playing 2nd cornet in his band at Lincoln Gardens on Chicago's South Side. This was an important engagement for Oliver and an example of the widening influence of New Orleans jazz that was now moving throughout the country. Oliver's band's time at the club inspired a number of young musicians from the Chicago area, including cornet player Bix Beiderbecke (Chapter 4, 1st Chorus). "Dippermouth Blues" is an excellent example of this band's style. It has an extended solo by King Oliver that allows us to hear this important musician at the height of his popularity.

Armstrong's respect for his mentor, Oliver, was shown by the fact that Armstrong chose never to overshadow the leader and to work in a supporting role, even though at this point he had surpassed his idol in both strength and soloing ability. The band's pianist, Lil Hardin, who soon married Armstrong, encouraged him to leave the band and go out on his own. When Fletcher Henderson, a leading New York City dance-band leader (Chapter 5, 1st Chorus), offered Armstrong a chair in his band in 1924, he accepted and moved to New York. Armstrong, while at first seen as a player from what some perceived as an already old-fashioned New Orleans tradition, quickly made a powerful impact and raised the level of Henderson's band, while also establishing himself as a major soloist. During this time he also recorded with classic blues singers such as Ma Rainey as well as clarinetist and soprano saxophonist Sidney Bechet (discussed this chapter, 4th Chorus), an important New Orleans soloist who preceded Armstrong.

Armstrong left Henderson's band in 1925 and returned to Chicago where, like all freelance musicians, he played a variety of jobs. But most importantly, from 1925 to 1928 he put together a band, the Hot Five, and when expanded, the Hot Seven, just for recording in the studio, which made classic recordings that both typified and stretched the New Orleans concept. While still using the polyphonic group improvisation style, these recordings also allowed players to expand their solos, an important innovation that helped to lead to what became a style of music dominated by powerful soloists. Lil Hardin Armstrong played piano on some of the recordings, while the rest of the band originally included New Orleans players: Johnny Dodds on clarinet, Johnny St. Cyr on banjo (both were in Oliver's band at the time), and Kid Ory on trombone. The Hot Seven had added tuba and drums.

Armstrong played in numerous settings during this period in Chicago and developed a powerful relationship with the influential pianist Earl "Fatha" Hines (1903–1983; see Chapter 4 on Chicago jazz). Armstrong's trumpet playing was always brilliant. After joining Luis Russell's orchestra, an integrated band, Armstrong's

Louis Armstrong with his Hot Five. (Left to right) Armstrong (trumpet), Johnny St. Cyr (banjo), Johnny Dodds (clarinet), Edward "Kid" Ory (trombone), and Lil Hardin Armstrong (piano). Armstrong used a classic New Orleans lineup to accompany his own virtuosic performances.

© Pictorial Press Ltd./Alamy.

listening guide

"Hotter Than That" (1927) by Louis Armstrong and His Hot Five

OVERVIEW: "Hotter Than That" is an excellent example of a mature New Orleans style that includes polyphonic group improvisation. This performance also displays Armstrong's terrific melodic and rhythmic invention both as trumpeter and as vocalist. While Armstrong's playing and **scat singing** (a wordless improvised vocal) clearly stand out, the sophisticated guitar playing of Lonnie Johnson, the **tailgate trombone** of Kid Ory, the clarinet playing of Johnny Dodds, the dynamic pianism of Lil Hardin Armstrong, and the powerful New Orleans–style introduction and **out-chorus** (the last chorus or partial chorus of a tune when everyone plays forcefully for climactic effect) are all important elements of this Hot Five recording.

INSTRUMENTATION: Trumpet and vocal: Louis Armstrong; **Clarinet:** Johnny Dodds; **Trombone:** Edward "Kid" Ory; **Piano:** Lil Hardin Armstrong; **Guitar:** Lonnie Johnson.

The "front line" of trumpet, clarinet, and trombone is a common one in this style of music. Here, the rhythm section is comprised of piano and guitar. For this particular recording guitarist Lonnie Johnson replaces banjo player Johnny St. Cyr, who usually recorded with Armstrong's Hot Five and Hot Seven. Banjo was preferred at times as it had more ability to project its sound before the advent of amplification. Nonetheless, Johnson was an accomplished guitarist, among the first to play single-line melodies in jazz.

FORM: Thirty-two bars, ABAC. The form of this song consists of four 8-measure sections, the most common length for individual sections in popular songs and traditional jazz tunes. A and B combine to make a larger 16-measure section. A then repeats and is followed by C—a variation on B—also combining to make a 16-measure section.

STYLE: Armstrong is the most dynamic soloist here, and his tone is crisp, sharp, brassy, and focused. Notice that his trumpet style and vocal style, while similar, have distinct differences. Armstrong's trumpet soloing tends to be more on top of the beat, always pushing the time, while his singing is a bit more relaxed and perhaps even more elastic and flexible rhythmically. The trumpet can be a very percussive instrument, with the tongue explosively articulating notes or the beginnings of phrases. Though some play it in a very relaxed and laid-back way, trumpeters tend to be fairly aggressive with their rhythmic approach as they are generally called upon to lead the ensemble and do so with a confident rhythmic vitality.

MELODY AND HARMONY: There is essentially no composed melody in this tune as it is primarily a showcase for the front line's soloing prowess, and particularly for Armstrong, who plays a trumpet solo for one chorus and scat sings another. A unique element of this performance is Lonnie Johnson's guitar work as he trades melodic phrases with Armstrong. The **chord progression** (a sequence of chords) of this tune is based upon "Tiger Rag," a New Orleans jazz standard.

RHYTHM: There are no drums in this recording, but the guitar and piano create a forceful beat by playing solidly on all 4 beats of the measure. It is Armstrong's dynamic rhythmic approach that dominates this recording however. His trumpet playing is hot and intense from the first note as he forcefully drives the band by aggressively pushing the beat.

"Hotter Than That" listening guide continued

TIME	FORM	STYLE	MELODY AND HARMONY	RHYTHM	ACCOMPANIMENT
0:00	Intro	Armstrong leads an 8-measure introduction that features the Hot Five in a polyphonic New Orleans–style collective improvisation.			Full band plays
Chorus 1					
0:08	A	Armstrong's tone is bright and full with a percussive edge to it that swings the band. Feel the difference between the intensity of the music during Armstrong's solo and the clarinet solo that follows.	Rather than play a written melody, Armstrong jumps right into a hot improvised solo.		Guitar dominates the accompaniment during Armstrong's trumpet solo.
0:18	B			There is a 2-measure trumpet break (a common rhythmic technique during which the band breaks by strongly emphasizing a beat or a rhythmic figure while the soloist continues to play) at the end of B (0:25). When the band stops, Armstrong's rhythm is clear and strong.	
0:27	A	As the chorus comes to a close, Armstrong's intensity builds to a climax at C.			
0:36	C	Perhaps the most dynamic section of the trumpet solo.		Clarinetist Johnny Dodds takes a 2-measure break into chorus 2.	
Chorus 2					
0:45	A	Dodds plays in the clarinet's upper register to match Armstrong's intensity.		Dodds's rhythm is not quite as assured as Armstrong's.	
0:54	B			Dodds takes a 2-measure clarinet break (1:00).	
1:03	A	Notice that Dodds does not dominate the ensemble in the same manner as Armstrong.			Piano dominates the accompaniment during Dodds's clarinet solo.
1:11	C			Armstrong takes a 2-measure scat singing break (1:18).	

continued

TIME	FORM	STYLE	MELODY AND HARMONY	RHYTHM	ACCOMPANIMENT
			Chorus 3		
1:20	A	While Armstrong's voice is craggy, his musicality and melodic and rhythmic inventiveness make his vocals warm, appealing, and musically exciting.		Armstrong begins with simple, solid rhythms but in the second half of the section begins to play with the time.	Only guitar during Armstrong's scat singing solo. Johnson artfully manages to keep time on all 4 beats while also adding melodic fills to create a lively accompaniment.
1:29	B	Armstrong begins the section with a loose rhythmic approach and then solidifies the time toward the middle of the phrase and into his 2-measure vocal break (1:36).			
1:38	A			While Johnson keeps solid time, Armstrong begins a striking series of syncopations that confuse the meter for this entire A section.	
1:47	C			As Armstrong ends the syncopation at C, the swing becomes even more intense.	
1:56			In an unusual arrangement, Armstrong and Johnson trade bluesy melodic phrases in a **rubato** (rhythmically free) style without piano accompaniment.		
2:13					Lil Hardin Armstrong's solo piano break leads the band into the final chorus.
			Chorus 4		
2:17	A	This is a great, yet short and somewhat understated example of a solo in the tailgate trombone style. Ory's tone is edgy and intense. Notice that Ory's solo is considerably simpler than the others in this tune.			
2:26	B	Trombone solo continues.		Armstrong has a 2-measure break into the out-chorus.	

TIME	FORM	STYLE	MELODY AND HARMONY	RHYTHM	ACCOMPANIMENT
2:34	A	Armstrong leads the full band in a hot New Orleans–style out-chorus with a high, powerful repeated rhythmic figure.			
2:43	C			Armstrong's rhythmic assurance and aggressive approach during an exciting series of breaks insure that the beat stays steady and strong.	
2:50			Armstrong and Johnson again trade phrases to end the tune. Johnson's final chord leaves us a bit up in the air.		

In addition, Armstrong's scat singing is an example of his incredible rhythmic flexibility that influenced all American popular singing that followed. As guitarist Lonnie Johnson keeps a steady beat behind him, Armstrong pushes the beat, pulls it back, hesitates, syncopates, and stretches the time, doing whatever he can to be rhythmically expressive; yet it always feels right and swings like crazy.

ACCOMPANIMENT: Despite its short, 3-minute length, there is a great deal of variety in the accompaniment to this tune. Because of the limits of recording technology, the balance between piano and guitar is at times a bit problematic; but the texture of the accompaniment clearly changes throughout the tune. The 1st chorus is dominated by powerful guitar behind Armstrong, and the piano is heard as well. Lil Hardin dominates the accompaniment during Dodds's clarinet solo. She pounds out bass notes with her left hand, **comps** (short for "accompanies" and refers to playing the chord progression in support of a soloist) with her right hand on all 4 beats of a measure, and occasionally **fills** (bits of melody that fill space between the soloist's phrases) behind Dodds. Johnson alone accompanies Armstrong's scatting, and in this chorus Johnson is a bit freer rhythmically, while also filling a bit. Piano and guitar both play strongly behind Ory's trombone solo and the out-chorus.

Compare

- "Weather Bird" (1928) by Earl "Fatha" Hines (piano) and Louis Armstrong (trumpet); see Chapter 4, 2nd Chorus.

- "A Kiss to Build a Dream On" (1951) by Louis Armstrong with Sy Oliver's Orchestra. "A Kiss to Build a Dream On" gives us a chance to see Armstrong (or "Satchmo" or "Pops," as he is often called) in a bit of a different mode. Here he is more of a pop artist and entertainer, accompanied by Sy Oliver's Orchestra. While Armstrong plays and sings as well as always, the setting and the material are more in the pop tradition but with a New Orleans jazz feel, particularly in the solo section in the 2nd chorus. Armstrong takes this beautiful and nicely written popular tune and turns it into something very special, from both a vocal and an instrumental perspective.

read all about it

"What Is Swing?" by Louis
Armstrong

Walser, **Keeping Time,** *Chapter 18*
Louis Armstrong discusses how
swing developed out of his New
Orleans–style playing.

worth as a vocalist, something that other bands did not seem to appreciate, became evident, beginning with his recording of "I Can't Give You Anything but Love."

Armstrong was a hit in Europe in the early 1930s, and his success continued in the swing era. While clearly a jazz trumpet player, Armstrong had become a pop star; and he began to appear in movies as well. His choice of material and his performance style changed to appeal to a pop audience. While distancing himself from his New Orleans jazz background in some ways, this focus on entertaining the audience was still very much in the spirit of New Orleans musicians.

While Armstrong was always a popular artist, popularity can prove mercurial. Tastes changed in the 1940s, and new styles of jazz developed, leaving Armstrong, in some people's opinions, seeming old-fashioned. To some he even represented a negative stereotype with his obvious desire to entertain, an ever-present smile, and what some even referred to as pandering to white audiences. But Armstrong continued to just be himself—the consummate entertainer who made the entire world happy with his virtuosic trumpet playing and tasteful, swinging singing, regardless of the opinion of those who felt he was politically incorrect. He began to work with smaller groups again under the name of Louis Armstrong and His All Stars. He had a steady stream of popular records, including "Mack the Knife," "Hello Dolly," and "A Kiss to Build a Dream On"; worked with the best musicians; made movies; toured continually; and continued to function as an ambassador for jazz as well as America itself until his death in 1971.

QUESTIONS AND CONTROVERSIES
Louis Armstrong Takes a Stand

Not known for addressing racism directly, Armstrong surprised some fans and critics when he commented on the racial unrest that occurred in 1957 when nine black teenagers attempted to attend a Little Rock, Arkansas, high school, following an order that the schools had to be integrated by a local judge. Arkansas governor Orval Faubus defied the judge, ordering the National Guard to the school in order to keep the African American students out. Two weeks later, Armstrong was interviewed before playing a concert. "It's getting almost so bad a colored man hasn't got any country," Armstrong commented, criticizing President Eisenhower for having "no guts" because he failed to force Faubus to change his position. When Eisenhower finally sent in troops to forcibly integrate the high school, Armstrong sent a telegram to him stating, "If you decide to walk into the schools with the little colored kids, take me along, Daddy." The incident also inspired a jazz musician of a later generation, Charles Mingus (Chapter 13, 3rd Chorus), to compose a piece called "Fables of Faubus," as another response to this landmark in the growing movement for civil rights.

CODA Chapter Summary

How Did the Mixture of Different Ethnic Groups in New Orleans Influence the Development of Jazz?

- The mix of European, African, Latino, and Creole cultures in New Orleans created an opportunity for musicians to hear and absorb many different influences, including popular tunes, marches, rags, light opera, hymns and spirituals, and brass-band music.

Who Were Some of the Key Early New Orleans Jazz Musicians?

- Among the first performers and bandleaders were African American cornet players Buddy Bolden and Freddie Keppard and white bandleader Jack "Papa" Laine.
- The Original Dixieland Jazz Band was an all-white band from New Orleans that made the first jazz record.

What Was the Influence of "King" Oliver on Early Jazz Music and Its Performers?

- King Oliver was known for his blues-flavored playing on the cornet.
- His long residency in Chicago influenced many young, white, Midwestern musicians.

Why Is Sidney Bechet Considered the First Virtuosic Soloist in Jazz?

- Bechet was among the first clarinetists to play solos rather than primarily providing fills. He switched from the clarinet to the soprano saxophone early in his career, popularizing this instrument.

Why Is Louis Armstrong Among the Most Influential Musicians in the History of Jazz?

- As a trumpet player, Armstrong had a physical and technical ability that stretched the limits of what was thought possible on the instrument. His ability to reshape a melody to give it extra melodic and rhythmic interest helped him transform even the most common popular songs into jazz masterpieces.
- His craggy, rough-hewn voice and approach to shaping a melody set a new standard for jazz singers.
- Finally, he was an enthusiastic and unabashed entertainer, whose love of performing shone through in every setting.

Talkin' Jazz (Key Terms)

Arranging	Creole	Rubato
Chord progression	Fill	Scat singing
Comp	Out-chorus	Tailgate trombone
Composing	Polyphony	

Key People

Buddy Bolden	Original Dixieland	King Oliver
Freddie Keppard	Jazz Band	Sidney Bechet
Jack "Papa" Laine	Jelly Roll Morton	Louis Armstrong

Think About This (For Further Discussion and Study)

1. New Orleans was ethnically diverse, and the music of the city reflected this. Discuss various types of music that you listen to in relation to various cultural influences that may be present.
2. What music do you hear in your neighborhood, town, or city; and how has this influenced your listening?
3. Discuss the process through which African Americans in New Orleans developed jazz.
4. The Original Dixieland Jazz Band's "Livery Stable Blues" brought jazz to the public's attention. Can you think of a song that did this in a genre that you listen to?
5. What is your experience as you listen to old recordings? Is it difficult for you? If so, how?
6. Discuss the importance of Jelly Roll Morton to the development of jazz as well as his influence upon composition and arranging in jazz.
7. Examine King Oliver's solo in "Dippermouth Blues" in relation to his use of blue notes.
8. Discuss what makes Louis Armstrong's playing and singing important in the development of jazz.
9. If you have seen films of Armstrong, what impressions do you have of his performance style?
10. Try taking a song everyone knows and put scat singing syllables to it.

Look It Up (Key Resources)

Armstrong, Louis. *Satchmo: My Life in New Orleans*. New York: Da Capo Press, 1986.

Bechet, Sidney. *Treat It Gentle*. New York: Hill and Wang, 1960.

Brothers, Thomas. *Louis Armstrong in His Own Words: Selected Writings*. New York: Oxford University Press, 1999.

———. *Louis Armstrong's New Orleans*. New York: Norton, 2006.

Chilton, John. *Sidney Bechet: The Wizard of Jazz*. Basingstoke, UK: Macmillan, 1997.

Giddins, Gary. *Satchmo*, rev. ed. New York: Da Capo Press, 2001.

Hersch, Charles: *Subversive Sounds: Race and the Birth of Jazz in New Orleans*. Chicago: University of Chicago Press, 2007.

Lomax, Alan. *Mr. Jelly Roll: The Fortunes of Jelly Roll Morton, New Orleans Creole and "Inventor of Jazz."* New York: Duell, Sloan, and Pearce, 1950.

Magee, Jeffrey. "'King Porter Stomp' and the Jazz Tradition." *Current Musicology* 71–73 (Spring 2001–2002): 22–53.

Raeburn, Bruce Boyd. *New Orleans Style and the Writing of American Jazz History*. Ann Arbor: University of Michigan Press, 2012.

Riccardi, Ricky. *What a Wonderful World: The Magic of Louis Armstrong's Later Years*. New York: Pantheon Books, 2011.

Schuller, Gunther. *Early Jazz: Its Roots and Musical Development*. New York: Oxford University Press, 1968.

Williams, Martin. *Jazz Masters of New Orleans*. New York: Da Capo Press, 1978.

JAZZ GOES TO TOWN
1910-1930

MAJOR MUSICAL STYLES

1912– Present	• Blues
1917–1930	• Chicago jazz • New York jazz • Kansas City jazz

The movement of African Americans from the rural South to the industrial North and West accelerated in the early twentieth century. This social movement came to be known as "the "Great Migration." The opening of major rail lines facilitated travel north, and major hubs—particularly Chicago—attracted thousands of African Americans searching for new employment opportunities and more social freedom. The railroads themselves employed thousands of African Americans in jobs from porters to freight handlers. Transportation hubs became centers of distribution of all types of goods, and these centers needed workers to keep the goods moving. Thus, Chicago became one of the fastest growing cities in the early twentieth century, attracting not only African Americans but large immigrant populations from eastern and southern Europe as well, which continued unabated until

World War I cut off easy travel, followed by more restrictive laws that limited the influx of immigrants. The different ethnic and racial groups tended to stay within their own neighborhoods, with the largest black population settling in the city's South Side.

As African Americans moved north, it was natural for musicians and entertainers to follow them for employment opportunities. The same trains that carried workers out of the South offered musicians a means of traveling either to perform in a new city or to move from city to city seeking employment more easily. Thus, King Oliver was able to take his band in the early 1900s to Los Angeles to play, a trip that would have been difficult, if not impossible, just a few years earlier.

The migration of blacks northward and the large new immigrant populations also had an impact within the cities. New York offers just one example of how neighborhoods changed during this period of rapid population growth. As the city grew, African Americans were displaced from neighborhoods such as Manhattan's San Juan Hill and were settling uptown in Harlem, which became a center of black culture in the 1920s during the period known as the Harlem Renaissance. Major new performing centers, like the Apollo Theater, and dozens of smaller nightclubs blossomed there, some catering to white audiences who came uptown to be exposed to the new black music and dance and others catering to the local population.

Pullman porter at Chicago's Union Station. A job as a Pullman Porter was viewed as very desirable because the pay was good and porters were treated well.

Photo by Jack Delano. Courtesy Library of Congress.

Kansas City was another rail hub that would become important in the development of jazz. Musicians could use the city as a base for playing throughout the Midwest. Just as New Orleans was tightening its laws against nightlife, Kansas City's laws were enforced only loosely, if at all, encouraging clubs to stay open late, giving musicians many opportunities to play.

Besides the revolution in transportation, a new technological revolution would make it possible for local musical styles to spread throughout the country. The development of recording technologies and radio had an enormous impact on the growth of jazz. Radio links to nightclubs—such as New York's Cotton Club—carried musical performances for hundreds of miles. In the early days of radio, stations were not tightly regulated, and there was little competition

Harlem Street Musicians, 1943. Just as they had done in the rural South, musicians took to the streets to entertain in major cities, hoping to earn some pocket change from passersby.

Photo by Roger Smith. Courtesy Library of Congress.

outside of the major cities so that programs originating out of New York, for example, could be heard through much of the northeastern part of the country, quickly spreading the music to new listeners and would-be performers.

Some jazz musicians were at first reluctant to record their music for the new phonograph industry. While radio was fleeting, records were more permanent; and some players feared that if they made a record of their unique arrangements, others would steal their music from them and thus deprive them of their livelihoods. However, with the success of the first jazz recording made in 1917, the floodgates were open and musicians saw recording as another means of augmenting their income and promoting their music throughout the country. Jazz was a musical style that you had to hear, so while sheet music of jazz pieces continued to sell, it was these records that actually helped musicians learn the new musical style and begin to perform it in their own hometowns.

1910–1930

MUSICIANS/MUSICAL WORKS

1910	• Mary Lou Williams, pianist-composer-arranger, born • Artie Shaw, pianist-bandleader, born • Milt Hinton, bassist, born
1911	• Roy Eldridge, trumpeter, born • "Big" Joe Turner, blues vocalist, born
1912	• W. C. Handy's "Memphis Blues" is published • Gil Evans, arranger-composer, born
1913	• Woody Herman, saxophone-clarinetist-bandleader, born
1914	• Herman Blount (aka Sun Ra), pianist-bandleader, born
1915	• Billie Holiday (b. Eleanora Fagan), vocalist, born • Frank Sinatra, vocalist, born • William Thomas "Billy" Strayhorn, pianist-composer, born
1916	• Scott Joplin records his "Maple Leaf Rag" on a piano roll
1917	• "Livery Stable Blues" recorded by Original Dixieland Jazz Band, credited as "first" jazz recording • John Birks "Dizzy" Gillespie, trumpeter-composer-bebop pioneer, born • Thelonious Monk, pianist-composer, born
	• Tadd Dameron, pianist-composer-arranger, born • Ella Fitzgerald, vocalist, born
1919	• Lieut. James Reese Europe's Band records W. C. Handy's "Memphis Blues" (1919) • Nat "King" Cole, pianist-vocalist, born • Art Blakey, drummer-bandleader, born • Lennie Tristano, pianist-composer, born
1920	• Mamie Smith records "Crazy Blues," first major blues hit; launches the "classic blues" era • Charlie Parker, saxophonist-bebop pioneer, born • Dave Brubeck, pianist-composer, born
1921	• *Shuffle Along*, with music by Eubie Blake and lyrics by Noble Sissle, opens on Broadway; first musical written, directed, and starring black performers
1922	• Charles Mingus, bass player-composer-bandleader, born • Ramon "Mongo" Santamaria, bandleader-conguero, born
1923	• Clarence Williams and the Blue Five, "Cake Walking Babies (from Home)," featuring Sidney Bechet • King Oliver's Creole Jazz Band, "Dippermouth Blues," featuring Louis Armstrong • Tito Puente, percussionist-bandleader, born • Wes Montgomery, guitarist, born

1924	• Lovie Austin and Her Blues Serenaders, "Traveling Blues" • Earl "Bud" Powell, pianist-composer, born • Max Roach, drummer-bandleader, born
1925	• Callen Radcliffe "Cal" Tjader, vibraphonist, born • Charlie Byrd, guitar player, born • Jimmy Smith, organist, born (ca. 1925–1928) • Ramsey Lewis, pianist, born
1926	• Jelly Roll Morton and His Red Hot Peppers, "King Porter Stomp" • Miles Davis, trumpeter-bandleader, born • John Coltrane, saxophonist-bandleader, born
1927	• Bessie Smith and James P. Johnson, "Backwater Blues" • Louis Armstrong's Hot Five, "Hotter Than That," featuring Lonnie Johnson (guitar), Lil Hardin Armstrong (piano) • Frankie Trumbauer and His Orchestra, "Singin' the Blues," featuring Bix Beiderbecke

	• Duke Ellington and the Washingtonians, "Black and Tan Fantasy" • Duke Ellington's Washingtonians begin a 5-year run at Harlem's Cotton Club • Gerry Mulligan, baritone saxophonist, born • Antônio Carlos Jobim, composer-vocalist-pianist-guitarist, born • Stan Getz, saxophonist, born
1928	• Earl Hines and Louis Armstrong, "Weather Bird" • Paul Whiteman Orchestra, "There Ain't No Sweet Man (Worth the Salt of My Tears)" • Julian "Cannonball" Adderley, alto saxophonist, born • Horace Silver, pianist-composer, born
1929	• Chet Baker, trumpeter, born • Bill Evans, pianist-composer, born • Cecil Taylor, pianist-composer, born • Benny Golson, tenor saxophonist, born • Ray Barretto, conguero-bandleader, born

1910–1930

MAJOR SOCIAL DEVELOPMENTS

1910	• Beginning of the "Great Migration" of African Americans from the South to northern cities
1913	• Armory Show in New York introduces modern European art to American audiences
1914–1918	• World War I
1914	• Panama Canal completed
1919	• Prohibition (ban on the sale of alcohol) begins
1920	• Women get the right to vote
1920–1930	• The "Roarin' '20s"/The Jazz Age
ca. 1922–1930	• The height of the Harlem Renaissance, a flowering of the arts in New York's largest African American neighborhood

1923	• The Charleston dance craze sweeps America
1924	• Soviet leader Vladimir Lenin dies • J. Edgar Hoover appointed director of the Bureau of Investigation, a precursor to the FBI, which he helped found
1925	• Scopes trial challenges the right to teach evolution in the classroom
1927	• First "talking picture," *The Jazz Singer*, starring Al Jolson • Charles Lindbergh makes first solo flight across the Atlantic Ocean
1928	• First Mickey Mouse cartoon is released
1929	• The Great Depression begins

Romaine

CHICAGO JAZZ | LATE 1917-1930

4

WHY DID A THRIVING JAZZ SCENE DEVELOP IN CHICAGO IN THE LATE 1910s AND EARLY 1920s?

With its thriving and diverse music scene, Chicago, as early as 1917, provided excellent employment opportunities for musicians. The city's booming industries—particularly the meat packing business—along with its status as a center of distribution for goods moving both east and west had already attracted many southern and Midwestern African American workers as part of the Great Migration to the booming northern and Midwestern cities. Naturally, black emigrants to Chicago's South Side created a substantial audience for African American entertainment. In addition, early black jazz entertainers such as clarinetist Wilbur Sweatman had already been popular in Chicago with both black and white audiences as early as 1906. New Orleans instrumentalists such as cornetist Freddie Keppard, clarinetist Jimmy Noone, trombonist Kid Ory, Jelly Roll Morton, and later King Oliver's band with Louis Armstrong were among those taking advantage of these opportunities and were crucial to bringing the New Orleans style to Chicago (see Chapter 3). While these musicians worked in Chicago, that does not imply that they permanently resided in Chicago; many came and went as part of their touring and itinerant employment, as we have seen with Louis Armstrong, for example.

As jazz disseminated, the music was also beginning to evolve from its emphasis upon a polyphonic ensemble texture toward a music that featured individual soloists. Armstrong's virtuosity and invention influenced a second generation of jazz musicians who arrived in Chicago from around the Midwest such as cornetist Bix Beiderbecke and saxophonist Frank Trumbauer, as well as a group of young white musicians who became known as the Austin High Gang. Players such as these were also among the first to have their introduction to jazz through recordings, such as those by the Original Dixieland Jazz Band (see Chapter 3, 2nd Chorus).

The Austin High Gang all went to Austin High School in Chicago and included cornetist Jimmy McPartland, guitarist Dick McPartland, tenor sax player Bud Freeman, clarinetist Frank Teschemacher, and drummer Dave Tough, all of whom went on to significant musical careers. Other Chicago-based musicians, including clarinetists Benny Goodman (who went on to be one of the stars of the swing era, discussed in Chapter 7, 1st Chorus) and

In this chapter, we'll answer these questions:

- Why Did a Thriving Jazz Scene Develop in Chicago in the Late 1910s and Early 1920s?

- How Did Bix Beiderbecke's Style Differ from Those of Louis Armstrong and Other Early Jazz Trumpeters?

- What Was Paul Whiteman's Role in Popularizing Jazz?

- How Did Earl Hines Revolutionize Jazz Piano?

- What Role Did Women Play in the Early Decades of Jazz?

Photo: Courtesy Redferns/Getty Images.

Pee Wee Russell, banjo player Eddie Condon, and drummer Gene Krupa (who also was a star in the swing era), were also part of this scene. Together they became known as "the Chicagoans," and the style they played was called "Chicago jazz." Beiderbecke and Trumbauer were particularly influential upon this style, and they were among the first white jazz players considered to be jazz innovators.

1st Chorus Bix Beiderbecke and Paul Whiteman

HOW DID BIX BEIDERBECKE'S STYLE DIFFER FROM THOSE OF LOUIS ARMSTRONG AND OTHER EARLY JAZZ TRUMPETERS?

Leon "Bix" Beiderbecke

Leon "Bix" Beiderbecke (1903–1931) was born in Davenport, Iowa, a northern port city on the Mississippi River. His mother played piano and organ and Beiderbecke displayed an excellent musical ear at a very young age, eventually teaching himself both the piano and the cornet. The harmonic knowledge he gained from playing the piano greatly influenced his playing as he had a sophisticated harmonic sense that made his melodic invention particularly unique. While an excellent cornet player, his was not a virtuosic style in the mode of Louis Armstrong. Beiderbecke primarily played in the cornet's middle register and had a bell-like tone that he opened or burnished depending on the character of the solo or passage. As his melodies unfold it is almost as if we can hear him thinking as he carefully crafts his lovely solos that are often gentle in character yet also hot and swinging. This all set him apart as an individualistic soloist and as a leading cornet player of the period. While it is his cornet playing he is primarily known for, he also continued to play and compose for the piano, including a forward-looking and impressionistic, classically oriented composition, *In a Mist*.

One of Beiderbecke's earliest important influences was hearing the Original Dixieland Jazz Band's recording of "Tiger Rag" when he was 14, an example of the importance of those early recordings upon the dissemination of jazz throughout the country. Living on the Mississippi also gave Beiderbecke the chance to hear jazz as the steamboats came through town. His early interest in jazz alarmed his parents, who sent him to boarding school at Lake Forest Academy, just north of Chicago, hoping this would set him on the path to a "normal" career. This plan backfired as the school's close proximity to Chicago allowed Beiderbecke to easily travel to town to be part of the city's thriving jazz scene, including hearing Armstrong with King Oliver at the Lincoln Gardens nightclub and later with the Carroll Dickerson Orchestra.

Frank Trumbauer

In 1923 Beiderbecke joined the Wolverines, a group of northern whites who formed a traditional New Orleans ensemble. Their recordings from 1924 clearly show Beiderbecke's early maturity and his calm, thoughtful style; and his influence began to grow as a result. Later in the same year Beiderbecke joined the Sioux City Six, partnering with saxophonist Frank Trumbauer (known as "Tram"). Trumbauer's smooth, lyrical style also showed new stylistic possibilities and was extremely significant, influencing future saxophonists such as Lester Young (Chapter 6, 4th Chorus) and saxophonist-trumpeter-arranger-bandleader Benny Carter (Chapter 5, 2nd Chorus).

The Wolverines making a record at the Gennett studios. Bix Beiderbecke is seated holding a trumpet, second from the right. Note the acoustic horn used to make the recording on the back wall.

© *Pictorial Press Ltd./Alamy.*

Trumbauer's and Beiderbecke's styles were well matched and complementary. They continued to play together in Detroit bandleader Jean Goldkette's excellent bands and then moved on to work for one of the leading bandleaders of the day, Paul Whiteman. There, at the top of the music business, Beiderbecke and Trumbauer were star instrumentalists and became leading figures in jazz. "Singin' the Blues," recorded under the name Frankie Trumbauer and His Orchestra, displays both of their styles clearly and elegantly.

Beiderbecke unfortunately became a model for the tortured artist stereotype as he developed a dependence on alcohol that led to a tragic early death at the age of 28. Beiderbecke's influence was profound however, offering an alternative approach to the Herculean, but no less melodic, cornet playing of Armstrong. His solos have been **transcribed** and played by cornet and trumpet players ever since, instilling his musicality and gentle, yet hot, melodic invention into the repertoire of styles in jazz.

Paul Whiteman
WHAT WAS PAUL WHITEMAN'S ROLE IN POPULARIZING JAZZ?

Paul Whiteman (1890–1967) led a highly successful dance orchestra in the 1920s and 1930s and continued a successful career through the 1950s. He was an excellent musician and showman, as well as an extremely savvy businessman who brought together some of the best instrumentalists, including Beiderbecke and Trumbauer, as well as top arranger-composers such as Bill Challis and Ferde Grofé to produce numerous hits of a consistently high quality.

Whiteman was highly successful in performance, recording, and the sale of sheet music. His relationship to jazz has always been a source of controversy, however, as he had a self-proclaimed desire to make jazz more appealing to the masses.

listening guide

DOWNLOAD
Track Number 5

"Singin' the Blues" (1927) by Frankie Trumbauer and His Orchestra

INSTRUMENTATION: Cornet: Bix Beiderbecke; **C-melody saxophone:** Frankie Trumbauer; **Trombone:** Bill Rank; **Clarinet:** Jimmy Dorsey; **Alto saxophone:** Doc Ryker; **Piano:** Paul Mertz; **Guitar:** Eddie Lang; **Drums:** Chauncey Morehouse.

FORM: After a short introduction, the form of this Tin Pan Alley song is comprised of four 8-measure sections, ABA¹C. A and B comprise the first half of the tune, A¹ is a repetition of A with some variation and is the beginning of the second half of the form, while the ending section, C, is quite different from B. Early jazz was frequently blues-based (despite the title, this does not resemble a blues) or a multistrain format, so this Tin Pan Alley popular song signals the beginning of a change in repertoire in jazz, which went on to base a great deal of its repertoire on the use of popular songs.

STYLE: The individualistic styles of Beiderbecke and Trumbauer are the most significant aspects of this recording. Both of their styles emphasize simple, understated, and graceful melodic playing. Beiderbecke's playing markedly contrasts with Armstrong's as he has a much gentler approach to the cornet and does not attempt to display a virtuosic technique. For example, he plays in a rather narrow range of the horn, instead focusing on melodic content. While sometimes he seems to float over the ensemble, at other times he digs in with a subtle yet insistent swing and driving quarter notes. Beiderbecke's note choices are consistently lovely, and he varies his rhythmic figures throughout. Trumbauer's **legato** (smooth) and lyrical playing is full of expressive slurs and bends with a very light **vibrato**. Like Beiderbecke, he has a gentle approach that differs from the more intense playing we often hear in other early jazz. Here, Trumbauer plays the C-melody sax, an instrument essentially no longer in use.

MELODY AND HARMONY: Trumbauer is featured in the 1st chorus as he plays a mixture of the melody and an improvised solo. During Beiderbecke's solo on the 2nd chorus, as opposed to stating and slightly varying the melody of this tune—which was the common practice of the day—he uses the underlying chord structure of this tune to create his solo, hinting at a new direction in jazz. The harmony is interesting and varied throughout and moves through a variety of keys.

RHYTHM: As we find in all of these old recordings, the volume levels are problematic. The guitar is right up front and is clearly highlighted, while the piano is barely heard in the background. The drums are largely confined to cymbal splashes and choked cymbal sounds—the manual damping of a cymbal after it has been struck.

ACCOMPANIMENT: Eddie Lang's remarkable guitar playing is the essential element of the accompaniment for this entire arrangement. He manages to keep time and propel the music by playing a steady pulse while also playing fills and counterlines throughout. These fills and counterlines function in three ways as they are melodically important, they create the pulse, and they outline the harmonies. Without his guitar playing this would be an entirely different and less compelling recording.

"SINGIN' THE BLUES" LISTENING GUIDE

TIME	FORM	STYLE	MELODY AND HARMONY	RHYTHM	ACCOMPANIMENT
0:00	Intro	A largely unaccompanied harmonized introduction by the horns begins this tune.	The arranger, Bill Challis, was a leading arranger of the period. Here, he creates a sequence, a melodic figure that is repeated but at different pitches. He does it twice and then expands it to create a second, expanded sequence.		Colorful and rhythmic cymbal splashes are the only accompaniment here.
Chorus 1					
0:06 A 0:20 B 0:34 A¹ 0:49 C		This entire chorus is a Frankie Trumbauer solo that includes portions of the original melody, and his playing is gently sweet and lyrical. This style was influential upon other saxophonists with lyrical sensibilities, such as Lester Young and Benny Carter, as it offered a contrasting approach to the more aggressive playing style that was dominant. Important features are breaks at the end of the B and C sections. Note how Trumbauer's solo and Lang's guitar hook up together rhythmically.	Trumbauer plays in a very melodic style.	This recording is at a medium tempo and is played in a very relaxed manner. Consequently, the dancers would be dancing lightly and easily around the dance floor, perhaps taking a bit of a break from more uptempo material.	Eddie Lang's guitar is the most important element of both the rhythm and accompaniment, and he manages to merge several roles. Lang keeps solid time as he chunks along on all 4 beats but also regularly plays lovely and inventive melodic counterlines and fills that are extremely varied rhythmically. His lines function as countermelodies, but he also uses them to carefully outline the harmony of the chord progression. This is rhythm guitar playing at the highest level, particularly for the period. Cymbal splashes are used occasionally to decorate and color the solo. The piano is heard only lightly in the background.

continued

"Singin' the Blues" listening guide continued

TIME	FORM	STYLE	MELODY AND HARMONY	RHYTHM	ACCOMPANIMENT
Chorus 2					
1:03 A 1:17 B		The 2nd chorus is a Beiderbecke solo. His playing is gentle and relaxed, which makes his rhythmic phrasing and melodic invention seem simple; but his subtle rhythmic variation and tasteful note choices make this a very sophisticated solo. Note the regular use of blue notes. Beiderbecke is playing quietly and easily floats above the ensemble for much of the solo. He plays right on the beat but not forcefully. He ends the B section with a break.	Beiderbecke also plays in a very melodic style.	Lang's guitar continues to dominate the rhythm and accompaniment here as he plays time and counterlines throughout Beiderbecke's solo. Lang is much less active during this chorus than he was in Trumbauer's solo however. The piano is more audible but is still in the background.	
1:31 A¹ 1:46 C		At A¹ Beiderbecke rips into his first phrase and plays more forcefully for the first few measures, including sharply emphasizing 3 quarter notes. He then quickly returns to his lighter playing and ends his solo as simply and in as relaxed a manner as he started. This is a very understated yet profound solo. It helped to set in motion a new style of playing and was widely imitated.			
Chorus 3					
2:00	A	The whole group enters and plays a New Orleans–style ensemble.	The actual melody of the tune is played here for the first time.	The rhythm continues to be relaxed but is a bit more insistent for this ensemble.	Lang largely sticks to playing on all 4 beats.
2:15	B	Jimmy Dorsey (who went on to fame as a swing dance-band leader) plays a clarinet solo.	Dorsey continues the simple, melodic character of the other soloists. He also ends his solo with a break.		Lang returns to playing time and simple fills.
2:29	A¹	The ensemble again enters with collective improvisation.	The melody of the tune is played again, this time more forcefully by Beiderbecke.	The rhythm is again a bit more insistent for the ending.	
2:43	C	The polyphony continues and becomes stronger to end the song with a bit of a bang. Beiderbecke in particular plays more insistently.	We hear the melody here briefly but it disappears toward the end.	The tune ends with a cymbal splash.	Lang has a nice break in the middle of this section, highlighting his importance in this recording.

"Singin' the Blues" listening guide continued

Compare

"There Ain't No Sweet Man (Worth the Salt of My Tears)" (1928) by the Paul Whiteman Orchestra. This track gives us a chance to hear Beiderbecke and Trumbauer in a more commercial context. In "Singin' the Blues" they each improvised whole choruses, but here, while there are solos by Beiderbecke and Trumbauer, Beiderbecke's primary role is to play the melody with the orchestra. The melody is presented clearly here, while in "Singin' the Blues" it was initially largely avoided. As the featured soloist, Beiderbecke, however, still manages to make the melody hot; Trumbauer also is given a little room to display his sweet and pretty way with a melody. We also get to hear lovely orchestrations and how a mixed ensemble of winds and strings with vocals was used in popular music, as well as how "hot" jazz was fused with a popular and "sweet" orchestra style. A "sweet" style generally implies less "hot," which means, as is true here, less improvisation, a more straightforward presentation of the melody throughout the tune, and a lighter groove than a "hot" jazz band would normally create. The Bing Crosby vocal (see following section "Paul Whiteman" regarding Crosby's importance to Whiteman) is a crucial element in this recording and a nice introduction to this extremely popular singer. Here, he sings with the Rhythm Boys, a vocal trio.

The notion of uplifting jazz to a more legitimate place in the American mainstream by means of mixing it with a more European-based compositional sensibility—this style is often referred to as "symphonic jazz" (Whiteman is credited with creating this term) or "concert jazz"—necessarily implies that jazz needed to be legitimized somehow, a concept which is misguided at best. But Whiteman's was one of the first attempts to fuse the excitement of improvised jazz and other African American elements with a compositional approach drawn from European classical music. This fusion continues to challenge composers.

Paul Whiteman, the son of a prominent music teacher, began his career as a violist, including playing with the Denver and San Francisco symphonies. After forming his own band and performing in San Francisco, Los Angeles, and Atlantic City, he had great success at New York's Palais Royal and had hits in 1920 with "Whispering" and "Japanese Sandman." As Whiteman attempted to blend a dance band with an orchestra, some at the time referred to his efforts as "making an honest woman out of jazz." Whiteman's response was that "he never questioned her honesty, I simply thought she needed a new dress." The "new dress" presented the melodies and feel of jazz in a popular music style reminiscent of the European popular orchestra tradition and appealed to a different audience from the traditional jazz audience. It featured arrangements that were carefully crafted and extremely well played, and improvisation was limited to short solo spots.

While some question his place in the history of jazz, Whiteman certainly was responsible for creating some very important early concert jazz works. His 1924 concert at New York's Aeolian Hall, which he named "An Experiment in Modern Music," included his most famous commission in this vein, George Gershwin's *Rhapsody in Blue*, performed with Gershwin at the piano. *Rhapsody in Blue* helped to set in motion a movement that attempts to combine classically oriented

read all about it

"The Man Who Made a Lady Out of Jazz" by Hugh C. Ernst

Walser, **Keeping Time,** *Chapter 12*
The original program notes for Whiteman's famous Aeolian Hall concert.

Bandleader Paul Whiteman (center with baton) leads his Ambassador Orchestra, ca. late 1920s. Whiteman's large band could play everything from sweet dance music to lightly syncopated jazz.

Courtesy Chicago History Museum/ Getty Images.

compositional concepts with jazz, often resulting in more extended compositions than is usual for the genre.

Whiteman, sometimes referred to as the "King of Jazz," was responsible for other innovations and led the first dance band to have a full-time vocalist, Bing Crosby, who went on to become one of the most successful singers in American popular music. Crosby heard Armstrong at this time and was heavily influenced by Armstrong's approach.

Whiteman also decided to include jazz soloists in his orchestra as a means of creating a more jazzy sound. Besides hiring Beiderbecke and Trumbauer, Whiteman brought on board prominent players including violinist Joe Venuti, guitarist

IN PERFORMANCE
Jazz Guitar

One of the greatest early jazz musicians was Salvatore "Eddie" Lang, who helped popularize the guitar as a lead instrument in jazz. Early jazz bands had featured tenor banjos to provide chordal accompaniment because they were loud enough to be heard over a small ensemble. With the introduction of larger and louder guitars, the more mellow-voiced stringed instrument began to be used but again primarily as an accompaniment.

Lang helped to introduce the guitar as a melody instrument. Often working with his childhood friend, violinist Joe Venuti, Lang's approach influenced generations of musicians, beginning with guitarists Django Reinhardt and Charlie Christian (see Chapter 7, 1st Chorus). Lang and Venuti were both hired to play in Paul Whiteman's orchestra at the time that Bix Beiderbecke was a member of that group.

Eddie Lang, and cornetist Bunny Berigan. While these soloists did not have the same kind of room to play as they did in smaller band settings, they were now with a top band and making an excellent salary.

2nd Chorus Earl "Fatha" Hines and Louis Armstrong

HOW DID EARL HINES REVOLUTIONIZE JAZZ PIANO?

Earl Hines

Earl "Fatha" Hines (1903–1983), one of the great pianists in jazz, had a long and varied career. He worked as a solo pianist and accompanist, played in small groups with most of the important names in jazz, and was an influential big-band leader.

Hines was known for his ability to fuse a variety of styles into one forward-thinking approach that embodied the history of jazz-oriented piano styles up to that time. He thoroughly absorbed the stride piano school and was an adept accompanist, yet it was his melodic playing that made him stand out. Hines's major influences were the stride piano players from the East Coast, such as Fats Waller (Chapter 5, 4th Chorus) and James P. Johnson (Chapter 2, 1st Chorus, and Chapter 5, 4th Chorus). But Hines was much freer with his left hand, allowing himself to at times establish a clear stride pattern of bass notes and chords, while at others allowing the time to be more implied and not completely spelled out by the left hand. We can hear this in "Weather Bird" (this chapter, "Listening Focus") as both he and Armstrong are responsible for keeping the implied pulse present and swinging. Hines's groundbreaking style of this period was particularly influential in leading to a new modern jazz piano style with more emphasis on melodic invention in the right hand, which helped move the stride piano style into the swing era.

Hines's solo style is also known for his use of playing passages in octaves in his right hand while using phrasing that is closer to that of trumpet players than to that of pianists of the period. As often happens, his style developed from a practical concern. As he soloed with a large group it was difficult to be heard, so doubling his solo in octaves gave him much more force and volume and brought his solos out over the ensemble. His early background playing the cornet undoubtedly had an influence as well. One huge difference between horn players and pianists and guitarists, for example, is that horn players have to take breaths between phrases. This automatically provides shape to phrases. Pianists

Earl Hines poses with an oversized piano keyboard, ca. late 1940s. Photo Gilles Petard.

Courtesy Redferns/Getty Images.

JAZZ LIVES EARL "FATHA" HINES

Earl "Fatha" Hines was born and raised just outside of Pittsburgh. His father was a cornet player and bandleader, and Hines at an early age was able to recall and play songs on the piano that he heard at shows or concerts. He went on the road at 17 and moved to Chicago in 1925. One of his early gigs there was with Carroll Dickerson, and after meeting and quickly establishing a musical rapport with Louis Armstrong, Armstrong joined him in Dickerson's band. Their relationship continued and grew as both were becoming leading figures in Chicago and in jazz. Hines eventually even replaced Lil Hardin Armstrong for some of the Hot Five recordings, and their duet recordings produced some of the highlights of early jazz, such as "West End Blues" and "Weather Bird."

Hines hit it big when he became bandleader of an orchestra at Chicago's Grand Terrace Café, performances that were locally and nationally broadcast on the radio. Many important musicians came through this band, and eventually the band became a breeding ground for the players who were beginning to develop bebop (discussed in Chapter 8), including Charlie Parker and Dizzy Gillespie (Chapter 8, 1st Chorus), making this band an important bridge between swing and bebop styles, much the way that Hines helped to move piano playing from stride toward swing.

Hines rejoined Armstrong in the late 1940s and then began touring on his own again. After a brief near-retirement from music, Hines was "rediscovered" in the 1960s and became a star once again, both playing solo piano and playing with the biggest names in jazz.

and guitarists can play endless streams of notes, an approach that can often become shapeless and even monotonous, so Hines's horn-style phrasing made him unique. He even managed to simulate a horn player's vibrato on a held note with a slight **tremolo** of his octaves.

listening focus

DOWNLOAD
Track Number 6

"Weather Bird" (1928) by Earl "Fatha" Hines (piano) and Louis Armstrong (trumpet)

LISTENING HIGHLIGHT, ACCOMPANIMENT: In a duet with a piano and an instrumentalist the normal relationship would be soloist and accompanist. Here, however, the relationship continually shifts. Additionally, when Hines does function as accompanist he does so with a freedom that goes beyond the normal role of the pianists of the period, namely, a stride style with left-hand bass and chords clearly delineating the beat and chord progression with the right hand playing chords and filling. The first strain, A (0:04), is an example of a relatively traditional accompaniment. At the first B strain (0:22), for example, Hines becomes freer and does not keep the stride left hand going at all times. He is also melodically active underneath Armstrong's melody, creating a complementary melody behind him. Though Armstrong dominates the texture at the second C strain (1:43), the roles are not clear. Hines sometimes accompanies, but at other times he is an equal partner, pushing the rhythmic envelope. The following C strain (2:00) is fascinating as it is primarily a Hines solo and Armstrong takes to an accompanist role as his melodies function more as counterlines that are meant to spell out the harmonies and support the soloist (2:02–2:12). Armstrong then takes over at the end of the strain.

IN PERFORMANCE
Spontaneous Interaction in Jazz

Professional musicians who have at least some common musical ground can generally play together effectively even if they have never met before. But once they become familiar with each other and develop a musical rapport, what happens between players takes on more depth. These musical partnerships allow players to become something more than themselves as they push and prod each other to "go for it."

Hines and Armstrong were working together regularly in different bands during this period and consequently were extremely familiar with each other's musicality as well as being personally well acquainted. It was an exciting time as both young men were enjoying blossoming careers and burgeoning musical styles. They clearly had fun together, and this joy is palpable in "Weather Bird." It even feels casual, almost as if they are playing in our living room for fun. This kind of "live" feel is quite difficult to capture in the recording studio and rarely happens, unfortunately. This is one reason that even though we are listening to recorded jazz in our studies, it is crucial for your jazz experience to hear jazz live and preferably in a nightclub as opposed to a concert setting. It is in the intimacy of a club that jazz is best experienced as you can see and feel the performers and almost be a part of the mutual exchange of ideas that occurs as you sit and listen.

In this performance there are a few examples of these players making adjustments as they go. As Armstrong ends his solo (1:14), he and Hines play a short interlude as a way into Hines's solo. Armstrong plays a repeated note and plays with the time to the point that we lose track of where the beat is. In fact,

he and Hines lose track as well, and where the beat is gets confused and a little off. Neither player gives any indication of this confusion, and Hines just jumps right back into the hard-driving tempo as if nothing had happened (at 1:23, the first C section). Without drums or bass and without a constant left-hand stride from Hines, the time of this performance is often implied and felt as opposed to being spelled out.

One of the most fascinating aspects of this recording is how it ends. Rather than a carefully worked-out conclusion, it seems as if the two players evolved this ending on the fly, as is common in live performance. First, it seems that both Hines and Armstrong are playing solos simultaneously. However, the character of what Armstrong is playing is an accompaniment figure; he is clearly establishing the chords with his note choices, allowing Hines a little more freedom with his own melody and comping. They then trade "4s" (each soloing for 4 bars at a time) back and forth. This finally breaks down a little as they seem to not quite know how they will end. Hines actually just stops and hopes Armstrong will make everything clear. Armstrong takes the lead, playing an ascending cadenza that clearly will reach a final note, which Hines then embellishes with a chord that ends the tune. This process is a constant one in live performance but more unusual in a recording as recordings are generally more carefully planned out and prepared. That type of spontaneity and looseness is part of what makes this a special recording, and it helps to give us insight into the way that players interact to create a piece of music on the spot.

3rd Chorus Lovie Austin and Lil Hardin Armstrong

WHAT ROLE DID WOMEN PLAY IN THE EARLY DECADES OF JAZZ?

Lovie Austin

Pianist and bandleader Lovie Austin (born Cora Calhoun, 1887–1972) from Chattanooga, Tennessee, studied classical music formally at Roger Williams College and Knoxville College. At this time, studying the piano was often part of a young woman's overall education, as opposed to the intention of leading to a career in music; but Austin took music seriously early on. As a youngster she would sneak off—along with Bessie Smith, another Chattanooga native (see Chapter 2, 1st Chorus)—to hear the great classic blues singer Ma Rainey.

Austin eventually settled in Chicago in 1923 and went on to be an important performing and recording artist, playing live shows, including vaudeville variety shows, and accompanying blues artists. Austin was the music director and pianist for the Monogram Theater, a vaudeville house on the South Side of Chicago, as well as being house pianist for Paramount Records. These were important positions, and both jobs required great versatility; so clearly Austin was a top Chicago musician. The great pianist-composer-arranger Mary Lou Williams (see Chapter 6, 1st Chorus) spoke of Austin reverentially as her most important influence and recalled seeing Austin in a theater playing piano with her left hand while writing out the arrangements for the next act with her right hand. Austin accompanied a who's-who list of performers in the 1920s, including Ma Rainey, Ethel Waters, Alberta Hunter, and Butterbeans and Susie, as well as leading her own band, Lovie Austin and Her Blues Serenaders. She remained active throughout her life, including recording as late as 1961.

Lil Hardin Armstrong

Lil Hardin Armstrong (1898–1971)—who we have already encountered as pianist for King Oliver and Louis Armstrong (see Chapter 3)—was also an important Chicago pianist. She was playing in several groups in Chicago, eventually leading to her playing with King Oliver, where she met Armstrong when he joined the group in 1922. She took it upon herself to acclimate Armstrong to Chicago lifestyle and to encourage him to be more professionally ambitious. They married in 1924, and she strongly encouraged Armstrong to take a more aggressive approach to his career by coming out from Oliver's shadow and allowing his skills to shine and blossom. Her influence upon his career was powerful, encouraging him to join Fletcher Henderson in New York as well as to return to Chicago as a featured artist and bandleader, where they were to collaborate on many of Armstrong's most important recordings. As Armstrong's career developed he, of course, toured extensively, while Hardin Armstrong continued a solid career as pianist and bandleader,

---

QUESTIONS AND CONTROVERSIES
Women in Jazz

As shown by Lovie Austin, Lil Hardin Armstrong, and other early pioneers, women have been active in jazz since its early history. Yet they have had a difficult time in the male-dominated jazz field and have also not been represented effectively in its history, though this is slowly changing. While they were not spotlighted like star soloists such as Armstrong and Beiderbecke, Austin and Hardin Armstrong were talented bandleaders, arrangers, composers, and promoters. It is certainly true that Louis Armstrong would have been unlikely to have as aggressively pursued a solo career without his wife's promotion and prodding. Still, the fact that both Austin and Hardin Armstrong were women led to limits in their overall careers; by the 1930s and 1940s they at times had to play off the novelty of their gender by leading all-women ensembles.

listening focus

"Traveling Blues" (1924) by Lovie Austin and Her Blues Serenaders

DOWNLOAD
Track Number 7

INSTRUMENTATION: Piano: Lovie Austin; **Cornet:** Tommy Ladnier; **Clarinet:** Jimmy O'Bryant.

"Traveling Blues" is an excellent example of Lovie Austin's skills as a powerful accompanist and thoughtful and skillful bandleader. She has created an interesting form and a piece that is exciting throughout. Her full sound, commanding rolling bass (in her left hand), an authoritative right hand, and her attention to detail regarding her place in the ensemble in support of the trumpet and clarinet help us to understand why she was an in-demand accompanist and music director, both for blues artists and for a wide variety of other acts. Certainly, her skills and the music she produced are worthy of much wider note than has been the case in much of written jazz history.

LISTENING HIGHLIGHT: FORM: "Traveling Blues" is an unusual hybrid form in two main sections. The first half consists of 5 choruses of the blues (0:00, 0:13, 0:26, 0:40, 0:53). The second half is more complicated and consists of five 16-measure phrases.

largely in Chicago. In the 1950s, during the revival of interest in New Orleans jazz, Hardin Armstrong recorded her memoirs; and in 1961 she made a final album of her piano playing.

There are many parallels between Austin and Hardin Armstrong's careers. Hardin Armstrong was also from Tennessee (Memphis), and both studied music formally for a time. Hardin Armstrong performed with many of the same artists as Austin, such as King Oliver and Alberta Hunter; and Jelly Roll Morton was an influence on both pianists during his time in Chicago. In fact, Austin used to create piano scores of Morton's music for him as he played for her at her Chicago home. The ability to read and notate music is another similarity between these two; **lead sheets** for King Oliver and Louis Armstrong were often done by Hardin Armstrong. Creating scores was an additional source of income for both of them.

Perhaps the most interesting similarity is that both women largely performed in an accompanist's role and were rarely featured as soloists. The accompanist's job is to make the ensemble and the soloists sound good in a supportive manner, and though not as glamorous as being a soloist, the role of accompanist is a crucial one and often goes unnoticed and underappreciated. How they fit into ensemble writing and comp for soloists can make the difference between a band or soloist being good and being great. In addition, both women, along with Mary Lou Williams, are examples of the importance of pianistic and musical ability, in both the private and the professional worlds, as a means for upward mobility for women, and for African American women in particular. Also, the development of musical literacy, such as the ability to notate and arrange music, provided women with a way into the professional jazz world. For example, this can be seen by Lovie Austin's work for Jelly Roll Morton and Mary Lou Williams's arranging for Count Basie. These female pianists also can be seen as a continuation of the nineteenth-century traditional belief that the ability to play piano was an important social skill for women.

CODA Chapter Summary

Why Did a Thriving Jazz Scene Develop in Chicago in the Late 1910s and Early 1920s?

- With its thriving and diverse music scene, Chicago, as early as the 1910s, provided excellent employment opportunities for musicians.
- The city's booming businesses had attracted many Southern and Midwestern African American workers. These black emigrants to Chicago's South Side created a substantial audience for African American entertainment.
- New Orleans instrumentalists, including Jelly Roll Morton and later King Oliver's band with Louis Armstrong, brought the New Orleans style to Chicago.
- White musicians from the greater Chicago area were attracted to the city's nightclub scene and were able to experience jazz firsthand from masters like Oliver and Armstrong.

How Did Bix Beiderbecke's Style Differ from Those of Louis Armstrong and Other Early Jazz Trumpeters?

- Armstrong's playing emphasized his virtuosity on the cornet (later trumpet), his ability to exploit the full dynamic and tonal range of the instrument, his imaginative and fiery solo playing, and his warm personality.
- Beiderbecke primarily played in the cornet's middle register and had a bell-like tone that he opened or burnished depending on the character of the solo or passage.
- Beiderbecke carefully crafted his lovely solos that were often gentle in character yet also hot and swinging.

What Was Paul Whiteman's Role in Popularizing Jazz?

- Whiteman led the most successful dance orchestra in the 1920s and 1930s. In his band, he brought together some of the best instrumentalists as well as top arranger-composers to produce numerous hits of a consistently high quality.
- Whiteman mixed jazz with a more European-based compositional sensibility to create what he called "symphonic jazz."

How Did Earl Hines Revolutionize Jazz Piano?

- Hines went beyond earlier blues-based and stride piano styles through his emphasis on melodic invention in the right hand.
- He based his solo playing on the way trumpeters phrased and shaped the melody, rather than on the style of other pianists. He played the melodies in octaves to increase the volume and impact of his soloing. He even managed to simulate a horn player's vibrato on a held note with a slight tremolo of his octaves.

What Role Did Women Play in the Early Decades of Jazz?

- Despite the prejudice and difficulties that they encountered, women often served important roles as bandleaders, accompanists, and arrangers in the early days of jazz.
- Lovie Austin was an important bandleader and performing and recording artist, playing live shows and accompanying blues artists.
- Lil Hardin Armstrong was a pianist, arranger, and composer who played with King Oliver's band in Chicago and then oversaw the early career of her then husband, Louis Armstrong. She later led several big bands and participated in the New Orleans revival.

Talkin' Jazz (Key Terms)

Lead sheet	Transcribed/Transcription	Vibrato
Legato	Tremolo	

Key People

Bix Beiderbecke	Eddie Lang	Lil Hardin Armstrong
Frank Trumbauer	Earl Hines	
Paul Whiteman	Lovie Austin	

Think About This (For Further Discussion and Study)

1. What were the conditions that set the stage for jazz in Chicago?
2. How did Bix Beiderbecke's trumpet style differ from Louis Armstrong's?
3. Discuss the differences between "Singin' the Blues" and "There Ain't No Sweet Man (Worth the Salt of My Tears)."
4. Discuss the various ways that Earl "Fatha" Hines revolutionized jazz piano playing.
5. Earl "Fatha" Hines and Louis Armstrong had a strong musical rapport, as can be seen in "Weather Bird." What artists who you listen to display this type of musical relationship, and how does it manifest itself? Can you think of examples of spontaneous interaction in music that you are familiar with?
6. Can you make any comparisons regarding women's involvement in early jazz and women's role in the workplace today?

Look It Up (Key Resources)

Dahl, Linda. *Stormy Weather: The Music and Lives of a Century of Jazzwomen*. New York: Limelight Editions, 1995.

Dance, Stanley. *The World of Earl Hines*. New York: Scribner, 1977.

DeLong, Thomas A. *Pops: Paul Whiteman, King of Jazz*. Piscataway, NJ: New Century, 1983.

Dickerson, James. *Just for a Thrill: Lil Hardin Armstrong, First Lady of Jazz*. New York: Cooper Square Press, 2002.

Kenney, William Howland. *Chicago Jazz: A Cultural History, 1904–1930*. New York: Oxford University Press, 1993.

Lion, Jean Pierre. *Bix: The Definitive Biography of a Jazz Legend*. New York: Continuum, 2005.

Placksin, Sally. *American Women in Jazz: 1900 to the Present, Their Words, Lives, and Music*. New York: Wideview Books, 1982.

Taylor, Jeffrey. "Earl Hines's Piano Style in the 1920s: A Historical and Analytical Perspective." *Black Music Research Journal* 12, no. 1 (Spring 1992): 57–77.

———. "With Lovie and Lil: Rediscovering Two Chicago Pianists of the 1920s." In *Big Ears: Listening for Gender in Jazz Studies*, edited by Nichole Rustin and Sherrie Tucker, 48–63. Durham, NC: Duke University Press, 2008.

NEW YORK JAZZ 1920s-1930s

5

1st Chorus Fletcher Henderson

HOW DID NEW YORK CITY BECOME A MAJOR JAZZ CENTER?

New York City has served as the jazz capital of the world since the late 1920s, and to a certain degree New York City is still considered "the place to be" to make a high-level career in jazz. New Orleans, Kansas City, Chicago, and Los Angeles were important centers as well in the history of jazz; but all the bands and musicians understood that New York was the place to "make it." In addition, New York City was rich with possibilities for performance, recording, publishing, and radio broadcasts. This is combined with the immigration from Europe that brought many great performers, songwriters, and composers. Important artists from other areas came to New York City to perform and record, including Louis Armstrong (who eventually made his home in New York) and Jelly Roll Morton, as well as Bix Beiderbecke and Frank Trumbauer, who, along with the arranger Bill Challis, left Jean Goldkette to join the most successful bandleader of the period, Paul Whiteman, also based in New York at the time.

We have already listened to some early bands and musicians centered in New York, such as the society and military bands of James Reese Europe and the stride pianist James P. Johnson. In the following choruses we will examine other bands and musicians who reigned supreme in New York City, such as the bands of Fletcher Henderson, Chick Webb, and Benny Carter, as well as that of the Cuban flute player and bandleader Alberto Socarrás, along with a deeper look at the stride piano style and one of its greatest practitioners, Art Tatum.

HOW DID POPULAR SONGWRITERS INFLUENCE THE JAZZ REPERTOIRE?

The business of writing, publishing, selling, recording, and performing songs was an important part of the music business as well as New York's cultural life; and New York City's Tin Pan Alley was the center for popular songwriters and music publishing from the late nineteenth century until the 1950s and 1960s. Originally on 28th Street, Tin Pan Alley in midtown Manhattan was a remarkable collection of brilliant composers and lyricists such as

Photo: Courtesy William P. Gottlieb Collection and Library of Congress.

In this chapter, we'll answer these questions:

- How Did New York City Become a Major Jazz Center?
- How Did Popular Songwriters Influence the Jazz Repertoire?
- What Role Did Fletcher Henderson Play in Developing the New York Jazz Scene?
- How Did the Successful New York Ballrooms and Nightclubs Influence the Development of Jazz?
- What Role Did Star Soloists Play in These Bands?
- What Are the Distinguishing Characteristics of Stride Piano?
- How Has Spanish-Caribbean Music Influenced Jazz?

read all about it

"Looking Back at the 'Jazz Age'" by Alain Locke

Walser, **Keeping Time,** *Chapter 19*
One of the leading intellectuals of the Harlem Renaissance gives his opinion on the importance of jazz and its popularity in the 1920s.

George Gershwin, Cole Porter, Irving Berlin, Jerome Kern, Richard Rodgers, and Oscar Hammerstein II, as well as music publishers, who were responsible for a huge portion of American popular song, much of it written for Broadway shows and revues. Many of these tunes have also become jazz standards and serve as the core repertoire for jazz musicians—a collection of songs, referred to as "standards," that all professionals must know. This area dominated popular music, even through the 1950s and 1960s, at which time the center of activity had moved to the Brill Building at 49th and Broadway in Manhattan with such pop songwriters as Carole King, Jerry Lieber and Mike Stoller, and Ellie Greenwich. Many of the early Tin Pan Alley songwriters and publishers were Jewish immigrants from eastern Europe.

The most common type of Tin Pan Alley song form combines two traditional forms, AABA (and its variation, AABC) and verse–chorus, becoming a form that includes a verse and an AABA refrain. The verse is generally played once, essentially serving as a long introduction. The AABA form then repeats as many times as the lyrics require. Jazz instrumentalists have traditionally relied upon this form (as well as the 12-bar blues discussed in Chapter 2) for a huge portion of their repertoire. They generally eschew the verse, however, making the AABA form central to the jazz repertoire.

Black songwriters also had success on Broadway and greatly contributed to both American popular song and the jazz repertoire. The violinist and composer Will Marion Cook (discussed in Chapter 3, 4th Chorus) had early success on Broadway, followed by pianist-composer Eubie Blake and the composer-lyricist Noble Sissle with their hit show *Shuffle Along* in 1921. Others followed, including Duke Ellington and Fats Waller, as well as numerous important songwriters in the Tin Pan Alley tradition such as Clarence Williams (Chapter 2, 1st Chorus), Spencer Williams, James P. Johnson (Chapter 2, 1st Chorus), Shelton Brooks, and Chris Smith. Blake and Sissle's *Shuffle Along* also helped to usher in the Harlem Renaissance, an important cultural movement in the 1920s and 1930s.

The Harlem Renaissance

Harlem, in upper Manhattan, was once an isolated white, middle- to upper middle–class neighborhood; but with accessibility through public transportation as well as a concentrated effort by realtors to attract both African Americans from the South looking for work as part of the Great Migration as well as educated middle-class blacks, Harlem became an African American neighborhood by 1920, its own city within a city. The musical life of Harlem was exciting, vibrant, and completely dominated by African American musicians. The Harlem Renaissance was a literary and artistic movement, primarily from 1920 until the mid-1930s, based upon the notion that creative endeavors had the ability to create racial pride and progressive social change that would improve African Americans' place in American society through cultural, intellectual, and artistic endeavors. While all arts and literature are generally included in the movement, the situation was more nuanced and complicated; and its relationship to jazz was problematic as there was a distinct split between the Harlem Renaissance in art and literature and the world of music and musical theater. Some in the New Negro movement (as it was dubbed by the author Alain Locke) believed that black "popular" music such as jazz, popular songs, and musical theater was not in the same "high-culture category" as musicians such as composer William Grant Still and composer-violinist-conductor Will Marion Cook who incorporated concert music traditions in their work.

Regardless of any splits or differences among figures in the movement, it is undeniable that the Harlem Renaissance brought African American culture and intellectualism into view in American society. A few well-known members of the movement were the writers Langston Hughes and Zora Neale Hurston; intellectuals and activists W. E. B. Du Bois, James Weldon Johnson, and Alain Locke; visual artists Palmer C. Hayden and Laura Wheeler Waring; and the actor Paul Robeson.

WHAT ROLE DID FLETCHER HENDERSON PLAY IN DEVELOPING THE NEW YORK JAZZ SCENE?

Fletcher Henderson

Also in New York City were some important early big bands that greatly influenced the swing era, including Fletcher Henderson's orchestra. Fletcher Henderson (1897–1952) was an early important composer-bandleader-pianist in New York City and influenced Duke Ellington's early approach (see Chapter 8). Henderson was originally influenced by Paul Whiteman's sound and success (see Chapter 4, 1st Chorus) and had the same ability to recognize, showcase, and develop talented players and arrangers.

Thanks to his success, Henderson attracted many of the greatest jazz musicians of the day to his band. Louis Armstrong (Chapter 3, 5th Chorus) was briefly a member of Henderson's band in 1925, followed by trumpeters Rex Stewart (who went on to fame with Duke Ellington) and Roy Eldridge (this chapter, 3rd Chorus), as was Coleman Hawkins (also discussed in the 3rd Chorus), one of jazz's most prominent tenor saxophone soloists. Saxophonist-arranger-composer Don Redman was an essential member of the band through both his playing and arranging. Redman's writing not only helped the band develop musically and commercially but also helped to create the soon-to-be standard big-band concept of trumpet, trombone, saxophone, and rhythm sections that worked independently and as an

Fletcher Henderson and His Orchestra, ca. late 1920s. Henderson's band was highly influential, and his arrangements formed the backbone of swing music in the 1930s.

© Pictorial Press Ltd./Alamy.

JAZZ LIVES FLETCHER HENDERSON

Born in Cuthbert, Georgia, Fletcher Henderson earned a degree in chemistry at Atlanta University (originally a primary school for freed slaves) and moved to New York City with the intention of continuing his studies. He shifted to music, however, and worked as a **song plugger** for W. C. Handy's (Chapter 2, 3rd Chorus) music publishing company and as an accompanist, including working with blues singer Ethel Waters. As Henderson established himself on the New York scene, he was selected as a bandleader by other musicians who believed that his education and personal and business manner would give them their greatest chance of success. His band gained early recognition through a long engagement at Roseland Ballroom in midtown Manhattan beginning around 1923, playing for an exclusively white clientele as was common at the time. Along with "hot" jazz, his band played a wide variety of standard dance music of the day.

In 1928, Henderson was in an automobile accident, in which he suffered injuries to his head and shoulder. According to his wife, this led to a declining interest in leading his own band. In 1931, he began arranging for a number of other orchestras, and by the mid-1930s he was writing arrangements for Benny Goodman's successful big band (see Chapter 7, 1st Chorus). In 1939, Henderson joined Benny Goodman's band, disbanding his own group. In the mid-1940s, Henderson again began leading his own bands on occasion and toured with Ethel Waters from 1948 to 1949. He suffered a stroke in 1950 that effectively ended his career and died 2 years later.

ensemble. When playing as an ensemble, this style at times moves away from the New Orleans concept, creating a homophonic sound that features a clear melody accompanied by a section (or sections) harmonizing and accompanying.

Henderson had other excellent arrangers, such as Benny Carter (see this chapter, 2nd Chorus), Edgar Sampson, and Fletcher's brother Horace. Henderson became a good arranger as well and was known for his use of call-and-response **head arrangements**, generally resulting from players spontaneously creating a series of riffs (this format will be examined further in the discussion of Kansas City jazz in Chapter 6). Head arrangements are often not written down but at times eventually become formalized in a chart. Henderson did this and sold his arrangements to other bands.

"New King Porter Stomp" is a Fletcher Henderson arrangement derived from the Jelly Roll Morton composition "King Porter Stomp" (Chapter 3, 3rd Chorus), an early Morton composition that provided hits for a number of big bands in a variety of ways. When finally published in 1924—it was composed around 1906—it appeared as both a solo piano piece and in a **stock arrangement** that any band could adapt to fit its own needs. Numerous groups recorded "King Porter Stomp," including an early version by King Oliver (Chapter 3, 4th Chorus). Fletcher Henderson's orchestra recorded the composition several times and became closely associated with it, and some of the elements in this recording come from earlier versions. Later, a Henderson arrangement of the tune was one of the key numbers for the legendary Benny Goodman concert at the Palomar Ballroom in Los Angeles (discussed in Chapter 7, 1st Chorus), and other prominent bands such as those of Chick Webb, Cab Calloway (both discussed in the 2nd Chorus of this chapter), and Count Basie (Chapter 6, 3rd Chorus) recorded it as well.

DOWNLOAD
Track Number 00

"New King Porter Stomp" (1932) by Fletcher Henderson's Orchestra

INSTRUMENTATION: Piano-arranger: Fletcher Henderson; **Trumpet:** Bobby Stark (1st trumpet solo) Rex Stewart (2nd trumpet solo), Russell Smith; **Alto saxophone:** Hilton Jefferson, Russell Procope; **Tenor saxophone:** Coleman Hawkins; **Trombone:** Sandy Williams (first trombone solo), J. C. Higginbotham (second trombone solo); **Bass:** John Kirby; **Drums:** Walter Johnson; **Guitar:** Freddie White.

FORM: ABBBBBBCC. Henderson makes significant changes in the form for this "New" version of "King Porter Stomp," making this less of a multistrain form. He uses the original A strain but skips the original second strain and makes the third strain—the trio—his second strain. From there soloists play over sax riffs for six choruses. Two shout choruses follow to close out the tune.

STYLE: Rather than focusing on the re-creation of the various melodies of the original four strains, this recording of the Morton composition appears as a head arrangement, becoming more of a vehicle for soloists and riffs based upon the chord progression of "King Porter Stomp."

MELODY AND HARMONY: The original Morton composition takes on new roles here. The original first-strain melody is essentially ignored while its chord progression is used. The second original strain is skipped entirely, and the third strain, the trio, is used as the basis for backgrounds behind the soloists rather than as a melody.

RHYTHM: The rhythm section here, compared to the early jazz recordings we have heard so far, has a lighter yet powerful groove. The use of string bass instead of tuba contributes greatly to this lightness. Riffing arrangements such as this, and this is true for much of urban blues as well, get their momentum from hitting a solid groove and just not letting up. Played live, the soloists often had the freedom to play as many choruses as they wished, and a live performance of this tune must have been wildly exciting for listeners and dancers. This is a developing swing sound, leading us to the swing era (see Chapters 7–9), as opposed to the New Orleans or Chicago music we have heard so far.

ACCOMPANIMENT: In addition to the rhythm section, the sax section creates a constant accompaniment to the soloists throughout the tune as they riff from beginning to end. The sax riffs swing very hard and create a terrific foundation for the soloists.

"NEW KING PORTER STOMP" LISTENING GUIDE

TIME	FORM	STYLE	MELODY AND HARMONY	RHYTHM	ACCOMPANIMENT
0:00	Intro	From the first beat this tune is hot. The trumpet, playing in a cup mute—a cardboard mute—quickly shows that this is a hot blowing tune dedicated to swinging hard for the dancers. Bobby Stark plays this first solo.	The introduction of this arrangement flows right into the A section, making it difficult to tell if this is really an introduction.	This arrangement is played at a fast tempo with the bass playing in 4 (on all 4 beats).	The presence of the bass, as opposed to a tuba, provides a fleeter and lighter sound.

continued

"New King Porter Stomp" listening guide continued

TIME	FORM	STYLE	MELODY AND HARMONY	RHYTHM	ACCOMPANIMENT
0:09	A	The muted trumpet just starts blazing with a hot solo. To make the trumpet in cup mute sound over the band the soloist has to blow harder than he normally might, giving the otherwise mellow sound of the cup-muted tone a nice edgy quality.	The 16-measure A section only happens once—it is played twice in Morton's version—and there is little beyond the chord progression that connects this to Morton's composition as the melody is not played by anyone.	The bass and drums play a solid and powerful groove which creates a momentum that builds throughout the arrangement.	While the bass and drums dominate the rhythm section, the constant presence of saxophone riffs is an essential element to the swinging accompaniment in this arrangement.
0:27	Interlude		This is the first time in this arrangement that Henderson uses Morton's melody, and he arranges the interlude for the full ensemble.		
0:32	B	Trumpet solo continues. His playing is melodic and has rhythmic punch.	Henderson skips the original second strain, jumping right to the trio.	The rhythm continues to chug along on all 4 beats. In this arrangement this is their primary function, and they do not particularly accent the ensemble or the soloist's rhythmic figures.	From here until the first shout chorus (C) the saxes play background riffs behind the soloists that are portions—or variations of portions—of Morton's trio melody.
0:50	B	Coleman Hawkins plays a tenor saxophone solo. His solo floats over the time a bit more than the trumpet solo and is a bit more florid, as is often the case with saxophone versus trumpet solos.			The other saxes continue to riff in the background.
1:09	B	Sandy Williams plays a trombone solo in straight mute. The straight mute is made of metal, so it has an edgier sound than the cardboard cup mute.			
1:27	B	Trumpeter Rex Stewart (who went on to make a big name for himself with Duke Ellington) plays a solo, also in cup mute.	At 1:37 Stewart plays a dramatic, long, held note (a high D-flat) that is then repeated in a rhythmic and syncopated fashion. He ends it by glissing (sliding) up to high F—these are very high notes for the trumpet and are virtuosic.	The rhythm section momentum is really building here, largely from its continued steadiness.	

"New King Porter Stomp" listening guide continued

TIME	FORM	STYLE	MELODY AND HARMONY	RHYTHM	ACCOMPANIMENT
1:46	B	J. C. Higginbotham plays a trombone solo in open horn.	Higginbotham uses a repeated riff throughout this chorus. At 1:53 he uses lip slurs—the quick alternation of two notes accomplished through the use of the lips and tongue only—which is a common technique for brass players.		
2:04	B	Trombone solo continues.	For this chorus the soloist growls into the trombone throughout for a bluesy sound and uses a combination of a repeated riff and more melodic playing.		
2:23	C	The full ensemble plays a shout chorus.	The brass and the saxophones each play a repeated riff. They are separate from each other yet also connect rhythmically at many spots.	The momentum continues to build.	
2:42	C	The full band plays a second shout chorus.	The brass and reeds play a bluesy call and response with each other. A short tag with a quick ritardando (slowing down of the tempo) ends this tune.	This is the climax of the arrangement and the rhythm's intensity is at its highest.	

Compare

Listen to these other versions of "King Porter Stomp"
- Jelly Roll Morton, piano solo, 1923 (see Chapter 3, 3rd Chorus)
- Benny Goodman, big-band arrangement, 1935

2nd Chorus New York Bands: Benny Carter, Chick Webb, Cab Calloway, and Jimmie Lunceford

New York City's many nightclubs, dance halls, and informal performance spaces encouraged musicians to form their own bands. The demand for musicians and bands from the mid-1920s to the early 1930s was great, thanks to the boom in the number of **speakeasies** and other illegal establishments that served up hot jazz, dancing girls, and smuggled-in alcohol. The Depression moved the action uptown to Harlem, where **rent parties** were often held as a means of raising money to pay for basic household needs, providing even more work for musicians.

Benny Carter

Saxophonist-trumpeter-arranger-composer-bandleader Benny Carter (1907–2003) was among those musicians drawn to the New York scene during this period. Carter was a gentle and soft-spoken man who was considered the epitome of a musician's musician. Although Carter had an uncommonly long and productive career, he was not particularly famous outside of the musical world; but he was important for numerous reasons. Carter was a lyrical and melodic alto saxophonist who helped to set the **lead alto style** for the bands to come. He was a composer, including the standard "When Lights Are Low," but most importantly a terrific and innovative arranger who helped to craft the overall approach to big-band writing and created an innovative style of ensemble writing for the saxophone section of a big band.

HOW DID THE SUCCESSFUL NEW YORK BALLROOMS AND NIGHTCLUBS INFLUENCE THE DEVELOPMENT OF JAZZ?

New York was home to several large dance halls that employed house bands to keep the dancers on their feet through closing time. One of the best-known and

JAZZ LIVES BENNY CARTER

Born in New York City, Carter began on trumpet after being inspired by his Harlem neighbor, Bubber Miley, Duke Ellington's early trumpet star (see Chapter 8, 1st Chorus). Later, Carter switched to alto saxophone as his primary instrument, though he continued to perform on trumpet as well as other saxophones and clarinet. Carter's first notoriety came during his stint with the Fletcher Henderson Orchestra. He then followed Don Redman, who he had worked with in Henderson's band, as the bandleader for the McKinney Cotton Pickers, an excellent and influential band out of Detroit.

Carter briefly formed his own band in New York but, after disbanding it, moved to Europe, where he stayed and toured extensively until 1938. After returning to New York, he again led a band, including playing at the Savoy Ballroom (discussed in "How Did the Successful New York Ballrooms and Nightclubs Influence the Development of Jazz?"). In 1942 he permanently relocated to Los Angeles, where he went on to compose and arrange music for film and television, helping to open opportunities for African American musicians in the Los Angeles studios. This included composer-arranger-producer Quincy Jones, who also became a top writer for film and TV as well as one of music's top producers (including Michael Jackson's album *Thriller*) and entrepreneurs. While working in the studios during this later period of his career Carter also became a popular arranger for many of the major jazz and popular singers, including Billy Holiday (Chapter 9, 1st Chorus), Sarah Vaughn, Louis Armstrong (Chapter 3, 5th Chorus), Ella Fitzgerald (Chapter 9, 1st Chorus), Ray Charles, Lou Rawls, and Peggy Lee.

After primarily working as a composer and arranger in the studios since the early 1940s, Carter began to perform more regularly again in the 1970s. His level of recognition was raised considerably as a result of touring and numerous awards, including Grammy awards for lifetime achievement (1987) and best jazz composition (1992). Before his retirement in 1997, Carter, nicknamed "the King" by his colleagues, had a nine-decade career as one of the most accomplished musicians in jazz.

listening focus

"Symphony in Riffs" (1933) by the Benny Carter Orchestra

INSTRUMENTATION: Trumpets: Eddie Mallory, Bill Dillard, Dick Clark; **Trombones:** J. C. Higginbotham, Keg Johnson, Fred Robinson; **Alto saxophones:** Benny Carter (lead alto), Wayman Carver, Glyn Paque; **Tenor saxophone:** Johnny Russell; **Piano:** Teddy Wilson; **Guitar:** Lawrence Lucie; **Bass:** Ernest Hill; **Drums:** Sidney Catlett.

Along with "Lonesome Nights" and "Keep a Song in Your Soul," "Symphony in Riffs" is a classic early example of Benny Carter's writing. The band is tight and exhibits many characteristics of the early big-band arranging style that Carter along with Fletcher Henderson, Don Redman, and others were beginning to create and standardize. Carter's lead alto sound, his writing for the saxophone section, strong soloists, and a two-part form are outstanding elements of this recording. This Carter composition was recorded many times, including by other major bands such as those of Artie Shaw (Chapter 7, 2nd Chorus), Tommy Dorsey (Chapter 7, 2nd Chorus), and Glenn Miller (Chapter 7, 2nd Chorus).

LISTENING HIGHLIGHT, MELODY AND HARMONY: The first section consists of 2 choruses. In chorus 1 the A sections (0:00 and 0:24) feature a bouncy, cheerful, and punchy brass melody, while the B section (0:16) features a piano solo over held notes in the brass. The A sections of chorus 2 (0:33) are an ensemble—a composed and harmonized melody over the chord progression (also referred to as the **changes**)—for his saxophone section and is an excellent example of the innovative arranging style Carter created for the big-band sax section. The lead alto plays the melody, and the other saxophones are written in a full-sounding harmony below it that follows the melodic and rhythmic contour of the melody—a homophonic texture, often referred to as "block-chord" style writing. At times, particularly the last A (0:59), the writing is rhythmically complicated and technically difficult, and sax sections have become extremely adept at playing this type of harmonized ensemble. Carter's lead alto sound is round, full, and smooth; and the extreme bending of pitches is a typical feature for him, as well as for another leading lead alto player, Johnny Hodges, who was a star with the Duke Ellington Orchestra (Chapter 8). The bridge (0:50) is a trombone solo over long held notes by the sax section.

A brass interlude (1:07) modulates to a lower key (from E-flat to D-flat) and leads to chorus 3 and the second distinct section of the piece. Chorus 3 (1:12) is a new section and is also AABA but in 4-measure phrases, which is unusual. The bridge of this section is quite interesting and a bit unusual, moving from A7 to D-flat major. The saxophones play another ensemble here. Chorus 4 (1:29) is over the same form and is a trumpet solo over saxophones playing long held notes. Chorus 5 (1:47) is a tenor sax solo with a punchy brass background for the A sections and long notes for the bridge. Chorus 6 (2:04) is a trombone solo over another smooth sax background. Chorus 7 (2:22) is a piano solo with drums and the bass in two. The 8th and final chorus (2:40) is a full-ensemble shout chorus that takes this tune out. The brass and reeds alternate and come together at the very end.

most successful was Harlem's Savoy Ballroom, which featured the country's hottest big bands and some of the most stylish and accomplished dancers. The undisputed king of the Savoy Ballroom was drummer Chick Webb, who led the house band at the Savoy from 1933 until his death in 1939. At the Savoy bands would face off in good-natured but intensely serious **battles of the bands**. The audience consisted of some of the most knowledgeable fans and dancers, and the dancers would pass judgment on whose band was superior that night. As the house band, Webb's band took on all comers and rarely lost a battle.

Chick Webb

William Henry "Chick" Webb (ca. 1905–1939) was from Baltimore and moved to New York in 1925, where he quickly became a bandleader. He was one of the top drummers of the 1930s, and despite his diminutive size and hunchbacked posture from a serious spinal deformity, his drumming was powerful and dynamic and included a wide variety of sounds including exotic wooden temple blocks (we hear them at 2:13 of "Go Harlem"). His playing was influential on other important swing drummers such as Gene Krupa, Jo Jones, Buddy Rich, and Sid Catlett.

Along with his drumming prowess, Webb was an excellent bandleader. The rhythm section, driven by his drumming, was the locomotive of the band; and it played a hard-driving swing with a powerful forward momentum. His bands were extremely well rehearsed and played with an exacting precision that fueled an intense swing. They also had uncommonly good control of their dynamics (how loudly or softly they played) and used them to dramatic effect (we will hear this in "Go Harlem"). Again, because of recording technology, we do not get to hear Webb's drumming as clearly as we would like in his recordings; and it is through those who heard him play live that we know of his incredible dynamism and the power of his band.

One of his best-known recordings is "Stompin' at the Savoy," which then became a swing staple and a hit for many bands, including that of Benny Goodman. The addition of the dynamic and hard-swinging 16-year-old vocalist Ella Fitzgerald

Chick Webb at the drums; notice the different percussion instruments he has lined up for his use.
© Pictorial Press Ltd./Alamy.

"Go Harlem" (1936) by the Chick Webb Orchestra

INSTRUMENTATION: Trumpet: Mario Bauza (a crucial figure regarding the incorporation of Latin music in jazz; Chapter 10, 1st Chorus), Bobby Stark (who we heard with Fletcher Henderson on "New King Porter Stomp" in the 1st Chorus of this chapter), Taft Jordan; **Trombone:** Sandy Williams, Nat Story; **Alto sax:** Edgar Sampson (and arranger of this tune), Pete Clark; **Tenor sax:** Teddy McRae, Wayman Carver; **Piano:** Don Kirkpatrick; **Guitar/banjo:** John Trueheart; **Bass:** Bill Thomas; **Drums:** Chick Webb.

LISTENING HIGHLIGHT, STYLE: As the house band at Harlem's Savoy Ballroom, Chick Webb's band knew dancing; and as a drummer and leader, Webb was in the perfect position to fill the dancers' needs with the correct tempos and the right rhythmic feels. "Go Harlem" is a terrific example of a groove that is pulsing yet subtle as Webb swings hard while not hitting you over the head with it. The dancers can choose how to handle this type of feel— they can smoothly glide across the floor or they can Lindy Hop like crazy. It suits everyone.

"Go Harlem" chugs along with a steady beat that never lets up. After the melody, the arrangement follows the typical pattern of moving back and forth between ensemble sections and short solo spots. The tune concludes with a restatement of the melody with solos mixed in and a *coda* (an ending section that is at times extended). An important factor at times here is the dramatic use of dynamics, and Webb's band paid more attention to this type of detail than most bands at this time. They do this very effectively as they come out of the bridge (B, 0:29) during the playing of the melody and quickly drop down to a whisper (*subito piano*) before building back up again as they play the last A section. While we cannot hear Webb as much as we would like, it is his drumming and overall approach that set the tone for this arrangement. Everything the band plays falls in line with his playing and is completely solid, precise, and right in the groove.

(Chapter 9, 1st Chorus), who would go on to become one of the great singers in jazz (or any style of music, for that matter), brought Webb's band national notoriety; and a novelty vocal tune, "A-Tisket, A-Tasket," was a huge hit. Every bandleader who was not a composer-arranger needed an arranger to help shape the style and sound of the band, and saxophonist-arranger Edgar Sampson played that critical role for Webb. His arrangement of "Go Harlem," a composition by James P. Johnson (Chapter 2, 1st Chorus) and Andy Razaf, is an excellent example of his writing.

The Cotton Club, another Harlem nightspot close by the Savoy, was also an incubator for great bands and a premier venue. Unlike the Savoy Ballroom, whose clientele was mixed but primarily African American from its Harlem neighborhood, the Cotton Club, while featuring black entertainment, was a whites-only nightclub. Fletcher Henderson's band performed there in 1923, and Duke Ellington had the house band from 1927 to 1931 and established his early reputation there (see Chapter 8). Two other top New York bands, led by Cab Calloway and Jimmie Lunceford, followed Ellington at the Cotton Club (in 1931 and 1934, respectively).

Cab Calloway

Cab Calloway (1907–1994) was a terrific singer, entertainer, and frontman. His trademark was a flamboyant style and a wildly outgoing and energetic stage persona. Calloway's show highlighted his performance, but he had a series of

read all about it

"The Caucasian Storms Harlem" by Rudolf Fisher

Walser, **Keeping Time**, *Chapter 16*
A white jazz journalist discusses the draw of the Harlem jazz clubs during the Roarin' '20s.

excellent bands behind him that featured top soloists such as tenor saxophonists Ben Webster and "Chu" Berry. He hired the then young and inexperienced trumpeter Dizzy Gillespie, who went on to become one of the innovators of bebop (Chapter 10, 1st Chorus), and the stalwart bass player Milt Hinton (Chapter 14, 3rd Chorus), one of the most recorded jazz musicians, anchored the band. Calloway specialized in novelty numbers, and "Minnie the Moocher" was a big hit for him, producing his signature line "Hi-de-ho!" The band was hugely successful, and live broadcasts from the Cotton Club helped to make Calloway nationally famous.

Jimmie Lunceford

Jimmie Lunceford's (1902–1947) band followed Calloway into the Cotton Club and was known for its precise ensemble playing and perfect appearance on the bandstand, as well as for its elaborate and accomplished showmanship. They put on an enthusiastic and energetic choreographed show with trumpet players flipping their horns, trombonists waving their slides in the air, the various sections swaying in rhythm, the drummer flipping his sticks, and the bass player spinning his bass. The band was also known for terrific arrangements, and trumpeter Sy Oliver was a particularly innovative arranger for Lunceford. Oliver's arrangement of "Organ Grinder's Swing" was a Lunceford hit and is a lovely arrangement that uses a wide variety of colors created through the use of clever combinations of instruments. For example, "Organ Grinder's Swing" begins with clarinet, muted trombone, and temple blocks and moves on to growling trumpet, baritone sax, bass, and drums. Oliver went on to fame with swing bandleader Tommy Dorsey (Chapter 7, 2nd Chorus) and, along with Fletcher Henderson and Benny Carter, helped to establish a big-band arranging style.

3rd Chorus Instrumental Masters: Roy Eldridge and Coleman Hawkins

WHAT ROLE DID STAR SOLOISTS PLAY IN THESE BANDS?

Besides the bands themselves, the major New York bands produced a group of noteworthy instrumental soloists who would go on to have long and successful careers. Many worked simultaneously with a big band and smaller ensembles and, thus, were able to establish themselves as major stars on their own.

Instrumental soloists were vital to the success and appeal of the big bands. Their playing brought an individual character to the band, and audiences looked forward to these bursts of personal expression as elements vital to the spirit of the music. Some soloists were extroverted and exciting, while others were more subdued and subtle. Some displayed incredible technical virtuosity, while others depended more upon a lyrical, personal style. Generally, the solos were short and just one part of the musical fabric within the context of big-band arrangements. At times, however, arrangements featured the star players of an ensemble, putting them in the spotlight as they stood up from their section or went out in front of the band.

After Louis Armstrong established the trumpet as a key melodic instrument in jazz, Roy Eldridge set a new standard for trumpet virtuosity, greatly influencing and inspiring the next great jazz trumpet virtuoso, Dizzy Gillespie (Chapter 10, 1st Chorus). Eldridge had a powerful and edgy sound, at times almost as if it was on the verge of being out of control. He was always in command, however, playing

"Rockin' Chair" (1941) by Roy Eldridge with Gene Krupa and His Orchestra

INSTRUMENTATION: Trumpets: Roy Eldridge, Norman Murphy, Torg Halten, Graham Young; **Trombones:** John Grassi, Jay Keliher, Babe Wagner; **Saxophones:** Mascagni "Musky" Ruffo, Sam Musiker, Walter Bates, Sam Listengart; **Piano:** Milt Raskin; **Guitar:** Ray Biondi; **Bass:** Ed Mihelich; **Drums and leader:** Gene Krupa; **Arranger:** Benny Carter.

LISTENING HIGHLIGHT, FORM: The primary texture is Eldridge soloing over saxophone backgrounds. This provides a nice contrast between his powerful, brassy sound and the mellow saxophones masterfully arranged by Benny Carter, who is known for his particularly effective saxophone ensemble writing. In the introduction (0:00), Eldridge plays a cadenza accompanied by only the saxophones. At A (0:21), the rhythm section joins in and continues through B (0:42) and C (1:03). The full ensemble comes in at the second C (1:46) for a big finish, which allows Eldridge to scream over the ensemble in true high-note trumpet player style. At the coda Eldridge plays an unaccompanied cadenza that ends on a powerful yet beautifully controlled high note to cap this bravura yet sensitive performance. Clearly, this cadenza is largely planned (they are often improvised) as we hear a call and response between Eldridge and a clarinet.

solos that regularly included flurries of rapid notes cascading all over the horn while playing either uptempo numbers or ballads, displaying the influence of saxophonists such as Coleman Hawkins on his playing.

Roy Eldridge

Born in Pittsburgh, Roy Eldridge (1911–1989) moved to New York in 1930. He had important early jobs with Teddy Hill and Fletcher Henderson and led small and large groups in the late 1930s. "After You've Gone" from this period was a classic feature for him that displayed his style at its best. His clarion calls, fearless breaks, and rapid yet highly melodic playing keep up a remarkable intensity. This intensity carried over to other areas as Eldridge was fiercely competitive in jam sessions, including those at New York's Minton's Playhouse, the early home of bebop (see Chapter 10). Eldridge joined drummer Gene Krupa's band as featured soloist in 1941 in an early example of racial integration. In "Rockin' Chair," a Benny Carter arrangement that Eldridge recorded with Krupa's band, he displays both his fearlessness and lyricism along with his virtuosity, ending on a signature high note.

Eldridge went on to play with many important bands as well as lead his own groups. The 1970s found him leading the house band at the well-known New York jazz club Jimmy Ryan's, where he continued to be an inspiration to trumpeters and up-and-coming musicians, such as the spectacular trumpet player Spanky Davis (1943–2014), who followed Eldridge into Jimmy Ryan's.

Coleman Hawkins

In much the same way that Louis Armstrong revolutionized the trumpet and created a new approach to playing it, Coleman Hawkins (1904–1969) brought the sax, and particularly the tenor sax, to the fore in jazz. With his strong and assertive, yet sensitive, approach to the tenor sax it became a fluid, melodic, and powerful instrument able to rival the trumpet as a jazz voice. Along with other terrific players that we have listened to, such as Benny Carter (this chapter, 2nd Chorus), Frank Trumbauer (see Chapter 4, 1st Chorus), and Sidney Bechet (see Chapter 3, 4th Chorus), Hawkins helped to create a new improvisational concept that involved the sophisticated use of chords for melodic and harmonic invention that is still the basis of jazz improvisation today.

Hawkins was born in St. Joseph, Missouri, and was already playing at local clubs when he was just 12 years old. He moved to Chicago and then Kansas City, where he was hired by well-known blues singer Mamie Smith in 1921, with whom he made his first recordings. Hawkins came to prominence, however, as a member of the Fletcher Henderson band, which he joined in 1923. While the Henderson band was helping to establish the swing style, Coleman Hawkins was sitting in the sax section from 1923 to 1934 setting the standard for jazz tenor saxophone playing. His earliest solos with Henderson display an older style of playing popular at that time. Saxophonists would pop the reed with their tongue (**slap-tongue**), making the sax almost a percussion instrument. Over the years, as documented through his many recordings, however, a wonderful maturation process took place; and his legato (smooth) yet rhythmically charged style emerged.

Coleman Hawkins, performing in New York City, ca. 1947. Hawkins is credited with bringing a new level of virtuosity to the tenor saxophone. Photo by William P. Gottlieb.

Courtesy William P. Gottlieb Collection and Library of Congress.

"Body and Soul" (1939) by Coleman Hawkins and His Orchestra

INSTRUMENTATION: Tenor saxophone and bandleader: Coleman Hawkins; **Trumpet:** Tommy Lindsay, Joe Guy; **Trombone:** Earl Hardy; **Saxophones:** Jackie Fields, Eustis Moore; **Piano:** Gene Rodgers; **Bass:** Oscar Smith; **Drums:** Arthur Herbert.

LISTENING HIGHLIGHT, MELODY AND HARMONY: Just as Roy Eldridge did in "Rockin' Chair," Hawkins takes huge liberties with the melody of "Body and Soul." Hawkins plays the melody of the first A (0:09) relatively straightforwardly with melodic fills between phrases. By the time he gets to the second A (0:30) he hints at the melody occasionally, and by the time he gets to the bridge, B (0:50), he has left the melody far behind. In its place he plays lovely nonstop melodic invention based upon the chord changes of the song. For many players, however, even though we may not hear them actually playing the melody, it is lurking in their minds and informing their soloing.

After leaving Henderson, Hawkins was hired for a tour in England. As was true for so many African American jazz players who toured Europe, he found some relief there from the racial tensions that were present in America, while also experiencing music fans who had a greater interest in his music than those at home. Hawkins wound up staying in Europe for 5 years. Upon his return he faced a new crop of serious rivals, including Ben Webster (Chapter 8, 2nd Chorus) and Lester Young (Chapter 6, 4th Chorus). Shortly after, Hawkins had a 1939 record date for his nine-piece band that he was working with in a New York City nightclub. After working through three difficult tunes and needing one more, a canny producer convinced a reluctant Hawkins to record an unrehearsed version of the popular and much performed tune "Body and Soul." The result is one of the classic recordings of jazz.

IN PERFORMANCE
"Body and Soul"

"Body and Soul" is an AABA Tin Pan Alley popular tune and a jazz standard that all jazz musicians must know. If someone on a job or at a jam session is going to call a jazz ballad, particularly for a saxophonist, the chances are good that they will choose "Body and Soul"; and most tenor players, at some point, use it as a feature for themselves. A primary reason for this is the immense popularity of Hawkins's amazing playing on his 1939 recording.

"Body and Soul," along with being a beautiful song, presents unique challenges to the player. It is in D-flat, an uncommon key in jazz; and the bridge presents a challenge as it moves relatively quickly through the keys of E major (also unusual in jazz) and C major. This is another reason it's become a test piece for saxophonists because it allows them to show off their talent and skill.

In the same way that Hawkins helped to transform the approach to soloing and the tenor sax, he also adapted to new styles. As bebop began to take shape, he performed with leaders of the movement, such as Dizzy Gillespie, pianist Thelonious Monk, and drummer Max Roach (all discussed in Chapter 10), and influenced many younger players, such as one of jazz's leading tenor sax players, Sonny Rollins. Hawkins spent his later career as a freelance featured soloist and bandleader.

4th Chorus Harlem Stride Piano

WHAT ARE THE DISTINGUISHING CHARACTERISTICS OF STRIDE PIANO?

Along with big bands in dance halls and nightclubs, Harlem produced a piano style referred to as the "Harlem style," "Harlem stride piano," or simply "stride piano," as the style was not exclusive to Harlem. Developing naturally out of ragtime, the main element of the stride style also gives the genre its name. The left hand of the pianist "strides" up and down the lower part of the piano as it booms out powerful bass notes on beats 1 and 3 and chords on beats 2 and 4. This is a virtuosic style of playing, and many players of this style had classical training and incorporated aspects of the classical repertoire into their playing and composing.

These pianists were held in great esteem and found work to be quite plentiful in saloons as well as rent parties thrown in apartments to quickly raise money for rent or other necessities. They were also fiercely competitive with each other, at times engaging in "cutting contests," which were public and informal competitions that were fun and exciting yet also quite serious. These pianists were well respected and known for their sartorial prowess. Technique was only part of their appeal and importance, however, as these pianists helped to expand the harmonic

IN PERFORMANCE
Jazz Harmony

One of the great joys in jazz, and one of its greatest accomplishments, is its use of traditional triadic harmony (chords based on the basic unit of the triad—3-note chords, major, minor, diminished, or augmented, based upon various configurations of major, minor, diminished, or augmented third intervals) and the way that jazz players and composers have taken these basic harmonic principles and stretched them. They have done this largely by increasing the level of intensity and color through the use of added tones. A chord has three basic tones—the root, 3rd, and 5th—and a fourth tone, the 7th, is common as well and ubiquitous in jazz. After that come 9ths, 11ths, and 13ths; and these can

be handled in a variety of ways as well. It is these added tones that help to create the colorful chords used in jazz. One way that this is reflected is in the reharmonization of a melody. A melody is originally written with a chord progression in mind, but the adventurous player or arranger can take this melody and put a variety of alternate chord progressions to it as well. Art Tatum was brilliant at this fine skill, and "Liza" shows Tatum taking the same melody and creating an impressive variety of **alternate changes** (alternate chord progressions) for this popular tune. He also places it in a variety of rhythmic contexts. Tatum was a supreme pianist but also a harmonic genius.

palette, not only of jazz but also of all Western music. Jazz has a very unique and sophisticated approach to harmony, and much of this tradition stems from its pianists.

Among these pianists, a number were pianist-composers, such as Eubie Blake ("I'm Just Wild About Harry"), James P. Johnson ("Charleston," see Chapter 2, 1st chorus), and Fats Waller ("Honeysuckle Rose"). They, along with Willie "The Lion" Smith, Earl Hines (Chapter 4, 2nd Chorus), Teddy Wilson (see his work with swing bandleader Benny Goodman, Chapter 7, 1st Chorus), and others, were part of an elite group of instrumentalists and composers. Their works were extremely sophisticated in all respects, with excellent melodic invention, harmonic sophistication, compositional distinction, and striking rhythms, including amazingly fast tempos and powerful swing. Pianist Art Tatum built upon their work and took jazz piano playing to new technical and harmonic heights.

JAZZ LIVES **ART TATUM**

From Toledo, Ohio, Tatum was born legally blind. He came from a musical family—his father, a church elder, played guitar and his mother, the piano—and he had perfect pitch, which helped him to learn to play by ear at a very young age. In 1927, he began playing on local Toledo radio and a year later, at a local club. In 1931, singer Adelaide Hall was passing through town, heard him play, and subsequently took him on tour as her accompanist; a year later, she brought him to New York to accompany her performance at Harlem's Lafayette Theater (a competitor to the popular Apollo Theater) and also used him for a recording session, his first appearance on record.

Tatum soon established himself as a leading pianist on New York's highly competitive jazz scene. In 1933, he won a famous **cutting contest** against Fats Waller, James P. Johnson, and Willie "The Lion" Smith with his version of the pop standard "Tea for Two." In the mid-1930s, Tatum toured the Midwest and then returned to New York in 1937; the next year, he made a tour to Europe, continuing to build his reputation as an innovative pianist. In 1941, he scored his only pop hit accompanying Big Joe Turner on "Wee Wee Baby Blues."

Besides for a brief period in the mid-1940s playing in a trio setting, Tatum performed and recorded as a soloist. His playing was so harmonically rich and rhythmically daring that it was probably difficult for others to accompany him. He recorded extensively in the late 1940s and 1950s, often for promoter-record label owner Norman Granz. From 1954 to his death, Tatum had a regular job at a small jazz club in Detroit. He died in Los Angeles of kidney failure.

Art Tatum, ca. 1946–1948. Tatum was highly influential as a pianist who opened up new rhythmic and harmonic possibilities for the instrument. Photo by William P. Gottlieb. *Courtesy William P. Gottlieb Collection and Library of Congress.*

listening focus

"Liza" (1934, Take D) by Art Tatum (piano)

LISTENING HIGHLIGHT, FORM: "Liza" is a typical AABA Tin Pan Alley tune with 8-measure sections. Tatum plays 5 choruses, and each is quite different. The 1st chorus (A 0:00, 0:11, B 0:20, A 0:31) is played rubato—the use of flexible rhythm, generally for expressive purposes. Though it is rhythmically free and does not sound like a fast melody, the harmonic and melodic rhythm is actually moving in cut-time—generally a fast tempo played with a 2-feel—and goes by very fast. The 2nd chorus is even more rhythmically free and has many long fills that stretch the form a bit. Tatum still manages to give a feel of tempo however. In this chorus, the A section (0:43, 0:53) elides (or overlaps) with B (1:01), which has a significant added tag that consists of an amazing **turnaround**. This turnaround leads into an extended last A (1:17), and through this extension he creates tension. The tension is then released at the 3rd chorus (A, 1:32, 1:37, B 1:43, A 1:48) when Tatum starts a series of incredibly fast choruses that boggle the mind with their technical and musical perfection as he stretches the limits of what a pianist can do. Chorus 4 (A 1:53, 1:58, B 2:04, A 2:09) flows directly from chorus 3. This is something that soloists often try to do, namely, to have the choruses of a solo be fluid enough so that the solo is of a whole rather than a series of choruses. Chorus 5 begins with a syncopated figure in the first two As (2:14, 2:19), and the bridge (B, 2:25) is a series of furious runs as Tatum's left hand continues to keep the tempo. Chorus 6 strays more from the melody and functions a bit like a shout chorus. Tatum makes extensive use of blue notes, and while the left hand continues to fly, his melody slows down and becomes a bluesy shout chorus that repeats for the first two A sections (2:35, 2:41). B (2:46) is a flurry of runs without a hint of melody, and the last A of the tune (2:51) gives us the melody one more time while finishing with a flourish.

Art Tatum

Art Tatum (1909–1956) learned from the masters, such as his idol Fats Waller, James P. Johnson, and Willie "The Lion" Smith. His dazzling piano technique was even further advanced than the others and inspired awe in jazz musicians as well as classical performers, conductors, and composers. Also, as was true for all of these great pianists, he played with great musicality and harmonic invention. His version of the popular tune "Liza" displays his astonishing virtuosity that evolved beyond the stride style, incorporating a number of techniques along with stride. Tatum was a major influence upon all jazz pianists who followed him and greatly expanded the harmonic palette of jazz.

Tatum worked effectively in a variety of group settings, but he was primarily a solo pianist; and there is good reason for that as playing solo allows him to reharmonize and change tempos at will without being concerned about others being able to follow his harmonic and rhythmic adventures. He mostly drew from the popular repertoire but also performed versions of classical material. He was also renowned for heading to after-hours sessions after work and continuing to play into the morning. He recorded extensively and worked continually and was revered by all jazz musicians, yet he did not reach the level of stardom that his virtuosic abilities would lead one to believe.

5th Chorus Spanish-Caribbean Influence on Jazz: Alberto Socarrás

HOW HAS SPANISH-CARIBBEAN MUSIC INFLUENCED JAZZ?

A Spanish-Caribbean influence has been present in American music since the nineteenth century and has been an extremely powerful influence on popular music in the United States. Of course, this is a cultural exchange as jazz and American popular music have also had a profound influence upon Spanish-Caribbean styles (the term Spanish-Caribbean will be referred to as Latin throughout the book, as is common practice). This exchange of musical styles led to the development of "Latin jazz," a hybrid musical style whose influence continues to steadily grow in jazz and in American popular music. New Orleans, the birthplace of jazz (Chapter 3), was heavily influenced by Caribbean music; and none other than Jelly Roll Morton (Chapter 3, 3rd Chorus) spoke of the importance of the Latin "tinge" to jazz style. Tango and *habanera* rhythms found their way into the stride piano style (this chapter, 4th Chorus) and into the music of W. C. Handy (Chapter 2, 3rd Chorus), including one of his most famous compositions, "St. Louis Blues," which contained a tango rhythm.

A wave of Caribbean dance styles swept American popular music from the turn of the century onward. Tango numbers such as "La Comparsita" and "Jalousie" were popular in the 1920s, as were the international hits of Cuban composer Ernesto Lecuona such as "Siboney" that combined traditional Cuban styles with forms and harmonic and melodic content influenced by Western classical music. The "rumba" era (rumba in this sense is a generic term and is different than traditional Cuban rumba) began in the 1930s spurred on by a huge hit, "El Manisero" ("The Peanut Vendor"), by the Cuban Don Azpiazú (Chapter 7, 4th Chorus). In the 1920s and 1930s a Latin influence could be found on Broadway and other theater productions, and Latin music was performed at ballrooms such as the Roseland Ballroom in midtown Manhattan.

Also in the 1920s, Latino musicians—particularly Puerto Ricans and Cubans during this early period—were heavily involved in the musical life of New York City. El Barrio—or East Harlem, a large Spanish-Caribbean community on the upper east side of Manhattan—created a demand for Caribbean music. While Latin musicians had been traveling to New York and other places in the United States for quite some time, the 1920s saw new Latin music created in the United States. In addition, many Cuban and Puerto Rican musicians had the advantage of excellent conservatory training as well as broad based practical professional experience. In New York this made them quite employable, and many wound up playing in American jazz ensembles. During the 1920s and 1930s, the American bands gained experience from their Latin counterparts, and the Latin players brought back to Latin ensembles skills learned in jazz bands. In this manner, bands from the 1930s led by Cuban flutist Alberto Socarrás and Puerto Rican trumpeter Augusto Coen, who played with Duke Ellington and Fletcher Henderson, became some of the first to incorporate both jazz and Latin styles.

Alberto Socarrás

Flutist-bandleader Alberto Socarrás (1908–1987) is one of many musicians who made an impact on jazz but has received very little credit or recognition. Born in Manzanillo, Cuba, Socarrás studied at the Santiago de Cuba conservatory of music and later moved to Havana, where he began a successful career including playing in a theater orchestra as well as an early Cuban jazz band.

After arriving in New York in the late 1920s, Socarrás quickly became immersed in the music scene with steady studio recording work and freelance performing, including being an early Latin jazz pioneer who moved freely between the worlds of Latin music and jazz. This includes being credited with playing the first jazz flute solo on record on Clarence Williams's "Shootin' the Pistol" in 1927, playing in Benny Carter's big band (this chapter, 2nd Chorus) as well as other jazz big bands, and becoming a featured soloist along with Augusto Coen in musical revues.

Socarrás led his own band which had a repertoire that included and combined Cuban, jazz, and light classical music and led a theater pit-band in the burgeoning Latin community of El Barrio that brought a jazz inflection to Latin material. Socarrás's band played at Harlem's Apollo Theater on a bill with Bessie Smith, played at the Cotton Club opposite Duke Ellington (Chapter 8) and Cab Calloway (this chapter, 2nd Chorus), played opposite Glenn Miller (Chapter 7, 2nd Chorus) at the Glen Island Casino (in New Rochelle, just north of New York City), as well as opposite the Ella Fitzgerald Orchestra (Chapter 9, 1st Chorus) after she took over the Chick Webb band (this chapter, 2nd Chorus). Socarrás's recording of "Masabi" gives us a picture of what a Cuban-influenced orchestra playing in a New York City ballroom or nightclub in the 1930s sounded like. This is essentially a "blowing tune," meaning its primary feature is improvised melody. So far we have heard improvising in jazz, yet it is important to note that improvising in some fashion can and does occur in many, if not most, styles of music from around the world; and in "Masabi" we hear a *típico*—traditional—improvisational style in a Latin context. This style generally features uncomplicated melodic playing with a laid-back feel, most often over chord progressions with one or two chords.

Socarrás recorded through the 1950s as well as with Tito Puente (Chapter 11, 3rd Chorus), and in the 1960s he benefited from the popularity of **charanga**,

Alberto Socarrás (standing, in white suit) and his band, August 1936, in New York City.
Courtesy BenCar Archives.

IN PERFORMANCE
Clave and Afro-Cuban Polyrhythms

Generally, styles of Cuban music were, and often continue to be, referred to by their relationship to a particular dance or genre, such as rumba, son, guaguancó, chachachá, or mambo. Each has an implied tempo range and rhythmic pattern connected to it. One common denominator is **clave**. Clave is a two-measure repeating rhythmic pattern with one measure being a 3-side and the other a 2-side. As a basic principle, one way or another, every instrumental and vocal part must fit with clave. Example 5.1 reflects a 3–2 clave (this can be reversed to be 2–3) with two typical accompanying rhythms, showing how multiple and independent rhythms interact and intersect with clave and each other.

Among the many reasons the Latin influence has been so important to jazz, the most important is the polyrhythmic character of the music. Many musicians over the years, including one of jazz's greatest stars, trumpeter Dizzy Gillespie (Chapter 10, 1st Chorus), have felt hemmed in by the specificity and lack of variation in jazz rhythm. Jazz, up until fairly recently—and it has now changed drastically as we will see in Chapter 15—has primarily been in 4/4 time (there are also many jazz waltzes, which are in 3/4) and has as its basic driving unit a common cymbal pattern and an emphasis on beats 2 and 4 (the backbeat) with the bass playing either in 2 or in 4, as seen in Example 5.2.

Latin music has a more varied and complex approach to rhythm. As mentioned, there are many types of rhythms, and each has a specific role, function, and prescribed rhythmic pattern. Also, jazz most commonly has one drummer, while a Latin band frequently will have a *bongocero* playing bongó, a *conguero* playing conga, and a *timbalero* playing timbal (or timbale), as well as other musicians in the band playing percussion instruments such as maracas, guiro, and claves. Clearly, this necessarily creates more complex rhythms through the use of polyrhythms as each percussion instrument plays a unique role in the overall rhythmic pattern.

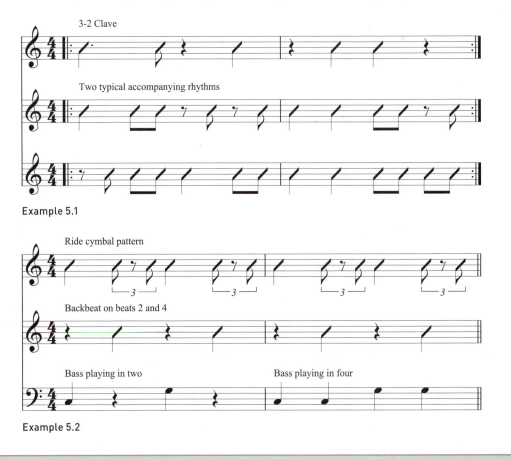

Example 5.1

Example 5.2

listening focus

"Masabi" (1935) by Alberto Socarrás y Su Orquesta Cubanacan

INSTRUMENTATION: Flute and leader: Alberto Socarrás; unknown personnel of four saxes, three trumpets, two violins, trombone, piano, bass, drums (a combination drum set that combines Latin percussion with elements of a standard drum kit), maracas; **Composer:** Roberto Ravelo-Friol.

LISTENING HIGHLIGHT, FORM: The form of "Masabi" is quite different from anything we have heard yet, and it is both simple and complex—simple because it is divided into two main sections and complex because the first section of the tune has a somewhat involved structure. The first section, which repeats twice, is more complicated than we have seen so far. It includes a 5-bar introduction, a 10-measure melody played by the saxes (0:07), a repeat of the melody (this time 12 measures) with Socarrás soloing over it (0:19), a solo section for Socarrás over a different chord progression (this time a simple V–I progression that is common in solo sections of many Latin styles), a 3-measure interlude (0:33), and finally a 7-measure solo section, again V–I (0:49). This entire section repeats verbatim (beginning at 1:00). The second section (1:48) is an "open vamp," meaning that in performance this chord progression could go on as long as the performers choose and the bandleader would "cue" the band to end the tune. It uses the V–I progression from the first section, and Socarrás on flute and a trumpeter (playing in **straight mute**) trade 10-measure solo "choruses" until a short ending (2:55) closes the tune. Normally, however, this second section would be a place for a **montuno**.

Clave is the essential pulse of this music. We hear the click of the clave pattern played by the claves—two sticks that are hit together—beginning at 0:07. Though the clicks are not always present throughout the tune, the clave rhythm is implied at all times.

a Cuban ensemble featuring flute and violin along with a vocalist and rhythm section. In later life Socarrás, a lovely and gentle man, concentrated on teaching, including being the go-to solfège teacher in New York City, particularly for Latin musicians. Socarrás employed his Cuban conservatory training, based on an old-school European system of solfège that uses syllables when singing ("do" for C, "re" for D, "mi" for E, "fa" for F, "sol" for G, "la" for A, and "si" for B), to help musicians (including this author) improve their ear and overall musicianship. While this system is taught at many conservatories, Socarrás brought an interesting twist to the lessons by insisting all exercises also be interpreted, in an improvised fashion, while finger-snapping clave (see "In Performance") and creating various phrasings that fit the clave pattern.

CODA Chapter Summary

How Did New York City Become a Major Jazz Center?

- New York has always been considered a major center for performing, recording, and music publishing.

- A large, thriving African American community in Harlem built an audience for jazz.
- During the prejazz years, bandleaders like James Reese Europe had trained and nurtured talented musicians who would go on to play significant roles in New York jazz.

How Did Popular Songwriters Influence the Jazz Repertoire?

- New York City's Tin Pan Alley was the center for popular songwriters and music publishing from the late nineteenth century until the 1960s.
- Many of these popular songs became jazz standards and serve as the core repertoire for jazz musicians—a collection of songs that all professionals must know.

What Role Did Fletcher Henderson Play in Developing the New York Jazz Scene?

- Fletcher Henderson led one of the most influential New York bands, employing master soloists including Coleman Hawkins and Louis Armstrong.
- His arrangements were used by leading bandleaders like Benny Goodman, becoming major hits during the swing era.

How Did the Successful New York Ballrooms and Nightclubs Influence the Development of Jazz?

- Dance halls like Harlem's Savoy Ballroom employed several bands a night to play for large crowds of dancers.
- Drummer Chick Webb's band was one of the most popular at the Savoy Ballroom.
- The Cotton Club produced lavish floor shows featuring singers, dancers, and jazz bands that attracted wealthy white clientele to Harlem. Duke Ellington's band was first established there, followed by popular bands led by Cab Calloway and Jimmie Lunceford.

What Role Did Star Soloists Play in These Bands?

- Trumpeter Roy Eldridge's clarion calls, fearless breaks, and rapid yet highly melodic playing set a new standard for the instrument, influencing the next generation of players, notably Dizzy Gillespie.
- Coleman Hawkins brought the tenor sax to the fore in jazz. With his strong and assertive yet sensitive approach to the instrument, it became a fluid, melodic, and powerful instrument able to rival the trumpet as a jazz voice.

What Are the Distinguishing Characteristics of Stride Piano?

- The left hand of the pianist "strides" up and down the lower part of the piano as it booms out powerful bass notes on beats 1 and 3 and chords on beats 2 and 4.
- Leading stride pianists included James P. Johnson, Fats Waller, Willie "The Lion" Smith, and Teddy Wilson.
- Their works were extremely sophisticated, with excellent melodic invention, harmonic sophistication, compositional distinction, and striking rhythms, including amazingly fast tempos and powerful swing.
- Pianist Art Tatum built upon their work and took jazz piano playing to new technical and harmonic heights.

How Has Spanish-Caribbean Music Influenced Jazz?

- A wave of Latin dance styles swept American popular music from the turn of the century onward, among them Argentinian tango and Cuban rumba.

- A Latin influence could be found in Broadway and other theater productions, and Latin music was performed at popular ballrooms.
- In the 1920s, El Barrio, a large Spanish-Caribbean community on the upper east side of Manhattan, created a demand for Latin music.
- Bands from the 1930s, such as one led by Cuban flutist Alberto Socarrás, began to incorporate both jazz and Latin styles.

Talkin' Jazz (Key Terms)

Alternate changes	Head arrangements	Speakeasy
Battles of the bands	Lead alto style	Stock arrangement
Changes	Montuno	Straight mute
Charanga	Rent parties	Turnaround
Clave	Slap-tongue	
Cutting contest	Song plugger	

Key People

Fletcher Henderson	Cab Calloway	Coleman Hawkins
Benny Carter	Jimmie Lunceford	Art Tatum
Chick Webb	Roy Eldridge	Alberto Socarrás

Think About This (For Further Discussion and Study)

1. What were the reasons for New York becoming a center for jazz? Can you name a center, or centers, for a style of music that you listen to?
2. Tin Pan Alley songs were important in the development of jazz. Considering a musical style that you are familiar with, can you name another style that it is dependent upon for its development?
3. Discuss the importance of the Harlem Renaissance. Do you think the arts can help society today? If so, how?
4. Considering the importance of ballrooms and nightclubs to jazz, what types of venues are important to the music you listen to, and how are they important?
5. Star instrumentalists such as Coleman Hawkins and Roy Eldridge were important to the success of big bands. Who is important in today's music? Are instrumentalists featured? If so, who and in what bands?
6. Discuss the characteristics of stride piano. Can you hear the differences in the various styles in the first part of Art Tatum's "Liza"?
7. Stride pianists were expected to dress well. What are the various expectations for entertainers today in terms of dress in various styles of music?

Look It Up (Key Resources)

Berger, Morroe, Edward Berger, and James Patrick. *Benny Carter: A Life in American Music*, 2 vols. Metuchen, NJ: Scarecrow Press, 1982.

Calloway, Cab, and Bryant Rollins. *Of Minnie the Moocher and Me*. New York: Crowell, 1976.

Chilton, John. *Roy Eldridge: Little Jazz Giant*. New York: Continuum, 2003.

———. *The Song of the Hawk: The Life and Recordings of Coleman Hawkins*. London: Quartet, 1990.

Dance, Stanley. *The World of Swing: An Oral History of Big Band Jazz*. New York: Da Capo Press, 2001.

Erenberg, Lewis. *Swingin' the Dream: Big Band Jazz and the Rebirth of American Culture*. Chicago: University of Chicago Press, 1998.

Glasser, Ruth. *My Music Is My Flag: Puerto Rican Musicians and Their New York Communities, 1917–1940*. Berkeley and Los Angeles: University of California Press, 1997.

Magee, Jeffrey. *The Uncrowned King of Swing: Fletcher Henderson and Big Band Jazz*. New York: Oxford University Press, 2008.

Roberts, John Storm. *Latin Jazz: The First of the Fusions, 1880s to Today*. New York: Schirmer Books, 1999.

———. *The Latin Tinge: The Impact of Latin American Music on the United States*. New York: Oxford University Press, 1979.

Schuller, Gunther. *The Swing Era: The Development of Jazz, 1930–1945*. New York: Oxford University Press, 1989.

Shipton, Alyn. *Hi-De-Ho: The Life of Cab Calloway*. New York: Oxford University Press, 2010.

Simon, George T. *The Big Bands*, 4th ed. New York: Schirmer, 1981.

Stowe, David W. *Swing Changes: Big-Band Jazz in New Deal America*. Cambridge, MA: Harvard University Press, 1994.

KANSAS CITY JAZZ 1920s-1940

6

1st Chorus Kansas City and Territory Bands

Both before the swing era and through it, the middle of America had a thriving music scene. It included hard-swinging bands such as Walter Page's Original Blue Devils, Bennie Moten's band, Andy Kirk's Twelve Clouds of Joy, and, most importantly, Count Basie, all of whom had great influence on the swing era. Some of these bands were located in a particular city, but most toured the Midwest and Southwest extensively.

WHY WAS KANSAS CITY A CENTER FOR THE EARLY DEVELOPMENT OF SWING MUSIC?

Kansas City, Missouri, the "Paris of the Plains," was an important city in westward migration because of both its position at the convergence of the Missouri and Kansas Rivers and the fact that it became a hub for the railroads as they moved west. It also was the major hub of musical activity for the Midwest and Southwest regions as well as a major center of jazz, and its relative isolation from Chicago, New York, and New Orleans helped to give it a unique sound. The political climate was also unique as Tom Pendergast and his corrupt and dominating political machine ran Kansas City from 1926 to 1939. The ready availability of alcohol, prostitution, and gambling under Pendergast's administration insured that Kansas City was depression-proof even in times of the severe economic challenges around the country during the Great Depression. Consequently, nightlife thrived with hundreds of clubs that had live bands and jam sessions, bringing musicians from around the country to take advantage of the available work. The sound of Kansas City had many sides and was both sophisticated and down-home, and everything from solo boogie-woogie pianists (see the 2nd Chorus of this chapter) to big bands could be found there. The blues was crucial to its sound and became the foundation of the early Count Basie band (see the 3rd Chorus of this chapter) as well as other bands and styles of the area.

As the city was rich in bands, the bands themselves competed for the top talent. It wasn't unusual for band members to be lured away by the chance of more regular work at better venues for better pay. Even the bandleaders moved from band to band on occasion; Walter Page, who led his own band, would eventually join Count Basie's group, which was more successful nationally.

Photo: Courtesy Redferns/Getty Images.

In this chapter, we'll answer these questions:

- Why Was Kansas City a Center for the Early Development of Swing Music?
- What Is Boogie-Woogie?
- What Were the Key Elements of Count Basie's Early Style?
- How Did Basie's Band Change in the Years After World War II?
- How Did Lester Young Create a New Style of Saxophone Playing?

Territory Bands

Bands that had an area they were known for touring regularly were called **territory bands**. Communities covering the huge expanse of America, the Midwest and the Southwest, from Texas to North Dakota and St. Louis to Colorado, all had ballrooms that regularly featured these territory bands as well as better-known nationally touring bands. These ballrooms were in steady use through the 1980s (and still are today to a much lesser degree) with numerous small bands, generally on the **sweet jazz** side, still able to work seven nights a week while touring the Midwest and Southwest in buses and cars.

Territory bands were based in a town, but that base was far less important than the areas, which were often quite large, that they toured. These areas were, in a way, governed by a particular band as other bands that wished to play the territory essentially had to ask permission from the leading band. Bands earned their place as leaders of the territory by being the hottest and most popular. Kansas City, with its many clubs and wild nightlife, was a favorite touring destination.

Walter Page's Blue Devils

One of the best-known and best of the territory bands was Walter Page's Original Blue Devils, who were based in Oklahoma City beginning in 1925. Walter Page (1900–1957) grew up in Kansas City and played there with Bennie Moten before creating his reputation as the leader of the Blue Devils. Along with bassist Wellman Braud from Ellington's band, Page is credited with helping to create the walking bass style, with the bass playing in 4, and had a huge sound as well. Page was known for having an extensive collection of arrangements that allowed the band to fit any circumstance and style. This is in contrast to many other territory bands as many had arrangements on the simpler side that were often played from memory or perhaps made up on the spot or developed over a period of time (so-called **head arrangements**). Page's band also featured an extraordinary stream of outstanding musicians such as tenor saxophonist Lester Young, singer Jimmy Rushing, and trumpeter-vocalist Oran "Hot Lips" Page (no relation), some of whom went on to star together in Count Basie's band.

IN PERFORMANCE
The Hard Life of a Territory Band Musician

During the 1920s and 1930s there were thousands of territory bands—both white and black bands and some all-female bands (see Chapter 7, 3rd Chorus)—providing steady work for many musicians who were consequently drawn to these bands from around the country. This was hard work however. These bands, often communally run with members sharing profits evenly, played anywhere they could, constantly on the move in whatever cars they had and under difficult conditions. They performed anywhere, in venues ranging from a ballroom to a field. And since the Midwest and Southwest cover such a vast area that is extremely diverse, these bands necessarily had to be able to play the music that was popular in each area and to please the various audiences they might encounter. Their material needed to be extremely varied, with waltzes and polkas, western-style hoedowns, sweet popular music, the blues, and swinging jazz all at their fingertips.

Page's Blue Devils band was known for outplaying all other territory bands, and Page always had his sights set on besting Bennie Moten's band, a top band in Kansas City. Head-to-head competition was the best way to accomplish this, so he moved his base to Kansas City. Moten, however, avoided battling the Blue Devils and little by little began hiring top members away from Page's band.

Bennie Moten

Bennie Moten (1894–1935) was a pianist and bandleader and a Kansas City native. Moten led what was considered to be the top band in Kansas City and helped to usher in and perfect the blues-based, riff-oriented sound that Kansas City and the Southwest were known for. One key to keeping his excellent pool of musicians was to work steadily, and Moten was a smart businessman in this regard.

In a savvy move, Moten and his guitarist-valve trombonist Eddie Durham brought Count Basie into the band to play piano as well as to work with Durham on helping to create a new musical direction for the band. The band began to incorporate some of the more polished aspects of the eastern bands into their bluesy sound as Moten's goal was not to just be a top Kansas City band but to compete with Ellington's, Fletcher Henderson's, and Chick Webb's bands. The addition of vocalist Jimmy Rushing, the Blue Devil's star singer, was a coup for the band.

Moten's band had a series of tours, mixed with residencies as a top band in Kansas City. They were continually in the process of reinventing themselves, eventually coming up with a successful sound that melded their hard-driving, stomping, and riffing style with a polished approach to arranging. After controversy surrounding a possible merger with another band, Moten was voted out as leader and Basie became the new leader. He had at his side bassist Walter Page, formerly leader of the Blue Devils. Moten continued to lead a band until his untimely death from an unfortunate accident during a routine tonsillectomy in 1935.

The Bennie Moten Orchestra poses for a studio portrait, United States, 1931. The Moten band was one of the best of the Kansas City outfits; it became the basis for Count Basie's orchestra. Basie is shown second from left; Bennie Moten is standing at rear center and vocalist Jimmy Rushing, at rear right. Photo Gilles Petard.
Courtesy Redferns/Getty Images.

listening focus

"The Count" (1940) by Andy Kirk and His Twelve Clouds of Joy

INSTRUMENTATION: Piano-arranger: Mary Lou Williams; **Trumpets:** Clarence Trice, Harold "Shorty" Baker, Harry Lawson; **Trombones:** Ted Donnelly, Henry Wells; **Saxophones:** John Harrington, Rudy Powell, Dick Wilson; **Guitar:** Floyd Smith; **Bass:** Booker Collins; **Drums:** Ben Thigpen; **Bandleader:** Andy Kirk.

LISTENING HIGHLIGHT, FORM: After an introduction, the form is AABA with standard 8-measure sections. The 1st chorus (0:10) features the trombone playing the melody for the A sections. The bridge (B) features the trumpet section. Chorus 2 (0:51) features Mary Lou Williams as piano soloist. It begins with a brief ensemble figure that leads into her solo on the A sections. The bridge (B) is a clarinet solo with the band playing background figures. A hot, yet relaxed, bluesy 16-bar trumpet solo follows (1:31) and almost functions as an interlude as it has a new, and simpler, chord progression and a spare accompaniment that features light comping by the guitar and drums using brushes. The 3rd chorus (1:55) returns to the original progression, but the form changes slightly. A tenor sax plays a solo on AAB, with the ensemble playing background figures throughout, including some wah-wah brass lines. The band plays an ensemble (AA), then the trombone plays the melody of A one last time, and the ensemble closes out with a tag ending.

Andy Kirk's Twelve Clouds of Joy

One of the local Kansas City bands that managed to be recognized nationally was Andy Kirk's Twelve Clouds of Joy. Andy Kirk (1898–1992) was raised in Denver, Colorado; studied music with Paul Whiteman's (see Chapter 4, 1st Chorus) father; and received his initial professional training when he joined an early touring band from Denver. He moved through several other bands while also hearing the jazz bands that were beginning to tour through Denver. Kirk wound up in Texas with Terrence "T" Holder's band, the Dark Clouds of Joy, and eventually became its leader. Kirk moved the band to Kansas City when hired for an extended engagement there.

Kirk, who played tuba and bass saxophone, was primarily known for his acumen as a bandleader, including the hiring of a string of brilliant musicians such as tenor saxophonists Ben Webster, Lester Young, and Buddy Tate. Kirk's band achieved national recognition through their hit recordings of "Christopher Columbus" and "Until the Real Thing Comes Along," as well as, of course, the power of their intense and compelling Kansas City swing feel, honed through the competition with other Kansas City and territory bands. The musical powerhouse that rocked this band, however, was pianist-arranger Mary Lou Williams. "The Count" is an excellent example of Mary Lou Williams's arranging and piano playing and clearly shows how valuable she was to the sound of Andy Kirk's band.

Mary Lou Williams

Mary Lou Williams (1910–1981) had a unique and important career as one of the few internationally known female instrumentalists and composers in jazz. Raised in Pittsburgh, Pennsylvania, Williams originally taught herself to play the piano at a very young age by listening to records and the family player piano. She was performing at parties before the age of 10, and by the time she was a teenager she was already a well-known professional musician in Pittsburgh. At 14 she was working on the Orpheum Theater circuit and soon was playing with Duke Ellington's early group, The Washingtonians.

When Andy Kirk and His Twelve Clouds of Joy began a long engagement in Kansas City, Williams joined her husband, saxophonist John Williams, part-time in the band, eventually becoming the band's pianist and arranger in 1931. Her remarkable arrangements, compositions, and piano playing drove the success of the band. Williams also wrote arrangements for other swing big bands, such as those of Benny Goodman (Chapter 7, 1st Chorus), Tommy Dorsey (Chapter 7, 2nd Chorus), and Earl Hines (Chapter 4, 2nd Chorus).

In the early 1940s, Williams formed a small group with her soon-to-be second husband, trumpeter Harold "Shorty" Baker from the Kirk band; and she soon joined Ellington as staff arranger. After leaving Ellington in the mid-1940s, she was hired to be pianist at the Café Society (see Chapter 9, 1st Chorus), a Greenwich Village nightclub that was the first racially integrated nightclub in the United States. Williams's remarkable versatility can be seen as around this time she became a mentor to early bebop (Chapter 10) pioneers such as pianist Thelonious Monk and trumpeter Dizzy Gillespie. Orchestrated versions of her extended and harmonically adventurous composition *Zodiac Suite*, originally written for solo piano and piano trio, were performed twice in New York, in 1945 and 1946.

After briefly retiring from performing in 1956, Williams converted to Roman Catholicism. She quickly returned to an active career that included writing jazz-based works on liturgical themes, performing, as well as business ventures including a record label and publishing company. Her playing and writing were largely couched in the blues in some fashion, and she was able to incorporate styles from multiple eras, including swing, bebop, and later the avant-garde, as evidenced by her performing with avant-garde pianist Cecil Taylor (Chapter 14, 2nd Chorus). Williams had a remarkable ability to continue to grow in her writing and playing and to stay current and modern, all while maintaining her musical personality.

Mary Lou Williams at the piano, ca. 1946. A talented pianist and arranger, Williams also was sympathetic to new trends in jazz and encouraged the young players developing bebop in New York during the early 1940s. Photo by William P. Gottlieb.

Courtesy William P. Gottlieb Collection and Library of Congress.

2nd Chorus Boogie-Woogie: "Big" Joe Turner and Pete Johnson

WHAT IS BOOGIE-WOOGIE?

Another style that was prominent in Kansas City and the Midwest and Southwest was **boogie-woogie**, a rocking and exciting blues piano style that features a constant and aggressively hard-driving, rolling, repeated left-hand figure that found a home in Kansas City. Some important boogie-woogie pianists are Meade Lux Lewis ("Honky Tonk Train Blues"), Albert Ammons, Clarence "Pine Top" Smith ("Pine Top's Boogie Woogie"), and Pete Johnson (1904–1967). Johnson was a popular fixture in Kansas City, and along with vocalist "Big" Joe Turner (1911–1985) helped establish the barrelhouse boogie-woogie style, while also pushing it toward a jazz style as well as toward rock and roll.

"Big" Joe Turner and Pete Johnson

Johnson and Turner were from Kansas City, both from fatherless homes. Johnson was sent to an orphanage when his father died but after dealing with difficult conditions there managed to escape and returned to his home. Johnson only made it to the fifth grade in school, at which time he began to work as a laborer with his uncle, who was also a working pianist. He began to play the drums, eventually switched to the piano, and soon was substituting for his uncle on **gigs** as well as playing at parties and in bars for tips.

Having left school in the sixth grade, Joe Turner also got an early start by helping a blind blues singer as he sang for change on the streets and in restaurants, as well as singing along with jug bands on the streets of Kansas City. Turner's singing career moved forward when he took a job as a singing bartender. While selling beer, Turner would also sing with the house band that included Pete Johnson; and they also worked together regularly as a duo. Turner would go outside and shout the blues in front of the club to bring in customers. Johnson and Turner developed a strong musical rapport and partnership and were an integral part of the night-life and musical scene of Kansas City.

Very few musicians, however, are able to stay in one place and continue to make a living. They are generally ambitious to establish national careers as they want others to hear them, of course; but that type of exposure is a necessity in order to expand one's career and to have it be more financially successful. Besides the kind of touring most of them were used to as part of the territory band tradition, all of these musicians and bands traveled to the other centers of jazz, Chicago and New York, with varying degrees of success.

For example, John Hammond, a top talent scout, record producer, and social activist, took Turner and Johnson to New York. They had broken up sometime before as Johnson evidently was spending money from their tips (which was how they were paid) as part of his womanizing at the club. Hammond got them a job at New York's Famous Door, a 52nd Street nightclub. But after that, work was scarce and they returned to Kansas City. Hammond was determined to bring them back to New York and included them in a famous Carnegie Hall concert he produced in 1938 that he titled "From Spirituals to Swing." The concert presented a range of performers who represented the history of African American music, including gospel, the blues, and jazz. "From Spirituals to Swing," a following engagement at Café Society, performances on Benny Goodman's national radio show, and their first recording, "Roll 'em Pete," all thrust Turner and Johnson into the national spotlight.

While both Turner and Johnson remained active through the 1940s and 1950s, it was Turner's signing with Atlantic Records in 1951 that took his career to its next level. For Atlantic, Turner recorded an early and influential rock-and-roll hit, "Shake, Rattle and Roll." The popular and short-lived rock-and-roll star Bill Haley's cover version of Turner's tune was a million-seller. Ironically, it was the popularity of rock-and-roll hits such as this that began to eclipse the popularity of older blues and jazz musicians such as Joe Turner and Pete Johnson. Turner was eventually inducted into the Rock and Roll Hall of Fame thanks to his pioneering work in that genre.

IN PERFORMANCE
Café Society, New York City

Barney Josephson opened the Greenwich Village nightclub Café Society, but shortly thereafter John Hammond and bandleader Benny Goodman invested in the club to keep it afloat. Hammond and Josephson saw it as an opportunity to present the artists they believed in as well as a range of African American musical styles. Josephson also put his integrationist philosophy to work by creating the first major nightclub to be integrated, and black and white customers were treated equally. The club also provided support for causes with a strong leftist political bent.

Café Society became known as home to a who's-who of jazz, including Kansas City musicians such as Joe Turner, Pete Johnson, and Mary Lou Williams, as well as Billie Holiday (she introduced the moving civil rights song "Strange Fruit" at the club; see Chapter 9, 1st Chorus), Hazel Scott, Sarah Vaughan, and an endless list of jazz stars and folk artists.

JAZZ LIVES JOHN HAMMOND

John Hammond (1910–1987) was a record producer and an extraordinary talent scout who promoted the careers of an incredible string of artists, including Kansas City musicians such as Count Basie, Mary Lou Williams, Joe Turner, and Pete Johnson, as well as Billie Holiday, Benny Goodman (and introduced Fletcher Henderson to Benny Goodman), Pete Seeger, Bob Dylan, Aretha Franklin, Stevie Ray Vaughan, and Bruce Springsteen.

A great-great-grandson of the industrialist and philanthropist Cornelius Vanderbilt and related to numerous influential politicians, Hammond was committed to social reform. He expressed this through his work in promoting African American music and the issue of racial integration in a variety of ways.

He produced "Spirituals to Swing," on December 23, 1938, at Carnegie Hall, presenting performers such as blues artists Sonny Terry and Big Bill Broonzy, boogie-woogie performers Meade Lux Lewis and Albert Ammons, gospel singer Sister Roberta Tharpe, Sidney Bechet and trumpeter Tommy Ladnier representing New Orleans jazz, blues singer Ruby Smith and pianist James P. Johnson for classic blues, and Joe Turner and Pete Johnson representing Kansas City boogie-woogie and blues shouters. Count Basie's jazz big band headlined the bill, while his terrific rhythm section (discussed in the 3rd Chorus of this chapter) functioned as the house band for the other artists. The concert was sold out and a huge hit. Joe Turner eschewed the microphone provided for him and thrilled the audience with his bold and powerful performance. With its emphasis on Kansas City artists and styles, this concert helped to solidify Kansas City's reputation as an important center of jazz. Hammond's involvement with Café Society (see "In Performance") is another example of his work in this essential area of social reform.

listening focus

"Roll 'em Pete" (1938) by Big Joe Turner (vocal) and Pete Johnson (piano)

LISTENING HIGHLIGHT, MELODY AND HARMONY: This is a standard boogie-woogie 12-bar blues with a I–IV–V chord progression. Unlike the stride style, boogie-woogie is not harmonically adventurous and sticks to a bit of a roots approach, keeping the harmony simple and straightforward. Turner's vocal is an excellent example of a traditional shouting blues. It's simple, leaves plenty of space in between phrases, and makes extensive use of blue notes and traditional blues melodies. Turner's singing on choruses 8–11 is much akin to a big band playing riffs at the end of tune as he uses the simple lyrics to create repetitive, swinging rhythmic phrases ("Yes, Yes," "Well alright, there," "Bye, Bye"). On chorus 11, "Bye, bye" is delivered with an extra layer of intensity and is an indication of where this song could go if they were playing an extended version in a live setting. The limitation of the length of a phonograph record at this time doesn't allow us to feel the full potential power of these two artists (this is almost always true for recordings), but it does give us an idea of the style and of where they might go if they had the chance.

3rd Chorus William "Count" Basie

"Count" Basie (1904–1984) led one of the most important big bands in jazz from 1935 until his death in 1984. He was a wonderful pianist known for his impeccable taste and musicianship rather than his technical prowess. His solos and accompaniment were generally sparse but always flawless and highly effective. Basie also had a great eye for talent in his choice of musicians and arrangers and knew how to showcase his band and musicians to their best effect. He and his band were steeped in the blues, and the band was known for an intense swing and a laid-back, relaxed feeling, a combination that is both difficult and rare. In addition, the concept of the Basie rhythm section set a new standard for big bands.

Basie was from Red Bank, on the New Jersey shore. His early listening experiences were hearing music at carnivals, circuses, and vaudeville shows. Basie was influenced by both ragtime and stride piano and spent time in New York City in the mid-1920s among the greatest stride pianists such as Fats Waller, who became his friend. Basie went on the road with vaudeville acts, and it was then, while on tour, that he first spent time in Kansas City, a musical environment that impressed him. During one tour, in Tulsa, Oklahoma, Basie's career took an important turn when he heard, and was tremendously excited by, Walter Page's Blue Devils (this chapter, 1st Chorus), which led him to join the Blue Devils, setting his career as a big-band player and leader in motion. Basie moved on to join Bennie Moten's band (this chapter, 1st Chorus), who was based in Kansas City, eventually becoming its leader. Basie then secured a job for his own band as the house band at that city's Reno Club. His popular radio broadcasts from the club established his career as a bandleader and led to his being "discovered" in 1936 by the important talent scout and producer John Hammond (see "Jazz Lives"), who arranged to have the band signed with a major booking agency.

WHAT WERE THE KEY ELEMENTS OF BASIE'S EARLY STYLE?

Early arrangements for the band were based on the blues and largely head arrangements that the band created. Head arrangements generally consist of a series of **riffs** (short, rhythmic, repetitive phrases). These riffs serve as the melody of the arrangement, as backgrounds behind soloists, and as polyphonic shout choruses that conclude the arrangements. Each section of the band makes up its own lines and creates its own harmonies. The players listen to each other, making constant adjustments, and eventually finalize an arrangement that essentially becomes a set routine without ever having been written down. These head arrangements have the potential to create a thrilling momentum as chorus builds upon chorus, creating a wildly intense groove that never lets up. They also provide room for soloists to "stretch out" (play long solos), which, in the right hands, can generate incredible excitement and energy. This type of flexible arrangement is terrific for dancing, and their skill with these arrangements was critical to the Basie band's early success. Another important factor in their success was Basie's uncanny ability to always set the correct tempo for a song or situation.

Count Basie folio, ca. 1940s. Collections like this were popular among home pianists who wanted to emulate the style of popular jazz players like Basie.
Courtesy BenCar Archives.

The Basie Rhythm Section

The Basie rhythm section—often referred to as "The All-American Rhythm Section"—created a driving, yet relaxed, 4-beat feel; and this groove is one of the band's most important trademarks and contributions. Basie sets the tone for the rhythm section and the band with his tasteful and spare piano introductions, accompaniments, and solos. Drummer Jo Jones contributed a propulsive, yet light, touch that kicked the band and the soloists with well-placed accents on his bass drum while keeping time on his cymbals. Freddie Green set the standard for big-band guitar accompaniment. He strummed chords on every beat with an insistent but relaxed feel, and his sound and style make the Basie rhythm section immediately recognizable. Anchoring the early rhythm section was bassist Walter Page (formerly the leader of the Blue Devils), who, from his long experience in these types of grooving bands, knew exactly how to drive a band with his big sound while also staying subtle and relaxed. This rhythm section bubbled along in support of the powerful ensembles and solos but also provided a crucial texture when they played on their own in between full-ensemble choruses and solos.

The early Basie band was full of great soloists such as saxophonists Herschel Evans, Buddy Tate, Illinois Jacquet, and Don Byas; trumpeters Harry "Sweets" Edison and Buck Clayton; and trombonist J. J. Johnson. The biggest star, however, was the tenor saxophonist Lester "Prez" Young (this chapter, 4th Chorus). "Sent

Jimmy Rushing at the microphone, ca. 1946. A popular blues-styled vocalist, Rushing was closely identified with the Basie band during the later 1930s and 1940s. Photo by William P. Gottlieb.

Courtesy William P. Gottlieb Collection and Library of Congress.

for You Yesterday (And Here You Come Today)" is an excellent example of Kansas City blues, an important early swing-era style. It features vocalist Jimmy Rushing, known as "Mr. Five-by-Five" for his short and thick stature, one of the great Kansas City blues shouters.

HOW DID BASIE'S BAND CHANGE IN THE YEARS AFTER WORLD WAR II?

This early version of the Basie band, with its swinging, bluesy style and power-house soloists, enjoyed great success through the 1940s. As was true for most bands after World War II, touring became economically difficult. Consequently, Basie broke the band up briefly in 1950 and toured with a smaller group. Basie re-formed the big band in 1952 and managed to completely change the band's style.

Basie's Arrangers
Along with its patented driving yet relaxed style, the band became known for its terrific arrangements and powerful and precise ensemble playing with the help of arrangers such as Neal Hefti, trumpeter-cornetist Thad Jones (who went on to

listening guide

DOWNLOAD
Track Number 12

"Sent for You Yesterday (And Here You Come Today)" (1938) by the Count Basie Orchestra featuring Jimmy Rushing

INSTRUMENTATION: Piano and leader: Count Basie; **Trumpets:** Buck Clayton, Ed Lewis, Harry "Sweets" Edison; **Trombones:** Eddie Durham, Benny Morton, Dan Minor; **Saxophones:** Earle Warren, Jack Washington, Herschel Evans, Lester Young; **Guitar:** Freddie Green; **Bass:** Walter Page; **Drums:** Jo Jones; **Vocal:** Jimmy Rushing; **Arranger:** Eddie Durham.

FORM: This is a classic 12-bar blues consisting of an introduction, 8 blues choruses, and a coda.

STYLE: "Sent for You Yesterday (And Here You Come Today)" is played in a typical Kansas City style. The riffs throughout this tune, bluesy and simple, are intended to create a steady swing for the dancers. Short solos such as those by these excellent soloists (Earle Warren, alto sax; Herschel Evans, tenor sax; Sweets Edison, trumpet) are quite common in big-band playing. Creating an effective solo within 1 or 2 choruses or playing fills between phrases is a particular skill and art.

MELODY AND HARMONY: The riffs and solos are full of blue notes, a crucial element in the blues. These are notes, most commonly the 3rd and 5th, of a scale, that are slightly flattened and give the blues its characteristic sound.

RHYTHM: This tune is in a moderate tempo but has an insistent and steady groove that builds in momentum. This building upon itself is a crucial feature of the blues and goes hand in hand with its simple and repetitive form. Blues by a big band or a blues band can go on for an extended period and build to a fever pitch, as can be seen in Duke Ellington's "Diminuendo and Crescendo in Blue," a live recording at the Newport Jazz Festival in 1956 that featured an extended 27-chorus solo by tenor saxophonist Paul Gonsalves. Blues players such as guitarist Albert Collins also made this type of extended solo over a solid groove a specialty.

ACCOMPANIMENT: The rhythm section chugs along steadily and gradually builds in intensity, leading up to powerful drum fills in the final chorus. Much of the accompaniment, however, consists of background riffs by the horn sections as well as horn fills between phrases.

"SENT FOR YOU YESTERDAY (AND HERE YOU COME TODAY)" LISTENING GUIDE

TIME	FORM	STYLE	MELODY AND HARMONY	RHYTHM	ACCOMPANIMENT
0:00	Intro		This 8-bar introduction begins with Count Basie playing solo for 4 bars in a stride piano style with a descending bass line. The saxophone section joins in for 4 more bars with a short riff that also accents this descending line.		

continued

TIME	FORM	STYLE	MELODY AND HARMONY	RHYTHM	ACCOMPANIMENT
0:12	1st chorus	The full ensemble plays the melody of the tune, which consists of three repeated 4-bar phrases.	The lead trumpet, as is usual, is most prominent in the harmonized ensemble. Lovely and expressive alto sax obligatos fill the space in between riffs.		
0:20	2nd chorus		The piano plays a chorus that is part solo and part slightly altered version of the melody.		The ensemble, dominated by the growling brass using plunger mutes, fills between Basie's phrases.
0:46	3rd chorus		The tenor sax plays a solo.		An ensemble background figure is again dominated by brass playing a simple riff using plunger mutes.
1:04	4th chorus	Jimmy Rushing's vocal is preceded by an inserted 4-bar figure borrowed from the introduction.		Rushing's voice is powerful and driving, yet his phrasing is relaxed, or laid-back.	A muted trumpet plays fills between Rushing's phrases.
1:27	5th chorus	The intensity begins to build behind Rushing's second vocal chorus.			The brass play a continuous riff behind the vocal, while the saxes fill between phrases.
1:45	6th chorus	This chorus begins with an inserted 4-bar trumpet break as Sweets Edison launches into a powerful and bluesy trumpet solo for a full chorus.		The rhythm section picks up in intensity, particularly Jo Jones on drums as he kicks the soloist with hits on his snare drum.	The saxes play a background riff behind the trumpet solo.
2:08	7th chorus	The 7th and 8th choruses are the shout choruses, or climax, of this tune as it builds to its highest point with the horn sections blowing intense, bluesy riffs.	The brass and saxophone sections play their own lines in a powerful call and response.		
2:26	8th chorus	The band keeps blazing, and the horns' riffs almost disguise the divisions between choruses to help build the intensity.	The saxophones seem to not take a breath during their riffs, adding to the power of this shout chorus.	Jones's powerful fills on the drums help to bring this tune home.	
2:43	Coda	This powerful and classic blues ends with the piano and saxes playing a relaxed 8-bar coda reminiscent of the introduction but with the piano and sax parts reversed.			

Compare

"Li'l Darlin'" (1957) by the Count Basie Orchestra. "Lil Darlin'" is a Neal Hefti composition and arrangement. Hefti was an important arranger for numerous big bands, but he was most associated with Count Basie. One of the most remarkable things about "Li'l Darlin'" is that along with being one of the prettiest original ballads in the big-band tradition, it is also one of the swingingest, a remarkable and difficult feat to accomplish. This arrangement and recording became a mid-period Basie standard, and it continues to be a popular tune with big bands of all levels, from student to professional.

lead the Thad Jones–Mel Lewis band and was one of jazz's great arrangers as well as a lovely and tasteful soloist), tenor saxophonist Frank Foster (his composition and arrangement "Shiny Stockings" is a Basie classic), and Quincy Jones.

Joe Williams

Basie kept the band's relationship to the blues, however, through his soloists and the vocalist Joe Williams, a singer very much in the blues tradition. Williams was not a blues shouter, however, and had a sophisticated and calm demeanor that matched the Basie vibe, plus he swung hard and was as comfortable with a jazz standard as he was with the blues. Basie and Williams's version of the classic blues "Everyday (I Have the Blues)" was a hit for the band and is a terrific example of their work together as well as of Williams's style.

The band's success in the 1950s and 1960s is an example of swing's continued success well after its heyday had supposedly passed. Their work accompanying popular vocalists such as Frank Sinatra (Chapter 9, 2nd Chorus), Ella Fitzgerald (Chapter 9, 1st Chorus), and Tony Bennett is further evidence that the swing style was still prominent well into the 1960s.

4th Chorus | Lester Young

Saxophonist Lester Young (1909–1959) gained fame as a featured soloist with the Count Basie Orchestra and took up the tenor sax mantle from Coleman Hawkins and ran with it. The inspired melodic fluidity of Young's playing makes him an important precursor to bebop alto saxophonist Charlie Parker (Chapter 10, 1st Chorus) and places him as one of jazz's greatest and most important and influential tenor saxophone soloists.

Young's mellow, less aggressive tone and melodic lyricism were particularly well suited for small group playing. The openness of the riff and blues–oriented Basie band was also a perfect medium for Young's style, giving him the room and the freedom to let his lyricism blossom and float over the rolling, rocking Basie rhythm section. A more heavily arranged accompaniment as heard in other bands would have inhibited a free-spirited soloist like Young.

"Prez," Young's nickname, was stylish and individualistic in other ways as well. He was known for his signature porkpie hat and was extremely creative with

JAZZ LIVES LESTER YOUNG

Lester Willis Young was born near New Orleans, received musical training from his father, and gained early experience touring the Midwest carnival circuit playing numerous instruments with his father's family band. Young went on to tour with important bands such as that of King Oliver and the Original Blue Devils, and in 1933 he based himself in Kansas City, where he joined the Count Basie band. Young joined Fletcher Henderson's band in New York City briefly in December 1933, but his less aggressive, melodic approach didn't sit well with the band, largely because he was filling the chair of the more burly-toned Coleman Hawkins. Returning to Kansas City, Young rejoined the Basie band.

Young also enjoyed an association on record with the great jazz vocalist Billie Holiday (Chapter 9, 1st Chorus), accompanying her on several sessions during 1937–1942. From 1940 to 1943, Young broke from Basie to play in smaller groups but returned to Basie's band for 10 months before being drafted into the army in September 1944. The result was disastrous, as his personality and personal habits did not fit with the regimentation of the service. He was convicted of marijuana use and spent 9 months in detention before leaving the service.

Over the next decade Young regained his place as a top tenor player, but alcoholism, and perhaps personal

frustration, took its toll. His skill and drive faded, but his lyricism was often still in evidence. He was admitted into a psychiatric hospital in late 1955 but recovered enough to continue to record and tour over the next few years. Young and Holiday reunited to perform a moving version of "Fine and Mellow" in 1957 for a performance on a television program, "The Sound of Jazz," produced by critic Nat Hentoff. Two years later, following a tour to Europe, Young finally succumbed to the longtime effects of alcoholism.

Lester Young on stage in 1940. Young's eccentric personality was reflected even in the way he held the saxophone.
© Lebrecht Music & Arts.

his language, inventing his own expressive slang vocabulary. He certainly was comfortable in the jazz world, which accommodated his nonconformist ways, perhaps because the jazz world has always been full of nonconformists and manages to handle musicians' eccentricities. However, Young's gentle yet insistent individualism made his relationship with the rest of society difficult.

His playing style is quite different from that of Coleman Hawkins. Young's playing is extremely linear. Rather than play in an almost vertical fashion that "spells" the chords, he rides over the chords, creating long, lyrical melodies that almost transcend the chord progression while still clearly articulating it. Young spoke of the lyricism of saxophonist Frank Trumbauer as a hugely important influence, mentioning Trumbauer's playing on "Singin' the Blues" as particularly important to him (see Chapter 4, 1st Chorus). Even today young jazz students and professionals are incorporating aspects of Hawkins's and Young's two styles, and combined, they help to define jazz improvisation.

Important early recordings that Young made with Basie include "Oh! Lady Be Good" and "Shoe Shine Boy"—both recorded by a Count Basie quintet under the

listening guide

"Lester Leaps In" (1939) by Count Basie's Kansas City Seven

INSTRUMENTATION: Piano and leader: Count Basie; **Tenor saxophone:** Lester Young; **Trumpet:** "Buck" Clayton; **Trombone:** Dicky Wells; **Guitar:** Freddy Green; **Bass:** Walter Page; **Drums:** Jo Jones.

FORM: "I've Got Rhythm," the basis for this tune, is a typical AABA tune, and the band plays 6 choruses. Young is primarily featured, but Basie and bassist Walter Page also get chances to shine.

STYLE: During his solo, Young floats over the band, mixing beautiful melody with a series of riffs, fitting in with the riffing style of both the melody and the arrangement. In addition, this Lester Young feature in a small group setting has an arrangement that is quite varied and that uses many typical stylistic arranging techniques.

MELODY AND HARMONY: The melody of this tune is a simple harmonized riff over the A section of the tune (0:08). The B section—the bridge—does not even have a melody.

RHYTHM: While the rhythm section calmly cooks, Young pushes this tune and makes it hot—with a cool demeanor—and his relaxed rhythmic intensity can be heard when he plays by himself during numerous breaks. His rhythmic sense is buoyant, on top of the beat, and gentle yet quite insistent, an important element in his unique and influential style.

In the 3rd chorus, during a stop-time section, it seems Basie did not realize—or he just forgot—that Young was still supposed to solo. Basie begins to play a solo at the start of the chorus, and it takes him almost an entire A section to realize his mistake! The fact that he does this probably indicates that there was little or no rehearsal for this particular cut. It also is indicative of a very different approach to recording from what we see in popular music today, where a recording is often labored over extensively to make it "perfect." This kind of relaxed looseness is refreshing and, like "Body and Soul," resulted in a classic recording.

ACCOMPANIMENT: The rhythm section is primarily supporting Young in this tune, but it also gives us a terrific chance to hear Count Basie's understated style.

"LESTER LEAPS IN" LISTENING GUIDE

TIME	FORM	STYLE	MELODY AND HARMONY	RHYTHM	ACCOMPANIMENT
0:00	Intro			The rhythm section plays a hot 4-bar intro that immediately sets a swinging tone.	
1st Chorus					
0:08	AA	The horns play the melody for the A sections of the 1st chorus. Even though the tenor sax is lower than the trumpet and would normally play a harmony below it, Young plays the melody.	The A section melody is a simple harmonized riff in a Kansas City style.	Bassist Walter Page plays in 4 throughout this tune. Basie and Jones play simply but add to the drive.	This recording displays Count Basie's understated yet uncannily effective style of accompanying and soloing.

continued

"Lester Leaps In" listening guide continued

TIME	FORM	STYLE	MELODY AND HARMONY	RHYTHM	ACCOMPANIMENT
0:19	B		The B section—the bridge—does not have a melody.		The rhythm section—displaying a typical Basie-esque restraint—plays through the bridge as if it is continuing to accompany a melody or a solo.
0:27	A		The riff melody is repeated for the last A.		
2nd Chorus					
0:35	AABA	Young begins his solo over the rhythm section.	During his solo, Young plays a seemingly endless stream of beautiful melody—it feels like he could go on forever—while also mixing in numerous riffs that are characteristic of the blues and riff-driven Kansas City style.		Notice Basie's tasteful fills throughout Young's solo.
3rd Chorus					
1:06	AA	Young continues to solo.		The rhythm section plays stop time, hitting only on beat 1 every 2 bars for the A sections of this chorus. This provides a series of breaks for Young to show his stuff. Young's rhythmic drive is highlighted during these breaks along with his lovely melodic sense.	Basie did not realize this section was stop time for Young and starts to solo during the first A.
	B			The rhythm section discontinues the stop time for variation.	
	A			The rhythm section again plays stop time for the last A of this chorus.	
4th Chorus					
1:38	AABA	The 4th chorus uses another typical jazz technique, "trading 4s." Basie and Young alternate 4-bar solos for the entire chorus.		Notice how much more space there is in Basie's solos than in Young's.	The rhythm section keeps chugging along in a powerful but understated and tasteful manner.

"Lester Leaps In" listening guide continued

TIME	FORM	STYLE	MELODY AND HARMONY	RHYTHM	ACCOMPANIMENT
			5th Chorus		
2:09	A	The A sections of the 5th and 6th choruses are a variation of trading 4s. The band hits a riff for 4 measures, and someone solos over the second 4 measures.	After a band riff, Young solos for the second 4 measures.		
2:17	A			After a band riff, Basie solos for the second 4 measures.	
2:25	B			Basie solos simply over the bridge.	
2:32	A		Again, after a band riff, Young solos for the second 4 measures.		
			6th Chorus		
2:40	AA	Bassist Page's powerful "walking" is featured for parts of the last chorus as the horns lay out and the rest of the rhythm section plays softly and simply.		After a band riff, Page's walking bass is featured for the second 4 measures of the first two A sections, with Basie playing light fills.	
2:56	B			Page continues his powerful walking, while the band plays underneath him, allowing his playing to shine.	
3:04	A	After one last band riff, the band hits a typical ending.			

Compare

Listen again to Coleman Hawkins's performance on "Body and Soul." How do the styles of these two innovative saxophonists differ? What sets Young's playing apart?

band pseudonym of Jones–Smith Incorporated (to sidestep a poor recording contract that Basie signed)—and "Lester Leaps In," with the Basie band. On "Lester Leaps In," Young is featured in an uptempo version of "rhythm changes," meaning that the chords of the song are based on George Gershwin's tune "I've Got Rhythm." Next to the blues, rhythm-change tunes are the most commonly played in jazz; and these are two types of tunes that Young thrived on. Adding to the lineage of instrumental soloists in jazz, his solos were so outstanding that saxophone players copied Young's solos as trumpet players have copied Armstrong and Beiderbecke.

CODA Chapter Summary

Why Was Kansas City a Center for the Early Development of Swing Music?
- It was the major hub of musical activity for the Midwest and Southwest regions. Its relative isolation from Chicago, New York, and New Orleans helped to give it a unique sound.
- Hundreds of clubs employed live bands and sponsored jam sessions. The proliferation of bands to meet the demand for live music led to competition for the best players and arrangers.

What Is Boogie-Woogie?
- Boogie-woogie is a rocking blues piano style that features a constant and aggressively hard-driving, rolling, repeated left-hand figure.

What Were the Key Elements of Basie's Early Style?
- Early arrangements for the band were based on the blues and often head arrangements that the band created based on a series of riffs.
- The Basie rhythm section created a driving, yet relaxed, 4-beat feel, which is one of the band's most important trademarks.
- Basie's piano playing was spare but tasteful.

How Did Basie's Band Change in the Years After World War II?
- Along with its patented driving, yet relaxed, style, the band became known for its terrific arrangements and powerful and precise ensemble playing.
- Basie kept the band's relationship to the blues through his soloists and the vocalist Joe Williams.

How Did Lester Young Create a New Style of Saxophone Playing?
- Lester Young gained fame as featured soloist with the Count Basie Orchestra. In contrast to Coleman Hawkins, Young had a mellow, less aggressive tone and melodic lyricism; and it was particularly well suited for small group playing.

Talkin' Jazz (Key Terms)

Boogie-woogie	Head arrangements	Sweet jazz
Gigs	Riffs	Territory bands

Key People

Walter Page's Original Blue Devils	Mary Lou Williams	Count Basie
Bennie Moten	"Big" Joe Turner	Lester Young
Andy Kirk's Twelve Clouds of Joy	Pete Johnson	

Think About This (For Further Discussion and Study)

1. Describe the conditions that led to Kansas City becoming a center of jazz.
2. Describe the elements of the Kansas City style.
3. What is a territory band, and who were some of the popular bands in the Southwest? Are there any modern-day equivalents of them?
4. Discuss the lifestyle of territory band musicians.
5. Discuss the importance of Mary Lou Williams to Andy Kirk and the Twelve Clouds of Joy, as well as to jazz in general.
6. After listening to "Roll 'em Pete," use your own words to describe the boogie-woogie piano style of Pete Johnson.
7. Describe the key elements of the Basie band's style, in both its early and later iterations.
8. Describe the key elements of tenor saxophonist Lester Young's style.

Look It Up (Key Resources)

Basie, Count. *Good Morning Blues: The Autobiography of Count Basie*. With Albert Murray. New York: Random House, 1985.

Dahl, Linda. *Morning Glory: A Biography of Mary Lou Williams*. New York: Pantheon, 1999.

————. *Stormy Weather: The Music and Lives of a Century of Jazzwomen*. New York: Limelight Editions, 1995.

Daniels, Douglas Henry. *Lester Leaps In: The Life and Times of Lester "Pres" Young*. Boston: Beacon Press, 2002.

Driggs, Frank, and Chuck Haddix. *Kansas City Jazz: From Ragtime to Bebop—A History*. New York: Oxford University Press, 2005.

Erenberg, Lewis. *Swingin' the Dream: Big Band Jazz and the Rebirth of American Culture*. Chicago: University of Chicago Press, 1998.

Hammond, John. *John Hammond on Record: An Autobiography*. With Irving Townsend. New York: Penguin, 1977.

Kernodle, Tammy L. *Soul on Soul: The Life and Music of Mary Lou Williams*. Boston: Northeastern University Press, 2004.

Kirk, Andy. *Twenty Years on Wheels*. As told to Amy Lee. Ann Arbor: University of Michigan Press, 1989.

Placksin, Sally. *American Women in Jazz: 1900 to the Present, Their Words, Lives, and Music*. New York: Wideview Books, 1982.

Porter, Lewis, ed. *A Lester Young Reader*. Washington, DC: Smithsonian Institution Press, 1991.

Ross, Russell. *Jazz Style in Kansas City and the Southwest*. Berkeley and Los Angeles: University of California Press, 1971.

Simon, George T. *The Big Bands*, 4th ed. New York: Schirmer, 1981.

Stowe, David W. *Swing Changes: Big-Band Jazz in New Deal America*. Cambridge, MA: Harvard University Press, 1994.

overview

III

FROM SWING TO BOP
1930–1950

MAJOR MUSICAL STYLES

1935–1945	• Swing • Big-band era • Jazz vocalists
ca. 1943–1950	• Bebop

The Great Depression that began in October 1929 marked the end of an era of growth and prosperity in the United States. For the African American community, which always suffered from more limited economic and social opportunities, the Depression only made living conditions worse. With work hard to come by, racial tensions grew as white and black Americans vied for the few jobs that were available. The Depression also hit the music industry hard, particularly the recording companies, which saw sales drop due to the popularity of "free" music transmitted by radio, a situation we see again today with the proliferation of "free" streaming music services and a continued drastic drop in CD sales and, more recently, digital downloads. Nightclubs that had prospered during the 1920s found it more difficult to survive in the 1930s, although the repeal of Prohibition in 1932, making it legal once again to serve and sell alcohol, did boost club attendance and led to renewed opportunities for musicians to perform.

The Depression era saw the rise of a new style of jazz, known as big band or swing music. During this period, jazz bands enjoyed great popular success, on record, on radio, and as attractions at large dance halls that had been built around the country. Many of the most successful bands were led by white musicians, including notably Benny Goodman, Artie Shaw, the Dorsey Brothers, and Glenn Miller, although Count Basie and Duke Ellington also prospered thanks to the increased popularity of jazz. Goodman was particularly controversial. On the one hand, he employed black arrangers, notably Fletcher Henderson, so that some said his band's success was an example of a white group cashing in on the creative work of black musicians. On the other hand, Goodman was among the first to feature African American musicians like Charlie Christian and Lionel Hampton in his smaller groups, helping to break down the color barrier in jazz.

In a reaction to the Depression, left-leaning social movements flourished, many advocating for equal rights for America's black citizens, as well as better working conditions and pay for the working poor. In the late 1930s to early 1940s, small clubs in major cities flourished, appealing to an integrated and politically progressive audience. Clubs like New York's Café Society were among the first to be open to integrated audiences, featuring a mix of black and white performers as well. Jazz musicians often played benefits for union groups and other progressive causes, as is still true today. Individual cases like the trial and conviction of a group of black teenagers, known as the Scottsboro Boys, who supposedly raped a young white girl in the rural South, became rallying points for the socially active.

African American artillery troops on march in Belgium, Nov, 1944.
Courtesy Library of Congress.

With the outbreak of World War II, many of the big bands lost key members who were drafted into the service. Ironically, with many men gone, all-female bands—many formed as "novelty groups" during the mid-1930s—were able to pick up more work. The war affected musicians' lives in other ways: gasoline rationing made it more difficult for bands to tour, and rationing of materials used in making records, as well as a musician's strike, led to fewer opportunities to record.

Although the army was not yet integrated, World War II brought together peoples of all races and backgrounds in a way that would have a lasting impact on American life. Soldiers got a chance to share not only the experience of warfare but also their interests in music, dance, and culture. The army produced special records known as V-Discs (for Victory Discs) that exposed soldiers to jazz and other popular forms of music, as did Armed Forces Radio and USO tours of popular bands. Because big-band jazz was among the most popular musical styles of the day, it was natural for this music to be prominently used as a morale booster for the fighting forces.

Thelonious Monk, Howard McGhee, Roy Eldridge, and Teddy Hill, outside of Minton's Playhouse, ca. September 1947, widely called the birthplace of bebop. Photo by William P. Gottlieb.

Courtesy William P. Gottlieb Collection and Library of Congress.

While the big bands offered excellent employment opportunities for musicians to perform, most bands catered to dancers, so solo space for players was limited by the commercial nature of the big-band medium. Consequently, a small group of musicians in New York began experimenting in informal settings—including an uptown hotel bar called Minton's Playhouse—developing a new style of music where the individual could excel. This music became known in the years immediately following World War II as "bebop." With this new musical style, pioneering musicians/composers like Charlie Parker, Dizzy Gillespie, and Thelonious Monk changed the way jazz was created and performed.

The bop lifestyle forecast the era of the beatniks of the later 1950s and the hippies of the 1960s; rebelling against society's norms, boppers dared to dress differently, developed their own slang, and played music that to some listeners sounded jarringly fast and aggressive. A controversy ensued as traditionalists criticized bop for its angular melodies, its fast rhythms, and its players' supposed disregard for pleasing the audience. We have seen aesthetic splits such as this in other eras as well, including in the 1980s with some of the neo-traditionalists' negative attitudes toward contemporary jazz styles that differed from "traditional" jazz (discussed in Chapter 14). Fortunately, attitudes have become more open, and most in jazz have always tended to have open minds regarding jazz styles as well as other types of music, including music from around the world.

1930–1950

MUSICIANS/MUSICAL WORKS

1930	• Don Azpiazú and His Havana Casino Orchestra, "El Manisero"
	• Clifford Brown, trumpeter, born
	• Ornette Coleman, alto saxophonist-composer, born
	• Theodore "Sonny" Rollins, tenor saxophonist, born
	• Tommy Flanagan, pianist, born
	• Jim Hall, guitarist, born
	• Muhal Richard Abrams, pianist-composer-arranger, born
1931	• Bix Beiderbecke dies
	• João Gilberto, guitarist-vocalist, born
1932	• Fletcher Henderson, "New King Porter Stomp"
	• Joe Zawinul, pianist-composer-bandleader, born
1933	• Benny Carter Orchestra, "Symphony in Riffs"
	• Shirley Scott, organ player, born
	• Wayne Shorter, saxophonist-composer, born

1935	• Count Basie forms a big band in Kansas City
	• Les McCann, pianist, born
	• Hammond B3 electronic organ introduced
1936	• Chick Webb Orchestra, "Go Harlem"
	• Carla Bley, pianist-composer-bandleader, born
	• Eddie Palmieri, pianist-bandleader, born
1938	• Big Joe Turner (vocal) and Pete Johnson (piano), "Roll 'em Pete"
	• The Count Basie Orchestra featuring Jimmy Rushing, "Sent for You Yesterday (And Here You Come Today)"
	• Benny Goodman Orchestra, "Swingtime in the Rockies"
	• Artie Shaw, "Begin the Beguine"
	• Lee Morgan, trumpeter, born
	• Freddie Hubbard, trumpeter, born

1939	• Coleman Hawkins, "Body and Soul"
	• Count Basie's Kansas City Seven, "Lester Leaps In"
	• Billie Holiday with Orchestra, "Strange Fruit"
1940	• Andy Kirk and His Twelve Clouds of Joy, "The Count," featuring Mary Lou Williams as pianist and arranger
	• Duke Ellington and His Famous Orchestra, "Ko-Ko"
	• Herbie Hancock, pianist-composer, born
1941	• Roy Eldridge with Gene Krupa and His Orchestra, arranger Benny Carter, "Rockin' Chair"
	• Armando Anthony "Chick" Corea, pianist-composer-bandleader, born
1942	• John McLaughlin, guitarist, born
	• Jack DeJohnette, drummer, born
1943	• The King Cole Trio, "Straighten Up and Fly Right"
	• George Benson, guitarist, born

1944	• Tommy Dorsey, "On the Sunny Side of the Street"
	• The International Sweethearts of Rhythm, "Blue Lou"
	• Glenn Miller, bandleader, dies while serving in World War II
	• Henry Threadgill, saxophonist-composer-bandleader, born
	• Woody Shaw, trumpeter, born
1945	• Charlie Parker and Dizzy Gillespie, "Salt Peanuts"
	• Keith Jarrett, pianist-composer, born
	• Anthony Braxton, saxophonist-composer, born
1947	• Ella Fitzgerald, with Bob Haggart and His Orchestra, "Lady Be Good"
	• Dizzy Gillespie Orchestra featuring Chano Pozo, "Manteca"
	• Woody Herman's Second Herd, "Four Brothers"
1949	• Charlie Parker with Strings, "Just Friends"
	• Tadd Dameron and His Orchestra, "Sid's Delight"
	• Miles Davis Nonet, arranger Gil Evans, "Boplicity"
	• Michael Brecker, saxophonist, born

1930–1950

MAJOR SOCIAL DEVELOPMENTS

1931	• Black teenagers known as the Scottsboro Boys imprisoned following charge of raping a young white woman
	• Empire State Building opens
1932	• Franklin Delano Roosevelt elected president; launches New Deal to bring country out of the Depression
	• Amelia Earhart is the first woman to fly solo across the Atlantic
1933	• Adolph Hitler named chancellor of Germany
	• Prohibition ends in the United States
1934	• Outlaws Bonnie and Clyde are killed in a stakeout
	• Board game Monopoly is introduced
1935	• Social Security is enacted

1936	• African American athlete Jesse Owens wins four gold medals at the Berlin Summer Olympics
1937	• Boxer Joe Louis becomes the heavyweight champion of the world
1938	• Hitler annexes Austria
	• First Superman comic published
1939	• World War II begins in Europe
	• Hattie McDonald becomes the first African American actress to win an Academy Award for her role in *Gone with the Wind*
	• Opera star Marian Anderson is initially denied permission to sing at a Washington, DC hall run by the Daughters of the American Revolution; instead appears at the Lincoln Memorial, attracting a crowd of 75,000 listeners

1940	• Richard Wright's *Native Son* published, addressing race relations in the United States
1941	• Japanese attack American battleships at Pearl Harbor on December 7, bringing the United States into World War II • Mount Rushmore completed • Training begins of the Tuskegee Airmen, first all-black flying force, who serve heroically in World War II
1943	• Singer Lena Horne and dancer Bill "Bojangles" Robinson star in all-black musical film, *Stormy Weather*
1944	• D-Day

1945	• United States drops atomic bombs on Hiroshima and Nagasaki; Japan surrenders • Hitler commits suicide • *Ebony*, African American weekly magazine, is founded
1946	• First tape recorder manufactured in United States
1948	• State of Israel founded • The military is desegregated by the order of President Harry Truman • Long playing record introduced by Columbia Records
1949	• Mao-Tse Tung's Communist Party takes control in China • Germany divided into East and West sectors

THE SWING ERA

7

By the mid-1930s jazz had come into its own. Louis Armstrong had revolutionized jazz musicians' approach to the genre, while also heavily influencing American popular music; and composer-arrangers such as Duke Ellington, Fletcher Henderson, and Benny Carter had developed a format and set an early standard for big-band music that was highly artistic and "hot" yet also commercially viable as dance music. While jazz was flourishing artistically, however, the Great Depression crushed America's economy. The economic crash cut record sales by 90% and the musicians' union membership by one-third (musicians have always been a hopeful and often impractical lot, yet it's surprising that this decrease was not even greater). Musicians and the music persisted however, and rising out of the economic and social ruin of the Depression, the mid-1930s swing era burst free as dancers and listeners across the country grabbed hold of swinging bands, vaulting jazz to the forefront of American culture as a popular music of the day.

WHAT IS SWING MUSIC?

Swing music is commonly defined as follows:

1. Music for dancing. During the swing era big bands played in large ballrooms for dancers, and the music had to get them up on their feet.
2. Music with a "swing" feeling. The rhythm had an easy, loping feeling that was created by emphasizing the weaker beats, or **off-beats** (2 and 4).
3. Swing music is typically performed by big bands divided into two sections: melody instruments (trumpets, trombones, and saxophones) and the rhythm section (piano, bass, guitar, drums).
4. Swing music became exceptionally popular in the mid-1930s thanks to the success of bands like those led by Benny Goodman.

"Swing" is used as a noun to categorize a style of music, but more importantly, swing as a verb is a feel. It is impossible to define it—in fact, nearly all music swings in its own way—but we have chosen recordings that will help you understand and feel it by getting your head bobbing, your feet tapping, and your fingers snapping. It is a style of music that is infectious in its enthusiasm and unflagging in its energy, and it has long transported its fans into

Photo: Courtesy BenCar Archives.

In this chapter, we'll answer these questions:

- What Is Swing Music?
- Why Is Benny Goodman Generally Credited as Launching the Swing Era?
- Who Were Some Other Popular Bandleaders During the Swing Era?
- What Were the Unique Challenges Faced by the "All-Girl" Bands During the Swing Era?
- How Did Latin Bands Continue to Influence Mainstream Jazz in the 1930s?

states ranging from the euphoric, ecstatic state of dancers who packed ballrooms across America to a relaxed memory of wonderful days gone by.

The swing era is the only time when jazz was one of America's popular forms of music and an important part of youth culture and the popular airwaves. This idea of the swing era is often discussed as limited to the mid-1930s to the mid- to late 1940s, at which time the big bands became less feasible economically and began to disappear as touring units. The swing culture continued in another, more subtle fashion, though, as many of the arrangers and players went to Hollywood, where they continued to dominate the recording of popular artists such as Frank Sinatra and Nat "King" Cole (see Chapter 9), as well as film and television music. Many bands also continued to tour.

1st Chorus Benny Goodman

WHY IS BENNY GOODMAN GENERALLY CREDITED AS LAUNCHING THE SWING ERA?

One event is often credited with launching the swing era. In August 1935, Benny Goodman, a sensational clarinetist and up-and-coming bandleader who had been featured on national radio, was in the midst of a national tour. Playing it safe, he was giving the public what he thought they wanted—**sweet jazz**, a somewhat easier listening and dancing style than **hot jazz**. The tour was not going well however. At the Palomar Ballroom in Los Angeles the band pulled out its hot **charts**, including some by Fletcher Henderson (Chapter 5, 1st Chorus). The crowds had been hearing these arrangements on Goodman's "Let's Dance" radio broadcasts from New York, and when they got the music they were expecting, the response was tremendous. It was around this time that swing became ubiquitous on radio and in dance halls. Countless bands, both well known and locally popular, toured their local territories, the country, and the world, creating huge hits and making stars out of their leaders, soloists, and vocalists.

The reality of the growth of "swing" is, of course, much more complicated. For example, bands had already been playing and developing this swing style in the 1920s and early 1930s. There were also many bands that were on the "sweet" side, playing popular dance music that was a hybrid of jazz-oriented music and popular music. These bands (sometimes pejoratively labeled "Mickey Mouse" or "Mickey" bands), such as those of Guy Lombardo and Kay Kaiser, were extremely successful, remaining popular even well into the 1980s. Another way to distinguish sweet from hot is to think of sweet as more commercially oriented, "prettier," and more middle-of-the-road, tailored to please a wide variety of audiences. Hot is often a more extroverted, rhythmically dynamic style with more emphasis on jazz soloists.

More importantly, however, many of the bands were playing music on both the hot and sweet sides. This is one of the most important and interesting facts about swing music: the movement had its finger on the pulse of the commercial marketplace yet was also producing innovative and hard-driving music that pleased jazz lovers. It appealed to youth culture, while suiting the political and economic climate, and became an important musical expression of the country.

It's difficult to pin down the time frame of the swing era, but it blossomed through the early 1930s and was an important part of popular culture from 1935 to 1945. The era really began in the 1920s, however, as we saw with composer-arranger-bandleaders such as Henderson and Benny Carter (see Chapter 5). The onset of World War II (1939), and the resultant patriotic energy that accompanied

QUESTIONS AND CONTROVERSIES
Race in the Swing Era

Race has always played a role in jazz, socially, musically, and economically; and we see it rearing its head again during the swing era. While there began to be some integration, bands were almost entirely segregated. Also, some of the white bands of this era soared to great economic success, while many of the black bands struggled. For example, in 1934, Fletcher Henderson was forced to disband his band (partially because of his lack of band-leading acumen) and took

employment with Goodman as chief arranger. In fact, some of the tunes from the old Henderson band that had not made money for Henderson became hits once Goodman played them. Swing bands that tried to tour the South with integrated lineups—as Artie Shaw did when he hired singer Billie Holiday to join his band—faced harassment on the road; although socially progressive, Shaw had to let Holiday go because it was too difficult to tour with an integrated band.

it, helped to fuel the swing era; and the war's end in 1945 in many ways signaled the beginning of the end as the swing bands were beginning to fade and bebop (see Chapter 10) was changing the music scene.

Still, numerous bands managed to survive and even thrive as they adapted to a changing musical scene. Swing music continued to be an important element in American culture through the 1960s, less through touring bands and more in the recording, television, and film studios of Los Angeles and New York City. Big bands are still an important part of jazz, though they are difficult to support economically; and while many are still playing swing-influenced music, others are forging new and ambitious musical ground as they draw their inspiration from wider sources and expand the notion of jazz composition.

An all-star big band recording a special broadcast for the troops during World War II, during August 1945. Count Basie (piano), Illinois Jacquet (sax), Tommy Dorsey (trombone), Artie Shaw (clarinet), Ziggy Elman (trumpet), Buddy Rich (in rear on drums), Lionel Hampton (vibes), unknown player (bass).
© Everett Collection Inc/Alamy.

Because of the incredible amount of musical activity of this period, we will devote three chapters to the swing era. The remainder of this chapter examines popular headlining bands of the swing era, such as those of Benny Goodman, Artie Shaw, Tommy Dorsey, Glenn Miller, and an all-woman big band, the International Sweethearts of Rhythm, as well as the beginnings of the rumba craze of the 1930s with Don Azpiazú and His Havana Casino Orchestra. Chapter 8 focuses on Duke Ellington, while Chapter 9 examines some of the vocal stars of the swing era.

Benny Goodman's tremendous success can be traced to a confluence of circumstances. First, Goodman was an outstanding clarinetist who helped set the standard for swing-style clarinet playing. As a precocious youth in the Chicago slums (his father, a Polish immigrant, was a worker in the Chicago stockyards), he was fortunate enough to receive excellent formal classical training from a clarinetist from the Chicago Symphony who taught at a settlement house. He also had the Chicago jazz scene at his feet (see Chapter 4), including clarinetist Jimmy Noone, who was a huge influence on Goodman, as well as New Orleans clarinetists Johnny Dodds (who we have heard with Louis Armstrong) and Leon Roppolo (from the New Orleans Rhythm Kings). By the age of 14 Goodman was already playing in a band with Bix Beiderbecke, and by the age of 16 he was playing in top Chicago bands. He absorbed both the jazz and the classical worlds, and his ability to fuse these styles eventually served him well in the music business.

Goodman's "hot" reputation was based on several things, but certainly the arrangements of Fletcher Henderson, Benny Carter, and Edgar Sampson (who also wrote for Chick Webb) were essential to his success. Goodman also had star soloists such as the phenomenal trumpeters Harry James (who went on to fame with his own band), Bunny Berigan, and Ziggy Elman; the exciting and showy drummer Gene Krupa (Goodman's fellow Chicagoan who also went on to lead a successful band and was featured on hit numbers such as "Sing, Sing, Sing"); and

Benny Goodman Quartet, ca. 1940. Goodman took a considerable chance by integrating his small groups. (Left to right) Lionel Hampton (vibes), Teddy Wilson (piano), Benny Goodman (clarinet), and Gene Krupa (drums).

© *Pictorial Press Ltd./Alamy.*

IN PERFORMANCE
Side Musicians

We always know who the bandleader is, and names like Benny Goodman, Artie Shaw, Duke Ellington, and Count Basie are the ones most casual listeners remember. The leaders stand up front, maybe they wear a different outfit, they make the announcements and introductions, and the band is usually named for them. But the leader is nothing without side musicians—the side musicians are the workers, and without them the job, whether playing a dance job or recording in the studio, doesn't get done. The swing era gives us an excellent opportunity to use some of this wonderful music to point out some of the necessary skills that go into being a successful side musician.

One of the most important and least noticed and appreciated big-band side musician responsibilities is to play effectively in an ensemble. For example, if there are four trumpets, they must precisely play the exact same rhythms. They also have to **articulate**—how they attack, sustain, and release a note—all of their notes in exactly the same way, their **phrasing**—where they take breaths and articulate—must be the same, their **dynamics**—how loudly they play—must match, and they must **crescendo** and **decrescendo**—get louder and softer—together. The arranger makes articulation and dynamic marks on the score to tell the musicians what to do, and the lead trumpet and lead alto interpret them and set the phrasing. The excellent side musician has to be able to hear how the lead players are playing the phrases and articulations and immediately imitate them. Each player in the section has slightly different responsibilities, but they are all working to support the lead player (who is also a side musician but has more responsibilities). Freelance side musicians are expected to fulfill these responsibilities almost intuitively as they are playing with many bands, perhaps even playing some of the same numbers but with different phrasings and articulations.

Small group side musicians have different types of responsibilities. Primarily, they must have a huge repertoire of tunes that they know as each band they play with has a different repertoire and often has no music for the side musician to read. They must be able to play the melody, of course; but they also have to know the chord progressions of the songs as they will be required to play improvised solos. They have to be able to play the songs in any key and should also be able to create harmony parts. If the small group features original compositions—such as the groups of pianist-composer-bandleader Horace Silver and drummer-bandleader Art Blakey (we will examine both in Chapter 11, 2nd Chorus)—the side musicians are also responsible for memorizing the tunes and chord progressions and doing so very quickly, probably in time for their first gig with the band.

Along with musical responsibilities, there are also the everyday professional responsibilities that go along with most jobs, such as being reliable, on time, and generally handling yourself in a professional manner. In the music business, however, at times these expectations are stretched a bit thin. While the lifestyle of swing musicians could be relatively normal compared to others who traveled for a living, including having families at home as well as other freelance work when they returned to their home base, often there were some differences. For example, many were career road musicians, meaning they went from band to band or perhaps played with a busy touring band for many years (for example, Harry Carney, Ellington's long-time baritone saxophone player, was with Ellington for 45 years). These musicians often spend very little time at home, which obviously can create difficulties in other parts of their lives. There were some superstitious quirks as well, such as some musicians believing it was bad luck to be the first to get on the bandstand, which could cause considerable delays as they sat and ate and kept a wary eye on the bandstand well past the time that they were due back to perform. Some side musicians had substance abuse issues, and this was common enough that, essentially, bandleaders were used to dealing with them.

Finally, imagine a big swing band full of high-level, professional, extremely experienced side musicians as this group of strong, grown men and women push as much air as possible through their horns—all night long—in a concerted and precise effort to create the amazingly powerful sound you hear in the recordings of these big bands. It is certainly a very dramatic and moving experience when you stand in front of, or play in, a big band. Side musicians don't get a lot of credit or recognition from the public, but savvy bandleaders, as well as side musician colleagues, greatly appreciate the good, solid player who toils in the trenches of the music business making it all happen.

listening guide

"Swingtime in the Rockies" (1938) by the Benny Goodman Orchestra

INSTRUMENTATION: Clarinet and leader: Benny Goodman; **Trumpets:** Harry James, Ziggy Elman, Chris Griffin; **Trombones:** Red Ballard, Vernon Brown; **Saxophones:** Hymie Schertzer, George Koenig, Arthur Rollini, Babe Russin; **Piano:** Jess Stacey; **Guitar:** Allen Reuss; **Bass:** Harry Goodman; **Drums:** Gene Krupa; **Arranger:** Jimmy Mundy. Recorded live at Carnegie Hall in 1938.

OVERVIEW: "Swingtime in the Rockies" was arranged by the arranger-composer Jimmy Mundy. It is a hard-swinging tune that is terrific for keeping the dance floors packed with energized dancers as the composition builds in intensity throughout the arrangement. The fact that this is a live recording adds excitement to the performance.

FORM: The form consists of 5 AABA choruses, one of the most common forms in jazz. The first 2 choruses are a series of riffs from all of the various horn sections. The other 3 choruses also consist of a series of riffs but feature solos, including an entire chorus by the leader, Benny Goodman, on clarinet.

STYLE: "Swingtime in the Rockies" is a riff-based tune that stems from the school of head arrangements that is so vital to jazz and jazz big bands. Composing and arranging a song in this style allows for complex interaction between the various riffs while still keeping the feeling of spontaneity.

MELODY AND HARMONY: While there are a variety of melodies in this tune, they function more as a series of riffs than as an actual melody. This style of tune takes us back to the riff-based style of Kansas City. The A section is a variation on "rhythm changes" (based on the George Gershwin tune "I Got Rhythm"), but the B section (the bridge) is not based on the Gershwin tune, making this one of many tunes that are loosely based on that basic chord progression.

RHYTHM: The rhythm section hits a groove and never stops. They vary their volume and level of intensity according to the dynamics of the arrangement. The maintaining of a constant groove builds a powerful intensity.

ACCOMPANIMENT: As is true for most big-band arrangements, the various horn sections are as much a part of the accompaniment as is the rhythm section. While the rhythm section keeps the groove, the horn sections provide backgrounds for the soloists and help to spur them on.

"SWINGTIME IN THE ROCKIES" LISTENING GUIDE

TIME	FORM	STYLE	MELODY AND HARMONY	RHYTHM	ACCOMPANIMENT
0:00	A	There is no introduction to this tune as the sax section jumps right into a swinging riff.		The rhythm section sets a fast tempo and, in typical swing style, chugs away solidly on all 4 beats. They build intensity throughout by maintaining this hard, solid groove.	

"Swingtime in the Rockies" listening guide continued

TIME	FORM	STYLE	MELODY AND HARMONY	RHYTHM	ACCOMPANIMENT
0:07	A		The sax riff repeats.		As is true for most big-band writing, both the rhythm section and the horn sections serve as accompaniment. For example, in this riff tune the various horn sections create an important accompaniment to the soloists.
0:14	B	It is hard to tell who has the melody here—it is more like two riffs on top of each other creating a swinging polyphony.	On the bridge, the trumpets join in while the saxes play a new and busier riff.	As the trumpets enter and crescendo (get louder), the rhythm section also begins to play a bit louder.	
0:22	A		The first sax riff repeats once more.	The rhythm section brings the volume back down once the brass is no longer playing.	
0:29	A		The saxes and trumpets have a call and response with short riffs. They end the section playing together.	The rhythm section gradually crescendos through the next few sections as the brass increases the intensity.	
0:36	A		The previous A section repeats.		
0:44	B		The trumpets take over with a rhythmic melodic line. It is less repetitive and a longer line, so it is not really a riff. The saxes play long notes underneath.		
0:51	A	For the first time this last A is a new riff.	The trumpets and saxes play a syncopated riff with a short ending.		The saxes play trills, while the trumpets hold steady notes. The trills add a dynamic quality to the figure.
0:58	A		The trombones play a short riff answered by the trumpets.		
1:05	A		The previous A section repeats.		
1:13	B	Notice the difference in the characteristics of the various soloists. The alto sax solo is melodic and rhythmically plays tightly in the groove.	We hear our first solo. An alto sax blows a short solo.	The rhythm section comes back down in volume to allow the soloist some room to build his solo.	The saxes riff underneath the alto sax solo.

continued

"Swingtime in the Rockies" listening guide continued

TIME	FORM	STYLE	MELODY AND HARMONY	RHYTHM	ACCOMPANIMENT
1:20	A		The trombone and trumpet A section repeats again.		
1:27	A		The leader and clarinetist Benny Goodman takes a solo over a band riff. Fittingly, it is the longest solo of the tune as Goodman plays over an entire chorus (once through the AABA form).		The drummer becomes gradually more dynamic.
1:34	A	Goodman has a legato style that almost floats over the hard-driving rhythm section and horn sections.	Goodman's solo continues over the same riff.		
1:41	B	It is hardest to hear the form here as the division is purposely not as clear.	Goodman continues his solo, this time with no band riff.	The rhythm section turns it on here, and the drummer plays louder and more aggressively.	
1:48	A	Here, for some reason, there are 2 extra bars to this A section. They create just a touch of anticipation and suspense.	Goodman's solo continues over the same band riff.	The rhythm section calms back down.	
1:57	A	The trumpet solo is the most aggressive of the three solos and is often in a riffing style that matches the character of the tune.	A trumpet solo over a band riff functions as the climax of this hot tune. Listen to how effectively he bends his notes.		The band gradually raises its level of intensity as it builds toward the end of the tune.
2:04	A	A riff-like solo is a very common improvisational device.	The trumpet solo continues.		
2:11	B		The trumpet solo continues as he plays in his upper register to rise up over the band's powerful riffing.		
2:18	A		The entire band blasts the original riff to conclude the tune.	The drummer powers the tune to a rousing finish.	

Compare

"Seven Come Eleven" (1939) by the Benny Goodman Sextet. Goodman's small-group recordings tend to be more adventuresome than his big-band records. We also get a chance to hear some of the key soloists in the band, including the innovative jazz guitarist Charlie Christian and vibes player Lionel Hampton. Bandleader-arranger Fletcher Henderson (see Chapter 5, 1st Chorus) lends a hand on the piano, though we rarely can hear him in this recording.

the sensational and influential guitarist Charlie Christian, who pioneered the use of the electric guitar in jazz and was an important early contributor to bebop (see Chapter 10).

Goodman also managed to fuse the worlds of popular Tin Pan Alley songs and a hot style in a way that seemed to resonate deeply with both sweet and hot dance-band fans, making him the kind of star that Elvis Presley or the Beatles would later become. He was also an exacting taskmaster as a bandleader (he was famous for "the ray," a brutally disapproving stare) whose band produced a tight and hard-swinging sound.

The early period of the Goodman band's great success culminated in a ground-breaking 1938 concert that presented a full night of jazz at New York's Carnegie Hall for the first time, and it was an integrated concert that also featured members of Duke Ellington's and Count Basie's bands. A recording of this concert displays the band at its peak.

In addition to his big band, Goodman led smaller ensembles that were important in both musical and social terms. In 1935 he began to perform and record with a trio that featured his charismatic drummer Gene Krupa and African American pianist Teddy Wilson. Creating an interracial group was daring and an early step toward breaking down racial barriers that unfortunately still exist today in some forms. Goodman expanded to a quartet and further pushed the racial envelope with the addition of the electrifying vibraphone (vibes) player Lionel Hampton (who went on to lead his own big band that was highly successful through the 1980s) and again later as the group expanded to a sextet and then a septet and included the sensational electric guitarist Charlie Christian (introduced to Goodman by John Hammond, discussed in Chapter 6, 2nd Chorus), who also encouraged Goodman to integrate his bands. Goodman's small bands were more intimate showcases for the players as a smaller group allows for a different type of playing. In a big-band setting, the band is necessarily loud, and a soloist often has to resort to playing loud and high to cut through the band. But a small group encourages a wider range of expression by also allowing softer playing, which results in a very different style, as well as by giving each musician a bit more room to "stretch out" (to play longer solos).

In the 1940s Goodman hired the arranger Eddie Sauter, an important progressive jazz composer and arranger. Mel Powell, a pianist, composer, and arranger who went on to become an important contemporary classical composer, also contributed to a more progressive sound during this period. Goodman remained

IN PERFORMANCE
Understanding Form

Form is a crucial aspect of all music. However, like nested boxes, the overall form of a work can itself be broken down further into shorter forms that can lead to further distinctions. For example, "Swing-time in the Rockies" as a whole can be broken down into 5 individual choruses of AABA. Each chorus can be broken down to 8-measure sections (A and B are both 8 measures long), and those in turn can be broken into 4-measure phrases. You can count 4 beats 8 times for each section, and each section goes by very quickly at this fast tempo. The trickiest aspect of following it, and even musicians can have a hard time with this, is to keep track of the A sections as there are actually 3 of them after the B section. It is easy to get lost as a result, but generally the section divisions are quite clear.

active until his death in 1986, including playing standard classical repertoire (such as Mozart's Clarinet Quintet in A Major, K. 581) and premiering classical compositions by composers such as Aaron Copland, Béla Bartók, and Leonard Bernstein, as well as the commissioning of works for clarinet with symphony orchestra.

2nd Chorus Big-Band Innovators: Artie Shaw, Glenn Miller, and Tommy Dorsey

WHO WERE SOME OTHER POPULAR BANDLEADERS DURING THE SWING ERA?

Artie Shaw

The extremely popular clarinetist-bandleader Artie Shaw (1910–2004) was an excellent clarinetist who had a terrific big band that recorded some of the major hits of the swing era, including "Begin the Beguine," "Stardust," and "Frenesi." Born in Manhattan's Lower East Side Jewish ghetto, Shaw, like Benny Goodman, was the son of recent immigrants. A professional at an early age, Shaw had an expansive musical life that saw him in the studios during the day and the jazz clubs at night.

Shaw's musical vision and goals were quite different from those of many of the other major bandleaders of the period. As a bandleader he doggedly pursued the goal of employing his interests in contemporary classical music and jazz through innovative instrumentation (for example, the extensive use of strings) and his choice of composers and arrangers, including his staff-arranger Jerry Gray (who arranged the hit "Begin the Beguine," see "Listening Focus"), the important African American composer and arranger William Grant Still (who arranged Shaw's hit "Frenesi"), Ray Conniff, and the composer Paul Jordan (who wrote some interesting extended compositions, including "Evensong"). Consequently, Shaw—as were Goodman and other swing-band leaders such as vibraphonist "Red" Norvo—was an early progenitor of **progressive jazz** composition (see Chapter 11, 1st Chorus). Through its use of compositional resources more often associated with classical music, such as extended forms and the use of various orchestral instruments, progressive jazz broadened the scope of jazz composition.

Shaw's hit, an arrangement of the 1935 Cole Porter popular song "Begin the Beguine," takes a brilliant multisection composition and makes it even better with his band's sound that combines hot and sweet styles in a convincing and unique manner. The popularity of this tune helped propel Shaw and his band to stardom. Interestingly, Billie Holiday was a vocalist with this band during this period, marking an early example of integration in the world of the big bands. Among other attempts to create racial integration, Shaw also hired trumpeter Hot Lips Page (Chapter 6, 1st Chorus) and saxophonist Benny Carter (Chapter 5, 2nd Chorus).

Though he was making huge sums of money as a result of his popular recordings, Shaw had lofty musical ambitions beyond the normal commercial swing-era fare. Ironically, these goals were somewhat thwarted by his huge hits such as "Begin the Beguine" and "Stardust," and he was bitter about the public's constant craving for these tunes at the expense of his more ambitious material. He seems to have been frustrated, or at least restless, in other ways as well: he was married eight times, including high-profile marriages to the starlets Lana Turner and Ava Gardner. He led many variations of his band and retired off and on for a variety of reasons, including nervous breakdowns, and essentially left public life precipitously in 1954.

listening focus

"Begin the Beguine" (1938) by Artie Shaw and His Orchestra

INSTRUMENTATION: Bandleader, clarinet: Artie Shaw; **Trumpets:** John Best, Claude Bowen, Chuck Peterson; **Trombones:** George Arus, Ted Vesely, Harry Rogers; **Saxophones:** Hank Freeman, Tony Pastor, Ronnie Perry, Les Robinson; **Piano:** Les Burness; **Guitar:** Al Avola; **Bass:** Sid Weiss; **Drums:** Cliff Leeman; **Arranger:** Jerry Gray.

LISTENING HIGHLIGHT, MELODY AND HARMONY: After an introduction that pits relaxed saxes against crisper brass figures (trumpets and trombones), the A section consists of Shaw's lovely and simple clarinet playing over a sax background (0:07). For the 2nd A, the sweet, commercial-sounding saxes play the melody as the muted brass section plays simple fills (0:34). B is a new melody that is passed around between the sweet saxes and the sassier and more biting brass section (1:01). The 3rd A is primarily a tenor sax solo version of the melody (1:28). The arrangement takes on new life as the C section features a powerful yet relaxed brass melody with a sax and clarinet background (1:55). Just as the tune seems to be winding down, the brass once again hits the 2nd C section melody (2:23). The tune then winds down once again before Shaw ends on a high note. While this tune does not particularly feature him, Shaw's solos, fills, and pieces of melody throughout add his unique flavor to the entire arrangement.

Glenn Miller

Trombonist-bandleader Glenn Miller (1904–1944) led one of the most popular big bands during the swing era. His reputation for being less jazz-oriented than the other headlining big bands is warranted but also casts his excellent band in an unnecessarily negative light. Miller had worked his way up through jazz bands as a side musician, soloist, and arranger, including playing in Benny Goodman's band. However, as a leader he took a commercial path playing in a simple and direct manner, while also creating a signature sound and repertoire that clearly had strong appeal for much of the swing audience.

Miller's huge hit "In the Mood" has essentially been a required dance number at parties when it comes time for a "swing" number. His other hits, including "String of Pearls" (with a lovely trumpet solo by Bobby Hackett), the pretty ballad "Moonlight Serenade," and the uptempo "Tuxedo Junction," helped define swing music for millions of listeners.

While Miller intentionally was not as "hot" as other bands, he did have a terrific band with a sound that still resonates with swing fans. During World War II Miller enlisted in the armed forces and led a large ensemble in the service until his tragic accidental death in a mysterious plane crash.

Tommy and Jimmy Dorsey

Two other influential and popular bandleaders of this era were trombonist Tommy Dorsey (1905–1956) and his brother, saxophonist-clarinetist Jimmy Dorsey (1904–1957). The Dorsey brothers are an interesting example of career swing musicians who worked their way up through the ranks of various bands, including

Tommy Dorsey, ca. 1940. Trombonist Tommy Dorsey's band was enormously popular in the 1940s, thanks to his lightly swinging arrangements and his vocalist, Frank Sinatra.

Courtesy BenCar Archives.

Paul Whiteman's popular ensemble (see Chapter 4, 1st Chorus). They both excelled as hot and sweet players and managed, with the help of skillful and canny arrangers, to create bands in the same mold that appealed to a wide variety of audiences who were neither too hip nor too square.

After briefly coleading a band, both men went on to form their own successful big bands. Tommy Dorsey's band featured vocalist Frank Sinatra (Chapter 9, 2nd Chorus), who went on to superstardom. While the band was extremely popular, being labeled a sweet band eventually frustrated Dorsey. In response, he hired Sy Oliver, Jimmie Lunceford's arranger (Chapter 5, 2nd Chorus), who added a hot element to the band while also keeping the commercial sound that made Dorsey's band popular. While this may not have been the best formula for artistic innovation, it appears to have made commercial sense. Tommy's band, including his use of strings (see "Listening Focus"), did manage to gently push the musical envelope at times.

While Tommy Dorsey may not have been the most inspired improviser, his ability to play the trombone in a beautifully legato and lyrical fashion was essentially unparalleled (it can be a rather awkward instrument because of its slide). An example of this is his famous hit "I'm Getting Sentimental Over You," which features a trombone rendition of this ballad's melody that is exceptionally smooth and expressive with a vocal-like quality. Sinatra, Dorsey's star vocalist, stated that he learned to phrase his own vocal lines from listening to Dorsey play every night.

Many top musicians passed through the Dorsey band, including trumpeters Bunny Berigan, Ziggy Elman, Charlie Shavers, and Doc Severinsen (well known as the bandleader for NBC's Tonight Show Orchestra when it was hosted by Johnny Carson) and drummers Buddy Rich and Gene Krupa (who both became star bandleaders), as well as vocalists Sinatra and Jo Stafford. The Dorsey brothers eventually reunited in the early 1950s when they hosted their own television show, attesting to their popular appeal.

As has been true for many of the better-known big bands (such as those of Glenn Miller, Count Basie, and Duke Ellington), the Tommy Dorsey band was taken over and continued to perform under the Dorsey name after his death. These bands that continue after the death of a leader are often referred to as **ghost bands**.

listening focus

"On the Sunny Side of the Street" (1944) by Tommy Dorsey and His Orchestra

INSTRUMENTATION: Bandleader, trombone: Tommy Dorsey; **Trumpets:** George Seaburg, Mickey Mangano, Dale Pierce, Roger Ellick; **Trombones:** Nelson Riddle, Red Benson, Tex Satterwaite; **Saxophones:** Buddy DeFranco (known for his terrific clarinet playing), Al Cooper, Al Klink, Gail Curtis, Bruce Branson; **Piano:** Milt Golden; **Guitar:** Bob Bain; **Bass:** Sid Bloch; **Drums:** Buddy Rich; **String Section**; **Harp:** Reba Robinson; **Tuba:** Joe Park; **Vocals:** The Sentimentalists; **Arranger:** Sy Oliver.

LISTENING HIGHLIGHT, MELODY AND HARMONY: In the intro we hear smooth strings, strong brass, and a powerful baritone sax honking out low notes. In the 1st chorus the trumpets in **cup mutes** play a version of the melody of the first 2 A sections. It has a mellow character as a result of the mutes yet also swings hard because of the interesting and precise rhythmic phrasing (0:16). The bridge creates a contrast as the trombones play full out with smooth saxes behind them, which then take over the last part of the bridge melody and carry over to play the last A (0:48). After the 1st chorus, there is an interlude with a growling trumpet over the rhythm section followed by a brief ensemble with brass and then reeds (1:24). The 2nd chorus features a vocal by The Sentimentalists (1:56). Their rhythmic phrasing is fun and hip, as are their extremely tight and effective harmonies, a common vocal group style of the period, and slightly altered and humorous lyrics. The rhythm section and subtle and effective string section support the vocal. The tune concludes with a short but full ending from the whole band.

3rd Chorus Women in Jazz: "All-Girl" Swing Big Bands

WHAT WERE THE UNIQUE CHALLENGES FACED BY THE "ALL-GIRL" BANDS DURING THE SWING ERA?

As we have already noted, the obvious racial segregation—most were either white bands or black bands—was a characteristic of the swing era. There are numerous political, social, cultural, and even practical reasons why this occurred. But while we examined the significant contributions and musical professionalism of Lovie Austin and Lil Hardin Armstrong (Chapter 4, 3rd Chorus), as well as the fact that Mary Lou Williams was an extremely influential member of Andy Kirk's band and an important pianist and composer (Chapter 6, 1st Chorus), we have yet to discuss the gender segregation that was present in the swing era.

For a variety of reasons, the top swing bands were male enclaves. But that does not mean that there were no female musicians to fill these bands or that women were not good enough to be in them. Thanks to new research, we now know that in fact there were plenty of excellent female jazz musicians who were ready, excited, and more than willing to play in jazz big bands—so many, in fact, that during the 1930s and 1940s there were hundreds of **"all-girl" bands** (while

read all about it

"It Don't Mean a Thing If It Ain't in the History Books" by Sherrie Tucker

Walser, **Keeping Time**, *Chapter 26*

Sherrie Tucker's work on women in the swing era has helped bring new attention to the achievements of these musicians. In this essay, she discusses some of the reasons that women's contributions to jazz during this period were not widely recognized.

the term "all-girl" might be archaic and politically incorrect today, it is how the bands were commonly referred to and is used here with this caveat).

The presence of so many female musicians and all-girl bands during this era has not, until recently, been a part of the written history of jazz; and it still generally plays a minor role, at best, in most histories. Other than a few musicians, swing-era women were not well represented in the popular press, and African American female bands, while they were covered in the black press during this period, have largely been ignored in jazz histories.

Regarding the white all-girl bands, Sherrie Tucker, in her influential study, *Swing Shift: "All-Girl" Bands of the 1940s*, points out that "despite their skill as musicians, their ability to reproduce images of idealized white womanhood . . . was a key element assuring their visibility in the entertainment industry and no doubt helped secure them a limited place in history as well" (p. 11). These bands had to not only sound good but also "look good." Female swing musicians consequently had a unique set of difficulties: heavier women were asked to lose weight, older musicians were required to try and appear younger, and those who wore glasses at times had to find ways to handle playing without them.

These all-girl bands were also generally ghettoized by being placed into particular types of venues; and unfortunately, their work was often not valued enough to be recorded, which necessarily limited their visibility and commercial potential. In addition, write-ups about the bands often emphasized their extramusical qualities, for example, depicting the all-girl bands as a novelty, rather than describing their musicianship. During World War II, these jazz women's place in the wartime effort was emphasized. Because many male musicians either joined the war effort or were drafted, there were new opportunities for the all-girl bands that already existed and created the need for more, consequently improving female jazz musicians' ability to find work.

Another way that women's roles in swing bands were marginalized is that most women were employed as vocalists. These big-band singers were often referred to as "girl singers" or "canaries," the latter a term that seems to allude more to their

QUESTIONS AND CONTROVERSIES
Women in Jazz

In the past some musicians and writers have expressed the unfortunate and obviously inaccurate and specious notion that jazz is a man's business and that women are not even able to play jazz well. A common feeling was that women were too small and dainty to handle big instruments like the tenor sax or electric guitar. Another common stereotype was that women were less able to endure the tough life of being on the road or even that the presence of women in a big band would be disruptive to the other musicians, much like the argument that was made about introducing women into the army.

The idea that women's smaller hands or less muscular frames would make them somehow less able to tackle the physical demands of playing jazz has happily been debunked by generations of players, and women are certainly hardy enough to endure the difficulties of being traveling musicians. Even though the jazz business is still more difficult for women, the situation has certainly improved; and there are many women in jazz, some of whom are particularly influential and examined throughout the book.

Clearly, their presence on the jazz scene, as well as the fact that until recently we have known so little about this, makes female jazz instrumentalists and all-girl bands an important topic in terms of a more complete and accurate history of jazz and the wider role of women in jazz.

place as cute and adorable decoration than to their musical value. This certainly does not convey the importance of, for example, Ella Fitzgerald's overall musical and commercial importance to Chick Webb's big band (Chapter 5, 2nd Chorus, and Chapter 9, 1st Chorus).

Phil Spitalny's "Hour of Charm"/Ina Ray Hutton's Melodears

Unfortunately, just like their male counterparts, the all-girl swing bands tended to be segregated along racial lines. Phil Spitalny's "Hour of Charm" was a white all-girl band that was one of the best known and most successful. In the world of all-girl big bands it became a touchstone for what a band could—and couldn't—be. The band, which included a string section and harp, perhaps for feminization, was nationally commercially successful for 20 years, including performing on live broadcasts for Armed Services and NBC radio, quite a feat for any band.

Ina Ray Hutton's Melodears was another successful all-white band. Financially backed by the powerful agent Irving Mills's organization (Mills also was Duke Ellington's manager and was instrumental in establishing his early success), the Melodears became one of the most popular all-girl bands of the 1930s. Originally a dancer, Hutton was known as the "Blond Bombshell of Rhythm" and served as frontwoman of the band, changing glamorous costumes throughout the night. The band was musically successful as well and included such excellent players as trombonist Alyse Wills, who also toured with Tommy Dorsey (see this chapter, 2nd Chorus).

The Prairie View Co-Eds

Many of the black bands came out of all-black educational institutions. Two of the most popular were the Prairie View Collegians and the International Sweethearts of Rhythm. The historically black institution Prairie View College in Texas (now known as Prairie View A&M University) sported a well-known dance band, the Prairie View Collegians. This band was decimated by band members being drafted or joining the military. In response, its leader, Will Henry Bennett, created a women's dance band, the Prairie View Co-Eds, to play for local dances as well as to perform at local military camps. Bennett recruited more players, such as the excellent trumpeter Clora Bryant (who went on to a long musical career in Los Angeles) and drummer Helen Cole; and the band wound up providing a rare training ground for female jazz musicians. The band eventually toured, including performances at Harlem's Apollo Theater.

The International Sweethearts of Rhythm

Founded in 1937, the International Sweethearts of Rhythm was an extremely popular all-girl band. Originally a product of Piney Woods Country Life School, a school for poor and orphaned African American children, the band broke away from the school's sponsorship in 1943. The Sweethearts was considered a black band, but the term "international" refers to the fact that some of the band's players came from mixed ethnic backgrounds and eventually also included two white players.

The band toured extensively, including appearances at major black theaters such as Harlem's Apollo and the Howard Theater in Washington, DC, dance halls, and US military camps with the USO (the United Services Organization). They were the first African American group to tour Europe with the USO to provide support and entertainment for the troops during World War II. As was true for all big bands, travel conditions were difficult, even though the Sweethearts had their own bus with sleeping berths. In addition, because of segregation laws, black bands had a much more difficult time on the road, often facing extreme difficulties finding acceptable food or lodging, as well as experiencing harassment from the police. The fact that the

The International Sweethearts of Rhythm, led by Anna Mae Winburn (in front, conducting), 1945. The Sweethearts were one of the leading all-female jazz bands. Photo Gilles Petard.
Courtesy Redferns/Getty Images.

Sweethearts traveled with two white players at times made things particularly difficult as southern authorities carefully guarded the "color line" based on Jim Crow laws that mandated racial segregation. Travel difficulties were even further exacerbated during World War II because of wartime rationing of gasoline and tires.

Tucker points out that "the proud history of black education traveled with the Sweethearts" and that they "reflected a history of African Americans providing basic education for poor black children." She further states that both the Prairie View Co-Eds and The International Sweethearts of Rhythm "served as reminders of the struggles of African Americans for education as a mode of resistance, freedom, and progress" (p. 165). The band disbanded in 1949.

We are fortunate to have a few recordings of this excellent band. They recorded several tunes for record labels, but they also performed live for the Armed Forces Radio Service's show *Jubilee*. This show was regularly recorded, and releases from this collection provide us with important historical recordings. The band also recorded **soundies** in 1947, giving us a great opportunity to hear how well the band played as well as how entertaining they were to watch, with the stylish bandleader Anna Mae Winburn leading the band and featured as vocalist. In these soundies, we hear that the International Sweethearts of Rhythm was a hot and hard-swinging band and featured strong star soloists such as trumpet player Ernestine "Tiny" Davis and tenor sax player Vi Burnside. This recording of "Blue Lou" is from a 1944 *Jubilee* broadcast.

4th Chorus Latin Styles During the 1930s

HOW DID LATIN BANDS CONTINUE TO INFLUENCE MAINSTREAM JAZZ IN THE 1930s?

Earlier in the text, we began our discussion of how Latin music has been an important part of American musical life, including its influence in early jazz in New Orleans as well as in Latino communities throughout the United States. We also discussed the Cuban influence in New York through listening to flutist-bandleader Alberto Socarrás in the context of early jazz big bands in New York City (Chapter 5,

listening focus

"Blue Lou" (1944) by the International Sweethearts of Rhythm

INSTRUMENTATION: Bandleader: Anna Mae Winburn; **Trumpets:** Tiny Davis, Ray Carter, Mim Polak, Johnnie Mae Stansbury; **Trombones:** Ina Belle Byrd, Helen Jones, Jean Travis; **Saxophones:** Vi Burnside, Rosalind "Roz" Cron, Willie Mae Wong, Grace Bayron, Helen Saine; **Piano:** Johnnie Mae Rice; **Bass:** Marganot "Trump" Gibson; **Drums:** Pauline Braddy.

LISTENING HIGHLIGHT, FORM: This arrangement consists of 4 choruses of an AABA tune by Edgar Sampson, arranger for Chick Webb, Fletcher Henderson, and Benny Goodman, among others. After a quick 4-measure introduction, the band plays the melody during the 1st chorus (0:04). The 2nd chorus features a tenor sax solo (0:37) and the 3rd chorus, a trumpet solo (1:10). The 4th and final chorus features the entire ensemble (1:43). At the bridge (1:59), the band shouts powerfully and features the drummer in a series of fills before playing the melody of the last A to take the tune out.

5th Chorus). This influence increased with the "rumba craze" of the 1930s as Latin bands regularly performed at ballrooms such as New York's Savoy and jazz bands began incorporating Latin styles into their repertoire for dancers.

The proximity of El Barrio, or East Harlem, and Harlem (they lay next to each other in upper Manhattan)—as well as the fact that these Latin bands and big bands played alongside each other in ballrooms and shared some of the same musicians—created an environment that encouraged a fusion of the styles. The same way that early big bands—and early New Orleans bands for that matter—played a wide variety of music for a diverse clientele, the Latin bands had to please traditionally oriented audiences who appreciated a nostalgic approach as well as younger dancers and listeners who expected some elements of swing that they were hearing all around them. As a result, the Latin bands were actually creating a new style that incorporated elements of jazz while also taking new approaches to their Latino roots.

Don Azpiazú's Havana Casino Orchestra

While Alberto Socarrás's band played a slightly generic version of Cuban music tailored to the tastes of the American public, the burgeoning Latino community in the 1930s in El Barrio (East Harlem) in New York City provided a market for authentic Cuban styles. These bands featured more traditional instrumentation such as a full percussion section, which normally includes some combination of bongó, conga, guiro, maracas, timbales, campana (bell), and claves. This new era in Latin music in the United States was ushered in by Don Azpiazú's Havana Casino Orchestra in 1930 with their huge hit "El Manisero" ("The Peanut Vendor"), a tune based on a Cuban street vendor chant and played in a Cuban style with a full percussion section. During a 1930 performance of "El Manisero" at Broadway's Palace Theater in New York City, Azpiazú's (1893–1943) show also introduced the **rumba** dance style to the American public. Many artists, including Red Nichols and Louis Armstrong, covered it; and a well-known instrumental version was recorded by bandleader Stan Kenton's (Chapter 11, 1st Chorus) big band in 1947.

"El Manisero" is still a standard (it has been recorded over 160 times and over 1 million copies of the sheet music have been sold) and, along with a few other

listening focus

DOWNLOAD
Track Number 14

"El Manisero" (1930) by Don Azpiazú and His Havana Casino Orchestra

INSTRUMENTATION: Bandleader-piano: Don Azpiazú; **Vocal:** Antonio Machín; **Trumpets:** Julio Cueva, Remberto Lara; **Saxophones:** Julio Brito, Alfredo Brito; **Bass:** unknown; **Percussion:** unknown.

LISTENING HIGHLIGHT, STYLE: Several things create a unique style in "El Manisero," such as the repeated **ostinato** and its polyrhythmic character. The rhythmic phrasing of the melodic lines, however, is particularly important to this Cuban style as the phrasing has a very different feel and approach from non-Latin popular styles. Without an understanding of this type of phrasing, a musician cannot effectively play this style of music. It has a relaxed, laid-back quality that is very appealing and idiomatic.

The trumpet soloist here plays with a **straight mute** (a metal mute that creates a sharp and nasal timbre) in a **tipico** (typical) soloing style. The tipico style is heard in both the lead trumpet's solos and fills behind the vocal. Unlike jazz improvisation that focuses on elaborating on the melody or harmony, tipico style focuses on phrasing and rhythm over a vamp with a simple chord progression. The melodies are kept simple, straightforward, and pretty. In addition, the trumpeter uses a fast vibrato to further the excitement of the performance.

important tunes such as "Siboney" and "Mama Inez," typifies the Cuban style heard in the United States during this period. While these types of compositions are popularly referred to as "rumbas," many were actually derived from a Cuban style, **son**, which is the main basis for **salsa**, an important Latin style based upon Cuban dance music and popularized in New York City.

While Cuban styles dominated during this period, other Latin forms were also extremely popular. For example, songs from Mexico in an "international" Latin style (meaning they are difficult to classify in a more specific manner) played an important role. "Cuando Vuelva a Tu Lado," better known to English-speaking audiences as "What a Diff'rence a Day Made," is a standard; and versions by singers from many styles, including jazz singers such as Dinah Washington (discussed in Chapter 9, 3rd Chorus) and Esther Phillips (who covered Washington's version but with a disco feel in the 1970s), have kept this song in the public eye. The Mexican folk tune "La Cucaracha" became so ubiquitous that its roots in Mexican folk culture have become obscured. As a final example, a Brazilian tune, "Aquarela do Brasil" ("Brazil"), became a hit during the late 1930s and is still popular to this day.

Other Latin Entertainers of the 1920s and 1930s

Along with its relationship to jazz and American popular music, Latin entertainers were becoming extremely popular during the 1920s and 1930s. Three of the most prominent Latin entertainers were the bandleaders Xavier Cugat and Desi Arnaz and the singer-dancer Carmen Miranda. Cugat (1900–1990), a Spaniard who moved to Cuba at the age of 5, was one of Latin music's most visible entertainers through recordings, radio, and film. He presented a hybrid of Latin styles in a manner that he believed was more palatable to American audiences than traditionally authentic Cuban music.

Desi Arnaz (1917–1986), who briefly worked with Cugat, was a frontman and entertainer and, like Cugat, helped to popularize Latin music with American audiences. His greatest visibility came in his role as the Cuban bandleader Ricky Ricardo on the *I Love Lucy Show*, where he also played Lucille Ball's husband (they were married in real life). Carmen Miranda (1909–1955) was born in Portugal and raised in Brazil, where by the 1930s she was already a star through her recordings, movies, and the radio. Her trademark was an outlandish hat covered with fruit. She performed on Broadway in 1939 and went on to become a Hollywood film star.

Another influential Latin musician was Puerto Rican pianist Noro Morales (1912–1964), who immigrated to New York City in the mid-1930s. His early professional experiences there were with Alberto Socarrás (Chapter 5, 5th Chorus) and trumpeter-bandleader Augusto Coen. These experiences introduced him to a sound that incorporated elements of the swing big-band style, including a similar instrumentation and approach to arranging for a large ensemble.

Big-band leader Stan Kenton was inspired to seriously incorporate Latin styles into his music when he and his arranger, Pete Rugulo, heard Morales play in New York City in 1946. Kenton brought Latin styles into a wider public's consciousness while also incorporating them into progressive jazz (see Chapter 11, 1st Chorus), a movement that helped to stretch and expand approaches to jazz arranging and composition. Morales also gave Chico O'Farrill, one of Latin jazz's most innovative arrangers, his first job.

Morales played in East Harlem with numerous groups and performed with Tito Puente (Chapter 11, 3rd Chorus) and Tito Rodriguez (who was a singer in Morales's band), two of the top bandleaders who successfully incorporated jazz big-band sounds into Latin big bands in the 1950s and 1960s (and, in the case of Puente, through the 1980s). Morales made his name, however, in the midtown Latin dance scene with a smaller group that played at clubs such as El Morocco and the Stork Club along with more rumba-oriented bands such as those of Xavier Cugat and Don Azpiazú that appealed to Anglo audiences. Morales had a hit in 1942 with "Serenata Ritmico" with a quintet that showcased his ability as a piano soloist and that presented music that was a fusion of American popular music and Latin styles.

CODA Chapter Summary

What Is Swing Music?

- Swing music is for dancing.
- It has a "swing" feeling, emphasizing the weaker beats, or off-beats.
- It is typically performed by big bands.
- It became exceptionally popular in the mid-1930s.

Why Is Benny Goodman Generally Credited as Launching the Swing Era?

- Goodman was an outstanding clarinetist who set the standard for swing-style clarinet playing.
- The arrangements of Fletcher Henderson, Benny Carter, and Edgar Sampson were essential to Goodman's band's success.
- Goodman fused the worlds of popular Tin Pan Alley songs and a hot style in a way that resonated deeply with both sweet and hot dance-band fans.

Who Were Some Other Popular Bandleaders During the Swing Era?

- Artie Shaw was an excellent clarinetist who had a terrific big band that recorded some of the major hits of the swing era, including "Begin the Beguine."
- Glenn Miller led a popular band that had a more "sweet" than hot style. He had a major hit with "In the Mood."
- Tommy Dorsey's band featured vocalist Frank Sinatra and successfully wed popular and swing elements.

What Were the Unique Challenges Faced by the "All-Girl" Bands During the Swing Era?

- There was a general prejudice against women playing jazz.
- Band members had to not only sound good but also "look good." Critics tended to focus on the players' looks and the novelty of all-female bands rather than on their musicianship.
- All-girl bands were generally ghettoized by being placed into particular types of venues.
- Their work was often not valued enough to be recorded, which necessarily limited their commercial potential.
- Until recently, most jazz histories have not recorded their achievements.

How Did Latin Bands Continue to Influence Mainstream Jazz in the 1930s?

- The proximity of El Barrio and Harlem—as well as the fact that these Latin bands and big bands played alongside each other in ballrooms and shared some of the same musicians—created an environment that encouraged a fusion of the styles.
- The popularity of the dance form the rumba encouraged dance bands to play Latin-flavored music.

Talkin' Jazz (Key Terms)

"All-girl" bands	Ghost band	Salsa
Articulation	Hot jazz	Son
Charts	Off-beat	Soundies
Crescendo	Ostinato	Straight mute
Cup mutes	Phrasing	Sweet jazz
Decrescendo	Progressive jazz	Tipico
Dynamics	Rumba	

Key People

Benny Goodman	Ina Ray Hutton's	Don Azpiazú's Havana
Artie Shaw	Melodears	Casino Orchestra
Glenn Miller	Prairie View	Xavier Cugat
Tommy and Jimmy Dorsey	Co-Eds	Desi Arnaz
Phil Spitalny's "Hour of	International Sweethearts	Carmen Miranda
Charm"	of Rhythm	Noro Morales

Think About This (For Further Discussion and Study)

1. Did Benny Goodman really launch the swing era?
2. When was the swing era, and how did it continue to thrive after the fade of the era itself?
3. Discuss racial issues in the swing era. How do they compare to today's issues surrounding race?
4. What are the qualities and elements of swing music?
5. Discuss the roles and duties of side musicians.
6. Discuss issues regarding women in jazz. How does the situation of female musicians in the current music scene compare to that in the swing era?
7. What do you think about all-women bands or festivals of only music by women? Is it a necessary or effective tool to improve the situation for women in the music business?
8. Discuss the differences in rhythmic approach between the swing recordings in this chapter and those in "El Manisero."
9. Clap clave along with the recording of "El Manisero." Also, go back to Chapter 5, 4th Chorus, and clap clave to Alberto Socarrás's "Masabi." See if you notice anything about how the relationship to clave and the phrase structure changes in this recording.

Look It Up (Key Resources)

Dahl, Linda. *Morning Glory: A Biography of Mary Lou Williams*. New York: Limelight Editions, 1995.

———. *Stormy Weather: The Music and Lives of a Century of Jazzwomen*. New York: Pantheon, 1994.

Dance, Stanley. *The World of Swing: An Oral History of Big Band Jazz*. New York: Da Capo Press, 2001.

Erenberg, Lewis. *Swingin' the Dream: Big Band Jazz and the Rebirth of American Culture*. Chicago: University of Chicago, 1998.

Korall, Burt. *Drummin' Men: The Heartbeat of Jazz—The Swing Years*. New York: Schirmer, 1990.

Levinson, Peter. *Tommy Dorsey: Livin' in a Great Big Way*. New York: Da Capo Press, 2006.

Placksin, Sally. *American Women in Jazz: 1900 to the Present, Their Words, Lives, and Music*. New York: Wideview Books, 1982.

Roberts, John Storm. *Latin Jazz: The First of the Fusions, 1880s to Today*. New York: Schirmer Books, 1999.

———. *The Latin Tinge: The Impact of Latin American Music on the United States*. New York: Oxford University Press, 1979.

Schuller, Gunther. *The Swing Era: The Development of Jazz, 1930–1945*. New York: Oxford University Press, 1989.

Shaw, Artie. *The Trouble with Cinderella: An Outline of Identity*. New York: Da Capo Press, 1979.

Simon, George. *The Big Bands*, 4th ed. New York: Schirmer, 1981.

Stowe, David. *Swing Changes: Big-Band Jazz in New Deal America*. Cambridge, MA: Harvard University Press, 1994.

Tucker, Sherrie. *Swing Shift: "All-Girl" Bands of the 1940s*. Durham, NC: Duke University Press, 2000.

DUKE ELLINGTON

8

WHY IS DUKE ELLINGTON CONSIDERED ONE OF AMERICA'S MOST IMPORTANT COMPOSERS AND BANDLEADERS?

Duke Ellington (1899–1974) was one of American music's most important composers and bandleaders. While a crucial part of the swing era and one of its trendsetters in the late 1920s and the early 1930s, Ellington's music transcends the swing era, the big-band genre, and even the jazz world. He created a sound, a compositional repertoire, and a musical institution that are unique and vastly influential. Though known for his incredibly rich and varied collection of short instrumental works in the jazz tradition, Ellington wrote music in many genres, such as jazz, blues, pop, soundtracks for film and television, suites, ballets, and extended works. Ellington was also a consummate pianist, showman, and entrepreneur and had one of the most illustrious and creatively productive careers in jazz and American music that spanned over 50 years.

Ellington was articulate yet careful with his words. As a person, he was handsome, suave, and scrupulously groomed and attired; and while his manner on stage was warm and welcoming, Ellington still kept his professional distance with a "cool" demeanor. His refusal to be limited by either musical or racial labels and stereotypes has been musically and socially inspirational, and Ellington's ability to create music steeped in the past while looking forward adventurously was another of his greatest strengths.

1st Chorus Early Ellington

Ellington was born in Washington, DC, to a middle-class family. Though having an early interest in visual art, Duke quickly gravitated to music, with a particular interest in stride piano, a style that he emulated as a young pianist and composer. Perhaps inspired by his father's entrepreneurial spirit—he was a butler but also contracted catering side jobs for social functions—while still in high school Ellington was leading his own band and sending out musicians to fill jobs he contracted in the Washington area.

Photo: Courtesy William P. Gottlieb Collection and Library of Congress.

In this chapter, we'll answer these questions:

- Why Is Duke Ellington Considered One of America's Most Important Composers and Bandleaders?

- What Were the Stylistic Hallmarks of the Early Ellington Band?

- What Impact Did the Hiring of Billy Strayhorn Have on the Ellington Band?

- How Did Ellington's Style Change in His Later Years?

WHAT WERE THE STYLISTIC HALLMARKS OF THE EARLY ELLINGTON BAND?

Ellington moved to New York City in 1923 and shortly after that began leading a band called the Washingtonians at the Kentucky Club. Many of the band members had worked with Ellington in his native Washington, and they became the nucleus of Duke's band as it moved forward. The band received excellent reviews, successfully toured and recorded, and secured professional management.

James "Bubber" Miley

An important personnel move, the addition of trumpeter James "Bubber" Miley, proved to be hugely influential on Ellington's style. Miley introduced a growling, gritty, bluesy sound to the band that sent Ellington in a new musical direction. "Black and Tan Fantasy" gives us an opportunity to hear Miley's effective blues playing. Miley also contributed the main melodic line of the piece. While it is a collaborative work between Ellington and Miley, the multisection character of the composition gives an early indication of Ellington's mastery of short-form compositions. This 3-minute piece is a study in contrasts, presenting three different moods in a remarkably short period of time. Another key player who also contributed to the piece's bluesy feeling was trombonist Joe "Tricky Sam" Nanton. Like Miley, Nanton used a mute to create a "wah-wah" effect, imitating a guttural vocal sound; he also was known for his growling low notes.

While most clubs at this time catered almost exclusively to segregated audiences, a few allowed both blacks and whites to attend. The title of this piece takes its name from these **"black and tan" clubs**.

Ellington and the band got one of their biggest breaks when they were hired as the house band for the Cotton Club, a top Harlem nightclub (see Chapter 5, 2nd Chorus). The clientele was all white, and the elaborate shows often catered to unfortunate African American racial stereotypes. It was, however, a terrific learning experience for Ellington because he had the opportunity to work with lyricists, accompany stage shows and dancing, and create vocal arrangements; and he developed a style that was referred to as his **jungle style**. Ellington became a star through the live shows and radio broadcasts from the club.

JAZZ LIVES BUBBER MILEY

James "Bubber" Miley (1903–1932) was born in Aiken, South Carolina, to a family of musicians. The family relocated to New York when Miley was 6 years old, and he was playing locally by his teen years. In 1920 he formed his first band and soon after joined blues singer Mamie Smith's group, the Jazz Hounds. When the group hit Chicago, Miley heard King Oliver (see Chapter 3, 4th Chorus) play using a mute and began to experiment with mutes himself. In 1923, he joined Duke Ellington's Washingtonians, introducing his new style that combined creative use of mutes along with a "growling" bluesy sound that came to be known as a **gutbucket** style.

Unfortunately, like his contemporary Bix Beiderbecke, Miley was a heavy drinker, leading to him missing dates so that Ellington was compelled to fire him in 1929. Miley continued to work with various other New York bands as he could, before succumbing to tuberculosis brought on by his alcohol abuse in 1932.

"Black and Tan Fantasy" (1927 Victor version) by Duke Ellington and the Washingtonians

INSTRUMENTATION: Piano and leader: Duke Ellington; **Trumpets:** Bubber Miley, Louis Metcalf; **Trombone:** Joe "Tricky Sam" Nanton; **Saxophones:** Otto Hardwick, Rudy Jackson, Harry Carney; **Banjo:** Fred Guy; **Bass:** Wellman Braud; **Drums:** Sonny Greer.

LISTENING HIGHLIGHT, STYLE: The initial melody is played by Miley, with Nanton playing in harmony, both in mutes. They bend many notes throughout in an expressive manner. It is the solos that follow that stand out here however. Miley and Nanton's solos are terrific examples of intense blues playing in a jazz-band concept, and their styles were influential upon the young Duke Ellington as he sought to create a sound and style for his early band. Miley begins with a quiet yet intense high note (0:57). Through his 2 choruses he goes on to give a tutorial in how to use a plunger mute, creating a wide variety of gritty and bluesy sounds, some of which are extremely vocal-like. His closing chorus (1:22) also includes a remarkable display of rhythmic flexibility and expressiveness in the first 8 measures. Miley's extensive use of blue notes is a major element of this solo as well as his overall style of playing.

Ellington's solo (1:46) manages to blend the sensibilities of the blues ("Black") with the second section's harmonic adventurousness ("Tan"). He solos on a blues but plays a harmonically sophisticated chord progression that expands its harmonic vocabulary ("Black and Tan"). Nanton's bluesy plunger solo (2:10), remarkably, produces an even more vocal-like sound as well as a number of sound effects including an intense growl that he uses throughout.

The Cotton Club was famous for its lavishly costumed reviews, featuring beautiful dancers. This photo shows Maude Russel and Her Ebony Steppers at the Cotton Club in the 1929 revue *Just a Minute.* Photo by Michael Ochs Archives. *Courtesy Getty Images.*

QUESTIONS AND CONTROVERSIES
Who Wrote Duke Ellington's Hits?

Duke Ellington freely admitted that he borrowed melodic ideas—and sometimes entire tunes—from his band members in shaping his music. Although Ellington added his own name at the time, today most scholars believe that "Caravan" was composed by Puerto Rico–born band member Juan Tizol. In addition to taking credit for entire pieces, Ellington is said to have borrowed riffs from saxophonists Johnny Hodges, for several of his bigger hits including "Don't Get Around Much Anymore," and Otto Hardwick, for "Sophisticated Lady." Hodges, for one, was angered for years that he didn't get credit for his contributions.

Of course, Ellington did much to enhance the material that these musicians created. And it wasn't unusual at the time for bandleaders to take credit for the work of their employees, who after all were paid to work for them. There also is a big difference from coming up with a short melodic idea and composing and arranging a song. Still, Ellington could have shared credit with his side musicians if he had wanted to, which would have meant they all would have benefited financially from their successful numbers. This led some of the key players to leave the band because they felt they could do better on their own.

To suit the needs of the shows at the Cotton Club, the band continued to expand in size. Ellington added musicians who would be with him through much of his career and who helped to shape the sound of his orchestra, such as Johnny Hodges (lead alto saxophone), Harry Carney (baritone sax), and Cootie Williams (trumpet). Duke was particularly known for featuring his musicians in solo spots as well as cleverly taking advantage of his side musicians' musical strengths by writing specifically for them and their playing styles. He also created what would be his signature sound, sometimes called the **Ellington effect** (a term coined by Billy Strayhorn, discussed in the 2nd Chorus). This unique sound and approach always set him clearly apart from other big-band writers.

2nd Chorus Later Ellington

WHAT IMPACT DID THE HIRING OF BILLY STRAYHORN HAVE ON THE ELLINGTON BAND?

Billy Strayhorn

Composer-arranger-pianist Billy Strayhorn was hired by Ellington as a staff arranger and pianist in 1939. Until his death in 1967 Strayhorn was a crucial composing and arranging partner for Ellington. Strayhorn's early interest in classical music influenced his rich harmonic approach throughout his career. Strayhorn's composition "Lush Life," written while he was still a teenager, is one of jazz's most beautiful and poignant ballads. Though some have said Ellington's and Strayhorn's works are indistinguishable and interchangeable, the two had distinctly different writing and playing styles that complemented each other's strengths. Strayhorn's compositions—such as the band's theme "Take the A Train," the lovely ballad "Chelsea Bridge," and collaborations with Ellington such as the hit "Satin Doll"—are central works in the Ellington repertoire. While one of jazz's great composers and

JAZZ LIVES BILLY STRAYHORN

William Thomas "Billy" Strayhorn (1915–1967) was born in Dayton, Ohio, although he was primarily raised by his grandmother, who lived in rural North Carolina. She owned a piano on which the young man learned to play hymns and popular songs. When he was a teenager, he attended school in Pittsburgh, Pennsylvania, where his mother and father lived, including a period studying classical music in a local conservatory. Inspired by Art Tatum (see Chapter 5, 4th Chorus), he started to explore jazz harmonies and arranging on the piano. Strayhorn began composing songs for local amateur and semiprofessional productions. In 1938, when Duke Ellington passed through town, Strayhorn showed him some of his arrangements, and Ellington hired him to join his band early the following year. He worked as Ellington's arranger/right-hand man for the next 25 years.

According to biographer David Hajdu, Strayhorn was openly gay, which was highly unusual for a jazz musician at the time. There was considerable prejudice in the jazz (and larger African American) community against gays, which must have made it difficult for Strayhorn. However, his long association with Ellington undoubtedly protected him from any repercussions in his career. Strayhorn was also a vocal supporter of Martin Luther King and the civil rights movement of the late 1950s and early 1960s. In 1964, he was diagnosed with cancer and 3 years later died from the effects of the disease.

Billy Strayhorn, working on a score backstage, ca. 1946. Photo by William P. Gottlieb.

Courtesy William P. Gottlieb Collection and Library of Congress.

arrangers, Strayhorn primarily spent his career out of the public limelight, which perhaps suited his introverted personality and his need for privacy. Yet Strayhorn's presence was crucial to Ellington's ability to be as productive as he was.

Along with Ellington and Strayhorn's formal arrangements, Ellington often worked directly with the band (often late at night after a gig) to create compositions and arrangements. Players would try ideas and discuss them back and forth, and Ellington would make decisions and eventually finalize the arrangements.

Jimmy Blanton and Ben Webster

Also in 1939, the addition of the innovative bassist Jimmy Blanton and tenor saxophonist Ben Webster inaugurated the "Blanton/Webster" edition of the band, which produced some of its greatest recordings, including the classics "Ko-Ko" and

Duke Ellington and His Orchestra, 1938. Note Sonny Greer's elaborate drum set, including bells and a large gong.

© *Everett collection Historical/Alamy.*

"Concerto for Cootie" (see "Compare"). While Ellington experimented with many types of formats, such as popular songs, extended compositions, suites, and movie soundtracks, the short-form composition was his greatest strength. Because of capacity issues surrounding the size of 78-rpm discs, popular music recordings were necessarily limited to around 3 minutes. "Ko-Ko" is an outstanding example of Ellington's ability to fit an incredibly exciting, engrossing, and action-packed composition into 2 minutes and 44 seconds; and the piece, based on a standard 12-bar blues progression, has the feel of a much longer work. This minor blues (in the particularly dark-sounding key of E-flat minor, an unusual key for jazz) has a dark, brooding quality; and it inexorably builds from its initial quiet intensity to a screaming climax.

While Ellington wrote many types of compositions, the blues is the foundation of his repertoire. Through that foundation Ellington sought to create what he referred to as "a genuine contribution from our race," stating that his music was "always intended to be definitely and purely racial" (Ellington 1939, 2, 16–17). Clearly, both his musical and social goals were lofty.

HOW DID ELLINGTON'S STYLE CHANGE IN HIS LATER YEARS?

The Ellington Orchestra played a Carnegie Hall concert in 1943 that featured an important yet controversial extended work, *Black, Brown and Beige*. Some jazz critics questioned Ellington's ability to write effective extended works, and some feel that *Black, Brown and Beige* is an inferior work compared to his shorter pieces. While Ellington primarily wrote in short form, he certainly had the ability to write longer works. *A Tone Parallel to Harlem*, a 1952 extended work, for example, is a particularly strong composition (discussed in "Listening Focus"). It is a powerful and effective piece that uses a great deal of **motivic writing**, meaning

"Ko-Ko" (1940) by Duke Ellington and His Famous Orchestra

DOWNLOAD
Track Number 15

INSTRUMENTATION: Piano and leader: Duke Ellington; **Trumpets:** Rex Stewart, Cootie Williams, Wallace Jones; **Trombones:** Joe "Tricky Sam" Nanton, Juan Tizol, Lawrence Brown; **Saxophones:** Johnny Hodges, Barney Bigard, Otto Hardwick, Ben Webster, Harry Carney; **Guitar:** Fred Guy; **Bass:** Jimmy Blanton; **Drums:** Sonny Greer.

FORM: "Ko-Ko" takes a simple 12-bar blues form and turns it into something almost unrecognizable as a blues. We hear in it an indication of the basic blues progression, I–IV–V; and there are timbral contrasts between choruses initially, but as the piece progresses through 7 blues choruses the divisions between choruses are sometimes quite veiled as the powerful ensemble and rolling polyphonic riffs create an almost impenetrable block of sound.

STYLE: "Ko-Ko" features the orchestra at its full-throated best and showcases two of its trombonists, Juan Tizol and Joe "Tricky Sam" Nanton. Valve trombonist Tizol was a longtime fixture in the orchestra and contributed to the repertoire as composer ("Caravan," "Perdido," and "Conga Brava") as well as filling the important role of music copyist, creating written parts and documenting arrangements. Nanton played in the Ellington band for much of his career and was an important featured trombone soloist. He was particularly famous for his use of the plunger mute to create a "wah-wah" sound, and he uses it here in combination with a metal mute inside the bell of the trombone to give his trombone an uncanny vocal-like quality. This type of sound, played by both Nanton and early Ellington trumpeter Bubber Miley, helped to create a distinctive, growling, bluesy sound for the orchestra. This raw sound, in combination with Ellington's and Strayhorn's supremely sophisticated and individualistic compositions and arrangements, created one of the most compelling sounds in American music, often referred to as the "Ellington effect."

MELODY AND HARMONY: Though this is such an effective and well-integrated composition based on a blues progression, in a way it is a riff tune taken to the highest level of sophistication and accomplishment while also maintaining an intense and raw quality.

RHYTHM: Drummer Sonny Greer plays a relatively understated role in this recording. It is the bass playing of Jimmy Blanton that stands out as the driving force of the rhythm section.

ACCOMPANIMENT: While this trombone-heavy composition features the low brass, the texture is quite full throughout, with all sections playing an accompaniment role. This all-in approach makes this one of Ellington's most intense pieces.

"KO-KO" LISTENING GUIDE

TIME	FORM	STYLE	MELODY AND HARMONY	RHYTHM	ACCOMPANIMENT
0:00	Intro	"Ko-Ko" has an exotic flavor, and the key of E-flat minor gives this composition a dark and brooding sound. The use of lower-register instruments—trombones and baritone saxophone—adds to the dark quality.	In this 8-bar introduction the trombones play a riff that is anchored by Harry Carney's distinctive and powerful baritone sax playing.	Jimmy Blanton plays in a hard-driving 4, and Sonny Greer on drums helps set the exotic mood on his tom-toms.	

continued

TIME	FORM	STYLE	MELODY AND HARMONY	RHYTHM	ACCOMPANIMENT
0:12	1st chorus	Juan Tizol's valve trombone melody functions as a theme to be used by the band in numerous ways throughout the piece, immediately setting this composition apart from the standard head–solos–head jazz arrangement.	Valve-trombonist Tizol plays a simple melody.	Blanton continues to play powerfully in 4, at times playing in a higher register than was common during this period. His sound is big and unusually percussive. Greer keeps insistent yet subtle time.	The sax section fills in between Tizol's phrases.
0:31	2nd chorus	The wailing vocal quality of "Tricky Sam" Nanton's trombone playing is eerily expressive and communicative.	Nanton plays a muted wah-wah trombone solo that consists of a series of short phrases.		Behind the trombone solo the saxes largely play sustained notes that draw from Tizol's initial line, while the trombones play a syncopated wah-wah figure with plunger mutes.
0:50	3rd chorus	The divisions of the 12-bar blues form as well as the sound of a typical blues progression become blurred.	Nanton continues his vocal-like wails.		The saxes and trombones continue in the background.
1:08	4th chorus	Ellington solos and pierces this texture by pounding dissonant piano clusters (that interlock with the syncopated wah-wah figure at times), glisses, and the use of the whole-tone scale, a symmetrical 6-note scale not often heard in jazz at that time. This all adds to the dark and almost sinister sound of this piece.	Ellington plays a piano solo, which is more a series of musical gestures than it is a traditional solo.		The saxes continue their rolling line, and the trumpets take over the syncopated wah-wah riff.
1:25	5th chorus	The full band plays a wild, almost chaotic polyphonic ensemble, with each section playing its own independent but interlocking line, noticeably raising the level of intensity.		Greer continues steadily with little fanfare. Blanton maintains his propulsive, edgy feel.	
1:44	6th chorus		The whole ensemble, again each section with its own line, trades 2-bar phrases with Blanton's dynamic and driving walking bass.		
2:02	7th chorus	"Ko-Ko" reaches its climax with this final chorus as the whole ensemble shrieks in a wildly intense and polyphonic shout chorus.	The sax section plays a riff, and the trumpets and trombones blast intense, thick, and almost dissonant chords. The power and intensity are similar to what a great rock band creates today.		
2:22	Coda	The composition immediately calms down as the trombone and baritone sax riffs from the introduction are repeated.	The full ensemble adds a 4-bar tag to end this powerful and compact compositional jewel.		

Compare

"Concerto for Cootie" (1940), like "Ko-Ko," was recorded by the Jimmy Blanton/Ben Webster version of the Ellington Orchestra but provides a strong musical contrast to "Ko-Ko." It features one of Ellington's star trumpet players, Cootie Williams, in a "concerto"—a classical music term for a work that prominently features a soloist. Williams presents a series of melodies and solos in this tune that combines an AABA tune (beginning at 0:17 and a final extended A at 2:38) and a C section (1:57). He creates numerous timbres by using various mutes and his open horn and is accompanied by the band throughout. Compared to "Ko-Ko," the feel of the band is relaxed and the melodies are simple and appealing, creating one of Duke's loveliest compositions.

QUESTIONS AND CONTROVERSIES
Classical vs. Jazz Composition

Some writers and critics compare Ellington's longer compositions to the work of classical composers (both favorably and unfavorably), which raises some essential questions regarding the reception of jazz composition and jazz in general. For example, should jazz composers be compared to classical composers when discussing issues of quality? Does differentiating jazz from classical music necessarily ghettoize it as a "popular" genre as opposed to "art music"? And does attempting to equate jazz with classical music, or to discuss jazz as "America's classical music," necessarily denigrate jazz by assuming classical music's cultural superiority? These are complicated questions that bring in social issues such as race as well as cultural issues. Taken on its own terms, however, Ellington's music holds a unique and lofty place in American music. Comparisons are not needed to understand Ellington's importance. (The relationship of classical and jazz composition is discussed further in Chapter 11, 1st Chorus.)

that a musical motive, or idea, is used many times in a varied manner. Most of jazz composition is not particularly motivic—a significant stylistic difference between jazz and classical composition—which makes this work stand out in both jazz and Ellington's repertoire.

Perhaps in response to criticisms of *Black, Brown and Beige*, as well as being aware of his greatest strengths, Ellington spent much of his later work composing *suites*—collections of small compositions intended to be heard as a unit. A group of songs in a suite creates an extended piece, but there is no assumed motivic connection between the pieces, essentially creating a series of short-form compositions that then form a larger work. One of these suites is *The Far East Suite*, composed jointly by Ellington and Strayhorn.

Ellington's reputation grew in the late 1940s and early 1950s, but the band had financial difficulties as well as a large turnover in important personnel. Ellington managed to keep the band working and recording and in July 1956 had a huge success at the Newport Jazz Festival as tenor saxophonist Paul Gonsalves galvanized and electrified the crowd with an incredible extended solo during *Diminuendo in Blue and Crescendo in Blue*. This performance thrust Ellington back into the limelight, and his career continued to blossom as he wrote film scores (*Anatomy of a Murder* and *Paris Blues*), numerous suites (including *Such Sweet Thunder*, based on Shakespeare texts; *The Far East Suite*; and *Suite Thursday*), and extended works (*A Tone Parallel to Harlem*, see "Listening Focus"). Duke recorded prolifically with his band as well as on albums that paired him with important contemporary players such as John Coltrane, Charles Mingus, and Max Roach. Late in his career Ellington concentrated on works that addressed religious themes, which became increasingly important to him, resulting in the albums *Concert of Sacred Music*, *Second Sacred Concert*, and *Third Sacred Concert*.

Ellington is recognized as among the most important jazz composers and one of America's greatest composers in any genre. His band thrived for over 50 years, an incredible feat. His continuous level of richly diverse productivity was also remarkable, leaving an extraordinary legacy.

Duke Ellington music folio, ca. 1945. This collection of Ellington hits emphasizes both the hot "rhythms" and the emotional "moods" that his pieces conveyed to listeners.
Courtesy BenCar Archives.

listening focus

A Tone Parallel to Harlem (The Harlem Suite) (1951) by Duke Ellington and His Orchestra

INSTRUMENTATION: Piano, leader, composer: Duke Ellington; **Trumpets:** Willie Cook, Clark Terry, Francis Williams, Ray Nance (on this recording session he also played violin and sang); **Trombones:** Quentin Jackson, Britt Woodman, Juan Tizol; **Saxophones:** Jimmy Hamilton, Russell Procope, Willie Smith, Paul Gonsalves, Harry Carney; **Piano:** Billy Strayhorn; **Bass:** Wendell Marshall; **Drums:** Louie Bellson.

Known also as "Harlem," this 13-minute, 47-second recording is an impressive work that is considered to be a premier example of Ellington's more extended compositions that resemble concert, or symphonic, works. Originally commissioned by the NBC Symphony Orchestra, the work was performed and recorded by the Ellington Orchestra but also presented in a version expanded to include symphony orchestra, orchestrated by Luther Henderson, Jr. In his biography, Ellington spoke of the work as a "tour" of Harlem, depicting various parts of the neighborhood and a variety of activities including a nightclub floor show and a sermon at a church service.

LISTENING HIGHLIGHT, FORM: While it has many fascinating aspects, how Ellington shaped this extended work formally stands out. The piece is not in movements, as are *Black, Brown and Beige* and Ellington's suites. As discussed by John Howland in his book *Ellington Uptown: Duke Ellington, James P. Johnson, and the Birth of Concert Jazz*, "Harlem" has three main sections, each with a wide variety of musical ideas and rhythmic feels. A long, slow introduction begins with a 2-note musical motive declaring "Harlem," a motive that is heard throughout the piece in many different ways. Section 1 (1:16) continues as a slow section, including many instances of the 2-note motive. Section 2 (4:39) takes off at a fast tempo (initially with a rumba beat), eventually moves into a series of 8 blues choruses, and ends with screaming brass, and the "Harlem" motive (7:16). A clarinet cadenza takes us into section 3 (7:19), which is again slow and includes the 2-note motive. A hymn-like melody stands out in this section (8:57) and is heard three times with different instrumentations. It is followed by a bridge (10:16) and then two final statements of the hymn (10:43 with full band and 11:13 featuring solo trumpet over a choir-like accompaniment without the rhythm section), each giving us a chance to hear Duke's use of colorful and varied orchestration. The piece has a concluding section (12:05) that includes the hymn, the 2-note motive, and screaming brass, bringing this Ellington masterpiece to a dramatic and stirring conclusion.

CODA Chapter Summary

Why Is Duke Ellington Considered One of America's Most Important Composers and Bandleaders?

- Ellington's band was one of jazz's trendsetters in the late 1920s and the early 1930s and played a crucial role in popularizing jazz during the swing era.
- However, Ellington's music transcends the swing era, the big-band genre, and even the jazz world.

- Ellington created a sound, a compositional repertoire, and a musical institution that are unique and vastly influential.
- Though known for his incredibly rich and varied collection of short instrumental works in the jazz tradition, Ellington wrote music in many genres, such as blues, pop, soundtracks for film and television, suites, ballets, and extended works.
- Ellington was also a consummate pianist, showman, and entrepreneur and had one of the most illustrious and creatively productive careers in jazz and American music that spanned over 50 years.

What Were the Stylistic Hallmarks of the Early Ellington Band?

- A hallmark of the early Ellington band was a growling, gritty, bluesy sound introduced by trumpeter "Bubber" Miley and trombonist "Tricky Sam" Nanton.
- Ellington was particularly known for featuring his musicians in solo spots as well as cleverly taking advantage of his side musicians' musical strengths by writing specifically for them and their playing styles. This, along with his colorful and unique orchestration, was known as the "Ellington effect."

What Impact Did the Hiring of Billy Strayhorn Have on the Ellington Band?

- Strayhorn was responsible for many of Ellington's greatest arrangements and hits, including the band's theme song "Take the A Train."
- Until his death in 1967 Strayhorn was a crucial composing and arranging partner for Ellington.

How Did Ellington's Style Change in His Later Years?

- Ellington continued to create classic short-form jazz compositions, inspired by new band members like Jimmy Blanton and Ben Webster, such as "Ko-Ko" and "Concerto for Cootie."
- However, he increasingly began focusing on longer-form works after World War II, at times emulating classical music forms.
- Late in his career Ellington concentrated on works that addressed religious themes, which became increasingly important to him.

Talkin' Jazz (Key Terms)

"Black and tan" clubs	Gutbucket	Motivic writing
Ellington effect	Jungle style	

Key People

Duke Ellington	Johnny Hodges	Billy Strayhorn
James "Bubber" Miley	Harry Carney	Jimmy Blanton
Joe "Tricky Sam" Nanton	Charles "Cootie" Williams	Ben Webster

Think About This (For Further Discussion and Study)

1. Discuss Duke Ellington's importance as a composer and bandleader. How did his work change jazz?
2. What were the stylistic qualities that made Ellington unique?
3. What is the "Ellington effect"?
4. Listen to an early and a late Ellington piece and discuss the differences and similarities between them.

Look It Up (Key Resources)

Dance, Stanley. *The World of Duke Ellington*. New York: Scribner, 1970.

Ellington, Duke. "Duke Says Swing Is Stagnant." *Downbeat* (February 1939): 2, 16–17.

———. *Music Is My Mistress*. Garden City, NY: Doubleday, 1973.

Ellington, Mercer, and Stanley Dance. *Duke Ellington in Person: An Intimate Memoir*. Boston: Houghton Mifflin, 1978.

Hajdu, David. *Lush Life: A Biography of Billy Strayhorn*. New York: Farrar, Straus and Giroux, 1996.

Hasse, John Edward. *Beyond Category: The Life and Genius of Duke Ellington*. New York: Simon and Schuster, 1993.

Howland, John. *Ellington Uptown: Duke Ellington, James P. Johnson, and the Birth of Concert Jazz*. Ann Arbor, MI: University of Michigan Press, 2009.

Tucker, Mark. *Ellington: The Early Years*. Urbana, IL: University of Illinois Press, 1991.

———, ed. *The Duke Ellington Reader*. New York: Oxford University Press, 1993.

Van de Leur, Walter. *Something to Live For: The Music of Billy Strayhorn*. New York: Oxford University Press, 2002.

SWING-ERA VOCALISTS

9

Besides the bands themselves, the swing era produced a group of vocalists who would go on to have long careers. Many worked simultaneously with a big band and smaller ensembles and thus were able to establish themselves as major stars on their own. This would prove important after the big-band era died as they could continue to perform in a variety of contexts as individuals.

In the swing era much of a night of dancing was instrumental, but there was always a featured vocalist or two, or even a vocal quartet, who would come on stage and bring a different type of entertainment to the show. While most big bands had vocalists, their level of importance to the band was quite varied. For example, Frank Sinatra became a huge star with Tommy Dorsey's band and was crucial to the band's success. Ella Fitzgerald became a vital element in Chick Webb's appeal and eventually became the bandleader. On the other hand, Duke Ellington had wonderful vocalists such as Ivie Anderson and Al Hibbler, but it was always the orchestra and the compositions that were featured.

In this chapter, we'll answer these questions:

- Who Were Key Jazz Vocalists During the Swing Era?
- How Did Some Vocalists Cross Over from Jazz to Become Popular Music Stars?

1st Chorus Swing Vocalists: Billie Holiday and Ella Fitzgerald

WHO WERE KEY JAZZ VOCALISTS DURING THE SWING ERA?

In this chapter, we will look at four vocalists whose careers were built during the swing era and then kept the swing style popular and up to date well into the 1950s and 1960s. They all have an instrumental quality to their singing, allowing them to appeal to the popular market, to more musically sophisticated listeners, and to musicians (who often tend to look down on singers as being less skillful than instrumentalists). These four singers each present a different approach to swing phrasing as well as contrasting vocal styles.

Billie Holiday

Billie Holiday (born Eleanora Fagan, 1915–1959) is the quintessential jazz singer. Though she sang standards from the popular song repertoire, there is no pop music in Billie Holiday. She has an intimate style, best suited for small bands, that forces us to listen to and feel every word she sings; and it is all

Photo: Courtesy Getty Images.

QUESTIONS AND CONTROVERSIES
What Distinguishes a Jazz Singer from a Popular Singer?

The intersection of jazz and popular music in the swing era is vividly evident in the work of the vocalists of the period. In fact, just what constitutes a "jazz singer" as opposed to a "popular singer" is controversial and very much up for debate. As is true for many instrumentalists, many singers have little use for this as a label or a boundary. For example, Ella Fitzgerald could scat sing a solo as exciting and profound as any instrumentalist, yet she also brought that same profundity to simpler popular tunes such as "A-Tisket, A-Tasket." Frank Sinatra never considered himself a jazz singer because of the wide variety of popular music that was a major part of his repertoire, yet his vocal approach and phrasing were influential to many jazz singers and certainly swing while drawing on the jazz tradition. Nat "King" Cole was a terrific and important jazz pianist and singer who also sang a wide variety of music including very light popular tunes such as "Ramblin' Rose" and "Those Lazy-Hazy-Crazy Days of Summer." Some decry their use of popular material, but these singers certainly brought integrity as well as a jazz sensibility to all of their material.

Billie Holiday performing in New York, ca. 1947. Holiday's smoky sound was one of the most unique among all jazz vocalists. Photo by William P. Gottlieb.
Courtesy William P. Gottlieb Collection and Library of Congress.

articulated through a jazz perspective on the blues. Her life was challenging in many ways, and she seems to communicate this to us through the emotions that imbue her music.

Holiday cited Louis Armstrong as a major influence on her singing, and indeed she is credited with furthering Louis Armstrong's revolutionary approach to phrasing. Armstrong sang very much like he played melodies on his trumpet, flattening notes, stretching the beat, and subtly manipulating the phrasing. He was also a talented scat singer, an important jazz singing technique. While Holiday is not a scat singer, her manipulation of a song's rhythm is incredibly careful and creative yet always feels spontaneous and natural. Her wonderful rhythmic phrasing and her emotional directness immediately stand out, and her fragile, gentle, and slightly nasal voice with its limited range has an incredible vulnerability that is heart-wrenching. Her delivery became even more emotionally vulnerable as her career moved along and as the difficulties of her life and upbringing, along with her drug and alcohol dependence, took a steady toll on her physically and emotionally.

Billie Holiday's life was difficult, and while we prefer not to dwell on sensational aspects of people's lives, with Holiday it is difficult not to discuss them. She was born to a single mother in Philadelphia and was raised from a young age in Baltimore by abusive family members. This in turn led her to reform school when she was 10. Holiday moved to New York City to live with her mother in 1929. Both mother and daughter supported themselves at times through prostitution and doing menial work such as cleaning homes.

Through all of this, Holiday created a singing career for herself in New York City. The producer-talent scout John Hammond (see Chapter 6, 2nd Chorus) heard her in 1933 and arranged her first recording date with Benny Goodman, as well as a series of star-studded dates led by the important pianist Teddy Wilson. These recordings included members of the Basie band, most significantly Lester Young (see Chapter 6, 4th Chorus) with whom Holiday developed a remarkably close personal and musical kinship; and it was Young who gave her the affectionate nickname "Lady Day."

Holiday sang with Basie's big band, and then Artie Shaw (see Chapter 7, 2nd Chorus) hired her to tour with his band; but she had to leave him because integrated bands were still not accepted. But because of her intimate style, Holiday is best known, and was better suited for, singing with smaller bands. She cowrote and made popular "God Bless the Child," "Don't Explain," and "Fine and Mellow" and is known for songs such as "Easy Living" and "Strange Fruit" (see "Listening Focus"), a haunting and emotional account of a lynching in the South that Holiday first sang at Café Society in New York City (see Chapter 6, 4th Chorus).

Beginning in the early 1940s, Holiday's life was plagued with drug addiction, alcoholism, and troubled relationships. She spent eight months in jail for possession of narcotics, resulting in the loss of her **cabaret card**, or license to perform in clubs where alcohol was served. Under New York City law, all performers had to have a cabaret card in order to legally appear in nightclubs; a drug arrest of any kind would lead to the loss of this license. Without it, Holiday could not work, significantly limiting her ability to make a living.

In the later 1950s Holiday's health suffered and her voice deteriorated, yet her direct and emotional approach to her singing and to her songs continued to be mesmerizing. Holiday continued to record and performed powerfully to two sold-out houses at Carnegie Hall in 1956. Another late-career performance that saw her in good form is the television feature "The Sound of Jazz." This wonderful

DOWNLOAD
Track Number 17

"Strange Fruit" (1939) by Billie Holiday with Orchestra

INSTRUMENTATION: Vocal: Billie Holiday; **Trumpet:** Frank Newton; **Saxophones:** Tab Smith, Kenneth Hollon, Stanley Payne; **Piano:** Sonny White; **Guitar:** Jimmy McLin; **Bass:** Johnny Williams; **Drums:** Eddie Dougherty.

LISTENING HIGHLIGHT, FORM: The form of "Strange Fruit," ABC, could almost be called **through composed**—meaning the composition does not rely upon formal repetition of sections in the way, for example, the form AABA does. Still, like most song forms we have seen, there are clear 8-measure sections, each divided into two 4-bar phrases (a 2-measure instrumental fill follows the 1st section). While all three sections are similar—they focus on the key of B-flat minor and its closely related chords—each section has some melodic differences. This version begins with an unusually long introduction. When the vocal starts (1:09) Holiday sings one time through the ABC form of the song.

"Strange Fruit" is a slow ballad, which of course befits the chilling and terrifically disturbing subject matter. The initial part of the introduction, a haunting melody played by a trumpet in cup mute over long notes from the other horns, is played rubato. The rhythm section featuring the piano goes into tempo to continue this long introduction (0:28). When the vocal starts, the bass keeps things moving by playing in an almost plodding 4.

QUESTIONS AND CONTROVERSIES
Billie Holiday and "Strange Fruit"

The lyrics for "Strange Fruit" convey devastating imagery depicting the lynching and burning of African Americans in the South. Billie Holiday is closely associated with the song as her rendition is emotionally striking, powerful, and direct. In fact, her version is so perfect and iconic that it is essentially *her* song; and until recently, the song was often credited to her as songwriter. It was, however, written by Abel Meeropol, a New York City high school teacher, social activist, and writer, who composed it under the pen name Lewis Allan. Until recently, Meeropol was better known for having adopted the orphaned children of Ethel and Julius Rosenberg after their controversial execution for alleged espionage in regard to passing secrets to the Soviet Union about the atomic bomb.

While much of the lyric straightforwardly portrays the horrific images of a lynching and the burning of a human being, the 2nd verse takes a different approach and ironically pairs the notion of a "gallant South" with "the bulging eyes and the twisted mouth" of an innocent victim killed because of the color of their skin.

version of the blues, "Fine and Mellow," gives us the opportunity to see Holiday in fine form and to experience her emotional reconnection with her longtime musical ally, Lester Young. Holiday died a sad death at age 44; as she lay dying in a hospital bed, she suffered the ignominy of her third drug arrest.

Ella Fitzgerald

Ella Fitzgerald (1917–1996) had an incredible set of vocal skills, including a 4-octave range, perfect intonation, a tonal quality that could range from light to husky, and an impeccable sense of rhythm. These qualities place her as one of the great singers of the twentieth century regardless of genre. She was right on top of the beat, always pushing it; and the power of her incredible timing and bright, hard-swinging style cannot be overstated. She swung as hard as, if not harder than, any instrumentalist in jazz; and her scat singing solos were instrumental gems. She also provides a dramatic contrast to Billie Holiday, in terms of both vocal approach and performance style.

Another important element in her style is that she radiated a wonderful and uplifting sense of joy and happiness that could be seen in performance and heard on recordings. Fitzgerald appeared to relish every opportunity to sing, treating each performance as if it was her last, always giving everything she had, physically and emotionally. Through her expression of joyfulness and pleasure, she was attempting to bring us to her blissful, almost ecstatic state by sheer will. You could not help but smile and feel terrific when watching her perform.

Fitzgerald was raised in Yonkers and moved to Harlem to live with her aunt upon the death of her mother. She soon dropped out of school and was essentially taking care of herself by the time of her first big break in 1934, when she won the famous Apollo Theater Amateur night at age 16 in front of a notoriously tough and boisterously vocal crowd. Bandleader-drummer Chick Webb (see Chapter 5,

Ella Fitzgerald performing ca. 1947; Dizzy Gillespie listens while she sings. Among her many talents, Fitzgerald was a pioneer in performing bop-like melodies as a scat singer. Photo by William P. Gottlieb.

Courtesy William P. Gottlieb Collection and Library of Congress.

listening focus

"Oh, Lady Be Good" (1947 version) by Ella Fitzgerald, accompanied by Bob Haggart and His Orchestra

INSTRUMENTATION: Vocal: Ella Fitzgerald; **Trumpets:** Andy Ferretti, Chris Griffin, Bob Peck; **Trombones:** Will Bradley, Jack Satterfield, Fred Ohms; **Baritone sax:** Ernie Caceres; **Piano:** Stan Freeman; **Guitar:** Danny Perri; **Bass and leader:** Bob Haggart; **Drums:** Morey Feld.

LISTENING HIGHLIGHT, MELODY AND HARMONY: This George and Ira Gershwin tune essentially becomes an instrumental feature for Ella. After singing the melody once, she takes off and scats an incredible solo straight through the entire recording. This tune is all about her and her soloing "**chops**"—meaning her musical skills. She soars through this jazz standard.

Fitzgerald's note choices during her scat solo are nothing short of amazing. Vocalists generally have different types of musical elements that they concentrate on, but their primary role is generally to present the melody of a song. Ella, however, is a scat singer almost without peer as she sings "the changes"—singing in such a way that we clearly hear how the note choices soloists make musically relate to the chord progression—with uncanny accuracy, at times even perfectly **arpeggiating** chords (singing the chords in a linear fashion as opposed to vertical). This is one of the many reasons that musicians love her singing. She is one of a small group of singers that we would refer to as a "musicians' musician." A few others are Sarah Vaughn and Carmen McCrae, as well as singers who specialize in scat singing and vocalese singing—the singing and setting of words to instrumentalists' solos—such as Eddie Jefferson, Jon Hendricks, and Kurt Elling (we will examine Elling's "She's Funny That Way," which he sets to a Lester Young solo, in Chapter 15, 3rd Chorus).

2nd Chorus) hired her (and later became her guardian) though she didn't physically fit the typical "songbird" (female vocalist) mold. She was such a hit with audiences that Webb actually tailored the band to feature her.

Though her young voice initially was best suited for light novelty numbers such as her breakout hit "A-Tisket, A-Tasket," Fitzgerald became a wonderfully convincing interpreter of all types of material, though she was never able to hide her ebullience. When bebop (Chapter 10) came to the fore, her marvelous scatting was given free reign, and her scatting set an extremely high standard for jazz vocalists that still stands today.

Throughout her career Fitzgerald recorded with all the greats of jazz. During the 1950s, she was featured with the popular touring "jam session" format presented by producer Norman Granz, Jazz at the Philharmonic. She also recorded a wonderful series of records with Granz, each featuring a composer or lyricist, including George Gershwin, Cole Porter, and Johnny Mercer. Her later career was made difficult by poor health and visual impairment due to diabetes, yet her positive and loving spirit was always present.

2nd Chorus From Jazz to Pop: Nat King Cole and Frank Sinatra

HOW DID SOME VOCALISTS CROSS OVER FROM JAZZ TO BECOME POPULAR MUSIC STARS?

Several major pop singing stars of the 1950s got their start during the swing era. Nat King Cole was a talented pianist who led a popular trio and became a vocal star almost by accident. He originally focused on his piano playing, singing only occasionally; however, once he began singing, he enjoyed great success on the pop charts, taking his jazz style in an entirely new direction. Frank Sinatra began his career singing with big bands, becoming a teen idol in the 1940s. During the 1950s, he transformed himself into a major pop singer, developing a style that highlighted his unique personality as the ultimate macho vocalist.

Nat King Cole

Nat "King" Cole (1919–1965), though not originally a big-band singer, rose to fame during the swing era as a result of his piano artistry and his vocal talent. Like Fitzgerald, his singing, playing, and performing always gave off great warmth and charm. His music, whether playing jazz piano or singing a pop song, always welcomed us in as if we were all good friends getting together to have some fun.

Nat King Cole at the keyboards, ca. 1947. Cole crossed over easily from jazz to pop styles thanks to his relaxed yet swinging vocal style. Photo by William P. Gottlieb.
Courtesy William P. Gottlieb Collection and Library of Congress.

Cole was raised in Chicago and influenced by the city's jazz scene at an early age. He began to lead his own group as a teenager and was first known for his innovative piano trio, the King Cole Trio, with a nonstandard instrumentation of piano, guitar, and bass (the most common piano trio is piano, bass, and drums). This format was then also used by other piano greats including Art Tatum and Oscar Peterson.

Cole was a terrific jazz pianist, and the arrangements for the trio were neat and slick yet felt spontaneous and light. He also sang with the trio, and his smooth, richly warm voice, with its perfect intonation and wonderfully precise yet relaxed and soft-edged swing, gradually came to the fore as the most popular element of the group's work. He sang standards such as "Sweet Lorraine" and "It's Only a Paper Moon," but it was a novelty number he composed, "Straighten Up and Fly Right," and a light blues number, "Route 66," that became hits and made him a star.

While Cole was a leading jazz performer as a pianist, as a singer-pianist he became a hugely successful pop star and was soon placed in orchestral and big-band settings with terrific arrangements, generally written by arrangers such as Billy May and Nelson Riddle from the swing era. Some of these were jazz-oriented, while others were more commercial in nature including the use of thickly layered strings. He also became the first African American to have his own television show, *The Nat King Cole Show*, a variety show on NBC that featured his playing and singing as well as many of the important jazz and pop artists of the day.

Along with Cole's popularity came a change in his material. His later repertoire included beautiful renditions of pop material such as "Mona Lisa," "L-O-V-E," "Smile," "When I Fall In Love," and "Unforgettable," bringing to them an unexpected beauty and seriousness, as well as his jazz sensibilities and instrumental and vocal skills. Cole was also quite involved with Latin music and recorded numerous albums in this style. His first, *Rumba à la King*, was recorded in Cuba and included the great Cuban trumpeter "Chocolate" Armenteros, who went on to a long career in New York City. Cole recorded another album in Cuba, *Cole Español*, this time entirely in Spanish.

Interestingly, it is a common occurrence for jazz artists who cross over to other genres, particularly pop music, to be criticized by jazz musicians, journalists, and critics, often for "selling out." Cole is no exception as many expressed disappointment at his supposed abandonment of his jazz roots. His range of material can be seen, however, as a continuation of the pop-jazz sensibility we see throughout the swing era, carried into the 1950s and 1960s, with songs such as "Ramblin' Rose" (which had a country music flavor), "(I Love You) For Sentimental Reasons," and "Those Lazy-Hazy-Crazy Days of Summer." Cole brought the same musical integrity to everything he did, which led to this long series of hit singles throughout his career. His daughter from his second marriage, Natalie, is also a popular singer; and her clever and lovely duo version of her father's hit "Unforgettable," with Nat Cole's singing edited in posthumously, was a huge hit. A committed smoker—he believed it helped his voice—Cole died at age 45 from lung cancer.

"Straighten Up and Fly Right," composed by Nat King Cole, was one of the King Cole Trio's biggest hits, charting on the Harlem Hit Parade (as the chart was known at the time) and the pop and country charts. Numerous artists from a variety of musical backgrounds have covered the tune. This is an excellent early example of a crossover style that led to Cole becoming one of jazz and popular music's biggest vocal and instrumental stars.

Cole attributed the lyrics to a folk tale that his father, a pastor in Alabama, used for one of his sermons. Like many African American folktales, the story

listening focus

"Straighten Up and Fly Right" (1943) by the King Cole Trio

INSTRUMENTATION: Piano, vocal, and leader: Nat King Cole; **Guitar:** Oscar Moore; **Bass:** Johnny Miller.

LISTENING HIGHLIGHT, RHYTHM: As a trio without drums, the King Cole Trio had a unique sound that required a different approach to playing. Since drums are not keeping time, it is up to the other players to create the time and the swing for the group. Notice that we don't miss the drums at all. It's also interesting to note that the guitarist doesn't feel it necessary to play on all 4 beats, as was common in swing big bands.

Since guitar and piano both have "comping" roles, it is challenging for them not to conflict with each other. Both Cole and Oscar Moore leave plenty of space for each other, which contributes to the light and airy feel that the group gets. This openness along with playing melodic lines together and in harmony throughout their arrangements are significant elements of the group's style.

hinges on a trickster figure—here the monkey protagonist—who seems to be taken in by the wily buzzard but actually outsmarts his opponent. Mixing the folk tale with African American slang, along with a terrific vocal delivery and slick musical arrangement, makes this an entertaining and musically rewarding song. This approach to jazz as entertainment takes us back to the joyous performances of Fats Waller (see Chapter 5, 4th Chorus) and ahead to other jazz performers who used humor so effectively during their performances, such as saxophonist James Moody and trumpeters Dizzy Gillespie and Clark Terry.

Frank Sinatra

Frank Sinatra (1915–1998) was one of the biggest vocal stars of the swing era. He went on to a long career as the standard-bearer of American popular song and its presentation through the medium of the big band. In his early career, Sinatra was a heartthrob. He had a romantic vocal delivery and slender, almost vulnerable little-boy good looks; and women screamed, sobbed, and swooned for him like they did for the Beatles in the 1960s. But he also had a masculine side to him—in later years it would be better characterized as a macho swagger—that appealed to men as well.

Influenced by Bing Crosby, Sinatra was initially primarily known for his smooth, lush voice and his emotion-laden performance of romantic ballads. As his career progressed, his command of phrasing, including long-lined phrases that required great breath control, came to set the standard for swinging a melody. His voice became deeper, stronger, and edgier; and he became a powerful, assured, and charismatic singer and performer.

Sinatra carefully crafted his vocals to present the meaning and intent of the lyric as effectively and directly as possible. His extensive early big-band background and studious approach to singing paid great dividends as Sinatra always cannily planned his phrasing to move with—and accentuate—crucial elements in

JAZZ LIVES **FRANK SINATRA**

Born in Hoboken, New Jersey, Sinatra's early singing career began with the Harry James Orchestra. He went on to great acclaim as the featured vocalist with Tommy Dorsey (Chapter 7, 2nd Chorus) and then began a storied solo career. After World War II, his career briefly declined as a result of several factors, including the changing musical tastes of young listeners, his lack of participation in the war effort, and negative reactions by the public regarding his romantic and personal life. In the early 1950s, he quickly revived his singing career while also expanding his forays into acting, including his 1953 Academy Award–winning performance in the movie *From Here to Eternity*, which relaunched his career. Sinatra continued to star in movies, including serious dramatic films; musicals such as *Pal Joey*, *Guys and Dolls*, and *On the Town*; and lighter fare such as the original *Oceans 11*.

Also in the 1950s, Sinatra began a series of LPs in collaboration with a number of top arrangers, such as Billy May, Alex Stordahl, and Don Costa. Sinatra had a particularly close and long relationship with Nelson Riddle, who often showcased Sinatra in a lush yet swinging sound that included strings and woodwinds in addition to a standard big band, bringing him full circle back to his work with the Tommy Dorsey band (we heard Dorsey's band with strings in Chapter 7, 2nd Chorus). Working with these arrangers, Sinatra also was an early artist to create **concept albums**, such as his favorite record, 1958's *Only the Lonely*, a remarkably lovely and moving collection of ballads arranged by Riddle. "Come Dance with Me," from an album of the same name, showcases his relationship with Billy May, who arranged and conducted the entire album.

During the later 1950s and early 1960s, Sinatra's persona took on a larger-than-life, rough, and blustery aspect and his antics as the de facto leader of the "Rat Pack," a group of stars that included Sammy Davis, Jr., and Dean Martin, sensationalized a Las Vegas–type lifestyle of drinking, gambling, brawling, and, of course, singing in the top Las Vegas venues. Rumors of his association with leading members of the Mafia were rampant in this era and continued to plague Sinatra over the years. From the mid- to late 1960s, he returned to the pop charts with songs like "Strangers in the Night" and the anthemic "My Way."

Although he announced his retirement in 1971, Sinatra was back to performing by the mid-1970s, becoming a fixture on the American entertainment scene. Late career successes include his hit recording of "New York, New York" in 1980 and his early 1990s albums *Duets* and *Duets II*, which paired Sinatra with a long list of pop singers from many styles, such as Aretha Franklin, Barbara Streisand, Tony Bennett, Stevie Wonder, Willie Nelson, and Neil Diamond. Sinatra died in 1998 following a series of heart attacks.

Frank Sinatra recording for Columbia Records, ca. 1947. Sinatra was a great master of the microphone, using it to develop his smooth, lush style. Photo by William P. Gottlieb.
Courtesy William P. Gottlieb Collection and Library of Congress.

IN PERFORMANCE
Swing Musicians in the Hollywood Recording Studios

This chapter concludes with swing music from the 1950s and 1960s, a time when few touring big bands were regularly on the road. Once that work dried up, many of the big-band players happily moved to Hollywood where film, television, and sound recording studios offered steady work and lucrative incomes. New York City studios also provided steady work for players. Things have changed, of course, as many films and television shows are now created and recorded by one person with a few assistants using computer-based systems. But back then recordings were often done in large studios with large groups of musicians, many of whom had spent their earlier careers on the road with big bands.

These players were eminently qualified for all types of work as their chops were in great shape from playing on the road continually, they had terrific ensemble skills (see "In Performance: Side Musicians" in Chapter 7, 1st Chorus), and they could generally **sight-read** music extremely well—meaning they could read their part correctly the first time they saw

a chart. Also, it was the arrangers from the big bands who were doing the orchestrations, so these were the perfect players to have on any session. A typical recording session of, for example, ten tunes for a singer such as Frank Sinatra or Nat King Cole might entail one rehearsal and then one or two recording sessions where all songs would be recorded in two or three takes. To put that in context, many contemporary pop albums take months or even a year or longer to record.

Large recording sessions were live, collaborative efforts between the vocalist or instrumentalist, an engineer, a producer, and up to perhaps forty musicians all in the same room recording with no overdubs. All were sharp and expected to take care of their jobs in a professional manner, and singers such as Sinatra and Cole were more on top of these sessions than anyone. These studios and sessions produced music that did not create the naturalness of a live performance but is a close second with its own kind of spontaneity.

the outstanding arrangements that his writers provided for him. He had no peer in this regard. In addition, throughout his career he always took care to give his arrangers credit during performances, a very unusual custom. His close relationship with his arrangers, as well as his appreciation of their work, helps to highlight the importance of the arranger to the success of musical stars such as Sinatra, Cole, and Fitzgerald.

Sinatra epitomizes the junction of pop and jazz and consequently exemplifies the confusion that surrounds labeling. He never spoke of himself as a jazz singer, yet, even with popular material, he generally performed in jazz-oriented contexts with big bands, including, for example, recording one of the hardest-swinging live vocal albums ever, *Sinatra at the Sands*, backed by a stellar and smoking Count Basie Orchestra conducted by Quincy Jones.

Jazz players and singers clearly influenced Sinatra, and the reverse is true as well because numerous jazz artists, from Louis Armstrong to Miles Davis, have extolled his virtues and his influence upon them. So while much of his material was firmly in the pop vein, as was true for Nat King Cole, his work and his acclaimed musical arrangements always reflected his jazz background.

"Come Dance with Me" (1959) by Frank Sinatra with Billy May and His Orchestra

INSTRUMENTATION: Vocal and leader: Frank Sinatra; **Conductor and arranger:** Billy May.

LISTENING HIGHLIGHT, STYLE: "Come Dance with Me" shows Sinatra at his peak. He displays his relaxed and romantic side during the 1st chorus (0:07-1:04) and a bit more of the powerhouse swinger in the 2nd chorus (1:14). His voice is confident, rich, and full with a little bit of gritty edge; and he is in complete control of his phrasing as well as his relationship with the band and the arrangement. His swinging style here is crisp and mostly on top of the beat, an approach that helps to propel the band.

In regard to the lyrics, Sinatra at first presents himself in a bit of an innocent, flirtatious manner as he asks a woman to join him on the dance floor: "Come on and dance with me/romance with me on a crowded floor." At the same time, his vocal style and tonal quality display a confident and muscle-bound swagger that doesn't expect to be denied.

Billy May's arranging for his band emphasizes crisp and powerful brass lines in the introduction, between Sinatra's vocal lines, in the short musical interlude (1:05), and in the powerful ending (2:05). Underneath Sinatra's vocal the saxes bubble along more gently, keeping things moving. The setting of this tune is a perfect example of the marriage of pop and swing styles that continues to show the influence of the swing era.

Listening to "Come Dance with Me" raises some interesting questions about the differences between pop and jazz. While there isn't necessarily a reason to try and differentiate, some issues are interesting and important to notice. In "Come Dance with Me" two things stand out: there are no solos in this recording and the instrumental interlude is quite short. In other words, this recording features the vocal performance above all else, which is much more common in pop music than in jazz, even in regard to jazz vocal performances. For example, a Billy Holiday recording might very well feature Lester Young's soloing and background playing as much as it does Holiday's vocal. But the arrangement of "Come Dance with Me" certainly reflects a big-band jazz perspective in support of a star popular vocalist.

3rd Chorus Louis Jordan and Dinah Washington

Louis Jordan

Two artists who are difficult to categorize and consequently often get lost in the shuffle of jazz history are saxophonist-vocalist-bandleader Louis Jordan (1908–1975) and vocalist Dinah Washington (1924–1963). Jordan is a fascinating combination of the soloists and vocalists examined in this unit so far. Like Nat King Cole, he is an instrumentalist and vocalist; but Jordan brings a heavy dose of rhythm and blues to his jazz and popular music approach, and he was a terrific all-around entertainer. Jordan, like Sinatra, was a Las Vegas mainstay. His combination of energetic rhythm and blues, blues, jazz, and pop made him a huge mainstream star.

Louis Jordan (right, with saxophone) and His Tympany Five, ca. 1946–1948. Jordan's swinging ensemble and humorous songs forecast the coming R&B explosion of the 1950s. Photo by William P. Gottlieb.
Courtesy William P. Gottlieb Collection and Library of Congress.

In contrast to Cole, Jordan's instrumental work and his 3-horn front line (Jordan's alto sax, trumpet, and tenor sax) were featured on his records, with his vocals as an additional element that appealed to a broader pop audience. "Choo Choo Ch' Boogie," a huge hit for Louis Jordan and His Tympany Five, is a fun example of his work. It is a jump blues novelty number with a boogie-woogie feel in the rhythm section, simple riffs by the horns, and a Jordan vocal. We also get to hear Jordan's alto sax soloing in a rhythm-and-blues style. A few other top sax players who have brilliantly bridged this R&B–jazz gap are King Curtis, Arnett Cobb, and Eddie "Cleanhead" Vinson. This type of sound and approach has been influential and can be heard in the sound of 1960s players such as Junior Walker and contemporary pop and R&B sax players David Sanborn and Lenny Pickett (the saxophonist and bandleader of NBC's *Saturday Night Live* TV show).

Dinah Washington

Dinah Washington was a terrific blues singer—one of the very best—and a wonderful jazz singer. But much of her popularity came from her crossover, or popular, hits, such as "What a Diff'rence a Day Makes." This effective recording features a syrupy string and chorus background throughout, yet Washington's full yet somewhat nasal sound with its fast vibrato is unmistakable and poignant. Her success performing popular material, however, should not overshadow or devalue her work as a blues and jazz singer. Her work, for example, with trumpeters

Clifford Brown and Clark Terry and saxophonist Cannonball Adderley is a powerful testament to her jazz artistry, while also managing to keep her deep blues feeling ever-present.

CODA   Chapter Summary

Who Were Key Jazz Vocalists During the Swing Era?

- Billie Holiday's wonderful rhythmic phrasing and emotional directness immediately stand out; and her fragile, gentle, and slightly nasal voice with its limited range has an incredible vulnerability that is heart-wrenching.
- Ella Fitzgerald possessed an extraordinary set of vocal skills, including a 4-octave range, perfect intonation, a tonal quality that could range from light to husky, and an impeccable sense of rhythm. Her more sunny tone and approach contrasts with Billie Holiday's darker sound.

How Did Some Vocalists Cross Over from Jazz to Become Popular Music Stars?

- Nat King Cole's singing, playing, and performing always gave off great warmth and charm. His recordings of pop songs like "Unforgettable" made him a major star in the 1950s, one of the few black artists to have his own show on main-stream television.
- Frank Sinatra transformed himself from a big-band singer and teen idol into a highly successful recording artist and actor. In the 1950s to early 1960s, he came to embody the ultimate swinging vocalist.
- Louis Jordan helped create small-combo R&B through his often humorous recordings.
- Dinah Washington was a terrific blues singer and a wonderful jazz singer. But much of her popularity came from her crossover, popular hits, such as "What a Diff'rence a Day Makes."

Talkin' Jazz (Key Terms)

Arpeggiating	Chops	Sight-read
Cabaret card	Concept albums	Through composed

Key People

Billie Holiday	Nat "King" Cole	Louis Jordan
Ella Fitzgerald	Frank Sinatra	Dinah Washington

Think About This (For Further Discussion and Study)

1. Discuss the importance of vocalists during the swing era.
2. Discuss the differences and similarities between the styles of Billie Holiday and Ella Fitzgerald.
3. Discuss the differences and similarities between the styles of Frank Sinatra and Nat King Cole.
4. Discuss the differences and similarities between the accompaniments for the four songs discussed in the 1st and 2nd Choruses.
5. What are the reasons that some of the vocalists discussed in this chapter were able to successfully cross over from jazz to become popular music stars? What crossover vocalists can you think of in contemporary music?

Look It Up (Key Resources)

Chilton, John. *Let the Good Times Roll: The Story of Louis Jordan and His Music.* Ann Arbor, MI: University of Michigan Press, 1994.

Clarke, Donald. *Wishing on the Moon: The Life and Times of Billie Holiday.* New York: Viking Press, 1994.

Cohodas, Nadine. *Queen: The Life and Music of Dinah Washington.* New York: Pantheon, 2004.

Epstein, Daniel Mark. *Nat King Cole.* Boston: Northeastern University Press, 1999.

Friedwald, Will. *Jazz Singing: America's Great Voices from Bessie Smith to Bebop and Beyond.* New York: Da Capo Press, 1990.

———. *Sinatra! The Song Is You—A Singer's Art.* New York: Da Capo Press, 1995.

Gourse, Leslie, ed. *The Billie Holiday Companion: Seven Decades of Commentary.* New York: Schirmer, 1990.

Holiday, Billie. *Lady Sings the Blues.* With William Duffy. London: Abacus, 1975.

O'Mealy, Robert. *Lady Day: The Many Faces of Billie Holiday.* New York: Da Capo Press, 1991.

Petkov, Steven, and Leonard Mustazza, eds. *The Frank Sinatra Reader.* New York: Oxford University Press, 1997.

Ramsey, Guthrie. *Race Music: Black Cultures from Bebop to Hip-Hop.* Berkeley and Los Angeles: University of California Press, 2003.

BEBOP AND BEYOND | 1940s

10

WHAT IS BEBOP?

Bebop developed in the early and mid-1940s, primarily among younger African American musicians. Already veterans of swing-era dance bands, they favored smaller groups such as a quintet that allowed for more solo improvisation than the highly regimented music of the big bands. Meeting for jam sessions in off-hour clubs, these musicians were also interested in exploring twentieth-century developments in areas such as classical composition and Latin music styles. They were particularly focused on the expansion of traditional notions of melody, rhythm, and harmony and worked to transform not only the musical vocabulary of jazz but also the role of each instrumentalist within the jazz ensemble. The repercussions of their explorations are still felt in jazz today.

Bebop was a wildly exciting music that challenged many aspects of jazz as well as the technical capabilities of instrumentalists. The music was also challenging from the audience's point of view. The melodies are quirky and technically demanding, particularly considering that the tempos were sometimes taken at breakneck speed. The solos often consist of a flurry of rapid notes and have a greater detachment from the actual melody of a song than was true in the swing era. Some audiences and musicians thought the music was too technical and didn't swing, and there was some initial controversy among musicians, critics, and audiences surrounding this music. In fact, even the notion of swing itself was changing from the typical big-band swing feel, becoming a bit subtler in bebop yet just as hard-driving.

The music was still commercially based, but perhaps the most important change was that this was no longer primarily music for dancing. Certainly, in some ballrooms and clubs people danced to bebop; but at the really fast tempos, who could dance? This music was primarily created for listening. It was born in the nightclubs, and this is where it lived, with forays into the concert hall as well.

In this chapter, we'll answer these questions:

- What Is Bebop?

- Why Are Charlie Parker and Dizzy Gillespie Considered the Prime Movers Behind the Bebop Movement?

- How Did Thelonious Monk and Bud Powell Create a New Role for Pianists in Bebop Music?

- What Role Did Big Bands Play in the Bebop Era?

Photo: Courtesy William P. Gottlieb Collection and Library of Congress.

1st Chorus Bird and Diz

WHY ARE CHARLIE PARKER AND DIZZY GILLESPIE CONSIDERED THE PRIME MOVERS BEHIND THE BEBOP MOVEMENT?

There were numerous musicians who contributed to the creation of this new style, such as alto saxophonist Charlie Parker, trumpeter John Birks "Dizzy" Gillespie, pianists Thelonious Monk and Earl "Bud" Powell, and drummers Kenny "Klook" Clarke and Max Roach. However, Parker (nicknamed "Yardbird," or simply "Bird") and Gillespie were the leaders of the movement; and it is their names that are most associated with bebop.

Charlie Parker

Alto saxophonist Charlie Parker (1920–1955) had an extraordinary melodic gift and regularly created solos that consisted of long-lined melodies, each of which was an elegant improvised composition unto itself. As we listen today, these gorgeous melodies seem to effortlessly flow out of his horn, and each has a rhythmic grace that seems almost casual yet also swings very hard. His playing feels natural and unstudied, yet the skill was hard-won through years of diligent practice and constant work. Building on the legacy of Coleman Hawkins and Lester Young, Bird profoundly influenced all jazz musicians who followed him.

While Parker's drive and determination are obvious in his astonishing musical accomplishments, he was a larger-than-life person with a self-destructive dark side that created a life very much on the fringe. Drug and alcohol dependence were a constant in his life, not only cutting it short but also seriously affecting his productivity and ability to function, both in music and in society. He was generally broke, he didn't show up for work at times and would even pawn his horn, and he was unreliable with friends and colleagues and in his relationships.

IN PERFORMANCE
Bebop Changes the Role of the Rhythm Section

The role of the rhythm section went through a huge revolution as bebop was created. The individual instrument's roles—for piano, guitar, bass, and drums—became more delineated and separated. The piano no longer had to supply both bass notes and chords as it did with ragtime or stride. Though it was not a new concept, the pianists, such as Thelonious Monk and Bud Powell, began to perfect the art of comping, laying down the harmonic foundation in a variety of ways, such as crisp rhythmic figures and more leisurely held chords. The bass, exemplified by Oscar Pettiford's playing, largely played in 4, essentially became the most important timekeeper. The

drums—in the hands of Kenny "Klook" Clarke, Max Roach, and Roy Haynes—also propelled the band but no longer by simply playing all 4 beats on the bass drum as was common up until bebop. The **ride cymbal** became a constant but lighter and more varied pulse, and the snare and bass drums were then used to play accents that would highlight the soloists or parts of the drummer's ride cymbal pattern. Hitting the bass drum accents was called **dropping bombs**. The beboppers set a new standard for the jazz rhythm section with a more open and loose rhythmic feel, and their influence is still prominent in contemporary jazz.

JAZZ LIVES CHARLIE PARKER

Charles Parker, Jr., was born on August 29, 1920, in the musical hotbed of Kansas City. He began his career as a seemingly no-talent saxophonist who suffered numerous musical embarrassments, but he persisted. Parker practiced incessantly, went on the road with territory bands, and eventually worked his way up to a chair in the prestigious territory band the Jay McShann Orchestra in 1938. In the spirit of this band and of Kansas City, Bird had a tremendous feel for the blues, eventually developing an extremely sophisticated approach to the genre.

Bird moved to New York City in 1939, where he initially washed dishes at a restaurant in Harlem and immersed himself in the musical life around him. Within a year, he returned to Kansas City to play with McShann's band again; but the relationship soured as a result of Parker's substance abuse, and Parker was fired and went back to New York.

Bird met Dizzy Gillespie in the early 1940s, and the two went on to become the faces of bebop, though for very different reasons and with very different approaches to business and to life in general. They joined Earl Hines's big band in 1942, and later both joined Billy Eckstine's big band, with Gillespie as musical director. Eckstine, formerly a vocalist with Earl Hines's big band, was one of the first to incorporate the new sound of bebop into a big-band context.

Parker and Gillespie worked together on and off until 1945. They took New York bebop to the West Coast for the first time for a tempestuous tour. When Gillespie returned home, Parker stayed, even more deeply affected by his substance abuse, and wound up committed to a state hospital. Bird returned to New York in the late 1940s, where he continued to work and record, including some of his most important material. Producer Norman Granz arranged for Parker to record an album with a string section accompaniment in 1949, fulfilling Parker's desire to record in a more classical idiom (see "In Performance: Jazz and Strings"). Parker, however, was in a steady physical decline as a result of his continued substance abuse. He died with a ravaged body at age 34.

Tommy Potter (bass), Charlie Parker, and Miles Davis (trumpet) at New York's Three Deuces, ca. 1947. Parker helped launch bop music along with Dizzy Gillespie, and his saxophone style was widely imitated for decades to come. Photo by William P. Gottlieb.

Courtesy William P. Gottlieb Collection and Library of Congress.

read all about it

To Be or Not . . . To Bop, by Dizzy Gillespie

Walser, *Keeping Time,* *Chapter 32*

In this excerpt from his autobiography, Gillespie addresses several common misperceptions about bebop and tries to set the record straight about the seriousness of the musical style.

Dizzy Gillespie

Dizzy Gillespie (1917–1993) was another crucial figure in the world of bebop and the next great trumpet virtuoso after Roy Eldridge (Chapter 5, 3rd Chorus). His playing style is unmistakable, and Gillespie's exciting and flashy style complemented Parker's melodic inventiveness, making them a remarkable combination that set the bar extremely high for anyone aspiring to play bebop from the outset.

Gillespie's style is marked by an astonishing fleetness and a tremendous range, often sending his solos into the stratosphere of the trumpet's upper register with flurries of high notes, while always remaining musically interesting. Gillespie, in contrast to Parker, was also an outgoing performer who created a wonderful, witty, and sharp-tongued rapport with his audience. His sense of personal style also distinguished him. For example, he played a trumpet with a bell bent upward, his cheeks puffed out enormously as he played, and he was often characterized with a cool, "hip" look, wearing a beret and big glasses and sporting a goatee. These were all part of his tremendous appeal.

While known for his antics, Gillespie was extremely thoughtful and professional in his approach to music, performance, and business. He brought a studious pianist's sensibility to bebop, helping to expand the harmonic language of jazz while also imparting his knowledge and concepts to his colleagues. In addition, he carefully cultivated an image and connected with the public as the face of bebop, while also slyly poking fun at the establishment along the way.

QUESTIONS AND CONTROVERSIES
Race and Economics in the Birth of Bebop

Speaking of the young bebop pioneers, Scott DeVeaux, in his book *The Birth of Bebop: A Social and Musical History*, discusses the birth of bebop as a reaction to racial and economic inequality. He gives several reasons why these musicians turned away from the more commercial swing styles to experiment with this new music.

- The swing era represented an important milestone for black musicians as it provided steady work for many. DeVeaux states, "As a class of skilled professionals who had proved their worth in open competition with their white counterparts, [African American] musicians were uniquely positioned to further the cause of black social and economic progress." This led many more to enter the business in order to attain "a level of material gain, social freedom, and respect from white America that could not even have been imagined a few decades earlier" (DeVeaux 1997, 27).

- The music business radically changed in the 1940s, however, when a downturn in the economy and the decline of the swing era itself led to fewer jobs and more competition for musicians all around. In DeVeaux's words, "the underlying inequities of race were felt with renewed force" (DeVeaux 1997, 27), as segregation, both in the music business and in society in general, gave an advantage to white musicians.

- Young black musicians—frustrated by both the racial and economic inequalities experienced in relation to both white musicians and older, better-connected African American players—reacted to this new reality by creating a new "space" for themselves. They created bebop, a new and revolutionary musical genre that focused on the virtuosic improvising soloist.

- These younger players were not as set in their musical ways and were more open to incorporating developments in other musical styles into jazz.

- The format of the jam session encouraged individual expression and experimentation over the fixed arrangements of commercial jazz.

This, in combination with these young players' musical aspirations, was the launching point for this foundationally important musical style.

JAZZ LIVES DIZZY GILLESPIE

From Cheraw, South Carolina, John Birks Gillespie was a precocious musician. His father was a bandleader, so the young Gillespie had access to a number of instruments and began to experiment on the piano when he was just 4 years old. By age 12, he was playing both trumpet and trombone and soon after received a scholarship to the Laurinburg Institute in North Carolina to play in their band. He then followed his family to Philadelphia, playing in local bands, and eventually reached New York by the mid-1930s. His excellent playing and overall musicianship helped him get early jobs with Teddy Hill's and Edgar Hayes's bands. Gillespie then hit the big time with Cab Calloway's popular big band in 1939 (Chapter 5, 2nd Chorus). While Calloway treated the band very well and provided an excellent model as an entertainer, Gillespie, as was true for many other young musicians, was ambitious beyond the confines of the big band.

After being fired by Calloway for his typically "dizzy" antics (this final time he was falsely accused, however), Gillespie went on to freelance in New York City, as well as be a leader in the musical movement leading toward bebop. He led the first bebop quintet at Kelly's Stables on New York's 52nd Street in 1943 with personnel that included bebop innovators Oscar Pettiford (bass) and Max Roach (drums), as well as Don Byas on tenor sax and George Wallington on piano. That same year, he joined Earl Hines's big band, where he first worked with Charlie Parker. The two moved soon after to Billy Eckstine's band.

In 1945–1946, Gillespie and Parker teamed up to create the signature front line of bebop. Their small-group recordings not only introduced the bebop style but established several pieces as standards, including Gillespie's "Salt Peanuts" and "Groovin' High."

After they broke up, Gillespie started his own big band, which was successful through 1950. The charts were exciting, and the band had an intensity coupled with a fun looseness. Gillespie also incorporated his interest in Afro-Cuban music into this band (see "Mario Bauzá").

An important element in Gillespie's presentation was his showmanship—he was fun, funny, lively, and engaging as he played, led the band, and danced across the stage. His humor could also be irreverent with a slight satirical edge in such a way that you were not always sure if he was laughing with you or at you.

Later in his career Gillespie led the life of an elder statesman of jazz, performing predominantly with small groups. He continued to be the face of bebop but also was a leading international jazz figure until his death in 1993.

Dizzy Gillespie, in his trademark beret and black plastic glasses, ca. 1947. A colorful performer, Gillespie came to embody the image of a bebopper in the public's mind. Photo by William P. Gottlieb.
Courtesy William P. Gottlieb Collection and Library of Congress.

After his early partnership with Dizzy Gillespie, Charlie Parker went on to become a bandleader and solo artist. As is true for most jazz musicians, Parker had a wide-ranging taste in music. This included a love of classical music, and along with this came a desire to play with strings. The *Charlie Parker with Strings* sessions gave him this opportunity. These recordings give us a chance to hear his uncanny melodic sensibilities, both in his ability to play written melodies gorgeously and in his lovely lyrical improvising. They were the best-selling recordings released by Parker in his lifetime and present Bird in a more "commercial" setting accompanied by a jazz rhythm section and a small string section. The strings, plus oboe and harp, add a "sweetness" to these recordings.

Mario Bauzá

Dizzy Gillespie is a premier example of a jazz artist who was extremely influenced by Latin music. Gillespie was first exposed to Cuban music and its rhythms by trumpeter Mario Bauzá (1911–1993). The two first worked together in Chick Webb's orchestra and then in Cab Calloway's band (both discussed in Chapter 5, 2nd Chorus). Gillespie's experience with Bauzá, combined with his frustration with what he perceived as the rhythmic limitations of jazz, led him to experiment with combining the two idioms in his short-lived but extremely exciting big band. This style came to be known as **cubop**, a fusion of Afro-Cuban music and bebop, an early form of Latin jazz. Bauzá introduced Gillespie to master Cuban percussionist Chano Pozo, whose brilliant and intensely energetic conga playing infused Gillespie's music with an authentic Cuban feel. Gillespie featured Pozo in 1947 concerts at Carnegie Hall and New York's Town Hall.

IN PERFORMANCE
Jam Sessions' Role in the Development of Bebop

Musicians working in the big bands had limited opportunity to build on their solo skills. Their solo slots were short, and they had to play essentially the same solo night after night. As a result, after work, when back in town from a tour, or at times when there was no work, players often congregated to try new things and to "stretch out" in **jam sessions**. These sessions were informal (in someone's house or apartment) or a bit more formal (in a nightclub), but players could play extended solos and try more experimental styles that were not appropriate for the big-band setting. These sessions also often functioned as cutting contests, a time for some serious competition between players. Bebop developed in this atmosphere of free experimentation among musicians, and two places that were particularly important in this regard were Minton's Playhouse and Monroe's Uptown House, both in Harlem.

Young players, more established veterans, players interested in new approaches, and others who were curious but cautious about new trends all came to these clubs to listen and play. These were places to learn and develop among your peers. Out of these settings, including jam sessions, and through the concentrated work of important musicians, many of them quite young, along with some open-minded veterans, came bebop, a new and extremely influential jazz style. After being formed in the jam sessions at places like Minton's, the music, fully formed, moved to 52nd Street, "Swing Street," in New York City in the later 1940s.

listening guide

DOWNLOAD
Track Number 18

"Salt Peanuts" (1953) by Charlie Parker and Dizzy Gillespie

INSTRUMENTATION: Alto saxophone: Charlie "Yardbird" Parker; **Trumpet and composer:** John Birks "Dizzy" Gillespie; **Piano:** Bud Powell; **Bass:** Charles Mingus; **Drums:** Max Roach.

OVERVIEW: This recording lets us hear the biggest innovators and stars of bebop. It features the two most prominent faces of the style, Charlie Parker and Dizzy Gillespie; but Max Roach and Bud Powell were also instrumental in the creation of this new style, and all of the players here went on to be amongst the most important instrumentalists and band leaders in jazz. The fact that this was a live performance from Massey Hall in Toronto allows us to hear this music as it was performed, as opposed to the shorter versions we hear on studio recordings. As is true for many live recordings, however, the recording quality is not as good as we would like. However, as opposed to some other live recordings, the drums are strong, so we can clearly hear the new style of drumming, especially when Roach "drops bombs" on his bass drum.

FORM: "Salt Peanuts" is a classic bebop tune by Gillespie. It is based on "rhythm changes," the chord progression for George Gershwin's "I Got Rhythm," and is consequently AABA. Also, the name of the tune and the lyrics are fun and silly, both elements of Dizzy's on-stage persona.

STYLE: The playing is fast and furious, and the players are all virtuosos. Dizzy and Bird's solo styles are different from each other, of course, as their instruments have different challenges and advantages; but their styles are also quite complementary, making them the original and ultimate front line for a bebop band. Their level of playing and excitement are so well matched that they complement and challenge each other.

The soloing style of bebop is often a rapid and steady stream of 1/8 notes. Of course, there are breaks where the player has to breathe; and they also vary the rhythms they play for much needed variety. Bird's playing is fast and furious, yet it is the beauty of his nonstop melodic invention that makes him stand out among all players of any era. The fact that he was able to do this at these speeds is remarkable and set a new standard that still stands today. Dizzy's style was so unique that most trumpet players were not able to follow his lead. His fearlessness and his ability to play extremely fast all over the horn, including way up into its upper register, display how heavily he was influenced by Roy Eldridge (Chapter 5, 3rd Chorus). This solo shows Dizzy at the top of his form, a level that few were, or are, able to match. In this solo, while largely playing lines of steady 1/8 notes, he breaks it up regularly with a variety of rhythmic figures.

While this is a small group and a new style, the band still employs ensembles and an arrangement reminiscent of a big-band chart. Both Dizzy and Bird are big-band veterans, so this makes sense.

MELODY AND HARMONY: "Salt Peanuts" has a quick and active melody, which is very much in the new bebop style. The bridge (the B section of the AABA tune), while using standard chord changes, emphasizes colorful notes of the chords, sometimes referred to as extensions of the chords, as well as blue notes.

continued

RHYTHM: The typical bebop tune is taken at a fast tempo, and "Salt Peanuts" is no exception. This is, of course, challenging for all instruments; but it is the rhythm section (piano, bass, and drums) that is responsible for keeping the time. In much of what we have heard before bebop the instruments in the rhythm section emphasized all 4 beats of a bar, but in this style each instrument has its own role (see "In Performance: Bebop Changes the Role of the Rhythm Section").

ACCOMPANIMENT: As discussed regarding the rhythm section, bebop created a new way to accompany soloists. The piano "comps," the bass "walks" (playing in 4), and the drums play a freer cymbal pattern that becomes more important than in earlier styles while accenting, on the snare and bass drum, important parts of melodic figures and other elements of players' solos.

"SALT PEANUTS" LISTENING GUIDE

TIME	FORM	STYLE	MELODY AND HARMONY	RHYTHM	ACCOMPANIMENT
0:00	Intro		After the drums start the tune, the horns play an introduction.	The tune is taken at a very fast tempo. This is typical for bebop and one of its challenges.	The drummer begins the tune alone on the hi-hat and then moves around the kit before the horns come in.
0:12	1st chorus	The melody uses octaves, creating a jumpy, almost comic feel. The bridge has leaping lines that are difficult to play, which is characteristic of bebop.	The melody is played by the trumpet (Dizzy) and alto sax (Bird). The sections go by very fast! If you want to follow the 8-bar phrases, you have to count in 2. The B section is at 0:24 and the last A, at 0:30.		Max Roach regularly "drops bombs" on his bass drum as accompaniment.
0:36	Interlude	This short ensemble uses bebop figures that also are reminiscent of a swing style but faster.	In between choruses is a fast ensemble unison figure for 8 measures.		
0:42	2nd chorus	Instead of playing the melody Bird solos fluently with controlled abandon over the bridge (0:55).	Bird on alto sax plays part of the melody on the A section, while Dizzy sings the second phrase using his fun and silly lyrics.		The accompaniment is simpler in the A section and more full for the bridge.
1:08	3rd chorus	Bird is playing on a borrowed plastic alto saxophone.	Bird begins slowly but then plays fast and furious, often a steady stream of 1/8 notes, but also breaks it up with rests (he has to breathe!) and a variety of rhythmic figures.		The solo sections that follow give us a chance to hear how the rhythm section accompanies a soloist. Unfortunately, the bass is not as clear as we would like.
1:33	4th chorus		Bird's solo continues. His playing is extremely melodic and fluid.		Powell is at times unsure of the form throughout this tune but everyone adjusts or keeps him in line.

"Salt Peanuts" listening guide continued

TIME	FORM	STYLE	MELODY AND HARMONY	RHYTHM	ACCOMPANIMENT
1:59	5th chorus		Bird continues and is now playing his 3rd chorus and sounding as if he is just getting warmed up and could go on forever.		
2:25	Interlude		Bird's solo ends with a brief interlude. He and Dizzy aren't together on this.	Roach accents beats 2 and 4 during the ensemble on his bass drum.	
2:31	6th chorus	While Bird had other trumpet players, such as the young Miles Davis, no one could quite match Dizzy. Howard McGee, however, is another terrific early bebopper.	Dizzy begins his solo. He plays effectively in all parts of his horn and displays confidence and fearlessness in his playing throughout his solo.		
2:57	7th chorus		Dizzy's solo continues. Like Bird, his solo is often a stream of 1/8 notes but he breaks it up regularly with other rhythmic figures. He ends the last A (3:16) with a repeated melody in the upper register		
3:24	8th chorus		Dizzy's solo continues.		
3:49	Interlude		The band plays a short interlude.		The rhythm section accents the interlude's rhythmic figures.
3:56	9th chorus		Powell plays a piano solo and brings a horn player's sensibility to his playing. Like Bird and Dizzy he plays a steady stream of 1/8 notes while breaking it up regularly with a variety of rhythmic phrases.	The piano solo calms the mood down a bit and shifts the timbre from horns to the rhythm section for variety. His playing is swift, fleet, and assured, even at this tempo.	During the piano solo, notice how Powell comps behind himself, and he does so in a variety of ways. Also, listen to Roach's playing on his cymbal, which is typical of the style, as well as his "bombs" on the bass drum.
4:20	10th chorus		Powell's solo continues.		
4:46	11th chorus		Powell's solo continues.		
5:11	12th chorus		Powell's solo continues.		
5:36	13th chorus	Roach plays an extended and virtuosic drum solo.		Roach gets a drum solo to end the tune and he makes the most of it by playing a huge variety of styles throughout.	
7:18		The tune ends with the band taking the tune out using the introduction of the song.			The rhythm section accents the rhythmic figures of the horn lines.

continued

Compare

Parker's "Mood" (1948), a slow blues, contrasts with "Salt Peanuts" and lets us hear Parker display his bluesy roots. While Bird plays a down-home blues including some standard blues licks, he also plays beautiful lyrical melodies throughout his solo. The singer and lyricist King Pleasure put words to Parker's melody and solo from this recording. His words to Bird's introduction, one of the most famous introductions in jazz, refer to Parker's Kansas City roots: "Come with me, if you want to go to Kansas City!" This recording includes drummer Max Roach as well as pianist John Lewis, who went on to lead an important group, the Modern Jazz Quartet (Chapter 11, 1st Chorus), which experimented with combining jazz and a classical chamber music sensibility.

IN PERFORMANCE
"Jazz and Strings"

The marriage of strings and jazz performance has often been a rocky and somewhat problematic one for a variety of reasons. For one, the average string player primarily plays in classical orchestral or chamber music contexts, and the approach to rhythm is quite different in these situations. While jazz bands tend to be aggressively on top of the beat, classical string players, particularly in an orchestral context, tend to have a slight delay in their attack. More importantly, classically oriented players frequently have difficulty effectively playing the swing style that comes naturally to jazz players and is essential to jazz. These are significant differences that create problems regarding ensemble playing as the different rhythmic approaches frequently have difficulty melding.

Regardless of these challenges, there have been many composers who have experimented in combining orchestras and jazz bands with varied levels of success. **Symphonic jazz** is one term that has been used to refer to this type of composition, and this style is frequently a melding of jazz, music for the theater, popular music, music for movies, and classical music. George Gershwin's *Rhapsody in Blue*, originally composed for Paul Whiteman's orchestra in 1924, is the most important early example of symphonic jazz.

So far we have heard strings used in two contexts, Paul Whiteman (Chapter 4, 1st Chorus) and Tommy Dorsey (Chapter 7, 2nd Chorus). Other big-band artists we have listened to, such as Artie Shaw and Benny Goodman, have used strings or have played in orchestral contexts; and composers in the "progressive jazz" and "third stream" styles often successfully incorporated strings in their works (Chapter 11, 1st Chorus). In addition, orchestrations used to accompany popular singers from the swing era, such as Frank Sinatra and Nat King Cole (both discussed in Chapter 9, 2nd Chorus), were arrangements of the highest caliber that combined a jazz big band with string sections extremely effectively. In contemporary jazz, saxophonist-composer Wayne Shorter (Chapter 13, 1st Chorus, and Chapter 14, 1st Chorus) is one example of a composer who has recently composed works for his jazz quartet and orchestra.

Individually there have been numerous excellent jazz violinists, including Stéphane Grapelli, Joe Venuti, Ellington trumpeter-violinist Ray Nance, and the avant-garde violinist Billy Bang; and there are now more string players than ever in all of the various styles of jazz being played, such as violinists Mark Feldman, Regina Carter, and Jean-Luc Ponty; violist Mat Maneri; and cellist Erik Frielander (see Chapter 15, 4th Chorus, regarding contemporary string players). In addition, string quartets such as Turtle Island String Quartet and the Kronos Quartet play jazz material very effectively. The melding of jazz and strings is a work in progress as more and more string players are able to cross, and even erode, musical boundaries successfully.

"Just Friends" (1949) by Charlie Parker with Strings

INSTRUMENTATION: Alto saxophone, leader: Charlie Parker; **Oboe, English horn:** Mitch Miller; **Violins:** Bronislaw Gimpel, Max Hollander, Milton Lomask; **Viola:** Frank Brieff; **Cello:** Frank Miller; **Bass:** Ray Brown; **Piano:** Stan Freeman; **Drums:** Buddy Rich; **Harp:** Meyer Rosen; **Arranger, conductor:** Jimmy Carroll.

LISTENING HIGHLIGHT, MELODY AND ACCOMPANIMENT: "Just Friends" is a 32-bar ABAC Tin Pan Alley tune that is a jazz standard recorded by innumerable artists and a part of most jazz players' repertoires. In "Just Friends" Parker is up front as a featured soloist, providing us with a chance to hear his uncanny melodic sensibilities, both in his ability to play the melodies of jazz standards gorgeously as well as in his lovely lyrical improvising. As Bird plays the melody in the 1st chorus (0:18–1:14) we hear him take two main approaches to presenting the song. The first is to largely play the melody while taking rhythmic liberties and adding slight embellishments. The second is to almost eschew the melody for periods while then returning at crucial moments.

Bird solos in the 2nd chorus (1:21–2:20), and his playing is assured, relaxed, and extremely lyrical, even as he plays streams of fast melodic lines. After a piano solo that features the rhythm section with the strings lightly behind them at times (2:21–2:48), Bird takes the tune out by barely paraphrasing the melody while still managing to imply it.

"Just Friends" is an example of combining two types of accompaniment, a standard rhythm section and a string section. The strings' role in this arrangement is vital while also being limited as they primarily function as a pad of sound underneath the main musical texture of the rhythm section and Parker's alto sax, though they do briefly play part of the melody in the 1st chorus (0:46). By limiting their role to long held notes, the issues surrounding rhythm (discussed in "In Performance: Jazz and Strings") are largely avoided while still bringing a particular type of lushness and richness that only a string section can create. Other than the piano solo, the rhythm section's role in this setting is less pronounced than is usual in jazz, partially because of the presence of the string section but also because this recording is focused on featuring Charlie Parker as a soloist.

"Manteca," a composition cowritten by Gillespie and Chano Pozo and arranged by Gil Fuller, featured Pozo on conga drum. "Manteca" is an example of how effectively jazz and Latin music can be combined, even at this early stage of the development of Latin jazz. Gillespie recorded numerous other compositions in this style, including "Cubana Be, Cubana Bop," a collaborative effort from Pozo, Gillespie, and composer-arranger-music theorist George Russell. Dizzy continued to maintain the Latin influence in his music throughout his career and often performed on a conga drum that he kept beside him during performances.

listening focus

"Manteca" (1947) by the Dizzy Gillespie Orchestra featuring Chano Pozo

DOWNLOAD
Track Number 19

INSTRUMENTATION: Trumpet, leader: Dizzy Gillespie; **Trumpets:** Dave Burns, Elmon Wright, Benny Bailey, Lammar Wright; **Trombones:** William Shepherd, Ted Kelly; **Saxophones:** Howard Johnson, John Brown, Joe Gayles, George "Big Nick" Nicholas, Cecil Payne; **Piano:** John Lewis; **Bass:** Al McKibbon; **Drums:** Kenny "Klook" Clarke; **Conga:** Chano Pozo.

LISTENING HIGHLIGHT, STYLE: In the introduction to "Manteca" we immediately hear features of both Latin music and jazz. The bass plays an ostinato, or vamp, over a conga drum rhythmic pattern; the horns join in with their own riffs; and Dizzy improvises over the whole texture in a mixture of jazz and "tipico" styles. The A section of this AABA composition consists of a call and response between saxes and brass and a final phrase with the whole ensemble (0:37). The bridge (the B section, 1:00) has a lovely melody of a very different character shared by the saxes and Gillespie.

After the band plays the form of the tune itself, predominantly in a Latin style, the feel of the composition changes as it moves into a more jazz-oriented swing section with solos while retaining a Latin flavor, largely as a result of Pozo's playing (1:48). A tenor sax plays a solo over the A sections with jazz background figures from the horns. The whole ensemble plays a powerful ensemble at the bridge before Dizzy takes over with a classic bebop-flavored solo (including some colorful notes), some of it screaming in the stratosphere (2:10). The band takes it out with the A section melody and a final vamp (2:32).

Mario Bauzá's band, ca. 1960. Bauzá was a leading Latino trumpeter and music director during the 1950s and 1960s. Photo by Herb Snitzer.

Courtesy Michael Ochs Archives/Getty Images.

2nd Chorus Thelonious Monk and Bud Powell

HOW DID THELONIOUS MONK AND BUD POWELL CREATE A NEW ROLE FOR PIANISTS IN BEBOP MUSIC?

Thelonious Monk

Pianist and composer Thelonious Monk (1917–1982) was also instrumental in the development of bebop and is certainly one of the most important composers in jazz. Many of his tunes are jazz standards that all jazz players must know, such as "Blue Monk," "Well You Needn't," the gorgeous ballad "'Round Midnight," and "Straight, No Chaser." Monk is also one of jazz's most enigmatic figures. He was an eccentric and reclusive person, and since he did not engage much with the audience, his stage presence was difficult to read.

As a result of the combination of well-crafted melodies and knotty, dissonant harmonies, Monk's music is extremely sophisticated while at the same time having a certain rough edge. Monk's playing and composing are angular and dense and have a completely individualistic character. For example, his use of dissonant clusters of notes as he plays melodies and solos, his stabbing left-hand comping rhythms, and quick upward and downward fills between phrases instantly identify his playing. No one sounds like Monk.

While Monk was a wonderful pianist, he had a distinct and nontraditional piano technique. It served him and his music well, but it wasn't the type of virtuosity we have seen in other pianists so far. Monk's playing and composing are more complicated than most. He is rhythmically and melodically quirky, cerebral yet accessible

JAZZ LIVES THELONIOUS MONK

Raised on Manhattan's West Side, Monk was largely a self-taught pianist. He played with such jazz greats as Coleman Hawkins and Roy Eldridge (both discussed in Chapter 5, 3rd Chorus), but it was as house band pianist at Minton's Playhouse in Harlem in the early 1940s that Monk came into his own as part of the early bebop movement. During this time, pianist Mary Lou Williams (Chapter 6, 1st Chorus) took Monk under her wing, nurturing and encouraging his talent. In the later 1940s, he played and recorded with Bird, Dizzy, and many others; but he was most known for leading his own groups. Many of Monk's early compositions became bebop standards, including "'Round Midnight" and "Blue Monk." While admired by musicians, his own

Thelonious Monk at Minton's Playhouse, ca. 1947. Monk was house pianist at Minton's, often cited as the birthplace of bebop music. Photo by William P. Gottlieb.

Courtesy William P. Gottlieb Collection and Library of Congress.

continued

recordings sold poorly through the mid-1950s; and his career stalled when he lost his cabaret card—a requirement for any musician who wanted to play in a New York City nightclub.

Monk's career began to pick up when he recorded his 1956 album *Brilliant Corners* and, with his cabaret card reinstated, began performing again around New York City. His famous residency at New York's Five Spot featuring saxophonist John Coltrane is celebrated for the collaboration of two jazz masters (see "Listening Focus"). Monk was busy performing and recording through the 1960s—even being featured on the cover of *Time* magazine in 1964—and had a number of successful records. He was known for numerous personality quirks and eccentricities and struggled mightily with what is now discussed as a mental illness or disorder, and by the early 1970s he essentially stopped performing and recording and at times was a recluse until his death in 1982.

and down-to-earth; and he has an edginess right on the surface. This is a unique combination that makes his music difficult to penetrate yet instantly mesmerizing.

Monk and his quartet had a famous extended stint in 1957 at the Five Spot in lower Manhattan that featured the up-and-coming tenor saxophonist John Coltrane (Chapter 13, 2nd Chorus). At this time, Monk was an established star in the jazz world as both a player and a composer, while Coltrane was still an up-and-coming performer on the tenor sax. After Monk heard him play, he hired Coltrane for what became a 6-month engagement at the Five Spot. A steady gig such as this or a long road tour has always been the best way for a band to create a sound. While professional musicians can quickly adapt to most any musical situation, it is only through regularly playing together that musicians are able to begin to connect to each other on deeper levels and build an intuitive musical rapport. It is this type of close relationship that creates the extra bit of magic that takes music to the highest level.

Discussing this engagement, the great trombonist J. J. Johnson, who had played with both musicians, recalled, "Since Charlie Parker, the most electrifying sound that I've heard in contemporary jazz was Coltrane playing with Monk at the Five Spot. . . . I had never heard that kind of performance—it's not possible to put into words. I just heard something that I've never heard before and I haven't heard since" (Gitler 1961, 19). This engagement led to a Carnegie Hall concert that presented the group at its peak. A CD of this landmark concert was released in 2005 as *Thelonious Monk Quartet with John Coltrane at Carnegie Hall*.

Bud Powell

Earl "Bud" Powell (1924–1966) was a very different sort of pianist from Monk, even though both helped to bring the piano into the age of bebop. His playing was swift and assured. His solos incorporated the same sort of melodic and harmonic ideas put forth by Parker and Gillespie as they were quick and long-lined and emphasized the right hand, essentially treating it like a horn as his left hand comped.

Raised in Harlem in New York City, Powell had music around him at an early age and played both classical music and jazz. His father was a pianist, as was his brother Richie (who later played with trumpeter Clifford Brown [Chapter 11, 2nd Chorus]; both were killed in the same car accident), and another brother played trumpet. Powell had early exposure to new approaches to jazz at the Uptown House in his neighborhood, through Thelonious Monk, one of Powell's primary influences, as well as Mary Lou Williams (Chapter 6, 1st Chorus). Art Tatum was another important influence for Powell, and Tatum's influence is especially evident in Powell's playing. After having played with Cootie Williams (Chapter 8,

listening focus

"Monk's Mood" (1957) by Thelonious Monk Quartet with John Coltrane

INSTRUMENTATION: Piano, leader: Thelonious Monk; **Tenor saxophone:** John Coltrane; **Bass:** Ahmed Abdul-Malik; **Drums:** Shadow Wilson.

LISTENING HIGHLIGHT, MELODY AND HARMONY: "Monk's Mood," an AABA composition, is an example of the harmonic and melodic richness of Monk's compositions. This recording gives us a chance to hear Monk play solo through the 1st chorus (0:08, bridge at 1:01, and the last A at 1:33). An interlude follows that functions as a joint **cadenza** (2:04). We then get to hear Monk as an accompanist as Coltrane plays an understated version of the melody for the 2nd chorus (2:34, bridge at 4:29, and the last A at 5:19). After the 2nd chorus, they jump to the bridge and last A, a common technique (6:14). Coltrane largely sticks loosely to the melody but also throws in flurries of notes.

With "Monk's Mood" we get to hear how thoroughly composed Monk's pieces are. Background harmonies as well as fills between melodic phrases are all carefully composed, and these various elements are virtually inseparable as together they create the overall character of the piece. And even though they are composed and the performances are only partially improvised, the way Monk plays them they always sound spontaneous due to a fascinating combination of rhythmic looseness, compositional rigor, and some well-placed and tasteful improvisation. The fact that he managed to recreate these pieces relatively verbatim yet was able to always make them sound fresh is remarkable. Along with this, in a way that he manages to make sound completely natural, Monk extensively uses the colorful notes of upper parts of chordal structures, a major characteristic and innovation of bebop.

Another noteworthy aspect of this recording is the deep communication that occurs between Monk and Coltrane and their accompanists. This entire performance is played rubato—with free and flexible time that allows for rhythmic expressivity from all players. This type of loose playing requires incredible and hard-won trust between players that only comes from experience with each other. It also requires an intense concentration, which is evident in this live performance.

2nd Chorus) and early beboppers such as tenor saxophonist Dexter Gordon, trombonist J. J. Johnson, and the influential trumpeter Fats Navarro, Powell joined Charlie Parker for an important record date in 1947. Around this time Powell's life became quite difficult. He had several violent altercations, including being beaten by the police, and was in and out of psychiatric institutions throughout his life. His emotional stability was erratic until his death in 1966.

Powell was an excellent and forward-looking composer, and his composition "Un Poco Loco" is so unique and advanced that it almost seems to have come out of the blue. The original recording has a variety of feels, with Latin rhythms and African-influenced rhythmic patterns from drummer Max Roach and powerful Latin-influenced rhythmic figures from Powell as essential elements of the piece. It is full of vamps, intense harmonies, and a colorful and varied melody and is a fascinating mixture of Latin and jazz styles while also expressing a modern approach to the harmonic innovations of bebop.

"Un Poco Loco" (1951) by Bud Powell

DOWNLOAD
Track Number 21

INSTRUMENTATION: Piano, leader: Bud Powell; **Bass:** Curley Russell; **Drums:** Max Roach.

LISTENING HIGHLIGHT, FORM: The tune itself is AABA but with 16-measure sections instead of the usual 8, making it feel like more of an extended composition. The A section is particularly intense and modernistic for the period. It largely consists of clave-like rhythmic figures and a colorful repeated melodic flurry, all of which focus on a particular colorful note of the upper parts of the various harmonies, in this case the sharp-eleven. As we saw with Monk, using these upper parts of chords is a defining bebop technique. The bridge (B section, 0:34) lightens up as it goes into a more standard Latin feel (from a jazz perspective) with a lyrical melody.

When Powell begins his solo (1:10), he follows an approach that is more typical of Latin music than jazz, which is to solo over a repetitive vamp, or montuno, as opposed to soloing over the form of the tune. In this case, however, the vamp is derived from two chords of the composition itself. Powell shapes his solo slowly and carefully, for example, with some initial repeated melodies (1:13), similar to what is frequently done in Latin music. He gradually opens up into a tasteful bebop-style solo over the vamp. After Powell's solo, Roach gets an extended solo (3:06), displaying a mastery of these various rhythms, while also staying within the context of the piece. Powell returns with the melody (3:34) to conclude this hybrid piece that feels much longer than its actual 4:46 length.

Bud Powell in 1963. Powell was one of the founding fathers of bebop piano, despite leading a difficult life marked by periods of emotional breakdown. Photo by Jan Persson.

© *JazzSign/Lebrecht Music & Arts.*

QUESTIONS AND CONTROVERSIES
Monk and Powell: Struggles with Mental Illness

Both Thelonious Monk and Bud Powell spent significant time institutionalized during their careers, and both received various diagnoses of mental illness. Monk, who had a family history of mental disorder, was eventually diagnosed with a chemical imbalance and given the controversial pharmaceutical drug Thorazine. Powell received electroconvulsive therapy during a stay at Creedmoor State Hospital and had psychological difficulties throughout his later life.

Racial issues again present themselves as the general working conditions for jazz musicians were quite poor, and the musicians' union did little toward breaking down racism in the music business. Jazz musicians worked long and late nights, and work was becoming scarcer for black musicians. Also, the constant availability of drugs and alcohol in many nightclubs, where jazz musicians worked, was problematic. It is entirely conceivable that issues such as these impacted more adversely upon Monk and Powell, who were already struggling with their mental health. Another example of the consequences of systemic racism is that both men were beaten by the police, a more common occurrence for blacks than whites, which may have contributed to their later difficulties. In addition, drinking and drug use took its toll over time on both musicians.

When Thelonious Monk and Bud Powell were performing at the height of their careers, both were original and innovative performer-composers without whom bebop would not have had the wide influence that it has enjoyed for over half a century.

3rd Chorus Big-Band Bebop

WHAT ROLE DID BIG BANDS PLAY IN THE BEBOP ERA?

Bebop was (and is) primarily a small-group music; but as noted before, the innovators were generally players from the big-band tradition, and the compositional opportunities, along with the power of the big band, still spoke to them. Dizzy Gillespie, for example, led an exciting big band that featured his playing and showmanship, as well as important composer-arrangers such as Chico O'Farrill, Gil Fuller, and George Russell. Also, beginning in the mid-1940s, many swing big bands incorporated the bebop aesthetic into their music, such as the bands of Cab Calloway, Earl Hines, and Billy Eckstine, and many of the white bands, such as those of Claude Thornhill, Boyd Raeburn, and Woody Herman, were also bringing this new element to their music.

Woody Herman

Bandleader-clarinetist-saxophonist-vocalist Woody Herman (1913–1987) was a vaudeville singer and tap dancer as a child. He became an instrumentalist by the time he was 12 and later worked as a big-band side musician. Herman went on to lead a successful swing band as early as 1936 with hits such as "Woodchopper's Ball" and "Caledonia," the latter featuring Herman as an effective blues vocalist; and his band regularly featured top players and forward-thinking arrangers.

Herman disbanded the band after World War II, but in 1947 he reemerged with his Second Herd, which had numerous players who were interested in

listening focus

"Four Brothers" (1947) by Woody Herman's Second Herd; Jimmy Giuffre (arranger)

INSTRUMENTATION: Clarinet, leader: Woody Herman; **Trumpets:** Stan Fishelson, Bernie Glow, Marty Markowitz, Ernie Royal, Shorty Rogers; **Trombones:** Earl Swope, Ollie Wilson, Bob Swift; **Saxophones:** Sam Marowitz, Herbie Steward, Stan Getz, Zoot Sims, Serge Chaloff; **Piano:** Ralph Burns; **Guitar:** Gene Sargent; **Bass:** Walter Yoder; **Drums:** Don Lamond; **Arranger:** Jimmy Giuffre.

LISTENING HIGHLIGHT, FORM: Giuffre's "Four Brothers," an AABA tune based on a popular song, displays its bebop influence through a relaxed and smooth melody harmonized for the four featured saxophonists punctuated by crisp brass hits. Though a big-band chart, it initially has the quality of small-band music. After the melody, Sims, Chaloff, Herbie Stewart, and Getz solo (in that order) and display distinct styles that all combine their swing expertise with their bebop influence. The band is then featured in a long ensemble section with a short spot for the bandleader, Woody Herman, on clarinet. A shout chorus (with terrific drum fills) featuring short solos by the "four brothers" ends this famous bebop big-band chart.

bebop and brought this sound to the band. This band was also known as the Four Brothers Band, named after its saxophone section and the Jimmy Giuffre composition "Four Brothers" (see "Listening Focus"). Saxophonist-clarinetist-composer-arranger Jimmy Giuffre (1921–2008) was a musician's musician, meaning he was well known and highly thought of by musicians but was not as well known to the general public. With his playing and writing he was involved in such diverse styles as free improvisation and carefully crafted compositions that contained classical influences.

In the Second Herd Herman employed an unusual combination for a big-band saxophone section. As opposed to the normal two altos, two tenors, and one baritone, he at times used one alto, three tenor saxes, and one baritone sax. And while many bands featured an aggressive saxophone soloist, Herman's players, Zoot Sims (tenor sax), Herbie Steward (alto and tenor sax), Stan Getz (tenor sax), and Serge Chaloff (baritone sax), had softer, more lyrical styles. Chaloff became a leading baritone player, and Sims and Getz both became major soloists and small-group bandleaders. Sims, and particularly Getz, went on to make careers based on this lyrical style that featured a full but soft-edged sound and an extremely smooth and linear approach.

Herman's persistence and the high quality of his band and arrangements helped him to keep his band regularly touring through the 1980s. It, along with the other big bands that managed to stay on the road, became one of the most important jazz "conservatories," turning out important young players for several generations by giving them the invaluable experience of touring with a top big band.

Tadd Dameron

Pianist-composer-arranger Tadd Dameron (1917–1965) is the arranger who is most closely identified with bebop. He was particularly known for his effective writing for "small" big bands, which combined the power of a big band and the

"Sid's Delight" (1949) by Tadd Dameron and His Orchestra/Big Ten

INSTRUMENTATION: Piano, arranger, leader: Tadd Dameron; **Trumpet:** Fats Navarro; **Trombone:** Kai Winding; **Saxophones:** Dexter Gordon, Sahib Shibab, Cecil Payne; **Bass:** Curley Russell; **Drums:** Kenny "Klook" Clarke; **Bongo:** Diego Iborra; **Conga:** Vidal Bolado.

LISTENING HIGHLIGHT, STYLE: Tadd Dameron's "Sid's Delight" features numerous players who made their name as bebop players and innovators. Drummer Kenny "Klook" Clark helped to free the bass drum from keeping a regular beat. Instead, he would "drop bombs," accenting ensemble figures or soloists' lines. Dexter Gordon was an important tenor sax soloist throughout his long and productive career. He set an example for how to bridge the gap between swing and bebop, while also being a standard-bearer for keeping the original melody, as well as its lyrics, in mind during a solo. Trombonist Kai Winding, along with bebop trombone pioneer J. J. Johnson, showed the way for all trombonists during the bebop era by helping to transform the trombone from a tailgating, riffing instrument into a technically adept horn that could successfully navigate and excel at playing the swift and tricky bebop style. The percussion section of conga and bongo (they enter for the solos) is quite prominent on this recording, adding a Latin influence to this determinedly swinging tune. Particularly featured in "Sid's Delight," however, is the tremendous trumpet player Theodore "Fats" Navarro (1923–1950). While Dizzy Gillespie was the leader of the bebop movement on trumpet, it was Fats's playing that actually influenced more trumpet players, including Clifford Brown (Chapter 11, 2nd Chorus); and his influence is still quite pronounced today. Navarro's career was unfortunately cut short by a lifestyle of drugs and alcohol, reminiscent of the life of Charlie Parker.

"Sid's Delight" is an excellent example of arranging for a "small" big band, which was one of Dameron's strengths. The arrangement incorporates the concepts of big-band arranging with an introduction and fully harmonized melody (0:00–0:45), an ensemble for the full band (1:59), a fun shout chorus (2:21), and room for three soloists. Navarro solos (0:46), giving a clinic in bebop trumpet style, followed by solos from Kai Winding on trombone (1:13) and tenor saxophonist Dexter Gordon (1:36).

intimacy of a small combo while giving soloists more room to stretch out. His compositions, such as "If You Could See Me Now" (composed for vocalist Sarah Vaughn), "Good Bait," "Hot House," and "Lady Bird," are all jazz standards. Dameron's arrangements melded his experiences in swing and bop as he created both lovely melodies and more bebop-oriented lines, and his harmonic approach was full and rich, articulating the chordal expansion so central to bebop.

CODA Chapter Summary

What Is Bebop?

- Bebop is a form of small-group jazz that developed in the early to mid-1940s.
- Although based on the harmonic progressions of popular songs, bebop melodies are quirky and technically demanding, with tempos that were sometimes taken at breakneck speed.

- The bebop rhythm section featured a more open and loose rhythmic feel. The individual instruments' roles—for piano, guitar, bass, and drums—became more delineated and separated.

Why Are Charlie Parker and Dizzy Gillespie Considered the Prime Movers Behind the Bebop Movement?

- Alto saxophonist Charlie Parker had an incredible melodic gift and regularly created solos that consisted of long-lined melodies, each of which was an elegant improvised composition unto itself.
- Dizzy Gillespie's style is marked by an astonishing fleetness and a tremendous range, while always remaining musically interesting. Gillespie, in contrast to Parker, was also an outgoing performer who created a wonderful, witty, and sharp-tongued rapport with his audience.
- Gillespie was also important in his early interest in Latin rhythms, resulting in a new musical style called "cubop."

How Did Thelonious Monk and Bud Powell Create a New Role for Pianists in Bebop Music?

- Monk's playing and composing were angular and dense. His use of dissonant clusters of notes as he plays melodies and solos, stabbing left-hand comping rhythms, and quick upward and downward fills between phrases instantly identify his playing. He also composed several tunes that became bebop standards, including "'Round Midnight" and "Blue Monk."
- Bud Powell was a very different sort of pianist from Monk. His playing was swift and assured. His solos incorporated the same sort of melodic and harmonic ideas as Parker and Gillespie as they were quick and long-lined and emphasized the right hand, essentially treating it like a horn.

What Role Did Big Bands Play in the Bebop Era?

- Bebop was primarily a small-group music, but the innovators were generally players from the big-band tradition, and the compositional opportunities, along with the power of the big band, still spoke to them.
- Woody Herman's Second Herd had numerous players who were interested in bebop. The band had an unusual saxophone lineup, known as the "Four Brothers."
- Tadd Dameron was particularly known for his effective writing for "small" big bands, which combined the power of a big band and the intimacy of a small combo while giving soloists more room to stretch out.

Talkin' Jazz (Key Terms)

Cadenza	Dropping bombs	Ride cymbal
Cubop	Jam session	Symphonic jazz

Key People

Charlie Parker	Thelonious Monk	Woody Herman
Dizzy Gillespie	Bud Powell	Tadd Dameron

Think About This (For Further Discussion and Study)

1. What are the characteristics of bebop?
2. Discuss any similarities and differences that you hear between swing music and bebop.
3. Can you hear why bebop was controversial in its early days? Can you think of musical styles that have been thought of as controversial during your lifetime? What are your attitudes toward new styles or developments in styles that you enjoy?
4. What is your experience as you listen to Bird and Dizzy stretch out a little during their solos on "Salt Peanuts"? Do you find it hard to concentrate on their solos?
5. What do you hear as the characteristics of Bird's and Dizzy's styles?
6. What are the characteristics of Thelonious Monk's and Bud Powell's piano playing? Discuss the similarities and differences that you hear between them.
7. Do you think the big band is an effective ensemble for bebop?

Look It Up (Key Resources)

Comb, Paul. *Dameronia: The Life and Music of Tadd Dameron*. Ann Arbor, MI: University of Michigan Press, 2013.

DeVeaux, Scott. *The Birth of Bebop: A Social and Musical History*. Berkeley and Los Angeles: University of California Press, 1997.

Fitterling, Thomas. *Thelonious Monk: His Life and Music*. Berkeley, CA: Berkeley Hills, 1997.

Giddins, Gary. *Celebrating Bird: The Triumph of Charlie Parker*. New York: Morrow, 1987.

Gillespie, Dizzy. *To Be or Not . . . To Bop: Memoirs*. With Al Fraser. Garden City, NY: Doubleday, 1979.

Gitler, Ira. "A Tranquil Frame of Mind: The Remarkable J.J. Johnson." *Down Beat*. May 11, 1961.

———. *Swing to Bop: An Oral History of the Transition in Jazz in the 1940s*. New York: Oxford University Press, 1985.

Groves, Alan, and Alyn Shipton. *The Glass Enclosure: The Life of Bud Powell*. New York: Continuum, 2001.

Kelley, Robin D. G. *Thelonious Monk: The Life and Times of an American Original*. New York: Free Press, 2009.

Korall, Burt. *Drummin' Men: The Heartbeat of Jazz—The Bebop Years*. New York: Oxford University Press, 2002.

Paudras, Francis. *Dance of the Infidels: A Portrait of Bud Powell*. New York: Da Capo Press, 1998.

Pullman, Peter. *Wail: The Life of Bud Powell*. Brooklyn, NY: Bop Changes, 2012.

Ramsey, Guthrie. *The Amazing Bud Powell: Black Genius, Jazz History, and the Challenge of Bebop*. Berkeley and Los Angeles: University of California Press, 2013.

Shipton, Alyn. *Groovin' High: The Life of Dizzy Gillespie*. New York: Oxford University Press, 1999.

Solis, Gabriel. *Monk's Music: Thelonious Monk and Jazz History in the Making*. Berkeley and Los Angeles: University of California Press, 2008.

———. *Thelonious Monk Quartet Featuring John Coltrane at Carnegie Hall*. New York: Oxford University Press, 2014.

Van der Blick, Rob, ed. *The Thelonious Monk Reader*. New York: Oxford University Press, 2001.

Woideck, Carl. *Charlie Parker: His Music and Life*. Ann Arbor: University of Michigan Press, 1996.

———, ed. *The Charlie Parker Companion: Six Decades of Commentary*. New York: Schirmer, 1998.

BUILDING THE MAINSTREAM
1950-1975

MAJOR MUSICAL STYLES

1949–1955	• Cool jazz
1950–1960	• Mambo
1955–1960	• Hard bop
1959–today	• Avant-garde
1960–1965	• Soul jazz
1960–1975	• Mainstream jazz
1962–1967	• Jazz samba
1967–1975	• Fusion, or jazz-rock

After World War II, America reached the heights of its international power and prestige. At home, the economy was booming and many city dwellers were moving to the newly created suburbs. The building of the interstate highway system—beginning in the 1950s—made long distance travel faster and safer. The G.I. Bill offered returning soldiers a chance to attend college, which led to a higher standard of living for the most educated workers. Scientific miracles—from the introduction of the polio vaccine to the splitting of the atom—held the promise of a new, more prosperous, and better world.

The 1950s was a time of contradictions. On the one hand, America had reached new heights of power and prosperity. On the other hand, the fear of the rise of communism gripped the country, as exploited by leaders like Senator Joseph McCarthy. "Radical" causes such as a push for racial equality, unionization of workers for better working conditions, and even criticism of the government itself all came under increased scrutiny. The execution of alleged spies Julius and Ethel Rosenberg sent a chill through the liberal community. While jazz music was not in and of itself considered subversive, many musicians were investigated for their involvement in performing at concerts to raise money for "left-leaning" organizations like the NAACP (National Association for the Advancement of Colored People), including older performers like Duke Ellington. Paradoxically, toward the end of the 1950s the State Department began sponsoring tours of jazz musicians to Europe and Africa as a means of spreading American culture and building "good will."

At the same time, college attendance boomed in the 1950s, offering a new audience and performing opportunities for jazz musicians. New technologies—including the introduction of the long-playing record which could hold up to 20 minutes per side (as opposed to earlier 78 discs, which were limited to 3–5 minutes) as well as magnetic recording tape—made it possible to record extended jazz performances. Live concert recording—previously difficult, if not impossible, to undertake—allowed jazz to be represented on record in a more natural, exciting way. New per-

Julius and Ethel Rosenberg, separated by a heavy wire screen as they leave a US court house after being found guilty of treason. *World Telegram* photo by Roger Higgins.

Courtesy Library of Congress.

formers like pianist Dave Brubeck took advantage of both of these developments, performing on college campuses and then issuing live albums to capture the moment. This in turn helped build audiences throughout the country, giving jazz a new acceptance among the educated and elite. In 1954, the first jazz festival was held in Newport, Rhode Island, a wealthy summer community not known for being particularly supportive of jazz. Nonetheless, the annual event became a milestone for the music, launching new careers and revitalizing older ones, through both the live concerts and widely distributed recordings of the events.

The civil rights movement was given a major boost in 1954 with the landmark *Brown v. Board of Education* decision by the Supreme Court, which found "separate-but-equal" segregated schools to be unconstitutional. It would take decades of struggle to achieve this vision, with the famous 1963 March on Washington led by Dr. Martin Luther King, Jr., symbolizing the triumph of his nonviolent movement's efforts to gain equality for African Americans. One of the landmark moments in the fight to desegregate schools came in 1957 when Governor Orval

The 1963 March on Washington was a landmark moment in the fight for civil rights.

Photo by Warren K. Leffler. Courtesy Library of Congress.

Faubus of Arkansas defied the federal government in its efforts to integrate the high school in the state's capital of Little Rock. The government ultimately sent in troops to accompany the first black students to attend the school. Bandleader-composer Charles Mingus was inspired by this event to compose "Fables of Faubus" (1959), one of the first jazz compositions to directly address civil rights. Over the next decades, the African American struggle to find a new cultural and social identity would be reflected in the work of composers and performers like Ornette Coleman and Cecil Taylor, leaders of the free jazz movement.

As the 1960s wore on, some felt that, despite the gains that the civil rights movement had achieved, equality was not coming quickly enough to African Americans. New leaders—like Malcolm X, who advocated black self-determination and a more active response to discrimination—challenged King's nonviolent approach. The assassination of Malcolm X in 1965 showed the growing tension within the African American community as the two philosophies engaged in a sometimes bitter battle. The war in Vietnam—disproportionately fought by blacks—was another flashpoint, as were the slow efforts to improve living conditions in America's inner cities. While the suburbs had flourished, the cities had become dumping grounds for the poor, with minimal services, poor housing, and underfunded schools. In 1967, rioting broke out in Detroit, which led to similar uprisings in other cities across the country. The 1968 assassination of Martin Luther King, Jr., represented a breaking point for the movement, with new organizations and new leaders—like the Black Panther Party's Eldridge Cleaver—rising to push for self-determination, as well as self-protection, in African American communities, even through violent means if necessary, as a response to the continuing indignities of discrimination. The free jazz movement was aligned with many of the more progressive black organizations of the period. The 1965 formation of the Association for the Advancement of Creative Musicians (AACM) in Chicago (followed 4 years later by the Art Ensemble of Chicago)—with their emphasis on black self-determination, honoring African American cultural traditions, as well as individual freedom of expression—reflected the social unrest of the time.

While jazz achieved a level of acceptance in the 1950s and 1960s—and occasional recordings like Dave Brubeck's "Take Five" or Stan Getz and João Gilberto's "Girl from Ipanema" appeared on the pop charts—younger listeners were increasingly turning to rock music, beginning in 1964 with the stunning success of The Beatles. The growth of the hippie movement—declaring freedom from rigid social rules—was reflected in the popular music of the day. Through the later 1960s, some rock musicians experimented with incorporating jazz instrumentation and harmonies into their music, notably groups like Blood, Sweat, & Tears and Chicago. Meanwhile, younger jazz players were attracted to the energy and relevance of rock music so that performers like Gary Burton and John McLaughlin began incorporating electric instruments and rock rhythms into their performances. This new musical style would come to be known as "jazz–rock" or "fusion music." Its free-form compositions, loud volume, and heavier rhythms all reflected the social trends of the day, including a general feeling of rebellion against established authority.

1951–1975

1951
- Duke Ellington and His Orchestra, "A Tone Parallel to Harlem (The Harlem Suite)"
- Bud Powell, "Un Poco Loco"
- Bill Frisell, guitarist-composer-bandleader, born
- John Scofield, guitarist-composer-bandleader, born

1952–1953
- Gerry Mulligan Quartet with Chet Baker, "Line for Lyons"

1952
- Joe Lovano, tenor and soprano saxophonist, born

1953
- John Zorn, composer-bandleader-alto saxophonist, born

1954
- Pat Metheny, guitarist-composer, born

1955
- Clifford Brown–Max Roach Quintet, "Joy Spring"
- Tito Puente Orchestra, "Mambo Inn"
- Charlie Parker dies
- Cassandra Wilson, vocalist-pianist-bandleader, born
- Mark Feldman, violinist-composer, born

1956
- Clifford Brown dies in an automobile accident
- Steve Coleman, alto saxophonist-composer-bandleader, born

1957
- Thelonious Monk Quartet with John Coltrane, "Monks Mood" and "Nutty"
- Geri Allen, pianist-composer-bandleader, born

1958
- Art Blakey and the Jazz Messengers, "Moanin'"
- Don Byron, clarinetist-composer-bandleader, born

1959
- Frank Sinatra with Billy May and His Orchestra, "Come Dance With Me"
- Dave Brubeck Quartet, "Blue Rondo à la Turk"
- Miles Davis Sextet with Bill Evans, "So What"
- Charles Mingus, "Fables of Faubus"
- Billie Holiday dies
- Lester Young dies

1960
- Kenny Garrett, alto saxophonist-composer-bandleader, born
- Maria Schneider, composer-arranger-bandleader, born

1961
- Bill Evans Trio, "Waltz for Debby"
- Wynton Marsalis, trumpeter-bandleader-educator, born

1962
- Charlie Byrd and Stan Getz, "Desifinado"
- Chris Botti, trumpeter-bandleader, born

1962 cont.
- Renee Rosnes, pianist-composer-bandleader, born
- Terence Blanchard, trumpeter-composer-bandleader, born

1963
- Shirley Scott, "Soul Shoutin'"
- Dave Douglas, trumpeter-composer-bandleader, born

1964
- Cal Tjader, "Soul Sauce (Guachi Guaro)"
- Diana Krall, vocalist-pianist-bandleader, born

1965
- Miles Davis Quintet with Herbie Hancock and Wayne Shorter, "E.S.P."
- John Coltrane Quartet, "Resolution"
- Terri Lyne Carrington, drummer-bandleader, born

1966
- Bud Powell dies
- Theo Bleckman, vocalist-composer-bandleader, born

1967
- Kurt Elling, vocalist-lyricist-composer-bandleader, born

1969
- Les McCann and Eddie Harris, "Compared to What?"
- Art Ensemble of Chicago formed
- Joshua Redman, tenor and soprano saxophonist, born

1970
- Brian Blade, drummer-bandleader, born
- Brad Mehldau, pianist-composer-bandleader, born
- Kurt Rosenwinkel, guitarist-composer-bandleader, born
- Erik Friedlander, cellist, born

1971
- Louis Armstrong dies
- Vijay Iyer, pianist-composer-bandleader, born
- Chris Potter, tenor and soprano saxophonist, born

1972
- Christian McBride, bassist-composer-bandleader, born

1973
- Art Ensemble of Chicago, "Barnyard Scuffel Shuffel"
- Mahavishnu Orchestra, "Birds of Fire"
- Nicholas Payton, trumpeter-composer-bandleader, born

1974
- Duke Ellington dies

1975
- Jason Moran, pianist-composer-bandleader, born
- Anat Cohen, clarinetist-saxophonist-bandleader, born

1950-1973

MAJOR SOCIAL DEVELOPMENTS

1950–1953	• Korean war
1950	• Senator Joseph McCarthy rises to power; beginning of anticommunist witch-hunt
1953	• Julius and Ethel Rosenberg executed as communist spies
1954	• Supreme Court decision on *Brown v. Board of Education* ends segregated schools • First transistor radio made, making it possible to "carry" music with you
1955	• Rosa Parks refuses to move to the back of the bus, sparking the Montgomery, Alabama, bus boycott • Disneyland opens in California
1957	• Congress passes Civil Rights Act, first bill since Reconstruction addressing equal rights in voting • Little Rock, Arkansas, schools desegregated despite opposition of Arkansas governor Orval Faubus
1959	• Cuban Revolution brings Fidel Castro to power • Alaska and Hawaii admitted into the union, becoming the forty-ninth and fiftieth states, respectively
1960	• Sit-in at a Greensboro, North Carolina, lunch counter inspires similar acts as part of the growing movement for civil rights
1961	• Inauguration of John F. Kennedy as youngest president • Vietnam War begins with arrival of first US military "advisors" • Berlin Wall erected separating East and West Berlin

1962	• Cuban missile crisis nearly leads to World War III • John Glenn first American to orbit the earth
1963	• March on Washington during which Martin Luther King, Jr., gives his famous "I Have a Dream" speech
1964	• Civil Rights Act passes, ending racial discrimination
1965	• Black Muslim leader Malcolm X assassinated in New York City • Major escalation of Vietnam War begun under President Johnson • First Moog synthesizer demonstrated
1967	• Detroit riots lead to "long, hot summer" of racial unrest in major US cities
1968	• Martin Luther King, Jr., and Robert F. Kennedy assassinated
1969	• Woodstock music festival held
1970	• Mounting protests to Vietnam War, including one at Kent State University where several protesters are killed by National Guardsmen
1971	• 18-year-olds gain the right to vote
1972–1974	• Watergate scandal leads to eventual resignation of President Richard M. Nixon
1973	• Abortion legalized in landmark *Roe v. Wade* decision • Paris Peace Accords lead to end of Vietnam War

JAZZ IN THE 1950s

11

HOW DID THE JAZZ WORLD CHANGE IN THE 1950s?

During the 1950s the jazz world opened wide. No longer could jazz be put easily into categories such as "swing" or "bebop." The music being produced from this time on began to show multiple influences, and while labels were still applied, musicians began to feel freer to broaden their scope. Consequently, there were numerous styles in the 1950s that were representative of the era and this more open aesthetic. Plus, these styles did not develop in neat chronological order, each one replacing the one that came before. In fact, "cool jazz," "hard bop," and "**progressive jazz**" were all developing through the 1940s and, in the case of progressive jazz, as early as the 1930s, embracing both swing and bebop while also bringing new influences to the music. Also, as we will see, the lines between styles are often unclear.

While soloists were still the backbone of the music, all three of these styles, as well as related styles such as "West Coast jazz" and "third stream," put more of an emphasis on composition and arranging. Composers and arrangers in these styles manage to smoothly integrate solos into the fabric of the compositions, creating a balance between the two. Also in the 1950s, Latin dance music—in this case, mambo—continued to be an important part of the scene with the ongoing vibrant flow of influence back and forth between jazz and Latin styles. Finally, avant-garde jazz, an entirely new style that challenged many conventions, began in earnest, destined to be an important part of jazz, where it still plays a prominent role in the music's evolution.

1st Chorus Cool Jazz/West Coast Jazz, Progressive Jazz

WHAT IS COOL JAZZ?

Bebop accentuated fast-moving, intricate lines, often at very quick tempos, creating a hard-driving, somewhat aggressive style. But in the hands of some musicians, including beboppers, the same principles of technical and intricate lines could be played with a more cool, laid-back approach, perhaps partially as a reaction to the fleetness, and sometimes almost manic quality, of bebop. A group of experienced musicians steeped both in swing and in bebop

In this chapter, we'll answer these questions:

- How Did the Jazz World Change in the 1950s?
- What Is Cool Jazz?
- How Did Cool Jazz Develop on the West Coast?
- What Is Progressive Jazz?
- What Is Hard Bop?
- How Did the Mambo Craze Continue the Latin Influence on Jazz?
- What Is Avant-Garde Jazz?

and with similar interests found each other and began to shape a style that was an outgrowth of bebop, **cool jazz**.

Gil Evans and Miles Davis, *Birth of the Cool*

One of the leaders in developing the cool style was arranger Gil Evans (1912–1988), who, along with Ellington, was one of jazz's great colorists. Evans made a name for himself as a bandleader and then as chief arranger for the popular Claude Thornhill Orchestra. Evans brought to that commercially oriented orchestra a quiet yet harmonically dense sound, as well as a bebop sensibility and the use of classical music themes. Evans had also been incorporating bebop into this sound by creating arrangements of bebop tunes such as Parker's "Anthropology" and Miles Davis's "Donna Lee." In addition, a "cool" sound was nothing new to jazz, as we have seen, for example, with Bix Beiderbecke and Frank Trumbauer (Chapter 4, 1st Chorus). Evans's small apartment in midtown Manhattan was the meeting place for other players, arrangers, and composers who were interested in this new sound as well as other areas of music such as contemporary classical composition. From these meetings and shared thoughts and concepts came a new sound that contrasted with bebop.

Miles Davis, who originally made his name as a young trumpeter with Charlie Parker (Davis will be discussed in detail in Chapter 13, 1st Chorus), was part of this informal group and used his imprimatur to get a record deal for a nine-piece band to play compositions and arrangements by Evans, baritone saxophonist-composer-arranger Gerry Mulligan, pianist-composer John Lewis, trumpeter-arranger Johnny Carisi, and Davis himself, all of whom wrote melodic, delicate, harmonically rich compositions and arrangements that featured Davis's playing.

Cool jazz compositions had a darker sound as well, partially from the use of unusual instruments for jazz such as French horn and tuba, both mellow, dark instruments. The soloing style of Davis, Mulligan, and alto saxophonist Lee Konitz also had a character that differed from bebop. The sound was dryer and lighter with less vibrato, and the long melodic lines they played tended to be extremely

Miles Davis and Gil Evans rehearsing ca. 1958. Evans and Davis worked together through the 1950s, with Evans's arrangements wedding a bebop sensibility and classical music harmonies and themes. Photo by Don Hunstein.
© D. Hunstein/Lebrecht Music & Arts.

listening guide

"Boplicity" (1949) by the Miles Davis Nonet

DOWNLOAD
Track Number 22

INSTRUMENTATION: Trumpet, leader: Miles Davis; **Trombone:** J. J. Johnson; **French horn:** Sandy Siegelstein; **Tuba:** Bill Barber; **Alto sax:** Lee Konitz; **Baritone sax:** Gerry Mulligan; **Piano:** John Lewis; **Bass:** Nelson Boyd; **Drums:** Kenny Clarke; **Arranger:** Gil Evans.

OVERVIEW: While Miles Davis did not write the arrangements for this record, he was the catalyst behind the organization of a nonet—a nine-piece group—that rehearsed and recorded twelve compositions in 1949–1950 that were released on the album *Birth of the Cool*. The players and arrangers consisted largely of the crowd that coalesced around the meetings at Gil Evans's apartment. It was an interracial group of players, most of whom had big-band experience; and some were key members of the bebop scene. This band performed these compositions during a single 2-week engagement at the Royal Roost, a midtown Manhattan nightclub, yet the album is one of the important recordings in jazz, largely responsible for the establishment of the cool jazz style, and influential upon West Coast jazz as well as upon jazz arrangers and the jazz world in general. "Boplicity" is a Gil Evans arrangement, and the musical partnership and friendship between Davis and Evans lasted throughout their lives and resulted in four collaborative albums.

FORM: This tune follows a typical AABA form but does so in a free manner, and while it sticks largely to that format, it manages to be a composition with a variety of aspects to it. After the initial melody, the composition moves on to solos, ensembles, and combinations of the two, loosely based upon the harmonic structure of the AABA tune, while also not being bound by its strictures. A great deal happens within its 3-minute length, and it almost feels as if the ending comes too soon.

STYLE: On this Miles Davis Nonet recording, Davis plays with a round, dark sound and a light, gentle, thoughtful, almost hesitant style, as is also true for the rest of the band. The music flows freely and has an emotional quality, but it is reserved and almost restrained. There are no loud passages that raise the roof. Instead, it is a brass-heavy ensemble that manages to be both dark in its timbre and light in its feeling. While brass instruments tend to be heavy and bold, there is an airiness in the sound of this band that results from both the arrangements and the playing styles of these instrumentalists. This is in contrast to the often more aggressive nature of both bebop and big-band swing. The horns here have a floating quality, and Davis in turn floats over the texture. Miles's ability to effectively weave in and out of the lead melody in the delicate ensembles while also moving in and out of his role as featured soloist is a testament to the level of his playing and musicianship during this still early point in his career.

MELODY AND HARMONY: Gil Evans cleverly and smoothly blends the melody, solos, and ensembles such that there is little separation between the various sections. Miles also moves smoothly through the various transitions, and while the music might sound simple, playing the lead melodic line while also being the featured soloist in these ensembles is a challenging task. As is true in big bands, the soloists play short solos interspersed with ensembles. The horns are generally harmonized in a lush and full manner and move together in parallel fashion.

RHYTHM: In this medium-tempo tune the rhythm section also has a light feel. The bass is prominent throughout as it walks in 4. The piano's role is primarily to accompany soloists

continued

during passages where the horns are not as full, and John Lewis gets a short solo as a brief but refreshing break from the sound of the horns. The composed ensembles are so rich and full that piano comping is unnecessary and could clash harmonically with the horns. The drums play an unassuming role as the bass propels the rhythm section.

ACCOMPANIMENT: A nonet is a cross between a small group and a big band (as we saw with Tadd Dameron's ten-piece band and "Sid's Delight," Chapter 10, 3rd Chorus), and they chose these particular instruments to give them the smallest possible group that would also still provide them with a full sound, multiple textural possibilities, and the dark, rich qualities of sound they were looking for. Consequently, we have the intimacy of a small band blended with the harmonic and textural possibilities of a big band, with a variety of combinations to play ensembles and to accompany soloists.

"BOPLICITY" LISTENING GUIDE

TIME	FORM	STYLE	MELODY AND HARMONY	RHYTHM	ACCOMPANIMENT
1st Chorus					
0:00	AA	Miles Davis and the other horns play gently and quietly in a "cool" style.	The lush harmonization is typical of Gil Evans and of this style in general.	The bass playing in 4 propels this tune.	Davis's lead melody line is harmonized by all of the horns.
0:28	B		The bridge begins with the saxophones playing the melody for variety, but Davis quickly reenters on the lead line.		
0:43	A		The A section repeats.		
2nd Chorus					
0:57	AA	Gerry Mulligan's sound has a lightness and airiness about it, which is unusual for the baritone saxophone, normally a big and heavy-sounding instrument. He is also playing in a melodic style that matches the "cool" aesthetic established by the arrangement.	Mulligan plays a solo on the A section.		The rhythm section accompanies the solo. We hear pianist John Lewis for the first time as he comps behind Mulligan.
1:25	B (loosely)	The style of this ensemble slightly changes initially with more polyphony as opposed to the parallel harmonization of most of the tune.	The horns play a 6-measure ensemble loosely based on the key of the bridge (B-flat), and Davis finishes the phrase soloing over the final chord progression of the B section (1:36).		As Davis solos at the end of the phrase, the horns comp simply for him instead of the piano.

"Boplicity" listening guide continued

TIME	FORM	STYLE	MELODY AND HARMONY	RHYTHM	ACCOMPANIMENT
2nd Chorus					
1:43	A (loosely)		The horns play a harmonized melody that creates a high point of the arrangement so far.	The melody of the first few bars of the ensemble turns the meter around a bit.	
3rd Chorus					
1:58	A		Davis solos over the ensemble on the first A section after a short send-off from the others. They accompany him at times as well.		For the first A the horns accompany Davis. Notice how Lewis generally chooses not to play when the horns are playing an ensemble or accompanying a soloist and comps for soloists when the horns are not present.
2:10	A	Davis solos alone. His tone is pretty and rich, and his melodic choices are tasteful and simple.			
2:26	B	Lewis plays quite simply and almost hesitantly.	Pianist Lewis solos on the bridge. The piano solo creates a needed timbre change before the ending.		
2:40	A		The horns take the arrangement out on the last A.		The bass continues to be the dominant member of the rhythm section.

Compare

"Will O' the Wisp" is a Gil Evans arrangement from the album *Sketches of Spain* (1960), which is the third of four full-length classic album collaborations between Davis and Evans. It is based upon an excerpt from the important Spanish composer Manuel de Falla's ballet *El Amor Brujo*. It features Davis playing in a **Harmon mute**—a metal mute that constricts the sound of the trumpet and gives it an intense, buzzy quality—a sound he was well known for. Along with Davis's sensitive and gentle playing, it features Evans's colorful and evocative use of the orchestra. Evans employs an expanded version of the big band to create a signature sound and style that is instantly recognizable and that builds upon his work on *Birth of the Cool*. Soprano saxophonist Steve Lacy describes the experience of playing Evans's colorful arrangements in a fascinating and enlightening manner: "Gil painted with his players. I felt like a color—a ribbon in the great spectrum. I'd never felt that before, and not much since then. It was a unique experience, to be a strand of color—there's no more you, there is just it" (Crease 2002, 206).

smooth in comparison to the more jagged style of some beboppers, such as Dizzy Gillespie.

This group, the Miles Davis Nonet that came to be known as the "Birth of the Cool" band, recorded twelve tracks in three recording sessions in 1949–1950. Several recordings were initially released shortly after the recording sessions: eight came out on *Classics in Jazz–Miles Davis* in 1954 and eleven finally came out in 1954 as the landmark album *Birth of the Cool*. A number of the Birth of the Cool band musicians went on to take these concepts in new and varied directions; two of them were John Lewis's Modern Jazz Quartet and the Gerry Mulligan Quartet.

The Modern Jazz Quartet

Pianist-composer John Lewis and the Modern Jazz Quartet had a unique sound and approach to performance that challenged many of jazz's established conventions. Under Lewis's musical direction, the group had an understated, calm, and stately style that drew on both jazz and classical music for its inspiration while emphasizing the role of composition in tandem with improvisation. Vibraphonist Milt Jackson, a leading performer on his instrument, provided a bluesy and hot foil to Lewis's more restrained piano style. Along with the use of classical chamber music techniques in their music, such as carefully composed **counterpoint**, they treated each performance as if they were playing in a concert hall. The quartet followed established performance conventions more associated with classical music, such as wearing tuxedos and entering and leaving the stage in a formal fashion. The group was rounded out by bassist Percy Heath and drummer Connie Kay and was one of the most successful and longest-lasting small groups in the history of jazz.

IN PERFORMANCE
Lennie Tristano's Influence on Cool Jazz

Lennie Tristano (1919–1978) was an influential pianist, composer, and teacher in the cool jazz vein. He combined his diverse musical interests in Art Tatum, Lester Young, bebop, and Johann Sebastian Bach and influenced cool jazz soloists such as saxophonists Lee Konitz and Warne Marsh. An important part of Tristano's teaching technique, which was carried on by Marsh and Konitz, was for students to both play and sing the various melodic lines and solos they were studying and writing. Tristano also experimented with techniques that presaged the avant-garde through freely improvising without basing the solos on a tune or melody as well as by experimenting with atonality.

Lennie Tristano performing in New York, ca. 1947. Tristano was an important composer and performer in the cool jazz style. Photo by William P. Gottlieb.

Courtesy William P. Gottlieb Collection and Library of Congress.

HOW DID COOL JAZZ DEVELOP ON THE WEST COAST?

West Coast jazz musicians represented a wide variety of styles in San Francisco's Fillmore District and in the extremely vibrant jazz scene on Central Avenue in Los Angeles that produced many important jazz artists, including saxophonists Dexter Gordon and Art Pepper, trumpeter Clora Bryant (Chapter 7, 3rd Chorus), trombonist-arranger Melba Liston, bassist-composer Charles Mingus (Chapter 13, 3rd Chorus), and arranger Gerald Wilson. A number of jazz musicians on the West Coast, however, had an affinity for the cool jazz style; and a subgenre of cool jazz developed as "West Coast jazz." What distinguishes the styles is not clear, but certainly a number of players are thought of as West Coast jazz stylists and generally have a relaxed, "cool," style. Also, there was a compositional style that developed around writers such as Jimmy Giuffre (Chapter 10, 3rd Chorus), trumpeter-composer-arranger Shorty Rogers, and Gerry Mulligan, as well as some progressive jazz composers and bandleaders. This style often included a great deal of **contrapuntal writing**, which previously was not a significant element in jazz composition. Small-group composing tended to be more delicate and transparent, while continuing to swing hard but in a relaxed fashion. Conversely, large-group writing in this style, often associated with progressive jazz, could be quite dense.

Gerry Mulligan and Chet Baker

Gerry Mulligan (1927–1996) was consistently a leading baritone sax player and displayed an unusually light and airy sound on what is normally a much

JAZZ LIVES CHET BAKER

Trumpet player Chet Baker (1929–1988) was born in Yale, Oklahoma. His father was a professional guitarist, and his mother played piano; both encouraged him to make music from a young age. He studied music in high school and then served two stints in the army; in his second enlistment, he was stationed in San Francisco and played with the army band. He began working jazz clubs in the area and in 1951 made a tour with saxophonist Charlie Parker, who was then working on the West Coast. Baker joined the Gerry Mulligan Quartet in 1951, performing with him for a year.

Baker's work with the Mulligan Quartet drove him to stardom. However, his addiction to heroin took a toll on his life and career beginning in the later 1950s. His career was an up-and-down affair after that, including jail time, a violent beating that left him without teeth, and a mysterious death after apparently falling out of his Amsterdam hotel window.

The 1988 documentary film *Let's Get Lost* did much to spread the romantic image of Baker as an individual who was too free-spirited and creative to survive in the more mundane everyday world.

Baker had a lyrical, gentle, and understated style. He had a limited range but played the horn well with a pretty bell-like tone, which suited his melodically oriented soloing; and he had a whisper-like vocal style to match. While a beautiful player, his place in jazz is confused. Early on he was touted as competition for Miles Davis, an unfair comparison for any trumpet player. He was also a compelling figure with his boyish good looks and wild, drug- and alcohol-fueled lifestyle, causing some to feel that his place in jazz is consequently overstated. This, however, does not do justice to his melodic gift, and it is the latter that allowed him to fit so well with Mulligan, an equally gifted lyrical player.

"Line for Lyons" (1952) by Gerry Mulligan Quartet with Chet Baker

INSTRUMENTATION: Baritone saxophone, leader: Gerry Mulligan; **Trumpet:** Chet Baker; **Bass:** Carson Smith; **Drums:** Chico Hamilton.

LISTENING HIGHLIGHT, MELODY AND HARMONY: The music of the Mulligan Quartet had a quality similar to classical chamber music both in the quietness and gentleness of the playing—along with Chico Hamilton's tasteful drumming (discussed in Chapter 14, 3rd Chorus)—and in the extensive use of polyphony (multiple contrapuntal melodic lines that are equal in importance and that generally interweave with each other). The group incorporated these elements into its composed melodic presentations as well as its improvisations. Along with this, without a piano, the two horn players were required to outline, or "spell," the chord changes, meaning that in their melodic lines they play important notes that clearly indicate the chord progression. Mulligan and Baker, as well as Mulligan's later band mates Brookmeyer and Farmer, all excelled at this fine art.

This Mulligan AABA composition quickly and smoothly shows the various ways that Mulligan and Baker interacted in this piano-less quartet. We first hear Baker playing the pretty melody, with Mulligan playing a carefully composed counterline. Mulligan solos with the bass and drums on the first two A sections (0:46), then Baker solos over the bridge as Mulligan accompanies him with a counterline (1:11). For the 2nd chorus, the two improvise interweaving lines (contrapuntal polyphony) on the first two A sections (1:35) before closing out the tune with the melody at the bridge and last A (1:59).

heavier-sounding instrument. An early and influential job for him was playing in Claude Thornhill's Orchestra, where he met Gil Evans. Mulligan eventually became part of the circle of friends and colleagues who converged at Evans's apartment and was the primary arranger for the *Birth of the Cool* material. While initially associated with New York City, Mulligan moved to the West Coast, where he wrote for Stan Kenton. He founded a quartet while living in Los Angeles, eventually becoming associated with West Coast jazz.

The Gerry Mulligan Quartet had an interesting twist: it was "piano-less," which created a very different and more open sound. Mulligan initially led this group with the trumpeter Chet Baker, and the group was a hit and made both Mulligan and Baker into jazz stars. Later iterations of the quartet included valve trombonist-composer Bob Brookmeyer, who went on to become one of the most renowned contemporary jazz composer-arrangers, and Art Farmer, one of the top jazz trumpet and flugelhorn soloists for many years. Mulligan went on to have a long and productive career as a bandleader, instrumentalist, and composer-arranger that included small groups as well as his own big band.

Dave Brubeck

As is true with most of the musicians presented so far in this chapter, pianist-composer Dave Brubeck (1920–2012) is difficult to categorize, but his music is often referred to as West Coast jazz. He is also known for a "cool" approach as well as the use of classical compositional resources in his pieces, but his approach and style differ from those of Mulligan. Brubeck studied classical composition with Darius Milhaud (he named one of his sons after the composer) and brought that training to his jazz writing. While he had an extremely varied and productive career, it is the work with his quartet beginning in the 1950s which featured the cool, sweet-sounding alto saxophonist Paul Desmond that he is best known for. Their 1959 album *Time Out* was a huge success and the first jazz album to go "platinum" while also reaching number 2 on the *Billboard* pop albums chart. Two selections from that album, "Blue Rondo à La Turk" and "Take 5," were two of Brubeck's biggest hits, becoming nationally popular. This is particularly surprising as both of these songs use unusual meters, 9/8 and 5/4, respectively, both referred to as "odd" or "irregular" meters.

The Dave Brubeck Quartet remained together through the late 1960s, and then Brubeck formed a group with his sons to play in a more jazz–rock style. That group remained together through the early 1980s. Brubeck continued to compose and perform almost until his death.

read all about it
"A Jazz Summit Meeting"

Walser, **Keeping Time***, Chapter 46*
This roundtable discussion brings together several key performers of the 1950s and 1960s, including Dave Brubeck, Gerry Mulligan, Stan Kenton, Dizzy Gillespie, Charles Mingus, Cannonball Adderley, and George Russell—along with several critics—to discuss current issues in jazz.

WHAT IS PROGRESSIVE JAZZ?

Another style from the 1950s is progressive jazz. Many of the progressive jazz composers had an interest in classical music, and a number studied at classical conservatories. Few wrote with the actual intent of fusing the two styles; however, their compositional palettes were expanded through their absorption and study of classical composition. This movement is often associated with bands led by Red Norvo, Artie Shaw, and Benny Goodman as early as the 1930s and arrangers such as Eddie Sauter. It is primarily thought of, however, as flourishing during the period from the mid-1940s through the late 1950s in the work of composer-arrangers such as Sauter, Ralph Burns, George Handy, and Bob Graettinger.

The Dave Brubeck Quartet, ca. 1960. (Left to right) Paul Desmond (saxophone), Joe Morello (drums), Gene Wright (bass), Brubeck (piano). Brubeck's classic quartet did much to popularize jazz in the 1950s and 1960s.
© Pictorial Press Ltd./Alamy.

listening focus

"Blue Rondo à La Turk" (1959) by the Dave Brubeck Quartet

INSTRUMENTATION: Piano, leader: Dave Brubeck; **Alto saxophone:** Paul Desmond; **Bass:** Eugene Wright; **Drums:** Joe Morello.

LISTENING HIGHLIGHT, FORM: "Blue Rondo à La Turk" nicely contrasts Brubeck's heavier, more rhythmic style with Desmond's light, pretty, and airy sound. This sectional composition begins by gradually adding each instrument of the quartet on a repetitive, yet long-lined melody consisting of a series of rhythmic groupings (1–2, 1–2, 1–2, 1–2–3 followed by 1–2–3, 1–2–3, 1–2–3, two different groupings of 9/8) that is put through various melodic and harmonic permutations. Two short contrasting sections follow (1:18 and 1:38), and the piece eventually begins to transition to a blues in a more standard meter, 4/4 (1:51). Desmond plays a typically relaxed solo that leaves lots of space and combines lovely melodic playing with bluesy lines (2:12). Brubeck's solo follows (3:52) and alternates simple melody with a **block-chord style** (4:25–5:07), a hallmark of his as well as a typical piano technique. They take the tune out (5:33) by quickly alternating the original melody and a blues followed by the two contrasting sections heard earlier in the composition.

QUESTIONS AND CONTROVERSIES
Progressive Jazz and Third Stream

The bands and composers normally associated with progressive jazz were primarily white, and the progressive jazz genre is generally depicted in this manner. Yet music that was spoken of as **third stream**—a term created by composer-conductor-scholar Gunther Schuller to describe works that deliberately fused classical and jazz composition—such as works by African American composers Charles Mingus (*Revelations*; see Chapter 13, 3rd Chorus) and trombonist-composer J. J. Johnson (*Poem for Brass*) could easily be labeled as progressive jazz, as could extended works by Duke Ellington, such as *A Tone Parallel to Harlem* (discussed in Chapter 8, 2nd Chorus). Billy Strayhorn (also discussed in Chapter 8, 2nd Chorus) also had much in his writing that could be included in this category, and Jimmy Mundy's "Futile Frustration," written for Count Basie, is another example of a composition that could easily be called progressive jazz. This artificial division clearly involves racial and cultural issues and needs to be further examined.

Stan Kenton

The big-band leader most commonly associated with progressive jazz is the extremely successful Stan Kenton, who actually coined the phrase "progressive jazz" to describe the music he was performing with his band. He hired forward-thinking composer-arrangers such as Pete Rugolo ("Conflict" and "Mirage"), Bob Graettinger ("Thermopylae" and *City of Glass*), Bill Holman ("Invention for Guitar and Trumpet"), Bill Russo ("Improvisation"), and Johnny Richards. The less commercially successful

Boyd Raeburn Orchestra was important in this genre as well in the mid-1940s, particularly through the writing of George Handy, such as his composition for the band "Dalvatore Sally" as well as "The Bloos," composed for the multidisc collection *The Jazz Scene*, which very effectively combined a big band with a small chamber orchestra.

2nd Chorus Hard Bop

WHAT IS HARD BOP?

As cool jazz took a more relaxed approach to the bebop aesthetic, many musicians in the 1950s went in another direction. Instead of becoming more laid-back, they actually increased the intensity of the music through the use of a heavier blues and R&B influence, creating **hard bop**. This style has more of a hard edge and is generally associated with East Coast musicians, setting up an interesting contrast with the West Coast style. Many of today's jazz standards come from the repertoire of the three quintessential hard bop groups we will examine here: Art Blakey's Jazz Messengers, the Horace Silver Quintet, and the Clifford Brown–Max Roach Quintet.

Each of these bands has its own approach, of course, but they do have much in common. All three groups were dissatisfied with the typical melody–solos–melody format and were interested in going beyond standard AABA and blues forms. Their compositions often were a bit more formally complicated, with sophisticated small-group arrangements that included interesting introductions, ensembles, and endings; and original material was integral to these bands' styles and identities. In addition, Blakey and Silver's long-lasting groups, as was true for big bands, served as "finishing schools" for young musicians before jazz was part of any educational curriculum.

Art Blakey and the Jazz Messengers

Art Blakey (1919–1990), as both a drummer and a bandleader, helped to define and refine hard bop. His band, the Jazz Messengers, was one of jazz's most important small groups from the 1950s until Blakey's death in 1990 as he continued to explore and expand the hard bop repertoire. As a drummer, Art Blakey was profoundly influential and known for his unending energy and a powerful intensity that combined his roots in blues, swing, and bebop, as well as employing elements of African rhythms.

As a bandleader, Blakey had an unerring sense for choosing musicians and for helping them realize their potential. Early members of his band, trumpeter-composer Clifford Brown and pianist-composer Horace Silver (originally a coleader of the group), went on to create their own hard bop groups. The list of musicians who starred with Blakey and went on to stardom is impressively long.

Blakey expanded his group from the standard quintet to a sextet by adding a trombone to the trumpet and saxophone horn section, giving him what became his signature front line of three horns. Having three horns as opposed to two gave the composers and arrangers of the band an extra color as well as more opportunity to flesh out harmonies in the horn section. Blakey also relied on his side musicians to create original repertoire, and many of the compositions written for the Jazz Messengers by Wayne Shorter ("El Toro," "Ping Pong"), Benny Golson ("Along Came Betty," "Blues March"), and Bobby Timmons ("Moanin'") are now jazz standards.

IN PERFORMANCE
Art Blakey's School of Jazz

Although an exhaustive list of the impressive side musicians employed by Blakey would make up a box in itself, some of them are particularly worthy of note. Trumpeters Clifford Brown, Kenny Dorham, and Bill Hardman as well as three of the most important post-bop trumpeters, Lee Morgan, Freddie Hubbard, and Woody Shaw, all had productive stints in the band. Contemporary trumpet players such as Wynton Marsalis, one of today's leading jazz musicians; trumpeter-composer Terence Blanchard; and Wallace Roney gained their first international exposure with the Jazz Messengers. The thoughtful and lyrical tenor saxophonists Hank Mobley, Benny Golson (also a leading composer-arranger), and saxophonist-composer Wayne Shorter (who we will encounter in Chapter 13, 1st Chorus, with Miles Davis and in Chapter 14, 1st Chorus, with Weather Report), as well as players such as Kenny Garrett (Chapter 15, 2nd Chorus), Billy Harper, Donald Harrison, Jackie McLean, and Gary Bartz were all with the band. He hired trombonists such as Curtis Fuller, Slide Hampton (also an important composer-arranger), Julian Priester, and Steve Turre. The pianists he hired, such as Bobby Timmons, Cedar Walton, Ronnie Matthews, Joanne Brackeen, Wynton Kelly, Keith Jarrett, John Hicks, Benny Green, Mulgrew Miller, and James Williams, were all terrific soloists but also were (and are) some of the most sensitive accompanists in jazz. Finally, bassists Jymie Merritt, Wilbur Ware, Reggie Workman, Stanley Clarke, and Lonnie Plaxico anchored the rhythm section at various times. As you can see from this list, the Jazz Messengers was an important finishing school for an incredible array of players.

Art Blakey and the Jazz Messengers, in performance in 1960. (Left to right) Lee Morgan (trumpet), Jymie Merritt (bass), and Art Blakey (drums). Blakey was an important hard bop bandleader and mentor to young musicians throughout his long career. Photograph by Lennart Steen.

© Lebrecht Music & Arts.

Horace Silver

Pianist-composer Horace Silver (1928–2014), a founding member of the Jazz Messengers in 1954 along with Art Blakey, left that band in the mid-1950s to lead his own groups. Defined by his funky, bluesy, and lyrical yet spare piano style and featuring one of the most impressive and varied bodies of original composition in jazz (including "The Preacher," "Song for My Father," and "Nica's Dream"),

"Moanin'" (1958) by Art Blakey and the Jazz Messengers

INSTRUMENTATION: Drums, leader: Art Blakey; **Trumpet:** Lee Morgan; **Tenor saxophone:** Benny Golson; **Piano:** Bobby Timmons; **Bass:** Jymie Merritt.

LISTENING HIGHLIGHT, STYLE: "Moanin'" combines blues and gospel influences with a bop sensibility. The A section melody (0:00) features a gentle call-and-response blues figure, while the bridge (0:29) has a more driving melody along with a classic Art Blakey rhythmic feel that features a powerful backbeat that exemplifies the blues and R&B influence that is often present in hard bop.

The front line featured two up-and-coming soloists, Lee Morgan on trumpet and Benny Golson on tenor saxophone, both of whom went on to stardom. Morgan begins his solo with an intense blues phrase that immediately grabs the listener (0:59). His playing is melodic and filled with great rhythmic diversity. It also is characterized by the shaping, bending, and smearing of notes, which greatly adds to its expressiveness and instantly identifies his playing. Bobby Timmons's solo (5:02) is a great example of the hard bop piano style as it is full of blues and gospel-like phrases and rhythms. He uses numerous pianistic techniques such as locked hands harmonization (block-chord style) and the melody played in octaves with little rolls at the end of phrases as we heard from Earl Hines in the early days of jazz.

JAZZ LIVES BENNY GOLSON & LEE MORGAN

Benny Golson (b. 1929) has consistently been a leading tenor sax player as well as one of jazz's top composers and arrangers. Born in Philadelphia, he got his start playing in 1951 as a member of Bull Moose Jackson's combo, which played primarily R&B-styled music; pianist Tadd Dameron (Chapter 10, 3rd Chorus) was also a member of this band. When Dameron formed his own group, Golson joined him, playing with him from 1953 to 1954, and then worked with various ensembles before joining Blakey's Jazz Messengers in 1958. His compositions for Blakey and for the Jazztet, a group he led with the lovely and understated trumpeter-flugelhornist Art Farmer from 1959 to 1962, stand out as a powerful body of work; many of these have become jazz standards, including "Along Came Betty," "Stablemates," "Whisper Not," and "Killer Joe." In 1967, Golson moved to Los Angeles, where he became a successful composer for the Hollywood studios, including scores for the TV shows *Mod Squad*, *Mannix*, and *M*A*S*H*. Golson revived the Jazztet in 1982 and has since performed in a variety of settings while continuing to compose.

Trumpeter Lee Morgan (1938–1972) was one of the great soloists in the hard bop tradition. Morgan also hailed from Philadelphia and played with local groups before joining Dizzy Gillespie's big band in 1956. He joined the Jazz Messengers in 1958, remaining with Blakey through 1961. After making his reputation with the Jazz Messengers, he led his own groups and had numerous successful records, including his 1964 album *Sidewinder*, before his untimely death after being shot by his partner, Helen More, outside Slug's Saloon, a New York City nightclub. His style was filled with the blues and funky phrases mixed with a bebop sensibility. He played hard with an intense edge and an aggressive and fat sound.

The Horace Silver Quintet was one of the most consistently interesting small groups for nearly 50 years. His quintet consisted of the standard instrumentation of trumpet, tenor saxophone, piano, bass, and drums.

While this lineup is small and a necessarily limited instrumentation, Silver stretched it to its limits and used it skillfully in a varied manner, always managing to keep the music fresh and interesting. His clever use of two-part harmony for the trumpet and sax helped beef up the ensemble's sound, and most of his compositions included the extensive use of introductions, endings, and composed ensembles. In addition, his compositions were quite diverse in character, he wrote in unusual keys for jazz, and he used a variety of musical influences, including the rich rhythmic traditions of his Cape Verdean family roots and of Brazil, as well as Latin and African music.

In later years Silver expanded his compositional pallet with a series of records that each in turn integrated his quintet with brass, strings, woodwinds, chorus, and percussion and wrote songs and lyrics that reflected his spiritual and political beliefs. Though his music was firmly in the hard bop vein, through his compositions Silver managed to create a stylistic niche all his own.

Like Blakey, Silver regularly found and nurtured terrific new talent, many of whom went on to great fame: trumpeters Kenny Dorham, Blue Mitchell, Donald Byrd, Art Farmer, Woody Shaw, Randy Brecker, Tom Harrell, Carmell Jones, and Dave Douglas (Chapter 15, 2nd Chorus); saxophonists Hank Mobley, Junior Cook, Clifford Jordan, Joe Henderson, George Coleman, Michael Brecker, and Bob Berg; bassists Larry Ridley and Bob Cranshaw; and drummers Roy Haynes, Louis Hayes, Billy Cobham, and Idris Muhammad.

Clifford Brown and Max Roach

In 1954 Horace Silver and Art Blakey teamed with one of jazz's most gifted and lyrically profound soloists, trumpeter Clifford Brown (1930–1956). Brown was heavily influenced by trumpeter Fats Navarro (Chapter 10, 3rd Chorus) and went on to become one of jazz's most influential trumpet players. He had a warm, round sound all over the horn, and his articulation—the use of the tongue to define individual notes or mark phrase divisions—gives his playing an unmatched and unusual quality of lightness and clarity, even in the swiftest of passages. Brown also had an uncanny ability to combine small bits of melody into long and coherent lyrical lines in a seemingly endless fashion. There was also a buoyant, upbeat, and joyous quality to his playing.

Between 1954 and 1956, Brown joined with drummer Max Roach to create a band in the mold of hard bop but that clearly marked out new directions in modern mainstream jazz. They played a combination of original and standard material, and their arrangements were straightforward yet clever, featuring interesting small-group arrangements. Brown's recordings with this group still stand out and continue to influence the jazz field; Roach was Brown's equal in the technical mastery of his instrument.

Brown's achievements are all particularly remarkable as his career was cut short when he died a tragic early death at the age of 25 in a car accident (along with pianist Richie Powell, Bud Powell's brother) while on the road with his group the Clifford Brown–Max Roach Quintet. His playing combined technical mastery, a nearly unparalleled melodic gift, and an intense rhythmic focus and flexibility. In addition, he accomplished this level of virtuosity and musical maturity without the usual long-term professional experience. That Brown managed to accomplish so much in the mere 12 years that he played the trumpet is astounding, and it is intriguing to consider where his playing might have gone had he not died so young.

listening guide

"Joy Spring" (1955) by the Clifford Brown–Max Roach Quintet

INSTRUMENTATION: Trumpet and coleader: Clifford Brown; **Drums and coleader:** Max Roach; **Tenor saxophone:** Harold Land; **Piano:** Richie Powell; **Bass:** George Morrow.

OVERVIEW: "Joy Spring" is a light, pretty, and joyful Clifford Brown composition that has become a jazz standard. While this is a simple arrangement, it allows us to hear the subtleties of a quintet arrangement in the context of a working, touring group. The group makes "Joy Spring" sound easy, but harmonically it is quite complex as it moves through numerous keys throughout the tune. This composition and performance do not have the typical hard bop feel, in the same way that Bobby Timmons's "Moanin'" does, but instead shows how this hard bop group took the style, expanded it, and made it their own.

FORM: The form of this tune is AA¹BA, a variation on AABA (see "Melody and Harmony"). After the introduction and the melody, saxophonist Harold Land plays a 1-chorus solo (0:55), Brown follows with a 2-chorus solo (1:45), and pianist Richie Powell plays 1 (3:20). The horns then **trade 4s**—trading 4-bar solos—with Roach for an entire chorus (4:07), after which Roach plays a chorus as an unaccompanied drum solo (4:55). The introduction is played again (5:40), and then the entire melody ends the tune.

STYLE: Brown's solo style is immediately recognizable to everyone in jazz, and this gem of a solo is perfect from beginning to end. The entire solo is one long, gorgeous, and extremely singable melody. Brown's playing is incredibly clean—nothing is out of place—and he is in complete control of all aspects of his playing at all times. While his sound is warm and round, there is also a slight burr or edge to it that comes and goes at will. Brown was not a loud player but managed to create an intense sound nonetheless. Along with his melodic gift, the lighter character of his playing gave him the exceptional facility, flexibility, and accuracy that made Brown stand out as a trumpet soloist.

MELODY AND HARMONY: "Joy Spring" has a particularly lovely, long-lined melodic line. It differs from Tin Pan Alley melodies in that it is instrumental in character (as opposed to vocal), as is also true for most bebop melodies.

RHYTHM: This is a medium-tempo song with a light and bouncy feel to the melody. Roach plays the entire tune with brushes, adding to the gentleness and lightness of this recording. The bass plays in 4 throughout.

ACCOMPANIMENT: The arrangement, while quite simple, is very effective. Since this was a highly successful working group that was touring and performing on a constant basis, they are quite tight while also being relaxed. "Brownie" (Brown's nickname) and Harold Land play the entire tune in **octave unison**—playing the same notes an octave apart. The rhythm section accents rhythmic figures of the melody and plays fills together, adding a level of sophistication and tightness to the melody and the overall arrangement. Particularly notice how Roach handles this aspect of the group interaction throughout the recording; this is a crucial aspect of a drummer's role.

continued

"JOY SPRING" LISTENING GUIDE

TIME	FORM	STYLE	MELODY AND HARMONY	RHYTHM	ACCOMPANIMENT
0:00	Intro			The rhythm section's introduction has a brief piano melody but is dominated by rhythmic figures that they all play together.	The bass and drums support and accent the piano figures throughout this carefully arranged introduction by the rhythm section.
1st Chorus, Melody					
0:11	A	Trumpet and tenor saxophone play the melody in octave unison (the same pitch an octave apart).	"Joy Spring" has a melodic character very much like Clifford Brown's solo style. It is pretty, light, and melodically inventive, with an upbeat flavor.	The bass plays in 4 throughout the tune.	The rhythm section stops playing time and together accent melodic figures during the last part of A and A^1. This type of arranged rhythmic figure is an important element in small-group arranging.
0:23	A^1		The A^1 section is the same as A except that it is a half-step higher in key (A is in F major and A^1 is in G-flat major), making it a long sequence—a duplicated phrase at a different pitch degree.		
0:34	B		The B section is harmonically challenging as it moves quickly through a series of four different keys.		The rhythm section's arrangement of accents plays an even bigger role in the first half of the bridge.
0:45	A		The last A returns to the original key.		
2nd Chorus, Saxophone Solo					
0:55	AA^{1}BA	Tenor saxophonist Harold Land plays a 1-chorus solo. It is generally relaxed with space between phrases and includes a short, speedy passage on the bridge (1:22).			Max Roach accompanies simply with brushes. The bass continues in 4, and the piano comps throughout all of the solos.
3rd Chorus, Brown Trumpet Solo					
1:44	A	Brown plays a 2-chorus solo—he gets a longer solo than sax or piano on the recording as he is the featured horn player and coleader.	Each of Brown's phrases is gorgeous and sweet.	There is a slightly laid-back character to Brown's playing here.	

"*Joy Spring*" listening guide continued

TIME	FORM	STYLE	MELODY AND HARMONY	RHYTHM	ACCOMPANIMENT
3rd Chorus, Brown Trumpet Solo					
1:55	A¹	Brown leaves space between phrases, as opposed to playing a steady stream of 1/8 notes. He creates a great deal of rhythmic variety in his phrases.	This section begins with a bit more energy by briefly going to the upper register.		
2:07	B	In the beginning of this section Brown plays a sequence as he moves from one key to the next.	Brown shows his stuff on the bridge by playing quick lines through the frequent key changes.	He is more on top of the beat for the bridge as he plays swift lines consisting of 1/8 notes.	
2:19	A	While much of this solo is on the mellow side and in the middle register, Brown goes into his upper register here (where he plays with great accuracy), creating variety as well as a climax for this chorus. He finishes the chorus in a relaxed manner.	Brown continues to play one beautiful melody after another.		
4th Chorus, Brown Solo, continued					
2:31	A	Brown's articulation is crucial to his style, and here he alters it slightly on two notes to give a repetitive little rhythmic figure extra flavor.	Brown begins by emphasizing a blue note in a rhythmic phrase, then continues to create small, melodic phrases.		
2:43	A¹	As Brown plays these rhythmically relaxed phrases, he carefully and softly separates the notes with his articulation.		Brown again lays back on these phrases to create a relaxed feel.	
2:55	B		For the first half of this section Brown plays a sequence as he moves through two keys. The second half is also two phrases that are very similar over the next two keys, but it is not quite a sequence.		
3:07	A		The melody at the end of this solo is a remarkably lovely and relaxed ending to a jewel of a Brown solo.		

continued

TIME	FORM	STYLE	MELODY AND HARMONY	RHYTHM	ACCOMPANIMENT
5th Chorus, Piano Solo					
3:19	AA¹BA	Richie Powell plays 1 solo chorus. It is understated and relaxed.			A pianist, of course, comps behind his or her own solo, giving the advantage of being able to carefully integrate the left-hand comping with the right hand's solo.
6th Chorus, Trading 4s					
4:07	AA¹BA	Since Roach is a coleader, he, of course, also gets plenty of room to play. The horns first "trades 4s"—trading 4-bar solos—with Roach for an entire chorus.		Roach plays simply, tastefully, and straightforwardly during his "4s." We can mostly follow the time easily, which is not always the case in drum solos.	The rhythm section, including Roach, accompanies the horns during their "4s."
7th Chorus, Unaccompanied Drum Solo					
4:55	A	While some drum solos are "open," meaning they don't have to follow a form, in this type of music they frequently do.		Roach's last 4 of the 6th chorus leads directly into an unaccompanied drum solo for an entire chorus. While he plays a 32-bar solo, Roach does not emphasize phrase divisions. While still soloing in a relatively simple manner, there are numerous spots where it gets difficult to keep counting beats, measures, and sections. This is a common characteristic of drum solos.	
5:06	A¹			Drum solo continues.	
5:18	B			Drum solo continues.	
5:29	A			Drum solo continues.	
5:40	Intro		The introduction is played again to reintroduce the melody.		
8th Chorus, Melody					
5:50	AA¹BA	The entire melody is played to end the tune.			

Max Roach (1924–2007) was one of jazz's top drummers and bandleaders throughout his career. We have already encountered him as one of the innovators of bebop drumming ("Salt Peanuts," Chapter 10, 1st Chorus). Roach went on to perform with an impressive cross section of major jazz artists over the course of his career, spanning both traditional and more avant-garde styles.

As was true with Art Blakey, polyrhythms were a crucial element in Roach's playing. Roach had the ability to play different rhythms with his hands and feet; this independence helped to revolutionize jazz drumming. Along with being an important innovator on his instrument, Roach played a politically important role by being outspoken on numerous issues, including racism in the music business. Through his music he also addressed civil rights issues in a significant recording, *We Insist: Max Roach's Freedom Now Suite* (1960), featuring his wife at the time, vocalist Abbey Lincoln, and lyrics by the vocalist-lyricist Oscar Brown, Jr. Another example of his political involvement was his attempt to gain more control over his music by founding Debut Records with bassist-composer-bandleader Charles Mingus (Chapter 13, 3rd Chorus). Roach was also one of the first jazz performers to enter academia (the University of Massachusetts–Amherst), helping to set the trend for jazz pedagogy moving to schools and the academy from apprenticeships such as the big bands and small groups like Blakey's and Silver's.

Throughout his career Roach continued to evolve and grow and challenged traditional notions of jazz by being a major figure in many genres, including bebop, hard bop, and the avant-garde, as well as through expressing his openness to other forms such as rap and hip-hop at a time when it was not popular among jazz musicians to do so. Roach had a working piano-less quartet for many years and combined this group with a string quartet (the Double Quartet, which included his daughter, viola player Maxine Roach), played solo and duet concerts, and teamed with a brass quintet.

3rd Chorus The Mambo Craze

HOW DID THE MAMBO CRAZE CONTINUE THE LATIN INFLUENCE ON JAZZ?

Along with cubop (Chapter 10, 1st Chorus), another Latin music phenomenon, the "mambo craze," was creating a sensation in New York City from the late 1940s through the 1950s. The **mambo** originated in Cuba and became popular after bandleader Pérez Prado began promoting the dance and music in the late 1940s. The dance originally had no prescribed steps; instead, the dancer was supposed to "feel the music" and express those feelings through movement.

The place to be for mambo was the Palladium Ballroom in midtown Manhattan, just a few blocks from the 52nd Street clubs where bebop was being performed; and the craze eventually reached the rest of the country. Dancers from all cultures mixed at the Palladium, and dance they did! Three bands—"the big three"—ruled at the Palladium: Machito's band (Chapter 12, 2nd Chorus) and bands led by Tito Rodriguez and Tito Puente. Rodriguez and Puente had big bands with a full Afro-Cuban rhythm section of piano and bass and a percussion section of bongó, conga, and timbales, along with other players and singers adding in maracas, guiro, and claves.

Trumpeter Mario Bauzá (Chapter 10, 1st Chorus) originally brought **timbalero** Tito Puente (1923–2000) into Machito's band. Puente went on to become one of

JAZZ LIVES TITO PUENTE

Tito Puente—known as "El Rey" (the King)—was born in New York City to Puerto Rican parents. Along with the timbales he was an arranger and played vibraphone (or vibes), helping to popularize that instrument's use in Latin music, along with vibes players such as Cal Tjader and Louie Ramirez. After serving in the navy, Puente studied at the Juilliard School of Music in New York City, one of the country's most prestigious music conservatories. He began his career as a side musician in New York mambo-oriented bands, eventually becoming a top Latin bandleader during the mambo era. Puente remained at the forefront of Afro-Latin music and Latin jazz for over 50 years.

Puente led groups of all sizes, ranging from small Latin jazz groups to Latin dance bands with a powerful big band–influenced sound. His groups always had the top New York musicians in the Latin field, and as was true for most of the Latin bands, the personnel of his band, along with Latino musicians who specialized in Latin styles, also included jazz-oriented musicians from all cultures. Puente recorded hundreds of albums and received a Grammy Award for Best Traditional Tropical Album (2000) as well as a posthumous Grammy Lifetime Achievement Award (2003).

Puente's recording "Mambo Inn" is an example of the mambo style while also showing strong roots in jazz. In "Mambo Inn," the power of a big band is combined with a full percussion section, showing what an amazing experience it is to hear a Latin orchestra in full swing. This music has great intensity while still maintaining a relaxed feel. If you have any inclination at all to move to music, bands such as this drive you to the dance floor or at least to bopping your head and rocking to the beat in your chair. This is dance music at its best. Like the tune itself, its composers—Mario Bauzá, Bobby Woodlen, and Edgar Sampson—combined Latin and jazz backgrounds. Sampson (discussed as Chick Webb's arranger in Chapter 5, 2nd Chorus) was a jazz saxophonist and a composer and arranger who also worked with Puente and Tito Rodriguez as an arranger. The roots of mambo-style tunes such as "Mambo Inn" are clearly Cuban.

Latin music's biggest and most important stars beginning in this mambo era in the 1950s until his death. (A timbalero plays the **timbales** (or *pailas*), a Latin percussion kit that consists of two drums that resemble a cross between a snare drum and a tom-tom, a cymbal, and a campana—a cow bell—that is played while standing up.)

4th Chorus The Early Avant-Garde

WHAT IS AVANT-GARDE JAZZ?

While the various jazz styles we've discussed were being explored, the 1950s and 1960s also saw the rise of a number of musicians who were challenging the status quo of jazz with new approaches to improvisation, composition, group interaction, and the role of the rhythm section. This experimentation was referred to in several ways, among them being "the new thing," "free jazz," and **avant-garde**—a term that refers to those artists who hope to free themselves and their art from accepted traditions. Pianist-composer Cecil Taylor (Chapter 14, 2nd Chorus) and alto saxophonist-composer Ornette Coleman are considered the most important musicians of the jazz avant-garde of the 1950s and 1960s, and both eventually came to be acknowledged as hugely influential in jazz.

listening focus

"Mambo Inn" (1955) by the Tito Puente Orchestra

LISTENING HIGHLIGHT, FORM: The arrangements of bands of this sort generally used traditional formal elements such as a verse sung by a *sonero* (lead singer), *coros* (a sonero alternating with others singing a repeated chorus), mambos (instrumental interludes that include new written material for the rhythm section and the horns), *moñas* (repeated riff-like melodic lines), and solos. While the harmonic components of some elements of this music are often quite simple, the influence of jazz harmony in both the composition and arranging is quite evident in this recording.

In instrumental compositions such as "Mambo Inn," adjustments are made to the formal elements as there is no sonero, and elements from the jazz world enter in as well. After an introduction, the composition begins with an AABA tune (0:14). The A section is crisp, rhythmic, and brass-heavy, while the saxes play the bridge (0:34) in a smoothly romantic style. The tune is played once, and a montuno section follows, where the harmony is pared down to just one chord (1:04). The saxes start a line on their own over a bass vamp, and then the brass add their own on top of it. The baritone sax plays a solo (1:22), while the horns at times play riffs behind the soloist, creating great excitement. This leads back to the bridge, this time played by the trombones (2:11), followed by a big ending (2:19).

There was also a political component to much of the avant-garde, most notably in regard to the African American struggle for civil rights and self-determination. This included African American musicians taking control of their own economic and artistic freedom by creating cooperatives, alternative music schools, and record labels, as well as producing concerts (for example, the Association for the Advancement of Creative Musicians; see Chapter 12, 3rd Chorus).

Defining the avant-garde is difficult as there are a great variety of approaches to it, and **free jazz** has many elements in common with more traditional jazz. Initially, however, there were some characteristics of the avant-garde:

1. While the standard melody–solos–melody format is often used, avant-garde compositions frequently employ alternative approaches to form. Many formal strategies can be present. For example, forms can be clearly delineated and planned, sections can be "cued" (someone indicates when the next section should begin), or the form can be allowed to unfold through group interaction and improvisation.

2. A typical 4/4 swing is sometimes present, but a free approach to rhythm and meter is frequently used, while generally maintaining something resembling a jazz feeling.

3. Harmonic progressions are frequently less emphasized or absent, leaving freedom for players to develop their own approach to harmony and melody during their improvisations.

4. Players often use unorthodox and extended instrumental techniques as they experiment with timbre and sound.

QUESTIONS AND CONTROVERSIES
The Resistance to Free Jazz

When free jazz first arose, many musicians, critics, and scholars were outspoken regarding their distaste and distrust of the music, believing, for either musical or political reasons (or both), that it challenged some of the basic musical tenets of jazz. For example, one of the issues with free jazz is that some of the musicians (not all, by any means) choose not to master the same sorts of basic skills called for in more traditionally oriented jazz, such as knowing standard repertoire and being able to play changes—improvise based upon a harmonic progression—convincingly.

This type of initial resistance to avant-garde practices is common and has been true in most art forms. Art that is at first considered "way out," however, is often eventually accepted and absorbed into the mainstream in some way; and this is true for free jazz. The supporters and detractors of the "new thing" initially found little common ground, and consequently the avant-garde at first became an almost parallel jazz universe with only a few musicians able to function well in both worlds. Those—such as saxophonist John Coltrane (Chapter 13, 2nd Chorus)—who did bridge this gap and were accepted by both the more traditional jazz world and the avant-garde generally had already firmly established their jazz pedigree in the more traditional jazz world before incorporating avant-garde techniques.

While the avant-garde players have been somewhat marginalized in the jazz world and often have difficulty finding enough work to make a living, the music found, and continues to have, a dedicated following and has persisted as an important substyle within the jazz field. Along with this, the seeds sown during these early years of the avant-garde are still bearing fruit as many musicians are pursuing the musical possibilities opened up by the early avant-garde players and composers. In fact, throughout the development of the avant-garde the line between traditional and avant-garde practices has continued to become fuzzier. It is now common for musicians to feel free to use any techniques that seem appropriate for a particular composition or a particular group they are playing in.

In addition, numerous so-called avant-garde players are also powerful performers in traditional jazz styles, allowing them to bring these various styles together quite convincingly, to the point that the terms "avant-garde" and "free jazz," or "traditional jazz" for that matter, have begun to have little value for many musicians. Further stretching things, many of the avant-garde players and composers have also incorporated a multitude of styles from various cultures into their music (as is true for contemporary musicians in general), and many are using contemporary classical compositional techniques.

The supporters of these new styles passionately believed that the players and composers of the avant-garde were moving jazz in a new and positive direction while opening avenues of expression that built upon and expanded the jazz tradition.

Ornette Coleman

Alto saxophonist-composer Ornette Coleman (b. 1930) was an early innovator and leader of the jazz avant-garde. While initially a controversial and polarizing musical figure, Coleman has come to symbolize originality, perseverance, and commitment to a musical aesthetic against all odds. After moving to New York City from Los Angeles in the late 1950s, the Ornette Coleman Quartet played an engagement at the Five Spot in New York City in 1959 that proved to be both divisive and groundbreaking. It seemed musicians, audiences, and critics either loved the music or hated it; and the question of its ties to the jazz tradition was hotly debated. Nonetheless, it proved to be a provocative and powerful influence on jazz.

Originally from Texas, Coleman began his career touring with tent shows and rhythm-and-blues bands and eventually landed in Los Angeles after touring with rhythm-and-blues guitarist-vocalist Pee Wee Crayton. While always idiosyncratic, it was in Los Angeles where his unconventional, or avant-garde, work began to more fully develop. While it may be difficult to hear it at first, Coleman is strongly influenced by Charlie Parker and, like avant-garde pianist-composer Cecil Taylor, is steeped in the blues, yet his style is determinedly his own. He has an almost harsh tone and an eccentric approach to intonation that he compares to the freedom of the voice.

"Congeniality" is an example of the style of Coleman's first important group, the Ornette Coleman Quartet, with Don Cherry (pocket trumpet; a small, compacted trumpet), Charlie Haden (bass), and Billy Higgins (drums). The group played compositions consisting of melodies that seem straightforward and to be loosely in the bebop tradition yet are quirky and individualistic. With no piano player, the group could take a free approach to harmony. Its improvisation—often in a standard head–solos–head format—largely revolves around melodic invention. The intent is to give each player a great deal of freedom, so the result is particularly dependent on the musicians' ability to work with little framework. And while group interplay is always an essential ingredient in jazz, groups playing with open structures such as these have to be particularly sensitive to each other in order to make the music work effectively.

Don Cherry's loose, playful style fits well in this context as standard melodic clichés don't seem to be part of his aesthetic. Charlie Haden, a spectacular and sensitive bassist who was capable of playing in most any musical context, was perfect for this group as he was able to supply an improvised compositional approach that gave the tunes formal shape. Haden is also an unusually lyrical bass player, which added another component to the group. Drummer Billy Higgins, also an extremely versatile musician, brought an upbeat energy to the group and created a perfect balance of propulsion and a loose approach to time that Coleman was looking for. Interestingly, this group gives us a chance to hear musicians who came up after the big-band era with a different type of professional performing background from that of bebop players, for example, many of whom had played in big bands.

Over time, Coleman developed a musical theory called **harmolodics** in which "harmony, melody, speed, rhythm, time, and phrases all have equal position in the results that come from the placing and spacing of ideas" (Coleman 1983, 54–55). He based his compositions and improvisations on this and schooled his musicians in the theory as part of the rehearsal process.

In the late 1970s Coleman gravitated to a new sound with his group Prime Time, including electric guitarists Charles Ellerbee and Bern Nix, electric bassist Jamaaladeen Tacuma, and Ronald Shannon Jackson, and later Coleman's son Denardo Coleman, on drums. This group could be seen as related to jazz fusion (Chapter 14, 1st Chorus) due to its electric character, but it maintained the character of Coleman's innovative music while adding new timbres as well as the power of funk and rock.

Ornette Coleman on stage in 2003. Coleman has stretched the boundaries of jazz composition and performance through five decades of work. Photo by Marc PoKempner. © Picade LLC/Alamy.

listening focus

"Congeniality" (1959) by the Ornette Coleman Quartet

INSTRUMENTATION: Alto saxophone-leader: Ornette Coleman; **Pocket trumpet:** Don Cherry; **Bass:** Charlie Haden; **Drums:** Billy Higgins.

LISTENING HIGHLIGHT, FORM: In this upbeat tune, the group begins by playing the melodic theme four times (0:00, 0:12, 0:27, 0:41). This melody circles back around on itself, making it hard to hear where one statement ends and the other begins. The melody is still in sections, however, almost in a conventional manner, with three primary phrases (0:00, 0:05, 0:10), reminiscent of ABA. After the melody, Coleman plays a solo (0:57), which then dovetails seamlessly into Cherry's solo (3:44), keeping the cyclical concept of the melody present throughout. This creates a constant flow and a formal structure that is less dependent on sections and choruses than we have seen so far. The solos are also more extended than in the past and when performed live could have been considerably longer. After Cherry's solo, they move directly into a restatement of the cyclical melody (5:45).

During the melody, the tempo is constantly shifting, and at times there isn't really a tempo at all. The musicians move in and out of unison and harmony with each other, creating good compositional variety. The rhythm section does not always accompany the melody in the same way, which also creates variety, as does the fact that the tempo shifts. The solos, while definitely in a new style, are, in their own way, quite melodic and related to a bebop aesthetic. The soloists largely rely upon a stream of 1/8 notes while also playing lines that mix angularity with smoothness and challenging old concepts by taking them in a new direction.

Coleman's tone is unique and was influenced early on by his use of a plastic saxophone. His sound is bright, dry, and even a bit harsh at times; but its relationship to traditional alto sax playing in the mode of Charlie Parker, for example, is still clear. Cherry's use of a pocket trumpet—which has the same range as a trumpet but is very small and compact so consequently has a tighter, smaller, more veiled character to its sound—enables him to create a distinctive sound that separates his playing from that of more conventional trumpet players.

Later in his career Coleman began to write for traditional classical ensembles including compositions for winds (*Forms and Sounds for Wind Quartet*) and orchestra (*Skies of America*). He was the first jazz composer to receive the Guggenheim award for composition, and in 2007 he was awarded both the Pulitzer Prize and a Grammy Award for lifetime achievement.

Whether you like the music or not, it is good to appreciate the boldness of moving in new directions, especially considering that these musicians' livings depended upon being accepted, at least enough to work steadily. In retrospect, it is a bit hard to understand why many people were so disconcerted by this music, but it did upset the apple cart and, along with others such as pianist-composer Cecil Taylor, provided a new avenue of expression in jazz.

CODA Chapter Summary

How Did the Jazz World Change in the 1950s?

- Rather than featuring one dominant style (as in the swing and bebop eras), several different styles thrived simultaneously during this period, including cool jazz, progressive jazz, hard bop, and avant-garde jazz.

What Is Cool Jazz?

- Cool jazz arose as a reaction to the fast tempos and intensity of bebop. It featured more muted tonalities, longer and smoother melody lines, and fuller orchestrations.

How Did Cool Jazz Develop on the West Coast?

- A group of West Coast performers—including saxophonist Gerry Mulligan and pianist Dave Brubeck—used classical music compositional techniques, new instrumentation, and unusual rhythms to create their own type of cool jazz.

What Is Progressive Jazz?

- Progressive jazz features more richly orchestrated works with less emphasis on solo improvisation. Stan Kenton's orchestra was a leading performer in this style.

What Is Hard Bop?

- Hard bop features more soulful, R&B-flavored music than bebop, with a hard edge. Leading performers include Art Blakey, Horace Silver, Clifford Brown, and Max Roach.

How Did the Mambo Craze Continue the Latin Influence on Jazz?

- The popularity of mambo dancing enabled bandleaders like Tito Puente to enjoy great success in the 1950s. Puente's music was influenced by big-band jazz and in turn influenced contemporary jazz players.

What Is Avant-Garde Jazz?

- Avant-garde or free jazz developed in the late 1950s–early 1960s in the work of Ornette Coleman and Cecil Taylor. They sought to free jazz of its ties to conventional melody, rhythm, and harmony.

Talkin' Jazz (Key Terms)

Avant-garde	Hard bop	Third stream
Block-chord style	Harmolodics	Timbalero
Contrapuntal writing	Harmon mute	Timbales
Cool jazz	Mambo	Trade 4s
Counterpoint	Octave unison	
Free jazz	Progressive jazz	

Key People

Gil Evans	Dave Brubeck	Horace Silver
Miles Davis	Stan Kenton	Clifford Brown
Modern Jazz Quartet	Art Blakey and the Jazz	Max Roach
Gerry Mulligan	Messengers	Ornette Coleman

Think About This (For Further Discussion and Study)

1. Describe the characteristics of cool jazz.
2. Describe the characteristics of hard bop.
3. How is hard bop different from bebop?
4. Listen to Dizzy Gillespie on "Salt Peanuts," Miles Davis on "Boplicity," Chet Baker on "Line for Lyons," and Clifford Brown on "Joy Spring." Discuss the similarities and differences in all of their styles. Do you have a style you prefer?
5. After listening to "Mambo Inn," compare it to "El Manisero" (Chapter 7) and "Masabi" (Chapter 5). What are the similarities and differences between them?
6. Discuss the relationship between "Mambo Inn" and music by jazz big bands we have heard.
7. Discuss your experience listening to avant-garde jazz.
8. Do you see a relationship between avant-garde jazz and more traditional jazz?
9. Do you hear any relationship between Ornette Coleman's and Charlie Parker's playing? If so, what do you notice?

Look It Up (Key Resources)

Catalano, Nick. *Clifford Brown: The Life and Art of the Legendary Jazz Trumpeter*. New York: Oxford University Press, 2000.

Coleman, Ornette. "Pro Session: Prime Time for Harmolodics." *Down Beat*. July 1983.

Crease, Stephanie Stein. *Gil Evans: Out of the Cool—His Life and Music*. Chicago: A Cappella, 2002.

Easton, Carol. *Straight Ahead: The Story of Stan Kenton*. New York: Da Capo Press, 1991.

Gavin, James. *Deep in a Dream: The Long Night of Chet Baker*. New York: Knopf, 2002.

Gioia, Ted. *West Coast Jazz: Modern Jazz in California, 1945–1960*. New York: Oxford University Press, 1992.

Glasser, Ruth. *My Music Is My Flag: Puerto Rican Musicians and Their New York Communities, 1917–1940*. Berkeley and Los Angeles: University of California Press, 1997.

Goldshear, Alan. *Hard Bop Academy: The Sidemen of Art Blakey and the Jazz Messengers*. Milwaukee, WI: Hal Leonard, 2002.

Hall, Fred M. *It's About Time: The Dave Brubeck Story*. Fayetteville: University of Arkansas Press, 1996.

Hamilton, Andy. *Lee Konitz: Conversations on the Improviser's Art*. Ann Arbor: University of Michigan Press, 2007.

Klinkowitz, Jerome. *Listen: Gerry Mulligan—An Aural Narrative in Jazz*. New York: Schirmer Books, 1991.

Litweiler, John. *The Freedom Principle: Jazz After 1958*. New York: Morrow, 1984.

————. *Ornette Coleman: A Harmolodic Life*. New York: Morrow, 1992.

Loza, Steven. *Tito Puente and the Making of Latin Music*. Urbana: University of Illinois Press, 1999.

Mandel, Howard. *Miles, Ornette, Cecil: Jazz Beyond Jazz*. New York: Routledge, 2008.

McMillan, Jeffery S. *DelightfuLee: The Life and Music of Lee Morgan*. Ann Arbor: University of Michigan Press, 2008.

Ramsey, Doug, Dave Brubeck, Iola Brubeck, and Paul Caulfield. *Take Five: The Public and Private Lives of Paul Desmond*. Seattle, WA: Parkside Publications, 2005.

Roberts, John Storm. *The Latin Tinge: The Impact of Latin American Music on the United States*. New York: Oxford University Press, 1979.

————. *Latin Jazz: The First of the Fusions, 1880s to Today*. New York: Schirmer Books, 1999.

Rosenthal, David H. *Hard Bop: Jazz and Black Music, 1955–1965*. New York: Oxford University Press, 1992.

Silver, Horace. *Let's Get to the Nitty Gritty: The Autobiography of Horace Silver*, edited by Phil Pastras. Berkeley and Los Angeles: University of California Press, 2006.

Sublette, Ned. *Cuba and Its Music: From the First Drums to the Mambo*. Chicago: Chicago Review Press, 2004.

Washburne, Christopher. *Sounding Salsa: Performing Latin Music in New York City*. Philadelphia: Temple University Press, 2008.

THE 1960s

12

Just as during the 1950s when many different styles coexisted in the jazz world, the early 1960s saw a variety of approaches developed by different musicians to extend the jazz vocabulary. Many of these styles enjoyed great popularity in their heyday, returning jazz to the top of the pop charts in a way that had rarely been seen since the swing era. Among the most popular were soul jazz, a marriage of hard bop with R&B, gospel, and blues influences, and new styles of Latin jazz, as in the work of Cal Tjader, Mongo Santamaria, and the bossa nova–flavored hits of Stan Getz. At the same time, the avant-garde continued to develop, assisted by the growth of musician cooperatives such as Chicago's Association for the Advancement of Creative Musicians.

1st Chorus Soul Jazz

WHAT IS SOUL JAZZ?

A subgenre of hard bop (see Chapter 11, 2nd Chorus), **soul jazz** draws on the funky, soul approach seen in the music of Horace Silver and Art Blakey. Musicians such as organists Shirley Scott and Jimmy Smith, guitarist Wes Montgomery, pianists Les McCann and Ramsey Lewis, and alto saxophonist Julian "Cannonball" Adderley all added a blues, gospel, soul, and R&B accent to their music that embraced the accomplishments and appeal of black popular music.

The success of crossover artists who fused these various black music styles—such as the pianist-vocalist Ray Charles, alto saxophonist-vocalist Louis Jordan, and vocalist Dinah Washington—influenced the development of soul jazz, which, along with other styles of this period, broke down barriers between jazz and popular music styles while also highlighting how intertwined jazz and pop styles actually are. In addition, in the same way that many bebop players were big-band musicians, many soul jazz musicians had their early professional experiences with R&B and blues bands. Audiences reacted enthusiastically to soul jazz and its relationship to pop music, as can be seen by the numerous hits these players and their bands created that were regular fare on jukeboxes, harkening back to the days when jazz was a "popular" music.

Soul jazz is best represented in the work of several jazz organists, notably Jimmy Smith and Shirley Scott. The physical power of the electric organ and its relationship to the African American church and gospel music, as well as

Photo: Courtesy Getty Images.

In this chapter, we'll answer these questions:

- What Is Soul Jazz?
- What Were the Key Developments in Latin Jazz in the Early 1960s?
- How Did the Avant-Garde Jazz Movement Continue to Develop in the 1960s?

249

IN PERFORMANCE
The Hammond B3 Organ and Leslie Speakers

Traditional church organs are acoustic instruments, creating sounds through the use of large pipes powered by bellows. These instruments are large and expensive, and most black churches were too poor to afford them. In 1935, the Hammond Company introduced an electronic organ that offered several advantages. It was electrically powered and much more compact than a traditional church organ. It featured a tonewheel, a metal wheel that was used to create the organ-like sounds, rather than large pipes. It also had features that allowed the player to create vibrato. The B3 was an immediate success, with over 1,700 organs sold to churches in the first 3 years of its production. Smaller "spinet" models were produced that were even more portable, and many found their way into homes and nightclubs.

Inventor Donald Leslie worked for a department store that sold Hammond organs. Disappointed in the sound quality of these instruments, he experimented with creating an amplifier–speaker combination that would more accurately reproduce the sound of a church organ. He came up with a design featuring a rotating speaker in a cabinet to create a tremolo effect. Pop and jazz musicians found that if they set the speaker volume high enough, they could also create a fuzzy, distorted sound that fit the music they wanted to create.

soul music, blues, and R&B, has made it an important instrument in the soul jazz style. In jazz, the organ sound is almost completely identified with one particular instrument, the Hammond B3. It is most frequently played through speakers that have a unique revolving feature inside the speaker cabinet (called Leslie speakers).

The most common configuration for organ groups is the organ trio: organ, drums, and saxophone, with guitar at times replacing the sax. Jazz organists generally play the bass themselves with a combination of their feet on the organ's bass pedals and their left hand, making the organ trio a compact and economical unit. These trios became a popular fixture in African American bars and nightclubs in the 1950s.

Jimmy Smith and Shirley Scott

Jimmy Smith (ca. 1925–2005) is the biggest name in the jazz organ world, and he essentially created the classic Hammond B3 organ sound for jazz. His playing combined a rhythmic left hand, a "walking bass" played with his feet (and left hand at times), and a blazing right hand that skimmed across the keys. Smith, as is true for most organists, was first a pianist and eventually switched permanently to organ after being influenced by organist-arranger "Wild Bill" Davis. Smith recorded extensively, both with a trio and backed by a big band, as well as in collaboration with other popular artists, such as guitarists Wes Montgomery and Kenny Burrell. Smith in turn was an influence on such players as "Brother" Jack McDuff, Charles Earland, Richard "Groove" Holmes, Jimmy McGriff, and Shirley Scott.

Organist Shirley Scott (1934–2002), from Philadelphia, switched from piano to organ at least in part because of the popularity of Jimmy Smith. She went on to record extensively and had particularly strong partnerships with tenor saxophonists Eddie "Lockjaw" Davis and her husband Stanley Turrentine, who helped define the soul jazz style for the saxophone. Scott was a powerful player who emphasized

listening focus

"Soul Shoutin'" (1963) by Shirley Scott

INSTRUMENTATION: Organ: Shirley Scott; **Tenor saxophone:** Stanley Turrentine; **Bass:** Earl May; **Drums:** Grassella Oliphant.

LISTENING HIGHLIGHT, ACCOMPANIMENT: The organ functions like a piano by comping and soloing, yet it has a very different character. Its power and its ability to sustain a sound—the sound of a piano immediately begins to die out after striking a note, while an organ note stays steady as long as you hold down the key—allows it to function almost as a horn section normally would. In addition, the B3 can have a very percussive edge to its sound; we hear this in Scott's playing behind the melody (0:17). After Stanley Turrentine "strolls"—plays with just bass and drum accompaniment—for 2 choruses (0:53), we hear Scott's strong and full comping behind his sax solo (1:29). In addition, in Scott's solo (3:18), we hear her function almost as a horn section would in a big band. In her first 2 choruses, she riffs with bluesy melodies or big, full chords with her right hand and backs herself with short blasts from her left hand. In her 4th chorus she plays even fuller and more powerful chords with two hands (4:25), as well as playing a shout chorus at the end of her solo worthy of a full big band (4:43). When Scott sustains notes or chords, we can clearly hear the effect of the revolving speakers as the sound has an intense vibrato that helps to create the classic B3 sound.

a full two-handed rhythmic approach along with a heavy dose of the blues. We hear this in "Soul Shoutin'," a medium-tempo shuffle blues and a riff tune in the blues and Kansas City traditions. Unlike most jazz organists, Scott frequently worked with a bass player.

Wes Montgomery

Wes Montgomery (1923–1968) was one of the most important electric guitarists in jazz since Charlie Christian (see Chapter 7, 1st Chorus) and Django Reinhardt and a powerful influence on most jazz guitarists who followed, including Kenny Burrell, Grant Green, Pat Martino, Pat Metheny, and George Benson. Montgomery was initially primarily a straight-ahead player, as seen, for example, on the album *The Incredible Guitar of Wes Montgomery* (1960) and the live album *Smokin' at the Half Note* (1965). He developed a signature sound that came from often playing his melodies in octaves, and this has become a technique that all guitarists regularly use. He also later included a great deal of pop material in his repertoire, such as the Beatles tune "Eleanor Rigby," "Goin' Out of My Head" (arranged by Oliver Nelson, who also arranged for Jimmy Smith and countless others as well as leading his own bands), and "Windy," a popular tune by the pop group The Association that became Montgomery's biggest hit. Montgomery was

Shirley Scott, ca. 1960s. Scott was a pioneer organist in the soul jazz style. Photo by Michael Ochs Archives.
Courtesy Getty Images.

"Compared to What" (1969) by Les McCann and Eddie Harris

INSTRUMENTATION: Piano, coleader, vocal: Les McCann; **Tenor saxophone, coleader:** Eddie Harris; **Trumpet:** Benny Bailey; **Bass:** Leroy Vinnegar; **Drums:** Donald Dean.

LISTENING HIGHLIGHT, STYLE: McCann's relaxed but driving piano, a syncopated bass line by Leroy Vinnegar (not walking in 4), and a drum beat by Donald Dean that often accents all 4 beats as he hits the steel rim of the snare drum with the middle of the drum stick make "Compared to What" a hot groove tune. This fun live recording features McCann's topical soul jazz–style vocal as he comments on the political, social, and economic situation in the late 1960s. His straightforward and rough-hewn vocal style and a little cursing here and there along with an overall extremely relaxed and seemingly unrehearsed performance by the band give this recording an unusual intimacy and freshness. Before and in between vocals we hear Harris (2:28, 3:19) and McCann solo, along with Benny Bailey, an exciting yet underrated trumpet player who spent most of his career in Europe and who was more associated with bebop and hard bop. Bailey is clearly comfortable in this soul jazz setting as he plays a couple of powerful and funky solos using a plunger mute (4:10).

also a forerunner of the "smooth jazz" sound when he worked in a symphonic setting orchestrated by Don Sebesky on albums such as *Bumpin'* (1965). His tie to soul jazz can be heard on his two albums with organist Jimmy Smith, *The Dynamic Duo: Jimmy Smith and Wes Montgomery*, and *The Further Adventures of Jimmy and Wes* (both 1966), as well as in his own work, such as his funky version of the Beatles tune "A Day in the Life."

Soul jazz produced a number of hit records, which, at this point in the history of jazz, was unusual, as it continues to be. Here are brief looks at four soul jazz artists from throughout the 1960s and the tunes that made them popular.

Julian "Cannonball" Adderley

Julian "Cannonball" Adderley (1928–1975), a fiercely melodic alto saxophonist with a nonstop driving sense of unerring and flexible rhythm, was frequently spoken of as "the next Bird" and was known for his work with Miles Davis, including playing on Davis's 1959 album *Kind of Blue*. Adderley's roots were in bebop, but his groups, often including his brother Nat Adderley on cornet, helped to create and popularize the soul jazz sound. "Mercy, Mercy, Mercy," written by keyboardist Joe Zawinul (discussed in Chapter 14, 1st Chorus) and performed and recorded live by the Cannonball Adderley Quintet, reached number 11 on the *Billboard* charts in 1966.

Ramsey Lewis, Les McCann, and Eddie Harris

Ramsey Lewis (b. 1935) became one of the most popular jazz pianists in the 1960s when the Ramsey Lewis Trio had a surprise number 5 *Billboard* hit with their cover of the hit tune "The 'In' Crowd." The trio went on to have more cover hits with "Hang on Sloopy" and the traditional spiritual "Wade in the Water." All three became gold records by selling over 500,000 copies, and Lewis has a total of five gold records and three Grammy Awards. He led his own trio from early in his career and is a radio personality through his nationally syndicated radio show *Legends of Jazz*. Lewis continues to tour and is active as a jazz educator.

Pianist-vocalist Les McCann (b. 1935) began his career as a jazz pianist leading a trio in the mode of pianist Ahmad Jamal but also always had a funky, gospel, blues side to his playing. It was a live recording of a soul jazz tune at the famous Montreux Jazz Festival in Switzerland, however, that made his name as a soul jazz artist. McCann and Eddie Harris's album *Swiss Movement* and its hit single "Compared to What" sold over 1 million copies and made them both extremely popular soul jazz artists.

Eddie Harris (1934–1996) was a saxophone player in the soul jazz tradition and an early adopter of electronic technology that altered the sound of his tenor saxophone, for example, allowing him to double himself an octave apart. Playing in a lighter and more airy style than we hear on "Compared to What," he had the first jazz gold record with his cover of the theme for the movie *Exodus*. He was also a fine bebop player, but, like McCann, he was most successful as a soul jazz artist.

2nd Chorus Small Combo Latin Jazz; The Brazilian Influence on Jazz

WHAT WERE THE KEY DEVELOPMENTS IN LATIN JAZZ IN THE EARLY 1960s?

The 1950s and 1960s saw the rise of small-group **combos** playing Latin jazz. Small groups were, of course, already common in both jazz and Latin music. For example, Noro Morales led a popular Latin piano quintet (Chapter 7, 4th Chorus), and we have heard numerous small jazz groups already. Several players rose from the ranks of side musician in both jazz and Latin music to become popular bandleaders, including vibraphonist Cal Tjader, congueros "Mongo" Santamaria and Ray Barretto, and pianist Eddie Palmieri.

One version of these early Latin jazz combos was the piano–vibraphone quintet or quartet. Tito Puente (Chapter 11, 3rd Chorus) was one of the earliest musicians to bring the vibraphone into Latin music and Latin jazz, and jazz pianist George Shearing introduced a similar format in the jazz world when he hired vibraphonist Cal Tjader in 1953 and introduced a Latin sound into his combo. For another example, Shirley Scott—discussed in the previous chorus—delved into this style on the 1960 album *Mucho Mucho* that included organ, piano, vibes, bass, and two percussion, which she recorded as a guest artist with the Latin Jazz Quintet (a group that also recorded with guest soloists as surprising as the avant-garde alto saxophonist Eric Dolphy and tenor saxophonist Pharoah Sanders).

Mongo Santamaria

Ramon "Mongo" Santamaria (1922–2003) was one of the most outstanding conga players in Afro-Cuban music. He was born in Havana, Cuba, and had early experience in Havana's famous Tropicana Club. Mongo moved to New York in 1950, where he played with pianist George Shearing (with Cal Tjader), among many others. Santamaria went on to form his own combo—consistently one of the top Latin jazz groups—that combined an intense Afro-Cuban sound with a bluesy R&B flavor, setting a standard for small-group Latin jazz.

JAZZ LIVES CAL TJADER

The vibraphonist Callen Radcliffe "Cal" Tjader (1925–1982) was born in St. Louis, while his parents were performing there. His father was a tap dancer and his mother a pianist, and the duo toured vaudeville theaters before settling in southern California to open a dance school when he was 2 years old. Tjader was exposed to Dixieland jazz as a teenager and then won a local contest as a drummer before serving in World War II. On his return from the service in 1946, he studied music at San Francisco State College, where he met pianist Dave Brubeck (Chapter 11, 1st Chorus) and saxophonist Paul Desmond and joined with them playing drums in the short-lived Dave Brubeck Octet. Unable to support such a large group, Brubeck took Desmond and Tjader with him for trio work in San Francisco, and Tjader began playing vibes to fill out the group's sound.

In 1953, the popular jazz pianist George Shearing invited Tjader to join his group as percussionist and vibraphonist. While Tjader toured with Shearing on the East Coast he heard bands such as Machito, Tito Puente, and Noro Morales, all of whom influenced his style. Tjader went on to form his own group in 1954, one of the first American bands to dedicate itself almost exclusively to Latin jazz and that included master percussionists such as Willie Bobo, Armando Peraza, and Mongo Santamaria. Tjader developed a particular Latin jazz sound that came to be identified with the West Coast. His style has a smooth, mellow sound that is less edgy than that of his East Coast counterparts such as Santamaria and **conguero** Ray Barretto.

Tjader's greatest success came in 1964 with the album *Soul Sauce*; the title track was a reworking of Dizzy Gillespie and Chano Pozo's cubop composition "Guachi Guaro." Later he worked with Latin jazz pianist Eddie Palmieri on *El Sonido Nuevo* (*The New Sound*, 1966). Tjader continued to work with his own band until his death. Pianist Clare Fischer, one of jazz and Latin jazz's great arranger-composers who had one of the most sophisticated harmonic senses in the field, was a collaborator with Tjader; and conguero Pancho Sanchez was an important band member later in Tjader's career. Sanchez continued the West Coast small Latin combo tradition with his own band, which is still one of the premier Latin jazz units. In 1980, Tjader won a Grammy for Best Latin Recording for his album *La Onda Va Bien* (*The Good Life*). He died 2 years later from a heart attack.

Cal Tjader, ca. 1960s. Vibraphonist Tjader helped introduce a Latin influence into mainstream jazz. Photo by Michael Ochs Archives.
Courtesy Getty Images.

An early Santamaria composition was "Afro-Blue," which became a jazz standard after it was recorded by John Coltrane. Vocalist-lyricist Oscar Brown, Jr., created lyrics to the song as well. Mongo had a big hit in 1963 with pianist-composer Herbie Hancock's (Chapter 13, 4th Chorus) "Watermelon Man." Mongo's recording of that tune featured a young pianist named Chick Corea, who went on to become

listening focus

"Soul Sauce (Guachi Guaro)" (rough mix) (1964) by Cal Tjader

DOWNLOAD
Track Number 26

INSTRUMENTATION: Vibraphone, leader: Cal Tjader; **Piano:** Lonnie Hewitt; **Bass:** Terry Hilliard; **Drums:** Johnny Rae; **Percussion:** Armando Peraza, Alberto Valdes, Willie Bobo.

LISTENING HIGHLIGHT, STYLE: "Soul Sauce (Guachi Guaro)" neatly blends the piano-vibraphone tradition in Latin music with a jazz style, particularly in Tjader's vibraphone solo. Tjader's Latin jazz combo is similar to a small jazz group with a rhythm section and featured frontperson. In this case, however, the vibes are the featured instrument and the rhythm section, while including the standard piano, bass, and drums, also features three percussionists, including Willie Bobo and Armando Peraza.

This classic small-group **chachachá** packs a lot of action into 2 minutes and 30 seconds. It begins with Tjader alone and the chant "guachi guaro" as a break. The melody is attractive and simple, and the harmony is typical for a chachachá; but it is the groove that matters here, and the insistent piano figure and solid percussion drive this tune. After the initial statement of the melody (0:13), the piano has a classic-style break (0:26) with funky hand clapping on 2 and 4 (and the "and" of 4!). Then Tjader plays a lovely solo that reminds us of the melody (0:39). After another piano break (1:06), Tjader takes off again (1:19) until the opening break repeats (1:52) and the tune vamps out on the melody.

a top artist in acoustic and fusion-oriented jazz (see Chapter 14, 1st Chorus). Mongo continued to lead a band into the 1990s, and Santamaria also played with many of the later generation of top Latin jazz stars such as pianists Michel Camilo and Hilton Ruiz as well as with many jazz bands.

Mongo Santamaria, ca. 1960s. Santamaria was among the most outstanding conga players in Afro-Cuban music and an important composer. Photo by Tom Copi.

Courtesy Michael Ochs Archives/ Getty Images.

New York City Latin bands took Santamaria's lead and continued to combine R&B with Latin dance music by combining a chachachá groove with a backbeat on 2 and 4 to create a style called **boogaloo**. This was a natural development for young New York musicians as the streets of Harlem, East Harlem, and the South Bronx were filled with Latin, R&B, and soul music. Trombonist-vocalist Johnny Colon's "Boogaloo Blues" (1967) was a hit in this style, and conguero Joe Cuba had a popular boogaloo tune as well, "Bang Bang" (1966).

Ray Barretto

Conguero Ray Barretto (1929–2006) led his own Latin dance bands and Latin jazz combos but also became the first-call percussionist to add a Latin flavor for countless mainstream jazz bands. "A Deeper Shade of Soul," from Barretto's 1968 album *Acid*, is an excellent example of a rich fusion of Latin, jazz, soul music, and soul jazz, as well as a boogaloo groove. The fusion comes through in many ways including the English vocals and the horn lines. The horns directly refer to soul jazz by playing a small part of the melody for "Mercy, Mercy, Mercy" (1:19), the soul jazz hit by Cannonball Adderley (discussed in the 1st Chorus of this chapter), immediately followed by a horn line from the soul hit "Knock on Wood" (1:26). The rest of the band plays in a more typical Latin style of the period, which is also heard in the very traditional introduction that starts the tune. Barretto's more aggressive and fusion-oriented New York City style of playing contrasts sharply with Tjader's smoother and more mellow sound, yet both styles stem from many of the same roots.

Eddie Palmieri

Eddie Palmieri (b. 1936) has long been one of Latin jazz's most exciting pianists and bandleaders and continues to be in the forefront of the genre. Palmieri's Afro-Cuban roots are deep, and his dance-oriented music has always been popular with the hard core Latin audience. At the same time, he incorporates a powerful jazz influence in his music.

Born in New York City's South Bronx, some of Palmieri's early work was with Tito Rodriguez, the top mambo bandleader along with Tito Puente, yet the jazz pianists McCoy Tyner and Chick Corea also were powerful influences on him, as was his brother, keyboardist-bandleader Charlie Palmieri. His groundbreaking group, La Perfecta, featured vocalist Ismael Quintana and an aggressive two-trombone and one-flute horn section led by trombonist Barry Rogers. The edgy, all-out playing style of Rogers continues to influence the Latin trombone sound.

Palmieri has led a variety of ensembles through a productive career. In recent years his group has featured a front line of jazz-oriented horn players with Brian Lynch (trumpet), Donald Harrison (alto sax), and Conrad Herwig (trombone). Lynch and Herwig have continued to explore the genre on their own albums as well.

Bossa Nova

In addition to Cuban and Puerto Rican musical traditions, the musical relationship between Brazil and America has contributed to the richness of jazz and popular music. The Brazilian **samba** was popularized in the United States by the movie star Carmen Miranda in the 1930s and 1940s. In the 1950s, Brazilian artists such as composer-singer-pianist-guitarist Antônio Carlos Jobim (1927–1994) and guitarist-vocalist João Gilberto (b. 1931) created a gentle, swinging, musically refined style called **bossa nova** ("new flair"). Bossa nova, an outgrowth of samba, is less focused on rhythm than samba and puts more emphasis on sophisticated harmony and melody. Already a fusion of samba and jazz, bossa nova was ripe for a

listening focus

"Desafinado" (1962) by Stan Getz and Charlie Byrd

INSTRUMENTATION: Tenor saxophone, coleader: Stan Getz; **Guitar, coleader:** Charlie Byrd; **Bass:** Keter Betts; **Guitar, bass:** Gene Byrd; **Drums:** Buddy Deppenschmidt; **Percussion:** Bill Reichenbach, Sr.

LISTENING HIGHLIGHT, STYLE: After a brief bass and percussion introduction, this recording—edited down from the original version for radio play—features Stan Getz's pretty, relaxed, and straightforward melodic presentation of this lovely tune (0:11). His round, dark, and soft-edged sound is unmistakable and was perfect for bossa nova, a gentle style that revels in its own beauty. Byrd's active guitar accompaniment captures the Brazilian flavor while adding numerous **counterlines/countermelodies** throughout, and the percussion section lays down a solid yet relaxed bossa nova beat. The composition has a harmonic sophistication reminiscent of some of the best songs of Tin Pan Alley. This shortened version includes just 1 chorus (one time through the tune's form), while the full version features solos by Byrd and Getz.

further fusion with jazz. In addition, as a composer, Jobim was heavily influenced by American popular song as well as the cool jazz approach often associated with the West Coast (see Chapter 11, 1st Chorus).

After being introduced to bossa nova, the versatile American guitarist Charlie Byrd (1925–1999) toured Brazil, where he met Jobim and Gilberto and took a great interest in this new style of music. Byrd enlisted the tenor sax player Stan Getz, whose memorable solo on the composition "Early Autumn," written by Ralph Burns for the Woody Herman band (see Chapter 10, 4th Chorus), had made him a star, to record *Jazz Samba* in 1962. Jobim's "Desafinado" from this album was a major hit that vaulted bossa nova into the American consciousness. Getz received a Grammy for Best Jazz Performance for his solo in 1963 and went on to collaborate with Jobim and Gilberto, as well as vocalist Astrud Gilberto, João's wife, on the million-selling album *Getz/Gilberto* (1963). Hits from this album included "Girl from Ipanema" and "Corcovado" ("Quiet Nights of Quiet Stars"), which, along with "Desafinado," have been nearly ubiquitous bossa nova tunes since their release.

The music of Brazil has continued to influence jazz and popular music through numerous artists. Pianist-bandleader Sergio Mendes has long made a powerful contribution to contemporary music with early records such as *Herb Alpert Presents Sergio Mendes and Brasil '66* and its hit "Mas Que Nada," as well as later records *Brasiliero* (which won a Grammy in 1992) and the 2006 CD *Timeless* that mixes Brazilian styles with hip hop and R&B through the inclusion of guest artists such as the Black Eyed Peas, John Legend, Justin Timberlake, Erykah Badu, India.Arie, and Stevie Wonder. Percussionist Airto Moreira has worked with numerous jazz artists including Miles Davis, Weather Report, and Chick Corea's group Return to Forever, as well as recording and performing as a leader, often with his wife, vocalist Flora Purim. Brazilian instrumentalists including pianist Eliane Elias and trumpeter Claudio Roditi have consistently performed at the highest level in jazz and multiple Brazilian styles, as well as powerful and effective fusions of these types of music.

3rd Chorus The Association for the Advancement of Creative Musicians

HOW DID THE AVANT-GARDE JAZZ MOVEMENT CONTINUE TO DEVELOP IN THE 1960s?

While early avant-gardists such as Ornette Coleman (Chapter 11, 4th Chorus) and Cecil Taylor (Chapter 14, 2nd Chorus) were challenging the status quo of jazz through various types of free improvisation in New York City in the late 1950s and 1960s, the stage for a powerful musical and social movement was being set in a very different artistic and social environment in Chicago.

The South Side of Chicago is a product of both the Great Migration—an unprecedented relocation of black migrants out of the agricultural South to urban industrial centers from 1910 to 1930—and profound segregation. In contrast to New York City, which had a very dense and close environment that essentially forced a certain type of integration on most everyone, portions of Chicago's South Side and West Side were strictly black neighborhoods. The music world was also highly segregated, with the white scene centered on Chicago's North Side and a black music scene on the South Side. As the avant-garde took root in Chicago, an entire movement began in this environment.

Sun Ra

An early influential musician on the Chicago scene in the late 1950s was pianist-bandleader Herman Blount, who we know now as Sun Ra (1914–1993). While early on a conventional stride pianist, Sun Ra quickly challenged the musical orthodoxy with a band he labeled his Arkestra that, along with avant-garde playing, included a swing repertoire, classical influences, and the early use of electronics such as synthesizers. As Sun Ra also began to connect his music to notions of outer space and African influence, as well as philosophy and mysticism, the band reflected these extramusical influences. Just how Sun Ra's personal mythology related to

Avant-garde pianist-composer-bandleader Sun Ra, on stage in 1992. Sun Ra's Arkestra's stage performances featured elaborate costumes paired with Ra's highly original compositions. Photo © Estate of David Gahr.
Courtesy Getty Images.

the music was not always clear, but the fact that he always made people think and challenged orthodoxy had a profound influence on many other innovative musicians, including some of the young experimental Chicago players.

Sun Ra later established himself as a strong presence in New York and Philadelphia and carved out a prominent place in the jazz world while also remaining on its margins. He also set the tone for an interesting aspect of the avant-garde, which is its inclusionary character. Many musicians from this scene embrace elements of jazz from many periods as well as influences from other styles and cultures.

Muhal Richard Abrams

Pianist-composer-arranger Muhal Richard Abrams (b. 1930) is another prominent and influential musician who came of age in Chicago during this avant-garde period of the early 1960s. While certainly in contact with others, such as the well-trained musicians coming out of the South Side high schools, Abrams was determinedly self-taught. His studies led him down two paths that converged to create an individual compositional voice. He was playing with experienced jazz players and composers in Chicago while also studying a complex system of composition created by composer-theorist Joseph Schillinger. The **Schillinger system**, more than other twentieth-century musical theories such as 12-tone or minimalism, has influenced numerous jazz musicians. One of the system's goals is to create the ability to generate extended compositions from a small amount of musical material. To facilitate working on his new ideas, Abrams started a workshop ensemble, the Experimental Band; and he eventually played a crucial role in the creation of a music collective, the Association for the Advancement of Creative Musicians (AACM), which has had widespread influence both musically and socially.

Cofounded by Abrams, pianist Jodie Christian, drummer Steve McCall, and trumpeter Phil Cohran in 1965, the AACM is a musicians' collective primarily based in Chicago that has been extremely important in the development of experimental music in America well beyond the boundaries of jazz. These musicians examined new ways of approaching timbre and experimented regularly with extended instrumental techniques, as well as challenging the relationship between composition and improvisation. It has also been the most influential of a number of African American art collectives that have created strategies for artists to take control of their own careers through self-production and self-promotion.

Members of the organization include some of the biggest names in experimental music as instrumentalists and composers over the last 50 years, including saxophonists Henry Threadgill and Anthony Braxton, trumpeter Wadada Leo Smith, and violinist Leroy Jenkins. One of the most visible and successful groups to grow from the AACM in the late 1960s, however, was the Art Ensemble of Chicago.

The Art Ensemble of Chicago

The original members of the Art Ensemble of Chicago were saxophonists Roscoe Mitchell and Joseph Jarman, trumpeter Lester Bowie, bassist Malachi Favors Maghostut, and percussionist Famoudou Don Moye. They all played various other instruments as well, including found objects, whistles, bicycle horns, and instruments from around the world. The band was also known for a theatrical approach to music, at times donning costumes and painted faces. Their motto was "Great Black Music: Ancient to the Future." As was true with many of the avant-gardists, the band incorporated numerous influences into their work; and they were seemingly unafraid to juxtapose any type of music or stylistic approach, including the

read all about it

"Creative Music and the AACM" by Wadada Leo Smith

Walser, **Keeping Time,** *Chapter 50*
One of the early members of the AACM, trumpeter Wadada Leo Smith discusses its musical philosophy.

listening focus

DOWNLOAD
Track Number 27

"Barnyard Scuffel Shuffel" (1973) by the Art Ensemble of Chicago

INSTRUMENTATION: Trumpet, percussion: Lester Bowie; **Saxophones, clarinet, percussion:** Joseph Jarman; **Saxophones, clarinet, flute, percussion:** Roscoe Mitchell; **Bass, percussion:** Malachi Favors Maghostut; **Drums, percussion:** Famoudou Don Moye; **Piano:** Muhal Richard Abrams.

LISTENING HIGHLIGHT, FORM: Form and style are inextricably linked in "Barnyard Scuffel Shuffel." It begins with a dreamy Muhal Richard Abrams piano solo (here as a featured guest artist), almost in a stride style but with references to harmony both from modern jazz and from contemporary classical music. The rest of the band then slams us with a loud, aggressive, freely improvised ensemble performance that contrasts with the piano introduction (0:58). This section is a good example of **group** or **free improvisation** in a free jazz style. A unison melodic line over a walking bass briefly interrupts this ensemble (1:25) in a more traditional jazz style before the band returns to free jazz mode. The band then jumps into a **shuffle** (hence the twisted title of the piece), a rhythmic feel closely associated with the blues and rhythm and blues. This shuffle is played over a 12-bar blues progression with a sax solo played over riffing horns and the rhythm section (1:45). The ensemble again interrupts this interlude and startles us with an aggressive free jazz ensemble (3:02) before returning to the shuffle again. While the shuffle sections are clearly referencing a long-established jazz and blues style, the group plays it here in a unique way, giving even this style a different feel. The saxes and trumpet move freely from riffing to soloing throughout this ensemble, and they end with a unison line over the shuffle beat.

use of simple textures provided by their various small instruments. In fact, finding a representative example for this group is daunting as their material is so varied. On Lester Bowie's "Barnyard Scuffel Shuffel," the band races through a variety of styles and approaches; this eclectic and ever-changing recording is an

The Art Ensemble of Chicago, 1993. (Left to right) Lester Bowie (trumpet, seated), Roscoe Mitchell (saxophone), Malachi Favors Maghostut (bass), and Herb Walker (electric guitar). The group was known for its eclectic instrumentation and marriage of African music and rhythms with jazz.
© Lebrecht Music & Arts.

QUESTIONS AND CONTROVERSIES
Music or Noise?

To many listeners, especially to those unfamiliar with this type of music, free improvisations in a "free jazz" or avant-garde style, whether by a group or by an individual, can seem chaotic and difficult to understand. In many ways, this music can be an acquired taste and takes effort to understand on its own terms. This is because it often tends to avoid standard approaches to harmony and rhythm that we are used to, making it a style that is quite foreign to the average listener. Because of this, listening to free jazz requires an open mind.

The often aggressive, in-your-face nature of this music also initially alienated many listeners. The bands frequently played loudly, using many "ugly" and unusual tonalities to shock and startle their listeners. The fact that this music arose simultaneously with the civil rights movement gave it an extra political edge that also made some mainstream listeners uncomfortable. Just as twentieth-century art music based on improvisatory techniques was greeted with skepticism, free jazz had a hard time finding its audience.

It is important to remember that when bebop first came on the scene, it too was described as wild, "noisy" music. Swing music fans and even traditional performers like Louis Armstrong were vocal in their opposition to the music with its high-speed tempos, unpredictable melodies, and dissonant harmonies. Ironically, when free jazz first arrived on the scene bop had become part of the mainstream, and now some bop fans were the ones complaining about this noisy new musical style that was claiming a place in the jazz arena.

example of the various approaches that the Art Ensemble combines in a unique manner.

The many members of the AACM and other members of the avant-garde have played a large role in expanding jazz's musical possibilities, which has helped to encourage musicians to be more open and experimental. Their refusal to be pigeonholed and their interest in encompassing the various musical, social, cultural, and political influences they choose have served as inspiration for all types of musicians, even if at times their music can be difficult to understand and appreciate. The influence of the AACM continues to be strong today, as many of its members have spread around the country and pursue projects with their own groups and a variety of ensembles (Chapter 14, 2nd Chorus).

CODA Chapter Summary

What Is Soul Jazz?

- Soul jazz developed in the early 1960s as a marriage of hard bop with blues and R&B influences.
- Musicians such as organists Shirley Scott and Jimmy Smith, guitarist Wes Montgomery, pianists Les McCann and Ramsey Lewis, and alto saxophonist Julian "Cannonball" Adderley all added a blues, gospel, soul, and R&B accent to their music that embraced the accomplishments and appeal of black popular music.

What Were the Key Developments in Latin Jazz in the Early 1960s?

- Small combos led by musicians like vibes player Cal Tjader helped bring Latin timbres and rhythms into traditional jazz settings.
- Several players rose from the ranks of side musicians in both jazz and Latin music to become popular bandleaders, including congueros Mongo Santamaria and Ray Barretto and pianist Eddie Palmieri.
- The bossa nova, a Brazilian song form noted for its sophisticated melodies and harmonies, enjoyed popularity thanks to the collaboration of guitarist Charlie Byrd and jazz saxophonist Stan Getz with Brazilian composers-instrumentalists Antônio Carlos Jobim and João Gilberto.

How Did the Avant-Garde Jazz Movement Continue to Develop in the 1960s?

- Musician collectives like the AACM formed in Chicago to encourage experimentation while promoting self-sufficiency and empowerment among black musicians.
- This movement spread to other cities through similar collectives as well as the travels of original members of the Chicago collective.

Talkin' Jazz (Key Terms)

Boogaloo	Counterline/	Schillinger system
Bossa nova	Countermelody	Shuffle
Chachachá	Group or free	Soul jazz
Combo	improvisation	
Conguero	Samba	

Key People

Jimmy Smith	Les McCann	João Gilberto
Shirley Scott	Mongo Santamaria	Sun Ra
Wes Montgomery	Caj Tjader	Art Ensemble of Chicago
Julian "Cannonball"	Ray Barretto	Anthony Braxton
Adderley	Eddie Palmieri	
Ramsey Lewis	Antônio Carlos Jobim	

Think About This (For Further Discussion and Study)

1. What is soul jazz, and what are its major characteristics?
2. Do you hear a difference in overall approach between Cal Tjader's "Soul Sauce (Guachi Guaro)" and Tito Puente's "Mambo Inn"? Discuss the instrumentation of both.
3. Discuss the merging of bossa nova and jazz. How does Stan Getz's sound meld with the genre?

4. What were the cultural, artistic, and political issues that encouraged the formation of the AACM?
5. What is your experience as you listen to the Art Ensemble of Chicago's "Barnyard Scuffel Shuffel"?
6. Discuss the Art Ensemble of Chicago's approach to the blues in "Barnyard Scuffel Shuffel" (beginning at 1:49) compared to Shirley Scott's "Soul Shoutin'" and other forms of blues we have heard so far.

Look It Up (Key Resources)

Anderson, Iain. *This Is Our Music: Free Jazz, the Sixties, and American Culture*. Philadelphia: University of Pennsylvania Press, 2007.

Castro, Ruy. *Bossa Nova: The Story of the Brazilian Music That Seduced the World*. Chicago: A Cappella, 2000.

Ingram, Adrian. *Wes Montgomery*. Blaydon on Tyne, UK: Ashley Mark, 2008.

Jones, LeRoi (Amiri Baraka). *Black Music*. New York: Morrow, 1967.

Jost, Ekkehard. *Free Jazz*. Graz, Austria: Universal Edition, 1974.

Lewis, George. *A Power Stronger Than Itself: The AACM and American Experimental Music*. Chicago: University of Chicago Press, 2008.

Litweiler, John. *The Freedom Principle: Jazz After 1958*. New York: Morrow, 1984.

Maggin, Donald L. *Stan Getz: A Life in Jazz*. New York: Morrow, 2003.

Mathieson, Kenny. *Cookin': Hard Bop and Soul Jazz 1954–65*. Edinburgh, UK: Canongate, 2012.

Reid, S. Duncan. *Cal Tjader: The Life and Recordings of the Man Who Revolutionized Latin Jazz*. Jefferson, NC: McFarland, 2013.

Roberts, John Storm *The Latin Tinge: The Impact of Latin American Music on the United States*. New York: Oxford University Press, 1979.

———. *Latin Jazz: The First of the Fusions, 1880s to Today*. New York: Schirmer Books, 1999.

Spellman, A. B. *Four Lives in the Bebop Business*. New York: Pantheon, 1966.

Sublette, Ned. *Cuba and Its Music: From the First Drums to the Mambo*. Chicago: Chicago Review Press, 2004.

Szwed, John. *Space Is the Place: The Lives and Times of Sun Ra*. New York: Pantheon, 1997.

Washburne, Christopher. *Sounding Salsa: Performing Latin Music in New York City*. Philadelphia: Temple University Press, 2008.

Williams, Martin. *Jazz Masters in Transition, 1957–69*. New York: Macmillan, 1970.

Wilmer, Valerie. *As Serious as Your Life: The Story of the New Jazz*. Westport, CT: Hill, 1980.

FIVE VIEWS OF THE MAINSTREAM

13

There are a number of remarkably important jazz artists whose work cannot be confined to a category or a particular period. We have seen this already with the music of Duke Ellington, Count Basie, and Louis Armstrong. This is also the case for the five musicians discussed here: Miles Davis, John Coltrane, Charles Mingus, Bill Evans, and Herbie Hancock. Their careers have been marked by constant evolution that helped them move through a number of styles and bands while also shaping modern jazz.

Although it is somewhat misleading to speak of **mainstream jazz**, the term has been used to describe those artists since the 1960s whose work has formed the core of jazz for most listeners. Each of these artists is essentially universally accepted as a major innovator and stylist. All have long and varied careers as performers, their music is extremely well documented on recordings, and they have made significant contributions to the jazz repertoire through their compositions.

In addition, after significant side musician apprenticeships, all of these musicians led their own groups for the rest of their careers. As bandleaders, all had a terrific ability to choose and nurture musicians, so examining these bands also gives us a look at many of the major players from the 1950s to today. For example, Coltrane, Evans, and Hancock all had early apprenticeships with Davis that were extremely significant in their careers and in the development of their music.

Miles Davis stands out as one of the few musicians in any genre of music who was an innovator in several different musical styles: beginning with playing bebop with Charlie Parker to being a leader of the cool jazz movement to hard bop to modal jazz and then on to **fusion**. John Coltrane set the standard for modern saxophone playing. Charles Mingus was an innovator on the bass and is one of jazz's most important composers and bandleaders. Bill Evans's stylistic and harmonic approach to the piano has been one of the greatest influences on modern jazz pianists, and his approach to the standard jazz trio changed the way this type of group functioned. Finally, Herbie Hancock has become one of the standard-bearers for contemporary pianists. He continues to be involved in many streams of jazz, while also pushing the envelope stylistically and through his use of electronics.

In this chapter, we'll answer these questions:

- How Did Miles Davis Continue to Innovate and Change Throughout His Career?

- How Did John Coltrane Set a New Standard for Jazz Saxophone?

- How Did Charles Mingus Revitalize Jazz Composition and Arranging for Larger Ensembles?

- What New Innovations Did Pianists-Composers Bill Evans and Herbie Hancock Bring to Jazz?

Photo: Courtesy Getty Images.

1st Chorus Miles Davis

HOW DID MILES DAVIS CONTINUE TO INNOVATE AND CHANGE THROUGHOUT HIS CAREER?

Throughout his career Miles Davis (1926–1991) was consistently one of the major voices in jazz. His instrumental ability, musical vision, and fearless adventurousness made him one of the twentieth century's great musical innovators. He was involved in bebop, hard bop, and cool jazz from the ground up; was a groundbreaker in the area of modal jazz; helped electrify jazz with the introduction of the electric piano; and was one of the leaders in adopting elements of rock music and R&B to create what came to be known as jazz fusion. His constant restlessness and desire for musical growth extended to his side musicians as he pushed them to seek new musical territory as well, urging and even insisting that they become individual voices within the context of the musical settings he was creating with his groups.

Davis was greatly influenced by Dizzy Gillespie, but his trumpet skills were different from Gillespie's, as was his musical sensibility. From the beginning, Davis had a lyrical sense that transcended his initially limited trumpet chops, and his trumpet technique grew steadily throughout his career as he blossomed into an excellent trumpet player (contrary to the opinion of some who believe Davis to have been a flawed, or even a "bad," trumpet player). Davis's relationship with his audience was at times an issue as he lost interest in introducing tunes and even would turn his back on the audience, which is traditionally unacceptable in the performance world.

The combination of intense lyricism and sensitivity—he was one of jazz's most lyrical and sweet-sounding players—combined with a bad-boy image made Davis an enigmatic musician and public figure. He showed a tough and even violent side to the public at times; spoke his mind straightforwardly, to say the least; and was unafraid to state unpopular or controversial points of view in colorful language. Of course, there was a private side of Davis as well, and close friends speak of a gentle, and even delicate, person who was a good friend and an inspirational influence on their lives in a variety of ways.

The contrast between his sensitive, moody, and exceptionally beautiful playing and his gruff, rough image is one that is difficult for some to reconcile. But rather than reconcile this contrast, it is more illustrative to use these contrasting qualities to realize that a person's playing and personality are not necessarily intertwined and that what musicians show to the public, or what the media chooses to portray, is not necessarily what their friends, colleagues, and families see.

Miles Davis's Early Life

Davis was raised in East St. Louis in an upper middle-class family, the son of a dentist. He began his trumpet studies in the sixth grade and moved on to study with the principal trumpet player of the St. Louis Symphony. In addition, a local jazz trumpet player, Clark Terry—who went on to become one of the great trumpet soloists and stylists in jazz—took Davis under his wing; and while still in high school Davis was running in an edgy nightlife scene and gaining experience with numerous bands.

After high school Davis moved to New York City to study at the Juilliard School, one of the premier music conservatories in the country. While not particularly involved in his classes, Davis valued his studies with one of the top trumpet players and teachers, William Vacchiano, the principal trumpet for the New York Philharmonic, and later in life credited his short time at Juilliard for giving him a broad musical background. Along with this, Davis began to frequent the clubs where bebop was blossoming, while another legendary, yet often overlooked, trumpet player, Freddie Webster, helped Davis to insert himself into New York's music scene.

While Davis's trumpet chops during this early period were not as sharp as they eventually would be, his musicality evidently impressed Charlie Parker enough to hire him to play in his group on 52nd Street, as high a compliment as a young jazz musician could have hoped for as Parker was a leader of the cutting edge of the jazz scene. On early recordings with Parker we can hear Davis struggling with the trumpet a bit, but we also hear a clear and individual voice already breaking away from the powerful influence of Dizzy Gillespie. For example, his concentration on the middle and lower registers of the trumpet contrasted with Gillespie's exciting work in the upper register, and his playing was more broodingly melodic with a burnished tone that generally eschewed the use of vibrato.

Davis went on to follow a typical path, playing with big bands such as those of Benny Carter (Chapter 5, 2nd Chorus) and Billy Eckstine (Chapter 10, 1st Chorus); working at clubs; and spending time at jam sessions. Davis was a studious musician and cleverly managed to attach himself to important players such as tenor saxophonist Coleman Hawkins (see Chapter 5, 3rd Chorus) and pianist Thelonious Monk (see Chapter 10, 2nd Chorus). His persistence paid off, and by 1947 he was established as an important new voice.

While he became a fixture of the bebop scene, Davis began what was to become a constant in his life, a restless and continual search for new avenues of creativity and musical relevance. His first foray into new territory came with his involvement with Gil Evans and what came to be called the "cool jazz" scene (Chapter 11, 1st Chorus). After the success of their collaboration on *Birth of the Cool*, Davis and Evans continued to work closely together and created four classic jazz albums, *Miles Ahead*, *Porgy and Bess*, *Sketches of Spain*, and *Quiet Nights*, all featuring Evans arrangements for extended big band—performed by top New York City studio players—featuring Davis as soloist.

Davis in the 1950s

The early 1950s was a difficult period for Davis as he succumbed to heroin addiction, as was unfortunately true for numerous jazz musicians. As he recovered

---

IN PERFORMANCE

Miles Davis, Bandleader

Performers like Miles Davis could not always keep a regular group together for recording and performances, particularly early in their careers. Consequently, for different recording dates different side musicians would be hired to work with Davis, either by Davis himself or by the record labels; and Davis had an important string of records as a leader through the 1950s. Yet certain "classic" lineups have been identified as representing key moments in Davis's career.

In the mid-1950s, Davis formed what has become known as his "first great quintet," featuring tenor saxophonist John Coltrane (see the 2nd Chorus of this chapter); pianist Red Garland, one of the more accomplished accompanists in jazz; bassist Paul Chambers, the epitome of solidity; and Philly Joe Jones, an innovative drummer with a distinctive approach to the ride cymbal.

Davis's next great group was assembled to create and record the album *Kind of Blue*. This sextet featured John Coltrane and Paul Chambers from Davis's previous group, as well as Cannonball Adderley on alto sax (Chapter 12, 1st Chorus), Jimmy Cobb on drums, and the up-and-coming pianist Bill Evans (see the 4th Chorus of this chapter).

During the mid-1960s, Davis formed his "second great quintet." Davis drew on a new generation of musicians to form this group, including tenor saxophonist-composer Wayne Shorter, pianist Herbie Hancock (see the 4th Chorus of this chapter), bassist Ron Carter, and 17-year-old drummer Tony Williams. Hancock and Carter were extremely experienced rhythm section side musicians, and both went on to become premier performers as well as bandleaders. Shorter was coming off of great success with Art Blakey (Chapter 11, 2nd Chorus) as a player-composer and went on to become one of jazz's great saxophone stylists and one of its major composers, as well as a coleader (with pianist Joe Zawinul) of one of the most important jazz fusion groups, Weather Report (Chapter 14, 1st Chorus). He currently leads a quartet

and consistently puts out recordings, such as *Without a Net* (2013) and *High Life* (1997), both of which received Grammy Awards. Shorter continues to stretch the limits of jazz with his compositional output as well as his current group's approach to musical interaction. Shorter, Hancock, and Carter are currently three of the elder statesmen in jazz and are still helping to lead the way as jazz continues to grow and change. Drummer Tony Williams was a gifted young prodigy and went on to have a major impact on jazz and jazz fusion with a variety of innovations, particularly with his splashy ride cymbal sound that became the driving element of Davis's group as well as the pioneering fusion group that Williams went on to lead, the Tony Williams Lifetime (Chapter 14, 1st Chorus).

In the late 1960s, Davis turned to jazz–rock fusion. Musicians who passed through his fusion groups included saxophonist Dave Liebman; keyboard players Joe Zawinul, Chick Corea, and Keith Jarrett (all discussed in Chapter 14, 1st Chorus); drummer Jack DeJohnette (Chapter 14, 3rd Chorus); bassists Dave Holland and Marcus Miller; and guitarists John McLaughlin (Chapter 14, 1st Chorus), John Scofield (Chapter 15, 1st Chorus), and Mike Stern. Bands such as Weather Report, Return to Forever, the Mahavishnu Orchestra (all discussed in Chapter 14, 1st Chorus) and Herbie Hancock's bands were spawned from Davis's work in the 1960s and 1970s.

Miles Davis with Herbie Hancock (piano), Ron Carter (bass), and Wayne Shorter (sax) performing at the Newport Jazz Festival, 1967. Some consider this mid-1960s lineup the best of all of Davis's many groups. Photo by David Redfern.
Courtesy Getty Images.

listening focus

"So What" (1959) by the Miles Davis Sextet

DOWNLOAD
Track Number 28

INSTRUMENTATION: Trumpet, leader, composer: Miles Davis; **Alto saxophone:** Cannonball Adderley; **Tenor saxophone:** John Coltrane; **Piano:** Bill Evans; **Bass:** Paul Chambers; **Drums:** Jimmy Cobb.

LISTENING HIGHLIGHT, MELODY AND HARMONY: "So What" is an example of what is referred to as "modal jazz," meaning it focuses on a particular scale or scales. The form is a typical AABA with A being in D minor and B (the bridge) providing the only harmonic change in this tune, in E-flat minor. After a meditative introduction, bassist Paul Chambers plays the melody (0:34)—an extremely unusual occurrence as the bass almost never gets to play the melody—and the horns play a simple harmonized background line (0:50). After the melody, the band moves into a calm, swinging, medium tempo with the bass playing in 4 (1:30), drummer Jimmy Cobb playing in a relaxed and understated manner behind the soloists, and Bill Evans comping in a sensitive and tasteful manner, displaying his colorful harmonic style even in this modal composition and at a relatively early stage in his development.

Being modal, the harmonic structure is extremely open, allowing each player to take his own melodic and harmonic approach. Each solo is strikingly different, making this an excellent example of the individuality that is so important to jazz. Davis's playing here is a perfect example of his focus on lyricism as he plays a solo filled with thoughtful and beautiful melody, largely in the middle register, all with a relaxed yet still biting swing (1st chorus 1:30, 2nd chorus 2:30). After starting in a manner similar to Davis, John Coltrane's playing (1st chorus 3:26, 2nd chorus 4:20) quickly provides a contrast to Davis as he moves into what we now know as the very beginnings of his more mature style, one that is filled with flurries of notes that move all over his horn with an intense, hard-edged sound. Here, however, he is fairly restrained, probably in deference to the mellow vibe of the recording session and the style of this tune. Cannonball Adderley's ties to bebop are clear in his fleet melodic lines (1st chorus 5:16, 2nd chorus 6:10), and the precision and control of his time, one of his great strengths, is always driving yet still relaxed. Before the final melody statement, pianist Evans plays a spare yet beautiful solo (7:05) that uses clusters of notes in an unusual way. Evans's piano introduction and understated accompaniment style are also important to note here as the types of chords and chord voicings (the note choices a pianist makes when playing chords) he uses have proven to be quite influential. Chambers walks through the first A (8:02) before playing the melody out (8:15). Notice the "coolness" of the overall performance. After having briefly retreated from the "cool" style, Davis, never one to stay the same, is back to his restrained and almost detached yet emotionally charged coolness.

from his addiction he also revived his career, including moving out of cool jazz and leading the way to hard bop (Chapter 10, 2nd Chorus) with his album *Walkin'*. Miles became a top star in jazz and in 1957 released his first great quintet's record *Round About Midnight* (see "In Performance: Miles Davis, Bandleader").

After disbanding this quintet, Davis was searching for new directions and experimenting with moving away from complicated chord progressions and

read all about it

"'Out of Notes': The Problem of Miles Davis" by Robert Walser

Walser, **Keeping Time,** *Chapter 62*
An insightful essay on Davis's life and career.

orchestral settings. To this end he created the Mile Davis Sextet and recorded the landmark album *Kind of Blue*. One of the biggest-selling jazz albums ever, *Kind of Blue* is given credit for helping to advance the notion of **modal jazz**. Rather than relying upon chord progressions—a series of chords—as has been traditionally true in jazz, modal jazz tends to use a single mode or scale for an extended time as the basis of melodies and solos. One of the popular tunes from the album, "So What," is an example of this approach.

Davis in the 1960s

Following *Kind of Blue* and his large-scale orchestral work with Gil Evans, Davis put together a new group in the early 1960s, his "second great quintet" (see "In Performance: Miles Davis, Bandleader"). This group's output is represented by the albums *E.S.P.* (1965), *Miles Smiles* (1966), *Sorcerer* (1967), *Nefertiti* (1967), *Miles in the Sky* (1968), and *Filles de Kilimanjaro* (1968), as well as the later-released *Water Babies* (1976) that included material by this group from earlier recording sessions.

The "second great quintet" produced exciting and innovative music that still intrigues and perplexes jazz musicians for a variety of reasons. The rapport between the players was unusually telepathic, compositions by pianist Herbie Hancock and tenor saxophonist Wayne Shorter were breaking new ground, and Davis was intent upon driving the players to always do something new and fresh. Davis's playing was flashier and more aggressive with a new confidence and attitude, and the other players were all exceptional soloists. The band was well versed in hard bop but quickly left it behind as they investigated new harmonic, melodic, formal, and rhythmic territory.

This band's first album as a unit was a studio recording, *E.S.P.* The melody of Shorter's tune "E.S.P." is an early indication of his composing style as it is melodic and lyrical, yet more abstract and knotty with a different sort of complex harmony from jazz standards up to this time. The recording is intense from beginning to end, and after the brief and angular melody, the band takes off at a quick tempo.

Davis and Fusion Music

As rock, funk, R&B, and pop were taking over the musical landscape, the ever-fluid and searching Davis responded. With *Filles de Kilimanjaro* Davis began experimenting with the **Fender Rhodes**, an electric keyboard that was to become ubiquitous in jazz and popular music. Influenced by funk performers such as Sly and the Family Stone and James Brown, and later Prince, Davis changed personnel and added musicians such as keyboardists Joe Zawinul and Chick Corea, bassist Dave Holland, and electric guitarist John McLaughlin—a player who was fusing jazz with rock and the blues and who went on to create the important fusion group, the Mahavishnu Orchestra—for the album *In a Silent Way*, which explored a variety of textures including rock and pop sensibilities through a jazz lens.

Davis went even further and shocked the jazz world by fully embracing rock and funk textures with his electric album *Bitches Brew*, helping to establish jazz fusion, a style that had actually already been developing for some time (Chapter 14, 1st Chorus). Davis continued this trend with *Jack Johnson* and *Live-Evil*, and *On the Corner* went even further toward a funk aesthetic. While these albums sold well, much of the jazz world had difficulty with fusion music, particularly with Davis's embrace of it.

During the later 1970s to early 1980s, health issues—including sickle-cell anemia, which physically debilitated him, as well as falling back into drug

"E.S.P." (1965) by the Miles Davis Quintet

INSTRUMENTATION: Trumpet, leader: Miles Davis; **Tenor saxophone, composer:** Wayne Shorter; **Piano:** Herbie Hancock; **Bass:** Ron Carter; **Drums:** Tony Williams.

LISTENING HIGHLIGHT, STYLE: After the melody (0:28), Wayne Shorter plays with a round yet edgy sound and manages to find an interesting balance between lyricism and intricacy in his solo. Davis plays a longer solo (1:22) that is the highlight of this tune and handles the harmonic complexity with, for him, a new and more chromatic style that almost floats over the chords. His trumpet playing has become more assured, as we can hear in intense upper-register high points in his solo (1:42 and 2:42, and they are quite similar); and his playing is also much busier than we have previously heard. A young but mature Herbie Hancock plays a solo (4:02) that beautifully weds a bebop sensibility with a more modern harmonic conception, displaying a versatility that is still an important part of his musical aesthetic. Tony Williams plays a driving yet open type of swing feel that features a new approach to the ride cymbal, using it to push the music while creating a dynamic splashy sound color that dominates the texture. Bassist Ron Carter provides an extremely solid harmonic and rhythmic foundation that allows the other rhythm section players freedom in these areas. After Hancock's solo, the band takes the tune out (4:52).

addiction—led to Davis stopping performing and recording. In the mid-1980s, he managed a comeback with a series of albums such as *Star People*, *You're Under Arrest* (that featured a cover of Cyndi Lauper's "Time After Time"), *Tutu*, and *Amandla*. These records included important young players such as saxophonists Bob Berg and Kenny Garrett (Chapter 15, 2nd Chorus), guitarists John Scofield and Mike Stern, and bassist-producer Marcus Miller, with whom Davis then collaborated on several albums that featured leading fusion players such as keyboardist George Duke. Davis passed away in 1991.

Davis's legacy is one of the most profound in jazz. Along with his tremendous trumpet playing, his constant searching and innovation as a musician and bandleader—as well as his ability to recognize musicians' abilities and potential while also helping them develop—place Davis in a spot of his own in jazz and in American music.

2nd Chorus John Coltrane

HOW DID JOHN COLTRANE SET A NEW STANDARD FOR JAZZ SAXOPHONE?

Tenor and soprano saxophonist John Coltrane (1926–1967) is one of the most important modern jazz musicians. Over 45 years after his death his influence is still widely acknowledged. Coltrane's "free" yet highly structured soloing style set the standard for modern jazz saxophone playing. His classic quartet and their extended group improvisations established a modern group style, taking it to a level that has rarely, if ever, been matched.

John Coltrane, performing in New York in 1961. Coltrane set the standard for modern saxophone playing, blending elements of bebop and the avant-garde. Photo by Herb Snitzer. *Courtesy Michael Ochs Archives/Getty Images.*

Coltrane's shy appearance on stage is in great contrast to his ability to put himself on raw display, and his extended solos are a marvel of expressiveness, passion, organization, stamina, skill, and a seeking experimentation. Coltrane's dedication to music was inspirational to his peers and is evident in his music. Throughout his career he proved himself to be an all-around player, excelling at playing traditional material such as the blues (his album *Coltrane Plays the Blues*), ballads ("In a Sentimental Mood" from *Duke Ellington and John Coltrane*), and jazz standards. His later, more mature style amazingly seems to transcend yet embody these traditions while also interweaving his interest in South Asian and African music, as well as his personal spiritual quest.

Born in North Carolina, by 1943 Coltrane was living in Philadelphia, which had a thriving jazz scene and community, including saxophonist-composer Benny Golson (Chapter 11, 2nd Chorus), a close teenage friend and musical colleague of Coltrane's. Coltrane had early gigs with blues saxophonist-vocalist Eddie "Cleanhead" Vinson and Dizzy Gillespie (Chapter 10, 1st Chorus) and influential studies with guitarist-educator Dennis Sandole, which were to become pivotal in Coltrane's later harmonic explorations. Other early influences were Charlie Parker (Chapter 10, 1st Chorus) and alto saxophonist Johnny Hodges, the lead alto player for Ellington for many years, a superlative ballad player, a genre Coltrane clearly loved.

Coltrane in the 1950s

Miles Davis hired Coltrane for the group that came to be known as Davis's "first great quintet" (see the 1st Chorus of this chapter), placing Coltrane at the epicenter of the jazz world and vaulting both him and Davis to stardom. Coltrane, however, was suffering from heroin addiction, a scourge common to jazz musicians during this period, and was fired by Davis. Following this devastating blow, Coltrane quit using heroin, an experience that was also a spiritual awakening for the saxophonist.

Coltrane next played an important 6-month stint at the Five Spot in New York City with Thelonious Monk, culminating in a 1957 Carnegie Hall concert released as *Thelonious Monk Quartet with John Coltrane at Carnegie Hall* (2005). We have already discussed "Monk's Mood" from this recording (see Chapter 10, 2nd Chorus). Another tune from the Carnegie Hall concert, "Nutty," gives Coltrane more room to solo and display the beginnings of his mature style. In addition, we hear another style of composing from Monk as this is a much simpler and more straightforward composition than "Monk's Mood." Monk's soloing style is also highlighted more here.

Following his engagement with Monk, Coltrane briefly returned to playing with Miles Davis, recording, among other albums, *Kind of Blue* (1st Chorus of this chapter). It was around this time that the term **sheets of sound** was coined (by jazz historian and author Ira Gitler) to describe Coltrane's playing style. His solos became fast strings of arpeggios and runs, sometimes in odd groupings. This style was controversial with both audiences and critics.

Coltrane in the 1960s

While Coltrane had already been recording under his own name, he was now coming more into his own as a leader and composer. His album *Giant Steps* (1960), the first album consisting entirely of his own compositions, was a huge step

listening focus

"Nutty" (1957) by the Thelonious Monk Quartet with John Coltrane

INSTRUMENTATION: Piano, leader, composer: Thelonious Monk; **Tenor saxophone:** John Coltrane; **Bass:** Ahmed Abdul-Malik; **Drums:** Shadow Wilson.

LISTENING HIGHLIGHT, STYLE: The contrast between John Coltrane's extremely busy solo and Thelonious Monk's spare playing and composing style is fascinating in this live concert. For his solo (0:53–2:32), Coltrane almost immediately takes off with a flurry of runs and arpeggios, an early indication of the new direction for his playing. Coltrane's ability to balance this newfound proclivity toward an intense style while still playing effectively within Monk's group style, as well as referencing the melody at times, is an example of the musical discipline that was evident throughout his career. The melody of "Nutty"—an AABA tune with a bridge that is like the A section but in a different key—is quirky and spare, as is typical for Monk's composing style. Monk's solo (2:32–4:11) is fascinating because of his ability to work the melody of the tune in numerous ways, almost like a set of variations on his melody. His percussive playing style mixes spare playing with quick, off-kilter runs; and his comping is also spare and rhythmically intense. Monk's playing style influences the entire band, which here also has occasional quirky rhythmic aspects to it, often to accommodate Monk's playing.

forward. The title composition, "Giant Steps," exhibited his interest in chord progressions that were traditional harmonically and also experimented with cycles that moved through keys in ways that were unusual in jazz. The album also featured his beautiful ballad "Naima." Another record from this period that shows his new style is *My Favorite Things*, the latter featuring, for the first time, Coltrane on soprano sax on the title track, a song from the popular musical *The Sound of Music*. This record also marks the beginning of the establishment of his classic quartet, which eventually consisted of pianist McCoy Tyner, bassist Jimmy Garrison, and drummer Elvin Jones.

McCoy Tyner, one of the most influential of modern jazz pianists along with Bill Evans and Herbie Hancock (see the 4th Chorus of this chapter), helped to develop a piano style that relied on chord voicings based upon intervals of a 4th, which remains essential to contemporary pianists. Elvin Jones's dynamic drumming brought an incredible intensity to the group that was actually able to match Coltrane's—quite a feat—and his incorporation of an African-influenced 6/8 feel over a 4/4 meter was extremely influential. While bassist Jimmy Garrison did not have as visible a career outside this group as Coltrane, Tyner, or Jones, his playing with this group helped to set the standard for supplying a harmonic foundation while also allowing the music harmonic freedom.

Coltrane's musical interests were broad and included investigating music from India, Africa, and the Middle East. These influences increasingly found their way into his music through the use of drones and intense polyrhythms. These musical interests also intersected with a growing spirituality and a desire for his music to express and reflect these beliefs. The clearest musical reflection of this quest is *A Love Supreme*, an album-length, four-part suite and one of the classic recordings in jazz. Lewis Porter, a Coltrane biographer, states that the titles of the four sections—"Acknowledgement," "Resolution," Pursuance," and "Psalm"—"suggest a kind of pilgrim's progress, in which the pilgrim acknowledges the divine, resolves to pursue it, searches, and eventually, celebrates what has been attained in song" (Porter 1999, 232). Each section of the album consists of simple and even minimal initial musical material that provides the basis for improvisation, but the quartet was playing at such a high level and was so directed and focused that not much was needed.

listening guide

"Resolution" (1965) by the John Coltrane Quartet

DOWNLOAD
Track Number 29

INSTRUMENTATION: Tenor saxophone: John Coltrane; **Piano:** McCoy Tyner; **Bass:** Jimmy Garrison; **Drums:** Elvin Jones.

FORM: The overall form of the melodic statement is ABA. The A section, repeated three times, is a dynamic 8-measure melody with a relatively simple chord progression in E-flat minor. B is a 16-measure bridge that becomes modal in the same key, meaning that it centers around E-flat minor without an actual chord progression.

STYLE: This extraordinary quartet was innovative as a group, and each player has proven to be an important stylist who has been influential on his instrument. Under Coltrane's leadership, they set the standard for modern small-group jazz by combining the traditional and the avant-garde. They used traditional harmonic concepts while also stretching them to their limits, and the openness of their forms incorporated extended solo playing. Notice the group dynamic throughout as they both support and push each other to new heights.

MELODY AND HARMONY: The melody and accompanying chord progression serve as a primary basis for McCoy Tyner's solo. He plays in 8-measure phrases throughout, but midway through his solo he becomes freer and begins to be more modal, as opposed to strictly following the chord progression. This sets up Coltrane's solo, which is also in a modal vein and in 8-measure phrases. Both solos are quite long and move in and out of the central key. In free jazz, more typically, the phrase structure would be more open and there would not be a central key. These are all examples of the combination of traditional and more avant-garde techniques.

RHYTHM: In modern jazz drumming the tendency has been for the bass to create the harmonic foundation while also keeping solid time, usually walking in 4, thereby freeing the drummer a bit from timekeeping chores. Here, Elvin Jones is the engine that drives this quartet with his powerful, dynamic, and polyrhythmic drumming. Jimmy Garrison is a bit freer as a result, and, though he walks a great deal, he is not tied to that function, allowing him rhythmic freedom. While Garrison and Tyner both have typical harmonic functions of playing progressions or key centers, they are also free to move around as they choose, creating a roving harmonic world, while always coming back to the home key of E-flat minor, often with powerful chords and low notes in both the bass and piano.

ACCOMPANIMENT: The rhythm section of this quartet is astonishing. They have a remarkable empathy for each other that is so complete that it sounds as if they are reading each other's minds. Along with Coltrane they move through various rhythmic feels and keys, creating form as they go.

"RESOLUTION" LISTENING GUIDE

TIME	FORM	STYLE	MELODY AND HARMONY	RHYTHM	ACCOMPANIMENT
			Introduction		
0:00		This unaccompanied bass solo is an unusual introduction for a jazz composition.		Jimmy Garrison's introduction is calm but still manages to set up the tempo to come.	This composition begins with a subtle and lovely unaccompanied Garrison bass solo.
			Melody		
0:20	A		John Coltrane plays this simple but intense 8-measure, almost riff-like melodic line three times.	The band immediately hits a powerful groove at a medium fast tempo and never lets up. Elvin Jones displays a modern straight-ahead swing style but also at times superimposes a 6/8 feel over the 4/4 meter.	Garrison plays freely and does not walk in this section, allowing Jones to keep the time. McCoy Tyner comps with forceful chords but in a simple way that rhythmically complements the melody.
0:52	B	Coltrane's playing is quite melodic for the first 8 measures, and he then slightly confounds the meter for the next 8.	The bridge (the middle section) of the melodic statement consists of Coltrane soloing for 16 bars.	Halfway through the section (1:03) the band confounds the meter a bit.	Garrison begins by walking for this section, and Jones plays a straight swing.
1:14	A	Coming out of the bridge there is a real sense of release into the dramatic melodic line.	Coltrane again repeats the melody three times.		
			Solos		
1:47		Throughout this solo Tyner moves back and forth between melodic playing and flurries of notes, creating a nice contour that keeps us interested. Playing long solos that are interesting is a very difficult task, and few do it really well.	Tyner takes the first solo. One of his innovations is clearly heard here, with his strong and rhythmic left hand that defines the harmony while also opening it up. He often does this through the use of chords that consist of 4ths rather than the more traditional 3rds. He starts slowly with simple, melodic lines.	A typical feature can be seen around 3:23 as Tyner creates a polyrhythmic feel with 3/4 against 4/4. Jones joins him in this by accenting the 3/4 divisions, while Garrison continues to lay down the underlying 4/4 meter in support. They all come back together powerfully at 3:45, just before Coltrane's solo.	For the beginning of the solo the rhythm section takes the intensity down a notch. They do this to give Tyner room to build his solo. They gradually build it up, leading to Coltrane's entrance.

continued

"Resolution" listening guide continued

TIME	FORM	STYLE	MELODY AND HARMONY	RHYTHM	ACCOMPANIMENT
3:55		Coltrane's intense sound is immediately recognizable to all serious jazz fans. His upper register has an emotional and extremely dynamic quality.	Coltrane's solo provides a mix of lyrical playing and wild flurries of sound, and he plays all-out all the time here. This solo, however, is particularly lyrical for an intense tune of this sort. Though it is not as present in this solo, his style is often referred to as "sheets of sound"; and he creates these "sheets" through the use of lightning-fast scales and arpeggios up and down the entire range of his horn.	The rhythm section remains at full force to match the intensity of Coltrane's solo.	Jones propels the rhythm with terrific energy and a big sound on his drums, while bassist Garrison provides a solid harmonic support as he mixes walking with a looser rhythmic approach. Tyner's comping largely consists of chords built in 4ths. He moves freely through a variety of harmonies but always returns to a home key where he and Coltrane frequently meet.
Melody					
6:24	A		Coltrane and the rhythm section move seamlessly out of his solo, and he repeats the melody three times to conclude the second part of this extremely powerful recording.		

Compare

In contrast to the nonstop energy of "Resolution," "Naima" (1960) is a calm and reflective John Coltrane composition from the album *Giant Steps*. Its colorful use of extended chords and its gorgeous, almost plaintive melody have made this lovely tune a jazz standard. Coltrane plays the AABA melody simply and beautifully with little adornment. The consummate accompanist, pianist Wynton Kelly, plays an understated solo on the A sections (1:23); and Coltrane closes the recording by playing the bridge, last A, and a coda (2:49). Coltrane never solos on this tune, showing a different side of his musicality on this tune, named for his wife.

Coltrane's Later Career

The CD *Live at the Half Note: One Down, One Up*, from a 1965 live performance at a well-known downtown Manhattan nightclub (released in 2005), perhaps gives us the best picture of Coltrane and his classic quartet at the peak of its power, just before it disbanded. The music is wild and free; yet Coltrane's playing is highly structured, and the performances, while very open, still feel formally coherent. These recordings, as well as later performances, encourage us to examine Coltrane's relationship to the avant-garde.

Just after that recording, Coltrane put together a large ensemble along with his quartet that included, among other important avant-garde players, saxophonists Pharoah Sanders and Archie Shepp and the mainstream trumpeter Freddie

Alice McLeod Coltrane (1937–2007) was a pianist, composer, and bandleader who had a distinguished career separate from her second husband, saxophonist John Coltrane. She was born in Detroit, where her parents encouraged her to study classical piano. While attending Detroit Technical Institute as a teenager, she began playing organ for a local gospel choir. By the late 1950s, she was visiting Paris, where she heard Bud Powell perform, which inspired her to play jazz. In the early 1960s, she played with vibraphone player Terry Gibbs's group; while touring with Gibbs, she met John Coltrane, and the two were married in 1965. Alice Coltrane replaced McCoy Tyner in John Coltrane's group and played with him until his death in mid-1967. She subsequently led her own groups and recorded under her own name through the early 1970s. At that time, Coltrane gradually withdrew from the jazz world to pursue her interests in the Indian religions. She established the Vedantic Center in California in 1975. Renewed interest in her music led Coltrane to return to performing in the early 2000s, often with her son, saxophonist Ravi Coltrane. Coltrane died of respiratory failure in 2007.

Hubbard along with the little-known Dewey Johnson, also on trumpet, to record the album *Ascension*. This recording shows Coltrane in an environment more typical of music associated with **free jazz**, yet Coltrane was highly organized, and even compositional, with his use of motivic development and cyclic harmony.

Tenor saxophonist Pharoah Sanders and drummer Rashied Ali then joined the band, and this expanded group can be heard on *Meditations*. The music was changing and becoming wilder, and dissatisfaction among the original members led to the classic quartet disbanding. Coltrane's wife, Alice Coltrane, joined the group on piano. While Coltrane continued his structured playing, the group itself was losing its coherence, which is so difficult to create in free jazz. Coltrane continued to tour and record up until his death from liver cancer on July 17, 1967, at only 40 years old, having set the direction for modern jazz.

3rd Chorus Charles Mingus

HOW DID CHARLES MINGUS REVITALIZE JAZZ COMPOSITION AND ARRANGING FOR LARGER ENSEMBLES?

Charles Mingus (1922–1979) made his mark in the jazz world as an extraordinary bassist while playing with many of jazz's top musicians. His greatest contribution to jazz, however, was as a composer-bandleader, leading his own groups from the mid-1950s through the late 1970s. He developed a unique writing style that combined the polyphonic group concept of early New Orleans jazz and a down-home, bluesy feel with a modern harmonic and compositional sensibility.

Mingus ranks alongside Duke Ellington as one of jazz's most important composers and, like Ellington, created a completely individualistic body of work. As Ellington did before him, Mingus effectively employed the individual musical

Charles Mingus. Along with Duke Ellington, Mingus was a key bandleader and composer in jazz. Photo courtesy CSU Archives/ Everett Collection.

© Everett Collection Historical/Alamy.

personalities of his musicians in the compositional process, while always maintaining musical control.

Mingus combined imagination with an intense compositional rigor steeped in the traditions of jazz and flavored with compositional elements borrowed from the world of classical composition. His music sounds loose, improvised, and fresh, yet it is also extremely well conceived and highly controlled, an extremely difficult combination to achieve. One of Mingus's greatest strengths as a composer was his ability to blend styles effectively. His mature compositions drew heavily from early styles of jazz, while also being completely contemporary, a very rare quality.

Raised in the African American community of Watts in Los Angeles, Mingus was the son of a mixed-race couple. His attitude toward his mixed heritage, along with his place in a race-conscious society, was a source of difficulty for Mingus; and the choices he made about his personal identity had a powerful effect on the direction of his music. He had an interest in classically oriented composition early in his career—"Half-Mast Inhibition" is an early example—and developed a clear and effective voice in this type of composition. As he made choices about how his racial identification as an African American should impact his

QUESTIONS AND CONTROVERSIES
Mingus the Man

Mingus was an exciting personality but also a troubled and volatile person, so controversy swirled around him on a regular basis. This carried over to the bandstand and his relationships with musicians. For example, he was quickly "encouraged" to resign from Ellington's band after a very short stint following some violent altercations. More importantly, as a bandleader he was known to scream and at times even bully and belittle his side musicians both on and off the bandstand, ostensibly in the service of the music. While he certainly wasn't the most sanguine of leaders, he did manage to regularly have successful bands that articulated his exciting musical vision.

Mingus was also acutely aware of racism in society and felt responsible and compelled to react strongly to racial slights that he experienced. This led to many fights with club owners, record producers, and even his fellow musicians. Horace Silver describes one incident in his memoirs, *Let's Get to the Nitty Gritty: The Autobiography of Horace Silver* (edited by Phil Pastras). One night, while Silver was taking a break from playing at Birdland, he noticed Mingus in his car being questioned by some white police officers. Apparently, they were suspicious of this large black man who was seated next to a white woman, who just happened to be his wife.

Mingus saw me and shouted, "Horace Silver, I want you to witness that these men . . . want to arrest me because my wife is white." I knew if I got involved in the situation, I probably would wind up at the nearest precinct, so I ignored him and kept walking. Mingus held that against me for about 2 years after that. Every time he saw me, he would say, "You didn't support me when I needed your help." He finally forgave me. Mingus was very adamant about racial situations and was very outspoken about the way he felt. This put him in jeopardy when confronted by the police, because he didn't bite his tongue about the way he felt (Silver 2007, 56).

The anecdote illustrates an important element of Mingus's personality. In addition, it highlights that it was indeed dangerous to be a black musician working New York's nightclubs and provides two clearly divergent approaches to handling indignities and ill-treatment brought on by racism.

music, he moved away from writing fully notated scores toward an oral approach to teaching his compositions.

Central Avenue in Watts was a thriving commercial strip filled with clubs. It was an active hub of the high-level local music scene and a neighborhood where all of the top jazz musicians performed and hung out when in Los Angeles. Mingus grew up in this environment, where he could interact with the touring jazz stars as well as with the numerous local musicians who went on to become top artists. His early career, typically, was as a side musician, leading to jobs with Louis Armstrong, Lionel Hampton, and then the Red Norvo Trio, which gave him national exposure. After settling in New York City in 1951, Mingus became a popular side musician, including stints with Charlie Parker, Miles Davis, Duke Ellington, Bud Powell, and Stan Getz. A live concert where Mingus played with Parker, Gillespie, Bud Powell, and drummer Max Roach is documented on the now celebrated *Jazz at Massey Hall* album. In partnership with Roach—as an early example of their interest in self-determination both for artistic freedom and to combat the racial disparities in the music business—they created their own record label, Debut.

In the mid-1950s Mingus formed his group the Jazz Workshop. This ensemble had a regularly changing personnel, but a number of players were longtime members, particularly drummer Dannie Richmond, who helped to anchor the group. The Workshop served to articulate the complicated and unusual forms of Mingus's compositions. It was with the Jazz Workshop that he began to find his mature compositional style as he moved away from notated composition. Mingus taught the players the parts by rote, which created an ensemble looseness that gives a feeling of exciting spontaneity while also being extremely disciplined and controlled, a crucial element of Mingus's style.

Mingus wrote many types of pieces, including simple riff-based tunes such as "Better Git It in Your Soul" and "Boogie Stop Shuffle." Even with these, however, he broke the mold of the standard jazz format of melody–solos–melody by moving through a series of musical ideas with the solos becoming more a part of the overall musical fabric as opposed to being the featured element.

Along with this, Mingus was one of the most successful composers at creating extended works in the jazz idiom, as can be seen in the works "Pithecanthropus Erectus," "Cumbia & Jazz Fusion," and "The Clown." *Reflections*, an extended composition originally referred to as third stream (Chapter 11, 1st Chorus), combines fully notated, classically oriented composition and more jazz-oriented sections. He also wrote ballad material, such as "Goodbye Pork Pie Hat," dedicated to Lester Young (Chapter 6, 4th Chorus), a hauntingly beautiful ballad as lovely and poignant as any work in jazz.

"Fables of Faubus" is another gorgeous Mingus ballad. Again, it has an unusual form. Many different musical "feels" occur, which transform what could be a simple ballad into a more extended composition. The title refers to Orval E. Faubus, former governor of Arkansas, who defied a Supreme Court order to integrate the schools of Little Rock, Arkansas, in 1957, and is an example of Mingus's musical expression of his political beliefs. He was an outspoken social critic, particularly regarding issues of race, an area of great personal significance to Mingus; and this is often reflected in his music, including a later version of this composition that featured lyrics straightforwardly condemning Faubus for his outrageous actions.

Charles Mingus was a larger than life figure for a few reasons. He was a dominant figure on the bandstand, was politically outspoken, and had an

read all about it

"Beneath the Underdog" by Charles Mingus

Walser, **Keeping Time,** *Chapter 38*
Charles Mingus wrote a semifictionalized autobiography in 1971, from which three excerpts are reprinted in *Keeping Time*.

listening guide

"Fables of Faubus" (1959) by Charles Mingus

INSTRUMENTATION: Bass, leader, composer: Charles Mingus; **Alto saxophone:** John Handy; **Tenor saxophone:** Shafi Hadi, Booker Ervin; **Piano:** Horace Parlan; **Drums:** Dannie Richmond.

FORM: The form is a large AABA but is more formally complicated than usual as the A section is divided into two distinct parts—I refer to them in the Listening Guide as A^1 and A^2. In addition, the sections are unusually long and have unconventional lengths, yet the odd length phrases feel normal and natural. The first A is 19 measures with two phrases of 11 and 8 measures, the other A sections are 18 measures with phrase lengths of 10 and 8 measures, and the B section is 16 measures divided into 8-measure phrases. This makes for an exceptionally long form, and Mingus tailors the lengths of phrases to the needs of the melodies, as opposed to sticking within the normal 8- and 16-bar restrictions. After an introduction, there are 3 full choruses; and in a stylistically typical manner, the last melodic statement of the composition includes only the last half of the tune (BA^1A^2).

STYLE: Mingus carefully creates a timbral landscape that is constantly changing and fresh. While a relatively slick presentation for Mingus's bands, we still hear a hint of the looseness to the ensemble playing that belies the tightness of the band.

MELODY AND HARMONY: The expressive and beautiful melodies of the various sections have a bittersweet and soulful character, with a wailing quality at times.

RHYTHM: "Faubus" has a multisectional form with an ever-changing rhythmic feel throughout.

ACCOMPANIMENT: The rhythm section is responsible for the different rhythmic feels that characterize this composition.

"FABLES OF FAUBUS" LISTENING GUIDE

TIME	FORM		STYLE	MELODY AND HARMONY	RHYTHM	ACCOMPANIMENT
				Introduction		
0:00			The feel of the opening line is ominous, in keeping with the subject matter.	The introduction consists of a sliding, bending line played by the two tenor saxophonists. The trombone also joins in for the start of the line.	Charles Mingus sets a very relaxed feel by playing the bass "in 2" (2 beats to the measure instead of 4) and adding fills.	The piano and drums are out here.
				1st Chorus: Melody		
0:16	A	A^1	Two melodic lines moving contrapuntally immediately make this an interesting texture.	While the tenor saxes continue the line from the introduction in the background, the alto sax and trombone play the melody in harmony and octave unison.	The bass continues in 2.	
0:32		A^2	This swinging section contrasts nicely with A^1.	The horns all play a new melody (in octave unison) that has more of a swinging character.		The drums enter gently, and the bass "walks" in 4 (playing on all 4 beats of the measure) to create the swing feel.
0:54	A	A^1	A^1 repeats.			
1:10		A^2	A^2 repeats.			

"Fables of Faubus" listening guide continued

TIME	FORM		STYLE	MELODY AND HARMONY	RHYTHM	ACCOMPANIMENT
1st Chorus: Melody						
1:30	B			The tenor saxophone plays an emotional, almost wailing melody in its upper register as the trombone and the second tenor sax respond and fill.	At 1:46, for 4 measures, the rhythm section goes into a "double-time feel," meaning the tempo stays the same but feels like it is twice as fast. The alto sax emphasizes this by playing a solo in a double-time feel as the other horns fill.	The rhythm section is back in 2 and plays sparingly until the double time, when they play in 4, which provides contrast.
2:02	A	A¹	A¹ repeats.			
2:18		A²	A² repeats.			
2nd Chorus: Solos						
2:37	A	A¹	The soloist plays simply and in a bluesy style, in keeping with the nature of the tune.	Tenor sax solo.		The rhythm section creates a quirky off-beat accompaniment.
2:52		A²	The rhythm section's background figure (see "Accompaniment") is an example of how Mingus manages, like few other composers, to create a highly organized and planned composition that also has a feel of sponta-neity and improvisation.	Tenor solo continues, and as in the presentation of the A² melody, this section contrasts nicely with A¹.	The rhythm section switches feels and hits a swinging groove.	The bass, drums, and piano play figures together behind the soloist (3:08). This is clearly a prearranged figure, showing the careful nature of the accompaniment and the arrangement.
3:14	A	A¹		Tenor solo continues.	The feels of A¹ and A² are repeated.	
3:29		A²				
3:48	B		Since the form of the tune is long, each soloist takes one part of a chorus, here either A¹A²A¹A² or BA¹A². When performed live, the soloists would most likely play at least a full chorus, if not more. Jazz recordings generally are more compact than live performances.	Piano solo.		The rhythmic feel shifts in and out of a double-time feel.
4:18	A	A¹		Piano solo continues.		The rhythm section continues with the now routine rhythmic feels of A¹ and A².
4:33		A²				
3rd Chorus: Solos Continue						
4:52	A	A¹	The tone of each tenor sax player is unique, but this solo is also largely in a bluesy and simple style.	The second tenor sax solos.		The rhythmic feels continue to shift back and forth.
5:07		A²				

continued

"Fables of Faubus" listening guide continued

TIME	FORM		STYLE	MELODY AND HARMONY	RHYTHM	ACCOMPANIMENT
3rd Chorus: Solos Continue						
5:28	A	A^1		Tenor sax solo continues.		
5:42		A^2				
6:01	B		Mingus's solo is quite melodic and has great rhythmic variety. He bends notes in an expressive and bluesy manner, as was true for the horns.	Mingus takes a bass solo.		As is typical for a bass solo, the drums and piano play in a lighter and softer accompaniment style, yet together they still manage to convey similar shifts in the rhythmic feel.
6:31	A	A^1		Bass solo continues.		The rhythmic feels continue to shift back and forth yet more subtly for the bass solo.
6:46		A^2				
Final Melodic Statement						
7:05	B		The band returns to repeat the bridge to take the tune out.			
7:35	A	A^1	Final statements of A^1 and A^2 end this lovely and bittersweet composition.			
7:51		A^2				

Compare

Like "Fables of Faubus," "Boogie Stop Shuffle" is from the popular Mingus album *Mingus Ah Um* (1959). In some ways "Boogie Stop Shuffle" is a simple blues shuffle riffing tune reminiscent of the early swing era, anchored by Mingus on bass and drummer Dannie Richmond. On another level, however, it has an evolving character that combines the style of an open blowing tune with the feel of an extended composition through the use of various themes and rhythmic feels. The combination of thoughtful composition that almost does not feel composed is rare but is typical of Mingus and a large part of what makes his music so compelling and important.

uncompromising attitude toward music and the music business. These traits played out in his music, and he produced some of the most individualistic compositions and performances in jazz; but they also caused difficulties later in his career. Mingus's autobiography *Beneath the Underdog* gives a complicated and perhaps stretched picture of this complex and controversial man. He continued, however, to create excellent albums, including an extended suite, *The Black Saint and the Sinner Lady*; a collection of works for big band, *Let My Children Hear Music*; and

Cumbia and Jazz Fusion. Lou Gehrig's disease cut his career short, and he died in 1979, having recently completed a series of songs for the popular folk singer Joni Mitchell. The Mingus Dynasty Band, Mingus Big Band, and Mingus Orchestra, all led by his widow, Sue Mingus, carry on his musical legacy.

4th Chorus Bill Evans and Herbie Hancock

WHAT NEW INNOVATIONS DID PIANISTS-COMPOSERS BILL EVANS AND HERBIE HANCOCK BRING TO JAZZ?

Bill Evans

Pianist Bill Evans (1929–1980), along with Herbie Hancock and McCoy Tyner (this chapter, 2nd Chorus), is one of the more important contemporary jazz pianists and has been a profound influence on modern jazz piano styles. He is known for his lovely and introspective lyricism, and his sophisticated harmonic approach was extremely influential. In addition, his approach to the **piano trio** encouraged a new formal and rhythmic freedom. In Evans's groups, the members of the trio function more as equal partners, as opposed to the drums and bass acting strictly as accompanists.

From Plainfield, New Jersey, Evans started piano at a young age and studied flute. His early musical experiences as well as his studies in college primarily involved classical music, which greatly influenced his later style as his harmonic approach owed a great deal to twentieth-century classical music traditions. He worked professionally after college, including in a trio with guitarist Mundell Lowe and bassist Red Mitchell and as an accompanist for Billy Holiday (Chapter 9, 1st Chorus).

Evans moved to New York City in 1955, where he freelanced and began to make a name for himself. His association with composer and music theorist George Russell placed Evans more firmly in the jazz world, through, for example, his solos in Russell's "Concerto for Billy the Kid" and "All About Rosie," leading to his first record as a leader with the album *New Jazz Conceptions*. His association with Russell also led to Evans joining Miles Davis's band, one of the most high-profile gigs in jazz, in 1958. Evans recorded *Kind of Blue* with Davis (this chapter, 1st Chorus), an important album that helped to popularize modal jazz. Evans's accompanying throughout the record helped to define a modal jazz concept, including his use of chords built on 4ths, as opposed to 3rds.

In 1959 Evans formed a trio with bassist Scott La Faro and drummer Paul Motian, which shaped a new concept for the piano trio genre. La Faro was a particularly melodically gifted bass player, and the group perfected a style that, while still featuring the piano, gave the bassist and drummer more freedom and a role beyond accompanying that created a high level of interplay. The group had an uncanny intuitive interaction, as well as a sound that was lyrical, sensitive, and introspective; and Evans's harmonic approach was original, fresh, and colorful. La Faro died tragically early in a car accident just after the group recorded two live albums at the Village Vanguard, which are among the greatest live recordings in jazz.

Evans continued to perform and record with his trio, managing to keep a steady personnel, including bassists Chuck Israels and Eddie Gomez and drummers Marty Morell and Eliot Zigmund. He recorded in other formats as well in later years,

Bill Evans (piano), Larry Bunker (drums), and Chuck Israels (bass), 1965. Evans's cerebral piano style and composing were ideally suited to the small trios that he often led in the 1960s. Photo by David Redfern.
Courtesy Getty Images.

including *Symbiosis*, a jazz concerto written for him by Claus Ogerman for his trio and orchestra; *Affinity*, a quintet album that features harmonica virtuoso Toots Thielmans; and two duet recordings with vocalist Tony Bennett (see "Listening Guide: Compare"). Evans's last studio recording, *We Will Meet Again*, featured a quintet that included his last bassist and drummer, Marc Johnson and Joe LaBarbera, as well as the wonderful contemporary trumpeter Tom Harrell and saxophonist Larry Schneider. The record won two Grammy Awards in 1981. Evans died in 1980 after a long struggle with substance abuse.

Herbie Hancock

Along with Bill Evans and McCoy Tyner, pianist Herbie Hancock (b. 1940) is responsible for helping to shape jazz piano styles after the bop era. Though identified as a jazz pianist by most, Hancock has steadfastly refused to accept the limitations that others have tried to place upon him. He has had a career with many phases, and his music has spanned numerous styles from jazz to music influenced by hip-hop. Hancock's ability to produce such a variety of music at the highest level gives him a special and important place in the music world.

From Chicago, Hancock was a child prodigy and performed with the Chicago Symphony, one of the world's top orchestras, when he was 11. After early work with trumpeter Donald Byrd, Hancock recorded his first record, *Takin' Off*, in 1962. His composition "Watermelon Man" from that record became a hit for percussionist-bandleader Mongo Santamaria (Chapter 12, 2nd Chorus) and is now a jazz standard.

Hancock's next gig, and probably his biggest break, came when he was hired by Miles Davis for the group that came to be referred to as Davis's "second great

listening guide

"Waltz for Debby" (Take 1, 1961) by the Bill Evans Trio

INSTRUMENTATION: Piano, composer, leader: Bill Evans; **Bass:** Scott La Faro; **Drums:** Paul Motian.

FORM: The form is essentially AABC, a common variation on AABA; but it is a bit more complicated than that. The first two A sections (referred to here as A^1 and A^2) are the same but have different endings, with A^2 leading to B, the bridge. C, while beginning the same way as the A sections, also has a different ending and is considerably extended. All sections are 16 measures, except C, which is 32. They play 7 choruses of the entire form.

STYLE: The Bill Evans Trio is known for its innovative approach to interaction and a free yet dynamic approach to time, and this can be seen in this recording, a classic Evans composition.

MELODY AND HARMONY: Evans's lyricism and gorgeous use of harmony that have been so influential on modern pianists are always in evidence in this recording. Evans is known for his beautiful and colorful chord voicings, and we hear these throughout. The solos by both Evans and La Faro are lyrical and pretty.

RHYTHM: This is as gentle as jazz gets, yet, paradoxically, it is so gentle and lovely that it has its own type of intensity. It is a wonderful combination of light and buoyant, while also swinging very hard. "Waltz for Debby" begins as a waltz (3/4) and quickly changes to a swinging 4/4 for the remainder of the tune. The feel is light throughout, with Motian playing with brushes.

ACCOMPANIMENT: In this classic version of Evans's trio, bassist Scott La Faro helped to free the bass, as Ellington's bassist Jimmy Blanton did before him. La Faro plays throughout with a fascinating blend of a traditional bassist's role of providing a harmonic and rhythmic underpinning along with a melodic and rhythmically free approach that was also very influential. While drummer Paul Motian's playing is understated—here he uses brushes, which makes it especially so—his interaction with the trio as well as his sensitive and gently floating melodic style make his playing extremely effective.

"WALTZ FOR DEBBY" LISTENING GUIDE

TIME	FORM	STYLE	MELODY AND HARMONY	RHYTHM	ACCOMPANIMENT
			1st Chorus, Melody in 3/4 (Waltz)		
0:00	A^1	Bill Evans plays the melody straightforwardly throughout this 1st chorus.	"Waltz for Debby" has a lovely melody that mixes a simplicity that reflects a childlike sensibility—the tune was written for his niece—with melodic and harmonic sophistication.	The entire 1st chorus is just piano and bass. This allows the time to be a bit flexible when they choose.	Scott La Faro plays a melodic bass line that acts as a counterline to the melody as opposed to playing just the roots of the chords.

continued

"Waltz for Debby" listening guide continued

TIME	FORM	STYLE	MELODY AND HARMONY	RHYTHM	ACCOMPANIMENT
1st Chorus, Melody in 3/4 (Waltz)					
0:13	A²				
0:25	B		The melody takes on a different character at the bridge, providing contrast.	The feel subtly shifts for the bridge as La Faro plays more simply, and they create more of a typical waltz feel.	
0:41	C			The flexible sense of time is heard clearly at 0:50, as La Faro has to listen closely to Evans to follow him.	At 1:00 Evans and La Faro set up a new tempo and shift the meter from 3/4 to 4/4. La Faro effectively uses a bass pedal point—one repeated note under changing chords.
2nd Chorus, Melody in 4/4					
1:11	A¹	Evans swings the melody this time through.	Evans plays the melody again in the new tempo and meter but more freely this time and takes more rhythmic liberties with the melody.	The band goes into a light yet insistent swinging 4/4 with a new tempo.	Drummer Paul Motian enters on drums, playing gently with brushes. La Faro does not feel compelled to strictly play time or to play the roots of the chords as he mixes up his approach regularly, playing both a typical bassist's role and a freer and more melodic style. He plays largely in 2 but mixes it up.
1:22	A²				
1:32	B				
1:43	C				
3rd Chorus, Piano Solo					
2:04	A¹	Evans's right and left hands are working quite independently here. He solos with his right hand much the way a horn would, while his left hand comps.		Motian's role here is perhaps the most limited in scope as he generally acts as an understated timekeeper. His subtlety and taste fit in perfectly with the style of this tune however.	La Faro continues his dual approach, again largely in 2. He displays great empathy for what Evans is playing.
2:14	A²				
2:25	B				
2:35	C	Evans moves into his 2nd solo chorus seamlessly.			

"Waltz for Debby" listening guide continued

TIME	FORM	STYLE	MELODY AND HARMONY	RHYTHM	ACCOMPANIMENT
4th Chorus, Piano Solo Continued					
2:57	A¹	Evans changes styles here as his two hands are playing in more of "locked hand" style throughout this chorus. In this style the two hands work together as one, as opposed to the kind of comping he was doing for himself in the 3rd chorus.			Motian continues his understated timekeeping.
3:07	A²				
3:17	B			This bridge section is a good place to hear La Faro's melodic accompanying style.	
3:28	C	The locked hand style is particularly noticeable in this section.		La Faro contrasts the bridge by playing a more traditional role here. He uses the pedal point again at the end of the section (3:43), then transitions directly into his solo.	
5th Chorus, Bass Solo					
3:48	A¹	La Faro plays a solo. During his solo he plays all over the instrument but begins primarily in the middle and lower registers.		Evans comps softly for La Faro's solo. He frequently plays pieces of the tune's melody behind La Faro's solo.	As is typical for drummers, Motian plays even more softly and subtly during the bass solo, to avoid overpowering La Faro's solo.
3:59	A²				
4:09	B	In the bridge La Faro builds up to the upper register while still playing in all registers.			
4:20	C				
6th Chorus, Bass Solo Continued					
4:40	A¹	La Faro continues to solo all over the various registers of the bass, but in this chorus he concentrates more on the upper register, a frequent style for bassists when they solo. The upper register projects well over the rest of the rhythm section, while a solo spot also gives bassists a chance to show their "chops" in this part of the instrument.			

continued

"Waltz for Debby" listening guide continued

TIME	FORM	STYLE	MELODY AND HARMONY	RHYTHM	ACCOMPANIMENT
4:51	A²				
5:01	B				
5:12	C				
7th Chorus, Melody					
5:32	A¹	The trio plays the melody a final time and in the same style as the 2nd chorus.			
5:43	A²				
5:53	B				
6:03	C	Evans initially plays this final A section more forcefully than usual; then toward the end the trio brings the intensity down to finish with a gentle ending and a small tag.			

Compare

The lovely ballad "Some Other Time" (1975) shows Bill Evans in a different setting. In this first of two records with the fabulous vocalist Tony Bennett, Evans functions as accompanist to Bennett; and his accompaniment style still has the gentle feel we heard in "Waltz for Debby." Evans begins the tune with an introduction that features a simple and repetitive figure that recurs in various guises regularly throughout the tune. Evans's pretty and gentle solo (2:20) is often set over this figure, bringing all aspects of this recording together into one cohesive statement. Bennett's straightforward but wistful and moving rendition expresses the lyrics that speak of a warm love mixed with regret. His singing of the words "Oh well" at 0:32 and 1:02 says it all.

read all about it

"Soul, Craft and Cultural Hierarchy" by Wynton Marsalis and Herbie Hancock

Walser, **Keeping Time,** *Chapter 54*

In this joint interview, Marsalis and Hancock debate their different attitudes toward the influence of free jazz, popular music, and jazz–rock on mainstream jazz.

quintet." Along with bassist Ron Carter and drummer Tony Williams, Hancock helped to redefine the jazz rhythm section with an expanded and more open rhythmic, harmonic, and even formal approach. This can be heard in the Davis group's recording of Wayne Shorter's composition "E.S.P." (see the 1st Chorus of this chapter).

While with Davis, Hancock worked with other prominent groups as a side musician, recording many albums on Blue Note Records, as well as beginning an important solo career. His 1965 albums *Maiden Voyage* and *Empyrean Isles* were classics from this period and featured Hancock's rhythm section partners from the Miles Davis quintet of this period, bassist Ron Carter and drummer Tony Williams, along with Freddie Hubbard, one of the most influential trumpet players from the 1960s through the 1990s (discussed in Chapter 14, 3rd Chorus). "Maiden Voyage" and Dolphin Dance" have become jazz standards, and numerous bands from various genres have recorded versions of these songs.

Herbie Hancock, ca. 2000s. Hancock has been a leading composer, bandleader, and pianist in both acoustic and electric jazz styles for decades.
© Rob Lacey/vividstock.net/Alamy.

At this time Hancock was a leading voice as both a pianist and bandleader in jazz. Traditionally an acoustic music, jazz was undergoing significant changes during the 1960s and early 1970s as many musicians who were playing jazz were also well-versed and interested in other styles such as rock, R&B, and funk and were playing music that freely drew upon all of their interests. This type of music

QUESTIONS AND CONTROVERSIES
Is Fusion Music Jazz?

The early experiments with fusing rock elements such as electric guitar and a heavier, rock rhythm section were met with dismay by the jazz mainstream. For many it was a question of "selling out"; the feeling was that jazz musicians were chasing pop success by emulating the hit sounds and styles of the day. Others felt that the new music forsook the subtlety of group improvisation, advanced harmonies, and polyrhythms that marked the greatest jazz playing.

Of course, it is important to recall that every new style of jazz has been greeted with initial dismay by adherents of earlier styles. Jazz itself was touted by early critics as being a "barbaric" dance music that promoted dancing, drinking, and other sinful activities. When bebop arrived on the scene, as we have seen, many jazz musicians criticized the new music as being noisy. Where's the melody? they asked.

As bebop became the mainstream, new developments were targeted as being anti-jazz, starting with the avant-garde experiments of the late 1950s and early 1960s.

Fusion music is still controversial. Some feel that it laid the groundwork for **smooth jazz** (Chapter 14, 1st Chorus), the highly commercial style of musicians like saxophone player Kenny G and others who the hard core jazz audience feel have no part in the jazz pantheon. Yet, many developments that were part of jazz–rock—from using amplified guitars and keyboards, synthesizers, and rock and R&B harmonies and rhythms—are now commonly heard in mainstream jazz groups. What was once revolutionary is hardly noticed by critics or fans, and the fusing of various styles is now more the rule than the exception.

eventually came to be known as jazz fusion (discussed further in Chapter 14, 1st Chorus). Miles Davis was inspired by this new musical form and encouraged Hancock to experiment with the use of electronic keyboards, such as the Fender Rhodes. Davis's music took on a different aspect as a result (discussed in the 1st Chorus of this chapter), and Hancock's contributions can be heard on Davis records such as *In a Silent Way* and *On the Corner*. While reluctant at first, Hancock went on to fully embrace the use of a wide variety of electronic instruments as well as the notion of freely expressing all of his musical interests.

listening guide

DOWNLOAD
Track Number 32

"Actual Proof" (1974, excerpt 0:00–6:06) by Herbie Hancock

INSTRUMENTATION: Keyboards and synthesizers, leader, composer: Herbie Hancock; **Electric bass:** Paul Jackson; **Drums:** Mike Clark; **Alto flute:** Bennie Maupin; **Percussion:** Bill Summers.

OVERVIEW: Following the popularity of *Head Hunters*, the Headhunters released *Thrust* and again had commercial success. The composition "Actual Proof" has been influential with its jazz-funk groove, created by drummer Mike Clark and bassist Paul Jackson, and Hancock's powerful and impressive Fender Rhodes keyboard solo.

FORM: The form of "Actual Proof" is quite simple in that after an introduction it repeats one section many times for solos. The form, however, in some ways is complicated as it has an asymmetrical and unusual length of 15 measures. Also, while it is in 4/4, the last 3 measures change meter with 5/4, 4/4, and 3/4 bars.

STYLE: "Actual Proof" is about the groove. Compared to the music we have heard so far, the drums and bass are played with entirely new and different concepts. Hancock's Fender Rhodes solo is a classic jazz solo over this funky groove.

MELODY AND HARMONY: The melody essentially consists of three variations of a melodic fragment, and there is as much space between melody lines as there is actual melody. The harmony is sophisticated and reflects the contemporary jazz of the day.

RHYTHM: The funk-jazz groove is powerful but also a bit confounding as it is difficult to know where the beat or the measure divisions are because it is heavily syncopated, with the band frequently anticipating the first beat of the bar by an 1/8 note. To discover this, try clapping your hands to the beat or dancing to the groove—neither is easy!

ACCOMPANIMENT: The drumming here is as good an example of this particular style of jazz-funk drumming as there is. Mike Clark, along with Dave Garibaldi and others, developed a style that is often associated with the San Francisco Bay Area and has been popularized with this recording and by the R&B and funk group Tower of Power. Bassist Paul Jackson worked closely with Clark for many years in a wide variety of bands, and he created a style of his own that was extremely active. In fact, the bass almost dominates the texture with its nonstop syncopated activity, similar to what funk bass players do and to a style that is now common among many contemporary jazz players.

continued

"ACTUAL PROOF" LISTENING GUIDE (EXCERPT, 0:00–6:00)

TIME	FORM	STYLE	MELODY AND HARMONY	RHYTHM	ACCOMPANIMENT
Introduction					
0:00		The introduction immediately sets a powerful and classic jazz–funk groove with drums, bass, and synthesizer.		The drums are playing a complicated jazz–funk groove based on 16th notes, and the bass plays a syncopated and extremely active bass line.	Herbie Hancock essentially plays two keyboard parts, one a funky, spare, and spiky clavinet part and the other a complementary part that fills in the space with a rounder sound.
Melody					
0:31	A	The melody, played by layers of keyboards and synthesizers and with the lead line doubled by alto flute, is rhythmically interesting and a bit mysterious.		A crucial part of the melody is a break at the end of the form—where the meter changes—that is used every time to signal the end of the chorus.	
1:04	A				
Herbie Hancock Fender Rhodes Solo					
1:36	1st Chorus	After the melody, Hancock plays an extended solo on the Fender Rhodes. The Rhodes is a classic electric piano and perhaps the most popular one in jazz. It has a piano-like touch that allows for great expression, compared to many synthesizers; and when the keys are hit hard it gives a funky, slightly distorted sound that players like. Hancock's solo is an amazing display of virtuosity in terms of his melodic and rhythmic invention as well as the overall command of his instrument that he displays. In this tune Hancock, Paul Jackson, and Mike Clark set the standard for jazz–funk playing.	The solo is remarkable for many reasons and is a tour de force for all three players. Hancock, Clark, and Jackson show a remarkable intuitive empathy for each other. They each play independent lines at times, creating an exciting polyphony, then all of a sudden they will play a tight rhythmic figure together.		The bass—and at times the keyboard and drums—clearly marks the end of each chorus with the break from the tune itself, and the band frequently plays a rhythmic figure from the middle of the melody, for example, at 2:18, 3:13, and 4:08.
2:01	2nd Chorus		Hancock solo continues.		
2:28	3rd Chorus		Hancock solo continues.		
2:56	4th Chorus		Hancock solo continues.		

continued

"Actual Proof" listening guide continued

TIME	FORM	STYLE	MELODY AND HARMONY	RHYTHM	ACCOMPANIMENT
3:24	5th Chorus		Hancock solo continues.		
3:51	6th Chorus		Hancock solo continues.		
4:18	7th Chorus		Hancock solo continues.		
4:45	8th Chorus		Hancock solo continues.		
5:12	9th Chorus		Hancock solo continues.		
5:39–6:00	10th Chorus		Hancock solo continues.		

Compare

The Herbie Hancock composition and recording "Dolphin Dance," from his classic album *Maiden Voyage* (1965), melds the straightforwardness of hard bop with the adventurousness and openness of Hancock's experience with Davis. It features his rhythm section partners from the Miles Davis quintet of this period, bassist Ron Carter and drummer Tony Williams, along with tenor saxophonist George Coleman and Freddie Hubbard, one of the most influential trumpet players from the 1960s through the 1990s (Chapter 14, 3rd Chorus).

The pretty melody has a certain kind of simplicity as it uses several melodic elements over and over again in different ways. The relationship between the melody and the rather complex harmony is not simple however, and in it Hancock extensively uses the colorful extensions of chords discussed previously. The chords themselves are also complex, and with tunes such as this Hancock helped usher in new approaches to jazz harmony.

Hubbard's virtuosity and powerful, aggressive yet lyrical style are immediately on display in his excellent solo (1:19). Hancock, in this tasteful and almost restrained solo (5:43), begins by taking his time and playing rather simply while leaving plenty of space. He displays a terrific command of rhythm while swinging in numerous ways by both delaying and pushing the time. Hancock gradually builds the intensity of the solo but always stays within the mood of this lovely composition.

An early example of Hancock's work with electronics is the album *Fat Albert Rotunda*, which deftly melds jazz with pop and R&B rhythmic feels on tunes such as "Tell Me a Bedtime Story." Hancock continued to expand his use of electronic instruments, including a variety of synthesizers. Because of his place as one of jazz's finest pianists, the jazz establishment at times criticized Hancock's forays into electronically oriented music and popular styles. Hancock persisted, however, and went on to create a group called the Headhunters that allowed him to incorporate funk music and R&B styles into his compositions. *Head Hunters* (1973) and its hit "Chameleon," now a jazz standard, did this very effectively and brought Hancock to the attention of new listeners. His next album, *Thrust* (1974), is another example of this; and the tune "Actual Proof" is a leading example of combining funk rhythms with a jazz concept.

Hancock continued to have an extremely productive, diverse, and commercially and artistically successful career. Highlighting the importance of their work with Davis, Hancock, Wayne Shorter, Tony Williams, and Ron Carter maintained a powerful and productive relationship. The group V.S.O.P. united the entire second Miles Davis Quintet with trumpeter Freddie Hubbard replacing Davis; V.S.O.P. II included Hancock, Williams, Carter, trumpeter Wynton Marsalis (Chapter 14, 3rd Chorus), and his brother Branford Marsalis on sax; and Hancock and Shorter recorded a duo album, *1+1* (1997).

Hancock also recorded a series of albums that continued to include pop and R&B elements, including *Future Shock* (1983). A tune from the album, "Rockit," included the use of turntablist techniques such as those used in hip-hop and rap and became a crossover hit while winning a Grammy Award for Best R&B Instrumental. In a tribute to Miles Davis, the second great quintet again reunited, this time with trumpeter Wallace Roney filling in for Davis, and the group won a Grammy Award for *a Tribute to Miles* (1994). Hancock also won a Grammy Award for his 2008 tribute to vocalist-composer Joni Mitchell, *River: The Joni Letters*. In addition, his CD *Herbie Hancock's Imagine Project* (2010) won two Grammy Awards and was a collaboration with musicians from around the world that was conceived to express his ideas regarding the importance of global responsibility for world peace.

Hancock continues to be in the forefront of jazz while also being extremely productive on a variety of fronts. He has maintained his enthusiasm for bringing together all of his musical interests and has become an important spokesperson for jazz as an open and constantly growing art form. Hancock is currently a goodwill ambassador for the United Nations Educational, Scientific, and Cultural Organization (UNESCO), holds the Creative Chair for Jazz with the Los Angeles Philharmonic, and is Chairman of the Thelonious Monk Institute of Jazz.

CODA Chapter Summary

How Did Miles Davis Continue to Innovate and Change Throughout His Career?

- Miles Davis was an innovator in several different musical styles: beginning with playing bebop with Charlie Parker to being a leader of the cool jazz movement to hard bop to modal jazz and then on to fusion.
- He worked with arranger Gil Evans, who wrote for Davis's nonet in the late 1940s, pieces that would be recorded on an album called *Birth of the Cool*, which helped establish cool jazz. They also collaborated on four other classic albums with an expanded big band.
- His late 1950s sextet with pianist Bill Evans popularized modal jazz through the album *Kind of Blue*.
- His two "great quintets"—during the 1950s with John Coltrane, Red Garland, Paul Chambers, and Philly Joe Jones and in the 1960s with Wayne Shorter, Herbie Hancock, Ron Carter, and Tony Williams—are recognized as among the greatest of all small jazz combos.
- In the later 1960s to early 1970s, Davis began experiments with fusion music, incorporating funk and rock instrumentation and rhythms into his music.

How Did John Coltrane Set a New Standard for Jazz Saxophone?

- Coltrane's "free" yet highly structured soloing style set the standard for modern jazz saxophone playing.

- His style of playing solos, featuring fast strings of arpeggios and runs, sometimes in odd groupings, was described as "sheets of sound."
- His classic quartet and their extended group improvisations established a modern group style, taking it to a level that has rarely, if ever, been matched.
- Coltrane's musical interests were broad and included investigating music from India, Africa, and the Middle East. These influences increasingly found their way into his music through the use of drones and intense polyrhythms. These musical interests also intersected with a growing spirituality and a desire for his music to express and reflect these beliefs.

How Did Charles Mingus Revitalize Jazz Composition and Arranging for Larger Ensembles?

- Bassist Charles Mingus's greatest contribution to jazz was as a composer-bandleader, leading his own groups from the mid-1950s through the late 1970s.
- He developed a unique writing style that combined the polyphonic group concept of early New Orleans jazz and a down-home, bluesy feel with a modern harmonic and compositional sensibility.
- He was able to create structures that encouraged a loose, improvisatory feeling in his music, while he still maintained rigorous control over the group.
- Mingus was sensitive to issues of racism in America, reflected in his fierce independence as well as his compositions like "Fables of Faubus."

What New Innovations Did Pianists-Composers Bill Evans and Herbie Hancock Bring to Jazz?

- Bill Evans is known for his lovely and introspective lyricism, along with a sophisticated harmonic approach, which was extremely influential.
- His approach to the piano trio encouraged a new formal and rhythmic freedom. In Evans's groups, the members of the trio function more as equal partners, as opposed to the drums and bass acting strictly as accompanists.
- Herbie Hancock has been a leading pianist, composer, and bandleader. His early compositions including "Watermelon Man" and "Maiden Voyage" have become classics of mainstream jazz.
- Hancock has been willing to adapt to a wide range of musical styles. He is equally comfortable playing electric keyboards and synthesizers as he is the traditional piano. His fusion band, the Headhunters, enjoyed great success during the mid-1970s to early 1980s.

Talkin' Jazz (Key Terms)

Fender Rhodes	Mainstream jazz	Sheets of sound
Free jazz	Modal jazz	Smooth jazz
Fusion	Piano trio	

Key People

Miles Davis	Charles Mingus	Herbie Hancock
John Coltrane	Bill Evans	

Think About This (For Further Discussion and Study)

1. What are the various styles that Miles Davis was involved in? How was he innovative in these styles?
2. Describe Davis's playing style. How did it change through the years? Which period is your favorite?
3. Discuss John Coltrane's playing style as he progressed through playing with Thelonious Monk, Davis, and his own group.
4. Discuss the importance of Charles Mingus's composing.
5. What was significant about Mingus as a bandleader?
6. Compare the styles of Bill Evans and Herbie Hancock. What was the stylistic importance of each?
7. Does Hancock's "Absolute Proof" have a relationship to any music that you listen to?

Look It Up (Key Resources)

Carner, Gary, ed. *The Miles Davis Companion: Four Decades of Commentary.* New York: Schirmer Books, 1997.

Carr, Ian. *Miles Davis: A Critical Biography.* London: Paladin, 1982.

Chambers, Jack. *Milestones: The Music and Times of Miles Davis.* Toronto: University of Toronto Press, 1985.

Davis, Miles. *Miles: The Autobiography.* With Quincy Troupe. New York: Simon and Schuster, 1989.

Early, Gerald, ed. *Miles Davis and American Culture.* St. Louis: Missouri Historical Society Press, 2001.

Gluck, Bob. *You'll Know When You Get There: Herbie Hancock and the Mwandishi Band.* Chicago: University of Chicago Press, 2012.

Kahn, Ashley. *Kind of Blue: The Making of the Miles Davis Masterpiece.* Boston: Da Capo Press, 2000.

————. *A Love Supreme: The Story of John Coltrane's Signature Album.* New York: Penguin, 2002.

Kirchner, Bill, ed. *A Miles Davis Reader.* Washington, DC: Smithsonian Institution Press, 1997.

Mingus, Charles. *Beneath the Underdog: His World as Composed by Mingus.* New York: Vintage, 1971.

Pettinger, Peter. *Bill Evans: How My Heart Sings.* New Haven, CT: Yale University Press, 1998.

Pond, Steven. *Head Hunters: The Making of Jazz's First Platinum Album.* Ann Arbor: University of Michigan Press, 2005.

Porter, Lewis. *John Coltrane: His Life and Music.* Ann Arbor: University of Michigan Press, 1999.

Priestly, Brian. *Mingus: A Critical Biography.* New York: Da Capo Press, 1982.

Ratliff, Ben. *Coltrane: The Story of a Sound.* New York: Farrar, Straus and Giroux, 2007.

Santoro, Gene. *Myself When I Am Real: The Life and Music of Charles Mingus.* New York: Oxford University Press, 2000.

Shadwick, Keith. *Bill Evans: Everything Happens to Me—A Musical Biography.* San Francisco: Backbeat Books, 2002.

Silver, Horace. *Let's Get to the Nitty Gritty: The Autobiography of Horace Silver.* Oakland, CA: University of California Press, 2007.

Szwed, John. *So What: The Life of Miles Davis.* New York: Simon and Schuster, 2002.

INTO THE PRESENT
1975–TODAY

MAJOR MUSICAL STYLES

1960s–today	• Jazz fusion
1970s–today	• Smooth jazz
1980–1995	• Neo-traditional
1970s–today	• "Downtown"

The social upheaval of the 1960s and early 1970s culminated in the ouster of President Richard Nixon in 1974, following the Watergate scandal. Nixon had attempted to spy on his adversaries in the 1974 presidential election, and subsequently he and his associates tried to cover up their involvement in this effort. At the same time, as an outgrowth of the hippie and civil rights movements of the 1960s, new groups—ranging from women to Native Americans to farmworkers—advocated for increased opportunity and personal freedom. As a reaction, President Jimmy Carter was elected as an outsider who could come to Washington and restore American's faith in government. However, when Iranian revolutionaries seized members of the American Embassy's staff in Tehran, the country's mood darkened and Carter was dismissed as weak in foreign policy. A new conservative movement arose, which led to the election of President Ronald Reagan and a return to "traditional values" during the 1980s.

Since the "Reagan revolution" of the 1980s, the country has veered back and forth between periods of more liberal governance (the Clinton years of the 1990s) to a return to conservative values (the Bush years of the first decade of the twenty-first century) and then back again to a more moderate government under America's first African American president, Barack Obama. A polarized political landscape—in which conservatives and liberals vie for control, with neither side totally victorious—reflects a citizenry equally divided between more liberal and conservative tendencies. In many ways, society is more open than it has ever been; same-sex marriage—once unthinkable—is

When American hostages were seized by Iranian revolutionaries, US protesters gathered to urge Congress to retaliate.
Photo by Marion S. Trikosko. Courtesy Library of Congress.

now accepted in many states and widely supported by the population. On the other hand, the Tea Party movement arose in response to President Obama's election, promoting the most conservative values seen in many decades.

Throughout these changes, the African American community, particularly in the inner city, continued to suffer from lack of resources and attention. In 2005 the monster storm Hurricane Katrina brought attention to their plight when large sections of New Orleans were flooded. Aid was slow to come to residents, and many cited racism as a factor in the government's slow response.

The new conservatism of the 1980s was reflected in the world of the arts. The neo-traditionalists in jazz came to the fore, led by trumpeter-composer Wynton Marsalis, trying to restore the African American, blues-based tradition of jazz performance as a reaction to jazz–rock and fusion, the black avant-garde musicians of the 1960s and 1970s, as well as the success of white jazz players who had co-opted earlier styles. Marsalis, a tireless educator and promoter of jazz around the world, essentially became the "face" of jazz as the artistic director of Jazz at Lincoln Center

Damaged houses in Mississippi following Hurricane Katrina, 2005. The huge storm disproportionately affected the African American communities along the Gulf Coast, including inner-city New Orleans.
Photo by Carol L. Highsmith. Courtesy Library of Congress.

in New York City, the eventual outgrowth of the successful jazz program that he cofounded in 1987. Marsalis initially promoted a conservative view of the jazz tradition, elevating the music of Louis Armstrong and Duke Ellington as models representing "real" jazz, often at the expense of some contemporary jazz styles. As a result, he and Jazz at Lincoln Center became flashpoints for controversy surrounding a "definition" of jazz, a slippery notion at best, regardless of perspective. More recently, Jazz at Lincoln Center has opened its programs to many different jazz styles, which have been well received by critics and audiences alike.

At the same time as the neo-traditionalists were coming to the fore, alternate movements were arising to promote a more open view of the jazz field. Female musicians, traditionally limited to backstage roles in jazz, were finding new opportunities to work, not only as composers but as performers and group leaders. The downtown music scene that developed in New York beginning in the late 1970s, and continues today, represented a new spirit of adventure and exploration, Latino/Latina musicians continued to have a powerful influence on jazz, and European jazz musicians became leaders in extending jazz into new directions.

1975-TODAY

MUSICIANS/MUSICAL WORKS

1976	• Cecil Taylor, "Streams of Chorus and Seed" • Miguel Zenón, alto saxophonist-composer-bandleader, is born
1978	• Robert Glasper, pianist-composer-bandleader, born
1982	• Thelonious Monk dies after nearly a decade of not performing
1984	• Esperanza Spalding, bass player, born
1985	• Wynton Marsalis, "Delfeayo's Dilemma"
1988	• Chet Baker dies
1991	• Miles Davis dies • Jazz at Lincoln Center becomes an official department of Lincoln Center

1993	• Dizzy Gillespie dies
2005	• Terence Blanchard, "Child's Play"
2008	• Brian Blade and the Fellowship Band, "Rubylou's Lullaby"
2010	• Jason Moran, "Feedback, Pt. 2" • Steve Coleman and Five Elements, "Beba" • Cassandra Wilson, "Blackbird" • Regina Carter, "Full Time"
2011	• Miguel Zenón, "Silencio"
2012	• Lionel Loueke, "Freedom Dance" • Esperanza Spalding, "Little Fly" • The Robert Glasper Experiment, "Afro Blue"
2013	• Joshua Redman, "The Folks Who Live on the Hill"

1975–TODAY

MAJOR SOCIAL DEVELOPMENTS

1976	• US Bicentennial celebration
1977	• First home computer introduced
1979	• Iran hostage crisis • Three Mile Island nuclear plant meltdown
1980	• Ronald Reagan elected president, ushering in a new period of conservatism in America • First Walkman, portable cassette player, introduced
1981	• MTV makes its first broadcast • Sandra Day O'Connor, first woman appointed to the Supreme Court
1982	• CD (compact disc) audio format introduced
1984	• Apple McIntosh computer debuts
1986	• Iran–Contra scandal, in which money earned by selling arms to Iran was used to fund Central American rebels
1987	• Stock market crash
1991	• Iraq invades Kuwait leading to the Gulf War • The World Wide Web debuts
1993	• "Don't ask, don't tell" bill signed into law, allowing gays to serve in the military as long as they don't announce their sexual preference
1995	• Oklahoma City bombing • O. J. Simpson acquitted of murdering his ex-wife

1998	• First commercial MP3 player introduced
1998–1999	• President Clinton accused of having sexual relations with intern Monica Lewinsky; impeachment trial held, but Clinton acquitted
1999	• Napster debuts allowing for free sharing of music files
2001	• September 11 terrorist attacks • iTunes introduced for Apple iPod
2003	• US invasion of Iraq
2004	• Facebook is launched
2005	• Hurricane Katrina devastates New Orleans and other regions of the country • YouTube launched
2008	• Banking crisis leads to major recession
2009	• Barack Obama inaugurated as first African American president • Tea Party movement launches first protests • Spotify music service launched
2011	• Osama bin Laden, leader of al-Qaeda, killed by US strike force
2012	• Hurricane Sandy causes major damage to the East Coast
2013	• Boston Marathon bombing • Supreme Court strikes down the Defense of Marriage Act, allowing for same-sex marriage

MANY MOVEMENTS

JAZZ FUSION, AVANT-GARDE, NEO-TRADITIONALIST, MAINSTREAM, AND THE DOWNTOWN SCENE (1970s-1990s)

14

Jazz Fusion

WHAT IS JAZZ FUSION MUSIC, AND WHY IS IT CONTROVERSIAL AMONG JAZZ FANS?

During the late 1960s and early 1970s, many musicians who were playing jazz were also well versed and interested in other styles such as rock, R&B, and funk. Players including guitarist Larry Coryell and vibraphonist Gary Burton, flutist Jeremy Steig, saxophonist Charles Lloyd, keyboardist Barry Miles, trumpeter Miles Davis (Chapter 13, 1st Chorus), guitarist Pat Metheny, and pianist Keith Jarrett and groups like the Fourth Way, Herbie Hancock's the Headhunters (Chapter 13, 4th Chorus), Eleventh House, the Brecker Brothers (with trumpeter Randy Brecker and his brother, saxophonist Michael, one of the leading sax players of his generation, discussed in the 3rd Chorus of this chapter), the Tony Williams Lifetime, John McLaughlin's Mahavishnu Orchestra, Weather Report, and keyboardist Chick Corea and his group Return to Forever were playing music that freely drew upon all of their interests. Their music eventually came to be known as **jazz–rock fusion**, or fusion, which helped lead the way to the openness we see in today's music world.

Each band had its own approach to fusion, so the term is extremely broad. The music includes the use of electronic instruments such as electric pianos and synthesizers, electric guitars (while electric guitars had long been used in jazz, in jazz fusion the influence of other styles, including rock, changed the way they were used), electric basses, as well as instruments from around the world such as the Indian stringed instruments the sarod and sitar, and numerous percussion instruments. These bands played to varied audiences, including jazz, rock, and funk fans, and played in both jazz clubs and more rock-oriented venues that regularly featured eclectic concerts.

John McLaughlin

Born in England, John McLaughlin (b. 1942) originally came to the US jazz scene's attention in 1969 when drummer Tony Williams (from Miles Davis's second great quintet, Chapter 13, 1st Chorus) recruited him to play in the Tony Williams Lifetime. One of the earliest and most important jazz fusion groups, Lifetime included Williams, McLaughlin, and organist Larry Young.

Photo: Courtesy Getty Images.

In this chapter, we'll answer these questions:

- ● What Is Jazz Fusion Music, and Why Is It Controversial Among Jazz Fans?

- ● How Did the Avant-Garde Movement of the 1960s Continue to Develop over the Following Decades?

- ● Who Were the Neo-Traditionalists, and What Impact Did They Have on Jazz in the 1980s–1990s?

- ● How Did Mainstream Jazz Continue to Flourish and Grow in This Period?

- ● What Is the Downtown Scene, and What Role Has It Played in Jazz Music?

read all about it

"Jazz Pop—A 'Failed Art Music' Makes Good" by Robert Palmer

Walser, **Keeping Time,** *Chapter 51*
Pop music critic Palmer addresses some of the controversies that arose in the wake of jazz–rock fusion.

QUESTIONS AND CONTROVERSIES
The Fusion Fission

Many musicians embraced the new fusion style because it opened up a wider audience for jazz. Some musicians and critics, however, felt that fusion was overcommercialized, that it compromised the purity of jazz, or that it was not jazz at all.

During the 1960s and 1970s, there was a generation gap among jazz performers, with many of the old guard preferring traditional styles while younger musicians were fascinated by the innovations in rock music. Rock in general appealed to a younger audience, with jazz fans often being older and more conservative. Musicians—and businesses in general—often make their money by appealing to a young audience, so it is natural as business people that jazz players would want to tap into this audience. It is interesting to note, however, that relatively few of the musicians involved with early jazz fusion

gained significant financial rewards. A more important reason for the rise of fusion is that many creative artists like to renew themselves by trying new things and playing and collaborating with different players with diverse musical perspectives. This helps them to grow, change, and be creative in new ways.

The backlash against fusion was, in retrospect, rather short-lived. The music blossomed and grew and became quite popular with a variety of audiences. The notion of fusion—of various types—is now essentially a nonissue for all but the most conservative musicians. That does not imply that everyone in the jazz world appreciates fusion music or that they should, but various types of fusions are now ubiquitous in jazz and in music in general. So many elements of the fusion style are integrated into contemporary jazz that the issue is becoming less and less important.

McLaughlin also recorded several albums with Miles Davis, including *In a Silent Way*, *Bitches Brew*, and *On the Corner*, which were seminal works in the development of jazz fusion. McLaughlin became an in-demand studio guitar player and went on to form his own group, the Mahavishnu Orchestra, through which he also incorporated his spiritual beliefs in Eastern religions. It featured virtuosic playing by all of its members, and McLaughlin is considered to be one of jazz and rock's premier guitar players. The band played extremely loudly, making it seem more like a rock band than a jazz band, though its connections to improvisation and jazz, as well as South Asian musical styles, were crucial to the music. McLaughlin later formed Shakti, a group that more directly expressed his interest in Indian classical music and that included the well-known Indian musicians L. Shankar on violin and Zakir Hussain on tabla, a South Asian percussion instrument.

Weather Report

Weather Report was the most commercially successful band in the fusion genre and was extremely influential. With a revolving personnel, the band managed to stay together for 16 years, an unprecedented length of time for a fusion band. It is unique among early fusion groups in that its founding members, saxophonist-composer Wayne Shorter (b. 1933) and keyboard player-composer Joe Zawinul (1932–2007), were both top jazz players with long-standing and impeccable traditional credentials. Shorter came to prominence with Art Blakey (Chapter 11, 2nd Chorus) and Miles Davis (Chapter 13, 1st Chorus), for both his playing and his composing, and is considered a leading jazz composer and bandleader in his own right. Zawinul had also worked with Miles Davis and earlier with the Cannonball

listening focus

"Birds of Fire" (1973) by John McLaughlin and the Mahavishnu Orchestra

DOWNLOAD
Track Number 33

INSTRUMENTATION: Electric and acoustic guitar, leader: John McLaughlin; **Violin:** Jerry Goodman; **Keyboard:** Jan Hammer; **Bass:** Rick Laird; **Drums:** Billy Cobham.

LISTENING HIGHLIGHT, STYLE: "Birds of Fire" opens with a gong crashing and a synthesizer drone—a repeated figure intended to be heard in the background—immediately signaling that we are in for something unique. The violin and bass set up a repeated vamp in 9/4 that is broken up into groupings of 4 and 5 beats (0:41 and throughout the recording), followed by the entrance of the drums. In addition to the use of an odd meter (the divisions of the 9/4 figure), the use of a different instrumentation (electric violin) and the virtuosic playing heard throughout by all members of the band are typical of jazz fusion. While electric guitar had already been used in jazz for a long time, McLaughlin's sound, with its intense volume and distortion, comes from the rock world, not jazz, while his improvisatory style deftly mixes jazz and rock.

The 8-measure melody is played by guitar and violin (1:04 and throughout), immediately followed by a McLaughlin solo. The guitar and violin play the melody again, followed by an ensemble (2:18), which leads to another guitar solo (3:11). For this second solo, however, McLaughlin changes his tone to a darker, rounder sound, an example of using additional electronic equipment such as foot pedals to enhance and change the guitar's tone. While the drums aren't prominent in the mix here, Cobham plays intensely with a tight and technically controlled style. Rather than comping, the keyboard-synthesizer is primarily used here to create an active but drone-like environment for the rest of the band to play over, a style taken from South Asian music.

Adderley Quintet, for whom his "Mercy, Mercy, Mercy," an early crossover tune featuring a soul jazz approach (see Chapter 12, 1st Chorus), an earlier type of fusion, was a major hit.

Weather Report distinguishes itself from many fusion bands, including the Mahavishnu Orchestra, because it does not emphasize rock music influences. Instead, it relies upon keyboard-synthesizer textures for its signature sound. Its influences are much more clearly from jazz, funk, and R&B. The band also featured a series of high-powered drummers and percussionists who brought a range of rhythmic approaches to it, including a strong Latin influence.

Because Weather Report heavily emphasized keyboard and synthesizer textures, it frequently felt as if Shorter was somewhat overwhelmed and deemphasized in the musical texture. Additionally, the band in general featured instrumentalists with great virtuosity. While Shorter is a wonderful sax player, he generally makes his musical statements in more understated and subtle ways than by showing his considerable virtuosity. After the band broke up, however, and Shorter was on his own again, his compositional work on albums such as *Atlantis* (1985) and *High Life* (1995) showed how profound an influence, along with that of Joe Zawinul, his compositional aesthetic had upon Weather Report.

IN PERFORMANCE
New Audiences and New Venues

Jazz–rock fusion helped extend jazz's reach beyond concert halls and the nightclubs where most jazz artists had traditionally performed. New York's famed Fillmore East and San Francisco's Fillmore and Fillmore West, which were known for presenting primarily rock groups but also for featuring eclectic lineups, featured several early fusion bands, including Charles Lloyd's popular group in 1967 and 1968 and Miles Davis's *Bitches Brew* band in 1970. John McLaughlin's Mahavishnu Orchestra made its debut performances at New York's Gaslight au Go Go club in 1971, not at one of the well-known New York jazz venues. During its first year of existence, the group toured with well-known rock groups including art rockers Emerson, Lake, and Palmer; heavy rockers Blue Oyster Cult; and folk rockers The Byrds, among many others. Similarly, Weather Report initially appeared in venues like Los Angeles's Whiskey a Go Go and the Roxy, both clubs catering to rock audiences. By appearing in these venues, these groups were able to introduce jazz instrumentation, soloing, and rhythms to listeners who would otherwise have never heard the music. Many of these rock fans were turned on to jazz through this exposure.

Several other important players came out of the band as well. Bassist Jaco Pastorius in particular made his mark on the band and later as a bandleader with his mixture of virtuosity, great musicality, and a broad musical aesthetic that easily embraced jazz, rock, funk, and more. His approach to the electric bass, which often put the instrument out front as a lead instrument, had a powerful influence on bass players, which can be seen in the expanded role of the bass in contemporary jazz.

Chick Corea

Pianist-composer-bandleader Armando Anthony "Chick" Corea's (b. 1941) early career reflected much of what was going on in jazz fusion during the 1960s and 1970s. Corea's experiences included

- An early background in bebop and hard bop
- An interest in Latin music, including playing with Mongo Santamaria (Chapter 12, 2nd Chorus)
- Work with Miles Davis during Davis's early experiments with fusion; Corea succeeded Herbie Hancock in 1968 and played on such Davis albums as *Filles de Kilimanjaro*, *In a Silent Way*, and *Bitches Brew*
- Experience playing free jazz in the group Circle
- Interest in contemporary classical music, as well as the volume and power of John McLaughlin's band

Joining the fusion movement, Corea founded an extremely popular group, Return to Forever, in 1972; the group has had several iterations that show some of his evolution as a musician. Corea's compositions such as "Spain," "500 Miles High," and "La Fiesta" all have long and complicated forms, compelling melodies, and sophisticated harmonies and have become jazz standards. The multisectional composition "Spain" (1973) is an example of the band's use of multiple influences. The piece begins with Corea alone on Fender Rhodes playing a version of Rodrigo's *Concierto de Aranjuez*—a piece featured on the Miles Davis–Gil Evans classic

"Birdland" (1977) by Weather Report

DOWNLOAD
Track Number 34

INSTRUMENTATION: Saxophone, coleader: Wayne Shorter; **Keyboard, synthesizer, coleader, composer:** Joe Zawinul; **Bass:** Jaco Pastorius; **Drums:** Alex Acuña; **Percussion:** Manolo Badrena.

OVERVIEW: The 1977 album *Heavy Weather* was a high point for Weather Report commercially and artistically. "Birdland," a Joe Zawinul composition, has proven to be extremely popular and, along with other tunes from the record such as "Teen Town" and "Cucumber Slumber," displays the band's wide range of approaches and styles.

FORM: "Birdland" has four principal sections (ABCD in the table) that repeat in various forms and are connected by vamps and interludes that run together in an organic manner. While the sections repeat, the form is less repetitive than traditional tunes. There are solos throughout—Shorter at 3:07 and Zawinul as the band vamps out at 5:00—but they function more as part of the overall texture as opposed to being featured elements.

STYLE: "Birdland" is a heavily layered and carefully composed recording that also manages to feel loose and open, a rare and difficult combination to obtain. The powerful, full, and rich texture is reminiscent of a big band (see Chapters 5–7).

MELODY AND HARMONY: Each of the various sections of "Birdland" has its own melody, with section D generally noted as the main theme. When the band is in high gear, Shorter's sax plays the melody on top of carefully orchestrated keyboard textures.

RHYTHM: The tune is powered by a steady and insistent pop-rock drum groove that is played both lightly and more forcefully depending on the section.

ACCOMPANIMENT: The arrangement is reminiscent of orchestral and big-band textures, but here they are primarily created by a variety of electronic synthesizers. Zawinul uses the synthesizers as earlier big-band composers like Duke Ellington did; he treats each as a separate "part," combining them to create an overall sound. In this way, "Birdland" combines modern instrumentation with traditional jazz arranging.

"BIRDLAND" LISTENING GUIDE

TIME	FORM	STYLE	MELODY AND HARMONY	RHYTHM	ACCOMPANIMENT
0:00	Intro	Keyboardist Joe Zawinul plays a simple synthesizer bass introduction.			Zawinul's synth bass introduces the tune by itself, giving the tune room to gradually build in texture.
0:18	A	The bass playing a melody is unusual (we heard Paul Chambers playing the melody on "So What" from *Kind of Blue* [Chapter 13, 1st Chorus]) and exemplifies Jaco Pastorius's highlighted role in Weather Report, as well as his innovative playing.	Pastorius plays the A section melody on the electric bass using a picking technique that gives the bass a unique tone and a slight edge to its attack. He plays four 4-bar phrases, the second two up an octave.	The drums enter with a light pop-rock groove, including insistent taps on the metal rim of the snare drum on all 4 beats of the bar.	Pastorius's bass playing covers a variety of roles throughout the tune. While he plays the initial part of the melody on his bass, Zawinul plays a bass line on synthesizer, an interesting switching of roles.

continued

TIME	FORM	STYLE	MELODY AND HARMONY	RHYTHM	ACCOMPANIMENT
0:42	B	This section creates one of the high points of this tune.	The B section is an 8-bar melody played by Wayne Shorter on sax over a powerful, dense, and carefully orchestrated keyboard texture.	The drums continue the same beat but louder and with more intensity.	Pastorius shifts to a bass line below the melody that functions as a harmonic foundation as well as a careful counterpoint to the sax melody.
0:55	Interlude			As a brief interlude, the drums vamp on the funky groove.	
1:02	C	The new phrase is played five times with two different keyboard sounds.	A new 4-bar phrase is introduced by Zawinul.	The drums continue to groove.	The keyboards and drums are alone until Pastorius enters with powerful, low bass notes that he alters electronically (1:19).
1:31	C	The C section is expanded with the addition of a saxophone melody.			Zawinul fills out the texture with a variety of keyboard sounds underneath the sax.
1:45	Interlude		The band grooves hard in a brief vamp interlude.		
1:59	D	This new melody is the one most associated with "Birdland." The orchestration keeps expanding during the three 8-bar sections of this melody, creating another high point in the arrangement. The melody and keyboard textures become more heavily dense throughout, including Shorter now on soprano sax, as well as some wordless vocals by the band.	A new 8-bar melody is introduced and played three times.		Pastorius's careful and clever counterpoint on the bottom adds a great deal to this section.
2:36	Interlude		The band plays a vamp as an interlude.	The drums slightly change the groove (2:43).	Zawinul adds a synth bass (2:48).
3:07	Interlude continues	This sax solo serves as a continuation of the interlude as opposed to a new formal section.	Shorter plays a brief tenor sax solo over a repeated series of descending chords.		Zawinul plays the descending chords on the synth and adds flurries of notes and clusters with a piano sound. Briefly in more of a traditional role, Pastorius anchors the bottom notes of the descending chords.
3:28	A		After a brief vamp, Pastorius plays the A melody again.	The drums once again play the light pop-rock groove.	The A melody returns with a thinner texture behind it and gradually builds up, including Shorter's sax.

"Birdland" listening guide continued

TIME	FORM	STYLE	MELODY AND HARMONY	RHYTHM	ACCOMPANIMENT
3:58	B	The powerful sax-led B section melody hits hard after the quiet A section.	The B section melody returns.		The accompaniment becomes full and layered again.
4:11	C		The C section returns.	The drums continue to groove.	
4:23	D		The D section melody, effectively the theme of this tune, returns.		The orchestral textures keep expanding as the section continues, again including Shorter's soprano sax and wordless vocals by the band. Pastorius's counterpoint bass line anchors this section.
5:00			Zawinul solos on a synth as the band vamps on the theme and the recording fades out.		

Chick Corea performing with Miles Davis, October 1969. As a pianist-composer, Corea has been influential in acoustic and fusion jazz, emphasizing his Latin heritage in many of his compositions.
© Lebrecht Music & Arts.

recording *Sketches of Spain*—and moves on to a rolling, fast, yet relaxed Brazilian samba-infused groove from Corea and bassist Stanley Clarke. Brazilian drummer-percussionist Airto Moreira adds his own distinctive rhythmic feeling to the piece. Joe Farrell performs much of the melody on flute in unison with a wordless

read all about it

"Ferociously Harmonizing with Reality" by Keith Jarrett

Walser, **Keeping Time,** *Chapter 59*
An interview with Keith Jarrett illuminating his philosophy of performance.

vocal by Flora Purim. Corea, Farrell, and Clarke play extended and virtuosic solos. While this music was not typical of rock- or funk-oriented jazz fusion, it was a fusion of its own.

A later version of Return to Forever, for example, on *No Mystery* (1975), was more rock- and funk-influenced, while also featuring gentle Corea compositions that show his classical music influences, as well as the virtuosic performances of guitarist Al Di Meola, bassist Stanley Clarke, and drummer Lenny White.

Corea went on to perform and record in an amazing variety of circumstances such as various duo contexts, with Chick Corea's Elektric Band, with the Chick Corea New Trio, with a reunited Return to Forever, with the 5 Peace Band including John McLaughlin, and as a solo pianist. He has also composed in the contemporary classical vein, including a piano concerto, which he performed with the London Philharmonic Orchestra, and a piece composed for the Orion String Quartet. His playing is always fluid and very melodic, and he has a personal and sophisticated harmonic sense that has been quite influential. Corea is a model to many of the musicians who came of age in the 1970s and 1980s for the way he has freely moved in and out of various musical contexts while always sounding like himself, in both his playing and his composing. While his music is quite sophisticated harmonically and formally, it also has an appealing and accessible quality to it, a difficult line to straddle. He has recorded extremely prolifically, and his records have been nominated for 59 Grammy Awards and have won 20.

Keith Jarrett

Pianist-composer Keith Jarrett (b. 1945) has forged a unique career, and much of his music stands alone as his own personal fusion of jazz, classical music, folk music, and gospel, among other styles. After playing with Art Blakey (Chapter 11, 2nd Chorus) in the mid-1960s, Jarrett gained a great deal of attention for his late 1960s work with the popular and successful Charles Lloyd Quartet, a group led by the tenor saxophonist that crossed over by appealing to rock fans with its own brand of fusion that included open-ended improvisations over eclectic grooves. After this, like Corea, Jarrett played with Miles Davis for a year and a half. Besides this stint with Miles, when he played electric piano and organ, Jarrett is known for his work on acoustic piano.

During the 1970s, Jarrett primarily worked with his own quartet that featured saxophonist Dewey Redman and bassist Charlie Haden, both of whom had worked with Ornette Coleman (Chapter 11, 4th Chorus), and drummer Paul Motian, who worked with pianist Bill Evans (Chapter 13, 4th Chorus). These musicians brought the important influences of Coleman and Evans to Jarrett's music. Also during the 1970s, Jarrett began to perform and record as a solo pianist, and it is these recordings, particularly the live concert recordings, that Jarrett is most known for. His approach to these performances was unusual and compelling in that they were completely improvised. Jarrett is a riveting performer and improviser, and he has a prodigious technique that embodies both jazz and classical methods. The improvisatory nature of the concerts made them unpredictable and exciting.

The Koln Concert (1975) is an excellent example of Jarrett's improvisational playing. It is Jarrett's most popular, even iconic, recording and became the largest-selling album of piano music in history, showing his ability to appeal to a wide spectrum of audiences. The recording documents an amazing improvised performance that rolls effortlessly from one lyrical idea to the next, often over a series of vamps and ostinatos. The encore of the concert, listed as "Part IIc," moves from one beautiful melody and mood to the next. It brings to mind jazz, pop, gospel, and blues styles, all with an elegant and harmonically interesting accompaniment, the music seemingly just pouring out of Jarrett.

In the 1980s Jarrett returned to his early roots as an interpreter of jazz standards with a trio that included bassist Gary Peacock and drummer Jack DeJohnette (this chapter, 3rd Chorus), both supremely gifted instrumentalists known for their sensitive musicality. This trio has recorded numerous albums together, as recently as 2009. With these lovely and lyrical recordings, such as the ballad "It Never Entered My Mind" from *Standards, Vol. 1* (1983), we can hear the strong influence of Bill Evans in Jarrett's playing as well as the empathy and good taste of the trio. Jarrett's voice is often heard as he hums and sings along with his solo.

Jarrett continues to perform as a solo artist, and he also performs classical repertoire and composes works in a classically oriented style. He is a dynamic pianist with an extremely personal and easily identifiable style.

Pat Metheny

Pat Metheny (b. 1954) represents the second generation of jazz fusion players, many of whom grew up on rock music as well as jazz. As a result, his music seems to more easily appeal to rock and pop audiences and almost sits in its own genre, helping to account for his tremendous and continual success.

Metheny gained early visibility as a member of vibraphonist Gary Burton's group, one of the early jazz fusion pioneers. He quickly became recognized as an up-and-coming guitarist and by 1978 had created the long-standing Pat Metheny Group with pianist Lyle Mays that became Metheny's primary outlet. His work with this group has been extremely popular and placed Metheny at the top of the jazz fusion world. The melodies of his compositions and improvisations are unapologetically pretty; they are accessible to many types of listeners because of the combination of their beauty and simplicity with their often almost pop-like settings. *Still Life: Talking* (1987) won a Grammy Award for Best Jazz Fusion Performance and shows the range of material this band covers, as well as the styles and accessible melodies they are known for. From this album, "(It's Just) Talk" features a long-lined, simple, and pretty melody that mixes Metheny's round guitar tone with Mays's synthesizer textures over a pop groove with a strong Brazilian flavor. The harmony is a mixture of a pop-like progression and more adventurous jazz harmonies.

While Metheny's music is hard to characterize, he has a very personal and recognizable playing style. He is a remarkable guitarist with a full-bodied tone that he often enriches with a hint of **reverb**, and he frequently uses effects to vary his sound. His playing is fluid and clean and always melodic. Although he has continuously placed himself in different settings, his recognizable sound is always present while still suiting the musical context. For example, besides his fusion work, Metheny also excels in more traditional jazz environments and has recorded prolifically in this vein, solidifying his overall reputation as a top guitarist. His collaborations with such jazz musicians as guitarist Jim Hall (*Jim Hall & Pat Metheny*), bassist Charlie Haden (*Beyond the Missouri Sky*), Ornette Coleman (*Song X*), Brad Mehldau (*Metheny/Mehldau*), and Michael Brecker (*Pilgrimage*) illustrate his jazz chops. An excellent example of this is "Breakdealer," from *Unity Band* (2012). It is a hard-driving jazz fusion tune and primarily a vehicle for powerful and virtuosic solos by Metheny and saxophonist Chris Potter (Chapter 15, 2nd Chorus).

Smooth Jazz

A subcategory of fusion is smooth jazz, a studio-oriented style that often employs sophisticated production values not generally associated with jazz. Like fusion,

read all about it

"Resistance Is Futile!"
by Sarah Rodman

Walser, **Keeping Time**, *Chapter 69*

In this essay, critic Rodman gives a brief history of smooth jazz and why the music has endured.

this subgenre also has its roots in the late 1960s and 1970s and is represented by numerous artists, many of whom have more traditional jazz backgrounds as well. Some important artists are guitarists Wes Montgomery ("Road Song," 1969) and George Benson ("Breezin'," 1976); saxophonist Grover Washington, Jr. ("Mr. Magic," 1975); keyboardist-producer Bob James (his version of "Feel Like Makin' Love," 1974); saxophonists Dave Sanborn and Kenny G; and the group Spyro Gyra ("Morning Dance," 1979). Groups such as The Yellowjackets and Four Play keep this genre—sometimes referred to as "adult contemporary" for radio purposes—alive and well. While not particularly popular among more hard core jazz audiences, these bands draw large and racially diverse audiences with music that achieves a balance between artistic principles based in jazz, jazz fusion, and popular music styles.

Breezin' (1976) sent the top jazz guitarist George Benson's (b. 1943) career in a more pop-oriented direction and helped to create the smooth jazz genre. It won a Grammy Award for Best Pop Instrumental Performance, topped several album charts, and had two major hits, "Masquerade," with a Benson vocal, and "Breezin'." "Breezin'" features a light-pop guitar melody with sweet string accompaniment over a pop–jazz groove. Benson's guitar solo mixes jazz, blues, and pop styles, all played with a classic jazz guitar tone. The song is ubiquitous enough to essentially be a must-know tune for guitarists.

Trumpeter-bandleader Chris Botti (b. 1962) is a current smooth jazz star with a huge international following. Botti plays with a full and pretty tone—generally with a reverb effect added—and has remarkable facility on the trumpet. He tours constantly with his quintet, performing in clubs, concert halls, and large concert venues. Botti and his band also are frequently featured along with a large orchestra, in both recordings and live performances. He always has a top-flight band of strong jazz musicians who are also capable of mixing in pop, Latin, and fusion elements that blend to create a smooth jazz sound.

Botti is a personable and warm entertainer and has created a formula that in any given performance includes jazz, pop, smooth jazz, and classical styles that has proven to be extremely popular and successful. He also regularly features guest soloists and vocalists who make his shows quite varied and entertaining. *Impressions* (2012) features a wide variety of guest artists as well as a remarkable range of musical styles and influences. For example, along with Botti's solos throughout, the hymn-like "Losing You" features a vocal by country-music star Vince Gil, "Tango Suite" features pianist Herbie Hancock (Chapter 13, 4th Chorus), and "Per Te" features the pop–opera vocal star Andrea Bocelli, all in a full and extremely well-produced orchestral setting.

Conclusion

In its early days, as exhibited by the various styles of the artists discussed in this chorus, jazz fusion took on many forms and had even been foretold by soul jazz artists, jazz and R&B players such as Louis Jordan and Ray Charles, as well as Latin jazz and boogaloo musicians. The fusion movement continues today in a myriad of new forms and styles, although the notion of fusing various musical styles with jazz has become so ubiquitous that the term "jazz fusion" is at once meaningless and more specific; nearly all jazz is a fusion of sorts at this point, and the term "jazz fusion" now refers more specifically to rock- or funk-oriented jazz styles. This movement leads us smoothly into Chapter 15 because the concept of fusing styles is a dominant feature in today's jazz.

2nd Chorus The Avant-Garde Continues

HOW DID THE AVANT-GARDE MOVEMENT OF THE 1960s CONTINUE TO DEVELOP OVER THE FOLLOWING DECADES?

Cecil Taylor

Earlier we discussed saxophonist-composer-bandleader Ornette Coleman (Chapter 11, 4th Chorus), one of the most important of the early avant-garde performers and composers. Along with Coleman, composer-pianist Cecil Taylor (b. 1929) was also one of the innovators of "the new thing" of the 1950s and continues to be one of the most, if not the most, important musician of the jazz avant-garde. Taylor, however, sees himself very much as part of the jazz tradition, following in the footsteps of Duke Ellington (see Chapter 8), and states that his music is blues-based. The music establishment has not always seen him in this light, however; and Taylor has often been viewed as an "outsider." His music is challenging to the most avid of fans as individual compositions, whether solo piano or group performances, can easily last over an hour, at times with an almost unrelenting intensity. Taylor hunches over the piano as his hands fly over the keys producing a music that is as percussive and rhythmic as it is melodic and harmonic.

Taylor's art has always been uncompromising, including his method of performance. He incorporates his interests in dance and poetry into his performances, at times through collaboration with other artists and at other times through his own movement and recitations. Taylor has recorded extensively and has had an active performing career, yet he has often found it difficult to get regular bookings, despite the fact that he has long been at the top of his field and his performances are generally sold-out, highly anticipated events.

Taylor's career evolved in a different manner compared to most musicians in jazz as his unapologetically unique style did not lend itself to playing in other

Cecil Taylor, ca. 2000s. Avant-garde composer-pianist Taylor has been among the most influential jazz composers and performers over the last 6 decades.
© Barry Kornbluh.

people's bands. Consequently, the typical apprenticeship of jazz musicians was largely unavailable to him, and he has consistently led his own groups throughout his career. Taylor graduated from the New England Conservatory of Music and by 1956 was presenting his brand of avant-garde jazz at what became a nexus for the avant-garde, the Five Spot in New York City. His first group included soprano saxophonist Steve Lacy (who went on to become a leading voice on that instrument), bassist Buell Neidlinger, and drummer Dennis Charles; and they performed a mix of their versions of standard tunes and free jazz compositions. Shortly after the Five Spot engagement, Taylor was invited to play at the prestigious Newport Jazz Festival but largely remained out of the public eye while primarily performing in New York's Greenwich Village.

By the early 1960s Taylor began working with his most important collaborator, alto saxophonist Jimmy Lyons (1931–1986). Lyons had a lyrical sensibility and a cool, calm demeanor that provided a much needed contrast to Taylor's all-out intensity. In addition, while also a free jazz player, Lyons's soloing managed to clearly convey its roots in bebop and the blues, helping to root Taylor's music in the jazz tradition. Drummer Sonny Murray, and later Andrew Cyrille, brought to the band a rhythmic propulsion that swung yet did not rely upon the standard jazz 4/4 meter. Rather, it alluded to it while not conforming to any metrical structure, a crucial element in much of free jazz. Taylor primarily worked with small ensembles and a close group of players but also at times led a big band made up of free jazz improvisers who, based on Taylor's compositional instructions, created an incredibly complex, improvised polyphony as well as stand-out solos.

A later important Taylor collaborator was bassist William Parker, who played with Taylor for 10 years. Since 1996, along with being a bandleader and ubiquitous side musician on the free jazz scene, Parker has been the organizer—along with his wife Patricia Nicholson-Parker—of the Vision Festival, a yearly New York City festival dedicated to avant-garde music that has consistently featured a cross section of the most important artists in free jazz.

The Continuing Influence of the Association for the Advancement of Creative Musicians

Along with Taylor and Coleman, the influence of the Association for the Advancement of Creative Musicians (AACM; Chapter 12, 3rd Chorus) continues and has spread around the country through its many members who left Chicago to pursue their own musical interests. Early members Leroy Jenkins and Henry Threadgill (Chapter 14, 2nd Chorus) became ubiquitous on New York's experimental scene. Jenkins led the Revolutionary Ensemble and played in innumerable groups and settings. Threadgill has led a series of unique ensembles, as well as being a member of Air, a trio that had a great deal of critical success and that included fellow AACM members drummer Steve McCall and bassist Fred Hopkins.

Another AACM member, saxophonist-composer Anthony Braxton (b. 1945), has created a huge and wide-ranging body of compositions that defy category. Braxton composes for and plays the whole range of woodwinds. His work is influenced by a variety of jazz styles including free jazz, while he has also embraced contemporary classical compositional techniques. He has written for unusual combinations of instruments and for many types of ensembles ranging from small to gigantic groups. Generally, his compositions combine a desire for freedom with carefully thought-out and well-articulated musical forms and schemes. He often uses graphic notation of his own devising to create his scores.

listening focus

"Streams of Chorus and Seed" (1976) by Cecil Taylor Unit

INSTRUMENTATION: Piano, composer: Cecil Taylor; **Alto saxophone:** Jimmy Lyons; **Trumpet:** Raphe Malik; **Tenor saxophone:** David S. Ware; **Drums:** Marc Edwards.

LISTENING HIGHLIGHT, FORM: Taylor has a background in classical music as well as in jazz and takes an eclectic and unique approach to composition. His performances are improvised, but he employs a number of strategies to create frameworks for the improvisations, including compositional forms, groups of pitches that are to be used, and sequences of musical ideas that he refers to as "unit structures," as well as the use of gradually unfolding melodies that we hear in "Streams of Chorus and Seed." Here, along with Jimmy Lyons, the front line includes Taylor's frequent collaborator, trumpeter Raphe Malik (1948–2006).

As we listen to the first 7 minutes of this album-length composition from a live performance, we can hear that there is a compositional structure to "Streams of Chorus and Seed"; but it is not as clear as those seen in most music we have listened to previously. The horns play a gradually unfolding melody as the piece moves rather quickly from section to section. For example, the piece begins with a melodic fragment played freely by the horns (0:00), and after a short interlude by Taylor on piano (0:41), the horns begin a second fragment (0:49). The melody continues to unfold with a third (1:15). Throughout, the piece mixes the introduction of new melodies with group improvisation and individual solos. The rhythm section (in this case piano and drums as no bass is present) fills busily throughout, each adding an individual character to the piece, as opposed to working jointly to provide a rhythmic and harmonic foundation. While the melody has some harmonic implications, everyone freely improvises throughout and finds an individual relationship with the composed material. Malik then begins his trumpet solo (6:22, the first in a series of extended solos).

Another collective, the Black Artists Group in St. Louis, has also influenced the New York scene through three powerful saxophonists who were group members: Oliver Lake, Julius Hemphill, and Hamiet Bluiett. Along with saxophonist David Murray, they created the World Saxophone Quartet. Without a rhythm section, this quartet has to employ alternate strategies to create rhythm and movement.

Carla Bley

Pianist-composer-bandleader Carla Bley (b. 1936) has been one of the jazz avant-garde's most interesting and prolific composers since the 1960s, and an extensive and impressive list of artists and bands have played and recorded her compositions. Bley has performed with many of the important members of the avant-garde, and they in turn have been members of her various ensembles. She was an organizer of the Jazz Composers Guild in 1964, an organization created to support and promote avant-garde jazz and out of which grew the Jazz Composer's Orchestra. Bley's compositions and arrangements were also featured by bassist Charlie Haden's

Carla Bley, 2012. Bley is an important pianist-composer-bandleader. Photo by Rene Fluger. © CTK/Alamy.

Liberation Music Orchestra, an example of the avant-garde movement's interest and involvement in political issues. Her political stance includes the notion of control over one's work and career. To that end, along with trumpeter Michael Mantler, she created a record label, WATT Records, as well as New Music Distribution Services, which provided album distribution to independent musicians and record labels.

While she has led many types of groups, Bley is perhaps best known for her arrangements and compositions for her Carla Bley Big Band. Bley's work for big band combines references to traditional big-band writing with aspects of free jazz, and does so both seriously and irreverently—humor is an important element in her work. Both her writing and her soloists move in and out of avant-garde and more traditional styles, making her recordings and performances eclectic events. Bley continues to perform with her big band as well as with smaller groups, regularly working with bassist Steve Swallow, including with their group the Lost Chords.

"Fast Lane," an up-tempo Bley composition from *Looking for America* (2003), is an excellent example of her style. It is highly organized yet allows the various soloists to "stretch out" by playing extended solos, as well as to freely interpret the harmonic underpinnings of the piece. To encourage this she combines a harmonic structure with harmonic freedom through both her melody's harmonic implications and the various and more open contexts she provides for the soloists.

3rd Chorus Neo-Traditionalists and the Continuing Mainstream

WHO WERE THE NEO-TRADITIONALISTS, AND WHAT IMPACT DID THEY HAVE ON JAZZ IN THE 1980s–1990s?

As a reaction to the popularity of fusion music as well as the free and avant-garde jazz of the 1960s and 1970s, the 1980s brought in new movements to revive more traditional jazz forms and compositions. One reaction was the establishment of numerous repertoire ensembles, such as the American Jazz Orchestra conducted by John Lewis (Chapter 11, 1st Chorus), the Carnegie Hall Jazz Band led by trumpet player Jon Faddis, and the Smithsonian Jazz Masterworks Orchestra. The purpose of these bands was to perform important repertoire of the past as well as to commission compositions from living jazz composers.

Another reaction to fusion and free jazz, however, came from some musicians, critics, and scholars who felt strongly that jazz was losing touch with its roots, as

QUESTIONS AND CONTROVERSIES
Music Distribution

Carla Bley and Michael Mantler filled a major gap when they started the New Music Distribution Services because smaller independent labels and musicians recording their own albums didn't have the mechanism or resources for distributing their music that was available to the major labels. Bley and Mantler initially teamed with several labels to distribute each other's records, but it eventually became a service available to any independent new music artist, with New Music Distribution Services charging a fee for each record distributed. Financial difficulties eventually forced the business to close.

At this point, while there are still a few major record labels, the landscape of the music business has changed drastically and is literally going through major developments on a day-by-day basis. Online downloading distribution such as iTunes and Amazon,

streaming services such as Spotify and Pandora, and the illegal downloading of music have created an entirely new landscape that the major labels and independent artists and labels are still trying to figure out. Meanwhile, the distribution of music as a service is undergoing radical change.

The new paradigms that exist allow independent artists access to the same services as major labels, but it is still a complicated and expensive task that is generally beyond the grasp of most artists. In addition, between the fact that royalties for streaming services are extremely low and the fact that the illegal downloading of music is rampant, it has become very difficult for anyone other than major artists to make money on recordings. While some independent artists are finding their way through this morass, most artists lose considerable amounts when recording their own work.

---

well as its identity as an African American music. They believed that jazz should maintain its strong connections to the past—including the music of Duke Ellington and Louis Armstrong, as well as its relationship to the blues—implying that certain styles in jazz were more respectful of the jazz tradition and consequently more valuable and important. The young, extremely talented, and skilled trumpeter Wynton Marsalis became the de facto leader of this movement, sometimes referred to as **neo-classical** or **neo-traditional**, in reference to the notion of looking to the classic jazz of the past to confirm important values for contemporary jazz.

In so deliberately and almost aggressively looking to the past as a model, there was an inherent conservatism to Marsalis's—and his musical colleagues'—approach. This included Marsalis's personal style as well; he made a point of dressing in stylish suits and ties, more in line with the presentation of jazz in the past, to counter the trend toward a more casual presentation in jazz performance at the time. Perhaps because of the times, as well as Marsalis's growing influence, this approach to both music and style caught on with many young players and became a dominant movement. The unfortunate part of this, however, was that accompanying this neo-classical approach was a sometimes publicly displayed disdain for other styles of music such as jazz fusion and the avant-garde. This set off a continued debate—almost a feud—within the jazz world regarding the worth of these various approaches. One reason the "battle" became so intense is that Marsalis holds one of the most important positions in jazz, artistic director of Jazz at Lincoln Center, and has become the face of jazz in many ways.

read all about it
"Three Polemics on the State of Jazz" by Stanley Crouch

Walser, **Keeping Time,** *Chapter 66*
Crouch has been one of the primary supporters of the neo-traditionalist movement and is closely associated with Wynton Marsalis. This essay outlines his basic beliefs.

Lincoln Center is an artistic complex in New York City that houses the New York Philharmonic, the Metropolitan Opera, and the New York City Ballet, among other prominent cultural institutions. Marsalis was a cofounder of a jazz program at Lincoln Center in 1987, which, in 1996, expanded to become a co-constituent of Lincoln Center: Jazz at Lincoln Center. Marsalis serves as artistic director, and through this position has arguably become the best-known and most influential musician in jazz. Jazz at Lincoln Center has continued to expand, including establishing its own home with several performance spaces. It also has an extensive outreach and education program that has led to the expansion of jazz programs in schools throughout the country. Marsalis leads the Jazz at Lincoln Center Orchestra, a full big band, which regularly performs and tours, presenting both repertory and newly commissioned works. Yet while his playing and bandleading are the most visible aspects of his job, Marsalis is a tireless and effective educator who travels the world teaching, supporting, and encouraging young jazz musicians.

One of the representations of Marsalis's huge early success was a major-label recording contract (an unusual occurrence for jazz musicians at this point) with Columbia Records for both jazz and classical releases. The album *Black Codes (From the Underground)* (1985) from that period features Marsalis's brother, saxophonist Branford, as well as young musicians who were early members of Marsalis's band: pianist Kenny Kirkland, bassist Charnett Moffett, and drummer Jeff "Tain" Watts.

HOW DID MAINSTREAM JAZZ CONTINUE TO FLOURISH AND GROW IN THIS PERIOD?

While the neo-classical movement was influential and still continues, the later part of the twentieth century was also a time when the jazz mainstream continued to thrive while also moving forward and absorbing many aspects of the contemporary scene. Musicians experimented, crossed back and forth between mainstream and avant-garde, and created unexpected musical partnerships. In this chorus we briefly examine a few important players who, while upholding the mainstream tradition, also helped to set the stage for the jazz of today.

Trumpet

Trumpeter Freddie Hubbard (1938–2008) was the standard-bearer for the tradition of the bold, brash trumpet soloist from the early 1960s through the 1980s. Hubbard played with a macho swagger and was powerful and self-assured with a gift for melodic invention. He also displayed remarkable technical ability and a wide range, playing with a full and rich tone in all registers. He appeared to be infallible as he managed to play an excellent and flawless solo every time. As a result, Hubbard was the go-to trumpet soloist during this period (eventually alongside Woody Shaw) and exhibited a remarkable stylistic range. He played and recorded with a long list of performers including mainstream artists such as Art Blakey's Jazz Messengers (*Mosaic* and *Ugetsu*), Herbie Hancock (*Maiden Voyage*), and Wayne Shorter (*Speak No Evil* and others) and avant-garde artists Ornette Coleman (*Free Jazz*), saxophonist Eric Dolphy (*Outward Bound* and *Out to Lunch*), and John Coltrane (*Ascension, Ole,* and *Africa/Brass*).

Hubbard's solo on Hancock's "Maiden Voyage" (from *Maiden Voyage*, 1965, 2:24–4:24) is an excellent example of his playing that mixes fast runs, long held

JAZZ LIVES WYNTON MARSALIS

Wynton Marsalis (b. 1961) is from a prominent musical New Orleans family. His father, Ellis Marsalis, is a wonderful pianist and an educator who has taught generations of New Orleans musicians. His brother Branford is a leading saxophonist, and his brothers Delfeayo and Jason play trombone and drums, respectively. Marsalis was a prodigy on the trumpet and won early acclaim as an outstanding player. In 1980 while at the Juilliard School, a premier classical music conservatory, Marsalis was hired by Art Blakey and joined the Jazz Messengers (Chapter 11, 2nd Chorus), one of the few remaining old-school "conservatories" of the road. This gave him instant recognition, and he quickly became one of the most watched rising stars. Along with his maturing jazz playing, Marsalis was also a highly accomplished classical trumpet soloist and recorded in both genres, eventually pulling off an unprecedented and extremely impressive "double" by winning Grammy Awards for both jazz and classical recordings in the same year, which he did for two consecutive years (1983 and 1984). Marsalis also has regularly led his own groups since 1981 and has performed and recorded prolifically, including sharing the front line with his brother Branford and with a never-ending list of major jazz performers, including Miles Davis's rhythm section of the mid-1960s—Herbie Hancock, Ron Carter, and Tony Williams (Chapter 13, 1st Chorus).

Marsalis's early playing was reminiscent of that of Miles Davis. Over the years, he has also effectively incorporated older styles of playing into his performances, such as interpreting the playing of Louis Armstrong and mastering the somewhat lost art of using the plunger mute in the mode of the Duke Ellington Orchestra's trumpet soloists. Marsalis's style has matured into a more personal sound that still reflects these various influences as well as having a contemporary feel. He has also become a composer of note, including the Pulitzer Prize-winning *Blood on the Fields*, an extended composition for jazz big band and voice that draws from the entire history of African American music; and he receives numerous commissions from a wide variety of ensembles.

Wynton Marsalis, ca. 1990s. As a trumpet player-composer-bandleader-educator, Marsalis is often cited as the leader of the neo-conservative movement in jazz that began in the late 1980s. Marsalis co-founded Jazz at Lincoln Center where he serves as Artistic Director.
© *Doug Horrigan / Alamy.*

notes, aggressive playing, and sensitive playing throughout. In his clear articulation and flawless execution we hear the influence of trumpet players such as Clifford Brown as well as the influence that saxophonists such as John Coltrane (Chapter 13, 1st Chorus) and his "sheets of sound" had upon Hubbard (3:46–4:04). Hubbard plays confidently and strings together a series of beautifully crafted melodies as he builds his solo, varying the level of excitement throughout.

As a bandleader Hubbard recorded a splendid series of albums, including *Goin' Up* (1960), *Ready for Freddie* (1961), and *Night of the Cookers* (1965), a live album that also featured trumpeter Lee Morgan who preceded Hubbard with Art Blakey (Chapter 11, 2nd Chorus). As was true for many musicians of this period,

listening guide

DOWNLOAD
Track Number 35

"Delfeayo's Dilemma" (1985) by Wynton Marsalis

INSTRUMENTATION: Trumpet, composer, leader: Wynton Marsalis; **Tenor saxophone:** Branford Marsalis; **Piano:** Kenny Kirkland; **Bass:** Charnett Moffett; **Drums:** Jeff "Tain" Watts.

OVERVIEW: *Black Codes (From the Underground)* (1985) is an early album by Wynton Marsalis and his quintet. Marsalis's playing at this point had reached maturity, so this is an excellent example of his playing as well as his group concept and early compositional style.

FORM: While this composition has a typical head–solos–head format, the form of the tune itself is unlike anything we have seen to this point (see "Melody and Harmony").

STYLE: "Delfeayo's Dilemma" is in a modern post-bop vein. This recording is also a good example of the mainstream style of the period that harkens back to hard-bop styles but with a contemporary feel, in terms of both its rhythmic and its harmonic approaches.

MELODY AND HARMONY: The melody is somewhat reminiscent of the types of melodic lines used in Miles Davis's bands of the mid-1960s. The tune is 27 measures long, is played twice (the second time through is 25 measures), and consists of three phrases (0:00, 0:11, 0:19) separated by space for the rhythm section. The solo section is 28 measures, and while it uses harmonies from the melody, it is almost a tune unto itself. It's loosely divided into phrases of 6, 6, 8, and 8 measures.

RHYTHM: The rhythm section plays a tight arrangement behind the melody. During the solos they stick to traditional roles but display a modern sound and approach (see "Accompaniment"). Both the melody and solo changes have a measure of 3/4 near the end that adds a little hitch to the rhythm, while also helping to create a bit of form.

ACCOMPANIMENT: The accompaniment during the melody is carefully arranged and tightly performed. During the solos the rhythm section plays traditional roles: the bass walks powerfully throughout, anchoring the rhythm section; the drums play time, but Tain Watts's playing is extremely active; and the piano comps. Pianist Kenny Kirkland's playing is particularly noteworthy and an excellent example of contemporary comping techniques. The rhythm section's playing is hard-driving and both tight and loose, a very compelling combination; this is an excellent example of contemporary rhythm section playing.

"DELFEAYO'S DILEMMA" (1985) LISTENING GUIDE

TIME	FORM	STYLE	MELODY AND HARMONY	RHYTHM	ACCOMPANIMENT
0.00	Melody	The melodic phrases are more gestural than they are melodic. The interaction between the band members is very strong, and the arrangement is tightly conceived and performed. The band and soloists give a primer in a contemporary style that harkens back to older styles while also being contemporary.	Wynton and Branford Marsalis play the 3-phrase melody twice (0:00, 0:27). They move in and out of octave unison and harmony.	This is played at a fast tempo but has a very relaxed feeling. The rhythm section has a strong empathy for each other that only comes from touring and playing together a great deal.	The rhythm section has two functions during the melodic presentation: to play a carefully crafted arrangement behind the melody and to groove in the spaces between melodic phrases.
0:52	Solo 1: Trumpet	Wynton Marsalis begins his solo simply and quietly in the lower register, gradually gaining in intensity throughout his solo as his playing becomes more adventurous and moves throughout the range of his trumpet, winding up in the upper register toward the end (3:00). This solo displays his rich, dark, and full tone that is immediately recognizable, as is his playing style.	Marsalis's playing is smooth, flawless, and thoughtful; and he plays over all registers of the trumpet with ease, showing his virtuosic mastery of the instrument. On held notes (2:53) in the upper register we hear his trademark vibrato and sound that quickly identify his playing.	The rhythm section cooks in a relaxed fashion behind Marsalis's solo.	The rhythm section follows Marsalis's lead by starting quietly, leaving room for him to build the excitement of his solo. As he builds in intensity, so does the rhythm section, particularly Tain Watts on drums.
3:08	Solo 2: Tenor sax	Branford Marsalis's playing here is generally busier than Wynton's, with less space between phrases. Rhythmically, he mixes long streams of 1/8 notes with syncopated rhythmic figures.	Branford Marsalis plays the second solo.	Drummer Watts drives this solo relentlessly with his active and powerful playing.	Charnett Moffett continues his strong walking as Kirkland comps in a rhythmically exciting manner.
4:27	Solo 3: Piano	Kenny Kirkland's left hand displays the influence of McCoy Tyner (Chapter 13, 2nd Chorus) with his stabbing chords that are open harmonically. His solo is fleet and busier than both horn players' solos. A pianist doesn't have to breathe between phrases!	Kirkland plays the third and final solo. Notice that both Kirkland and Branford's solos are shorter than Wynton's as he is the featured player here.		
5:45	Melody	As in the opening melodic statement, the melody begins with a break for the horns.	Wynton and Branford again play the 3-phrase melody twice (5:45, 6:12) to end this recording.		The rhythm section plays their tight arrangement but in a slightly different way, indicating that there is flexibility within a basic framework.

read all about it

"Sonny Rollins and the Challenge of Thematic Improvisation" by Gunther Schuller

Walser, Keeping Time, Chapter 37
Famed jazz scholar Gunther Schuller analyzes Rollins's improvised solo on his 1956 recording of "Blue 7."

Hubbard felt the influence of jazz fusion and recorded a number of albums in a funk–jazz vein, including *Red Clay* (1970), *Straight Life* (1970), and *First Light* (1971), which received a Grammy Award. On these records Hubbard successfully navigated a line between commercialism and straight-ahead jazz.

Trumpeter Woody Shaw (1944–1989) built his style upon the work of Fats Navarro, Clifford Brown, Lee Morgan, and Freddie Hubbard. Eventually, he created a sound and style so personal that it is impossible to not recognize his playing. His experiences with the avant-garde saxophonist Eric Dolphy, including Shaw's first recording on Dolphy's album *Iron Man*, along with his study of the music of John Coltrane and pianist McCoy Tyner, helped him create a new and influential trumpet style. Shaw's soloing featured larger intervals than is usual for trumpet players, who generally play in a more linear style, as well as crisp and clean articulation. His style was extremely demanding, required a phenomenal trumpet technique, and to this day stands as the most innovative of modern trumpet styles.

After playing with Dolphy, Shaw spent time living in Paris. Returning to the United States, he continued on a traditional path of apprenticeships, such as playing and recording with pianist-composer Horace Silver's group (Chapter 11, 2nd Chorus) as well as recording an important experimental album, *Unity* (1966), with organist Larry Young. Like Hubbard, Shaw quickly became a first-call side musician, making numerous recordings with various artists on the Blue Note record label. Shaw began to record as a leader in 1970; *The Moontrane* (1974) and *Little Red's Fantasy* (1976) are early important albums.

Shaw's career hit its peak when Columbia Records signed him to a major recording contract, resulting in five releases, including *Rosewood* (1977), featuring his regular working band of the period. "Rosewood" from this album is a classic Shaw recording, featuring his playing and composing. His solo (3:31) displays his precision, his demanding intervallic playing style that he makes sound so easy, and his burnished sound that has a slight edge to it. In the late 1970s Shaw's appearances with saxophonist Dexter Gordon (upon his return to the United States after many years abroad) gave him further visibility. Until his death in 1989, Shaw continued to lead his band and collaborated with other artists as well, including recording two albums with Freddie Hubbard.

Saxophone

Tenor saxophonist Theodore "Sonny" Rollins (b. 1930) has been an important voice in jazz for over 60 years. His playing has been at a consistently high level and has remained both classic in its embrace of swing and bebop and contemporary in style. Rollins is known for his powerful, aggressive, and burly approach to the sax and for having the ability to "stretch out," playing long, brilliant, and energetic solos that are exciting and constantly engaging. Early in his career in the 1950s Rollins performed and recorded with pianists Bud Powell and Thelonious Monk (Chapter 10, 2nd Chorus) as well as the Clifford Brown–Max Roach Quintet (Chapter 11, 2nd Chorus). Rollins also worked with Miles Davis (Chapter 13, 1st Chorus), and the pair recorded several tunes composed by Rollins that have become jazz standards, including "Airegin," "Oleo," and "Doxy."

As a leader in the late 1950s, Rollins began to work with a piano-less trio, accompanied just by bass and drums, a style referred to as **strolling**. This texture is often used during the course of a performance for variety and is documented in a live performance on *A Night at the Village Vanguard* (1957). In the 1960s Rollins experimented with the avant-garde but soon returned to his more traditional style, including recording the soundtrack for the movie *Alfie* (1966). Through the

1970s and 1980s Rollins worked with a band that often featured elements of jazz–funk, but no matter what the setting, Rollins's style is the same. He has continued to work steadily and received a Grammy Award for Best Jazz Instrumental Album in 2001 for *This Is What I Do* (2000), as well as winning a Grammy Lifetime Achievement Award in 2004.

"St. Thomas," from *Saxophone Colossus* (1956), is one of Rollins's most recognizable recordings. Its relaxed calypso feel reflects Rollins's Trinidadian heritage. After the statement of the melody, Rollins's solo almost has a herky-jerky rhythmic feel and a rough-hewn, aggressive sound as he spins out a stream of melody. His solo is followed by an extended Max Roach (Chapter 11, 2nd Chorus) drum solo, after which the tune speeds up and picks up energy as Rollins continues to solo. We also get a chance to hear pianist Tommy Flanagan, one of the classiest pianists in jazz and a premier accompanist (see "Rhythm Section Players Under the Radar").

Saxophonist Michael Brecker (1949–2007) represents a different generation from Rollins since he grew up with rock and funk as much a part of his musical life as jazz. For musicians like Brecker, as well as his brother, the top trumpeter Randy, blending rock, funk, and jazz was a completely natural process. Their group Dreams was an early fusion band, and their later fusion band, the Brecker Brothers, which ran from 1975 to 1982, was quite successful with popular tunes such as "Some Skunk Funk." The Brecker Brothers band combined slick compositions that demanded their virtuosic technique and featured powerful jazz solos over rock and funk grooves. Both brothers also played and recorded with pianist Horace Silver (Chapter 11, 2nd Chorus) on the album *In Pursuit of the 27th Man* (1973), establishing their more traditional jazz roots.

Michael Brecker went on to become one of the most in-demand saxophone soloists. His aggressive and polished playing that melded jazz and R&B saxophone styles with a contemporary approach has already been extremely influential on generations of saxophonists. Playing and recording with such pop artists as James Taylor, Paul Simon, Billy Joel, and John Lennon and jazz artists such as Herbie Hancock (Chapter 13, 4th Chorus), Chick Corea (Chapter 14, 1st Chorus), and Pat Metheny (Chapter 14, 1st Chorus) has also made him one of the most recognizable of players. Brecker won fifteen Grammy Awards, including for his last album, *Pilgrimage* (2007), which featured Metheny and pianists Herbie Hancock and Brad Mehldau (Chapter 15, 1st Chorus). From this album, "The Mean Time" shows how these players created a genre that combines the concepts of jazz and jazz fusion so smoothly that there is no distinction between the styles. After being diagnosed with a rare blood disorder, Brecker died in 2007 from complications related to leukemia.

Rhythm Section Players Under the Radar

While the artists we discuss in this book are generally those who are recognized as top players, composers, and arrangers and receive widespread attention in books on jazz and in the media, there is a whole world of players at the highest level who, for one reason or another, do not receive the attention afforded others. Here, we take a little time to discuss four such musicians as representative of this group, all rhythm section players, as they are the backbone of so much that happens in jazz and often toil behind the scenes.

Pianist Tommy Flanagan, guitarist Jim Hall, bassist Milt Hinton, and drummer Jack DeJohnette have been mainstays in jazz throughout the second half of the twentieth century. These players have made an endless list of artists and their recordings successful, elegant, and refined. Each of them is known for his good taste, subtlety, and the ability to make those they are playing with sound better. They are selfless players who are able to adapt to any situation quickly and skilled at supporting instrumentalists and vocalists, a skill that musicians appreciate more than almost any other, making these players musicians' musicians. They have huge repertoires that include compositions from the entire history of jazz and are prepared on a moment's notice to play most any song, in any key, and any style that an artist might suggest. Fortunately, these players have also been bandleaders and coleaders throughout their careers and have recorded extensively in this capacity.

Pianist Tommy Flanagan (1930–2001), while having over thirty records as a leader or coleader, is a perfect example of an accompanist. Because of his skills in this area, he seems to have turned up everywhere and with everyone, including being a side musician on over 200 records. From Detroit, as a teenager Flanagan was already working in the house band at the Blue Bird Inn, a well-known Detroit nightclub, accompanying touring artists who came through town. After moving to New York City in 1956, Flanagan began an association with vocalist Ella Fitzgerald (Chapter 9, 1st Chorus); and he became her accompanist and musical director on and off until 1978. During this time he also worked as a side musician with a long list of performers and played on numerous important albums such as Sonny Rollins's *Saxophone Colossus*, John Coltrane's *Giant Steps* (Chapter 13, 2nd Chorus), and guitarist Wes Montgomery's *The Incredible Jazz Guitar of Wes Montgomery* (this chapter, 1st Chorus), as well as numerous albums for Ella Fitzgerald. Other venerable pianists of the same era, such as Sir Roland Hanna and Kenny Barron, cite Flanagan as an important influence.

After ending his association with Fitzgerald in 1978, Flanagan became more active as a leader of his own trio, playing with a succession of rhythm section accompanists such as bassists Peter Washington and George Mraz and drummers Kenny Washington, Lewis Nash, and Albert "Tootie" Heath. On "Day By Day" (*Montreux '77*, 1977) we hear Flanagan in his role as Fitzgerald's accompanist from a live performance at the Montreux Jazz Festival. Flanagan creates an arrangement for her, much as one would when writing for a big band. The trio, under his leadership, is tight, swinging, and exciting. Flanagan's short but hot solo displays his terrific touch and phrasing, as well as the understated elegance that characterizes his playing.

One of the premier guitarists in jazz, Jim Hall (1930–2013) also had an understated and lyrical soloing style developed largely through the study of horn players' solos, as opposed to the work of other guitarists. After growing up and studying in Cleveland, Ohio, Hall moved to Los Angeles in the mid-1950s when West Coast jazz was in full swing (Chapter 11, 1st Chorus). He began to gain recognition through his work with the popular Chico Hamilton Quintet, one of the more important West Coast–style bands that had an unusual instrumentation including drummer Hamilton and Hall on guitar, along with sax, cello, and bass. He then played and recorded with saxophonist-composer-arranger Jimmy Giuffre until 1960, developing, along with Giuffre, a style of composing and arranging that also incorporated interactive improvisation that was characteristic of cool jazz and West Coast jazz. "The Swamp People," from *Trav'lin' Light: The Jimmy Giuffre Three* (1958), featuring Giuffre on baritone sax, Bob Brookmeyer on trombone, and Hall on guitar, is an example of this style. It showcases the ability of these three players to mix the playing of a carefully composed piece while also improvising complicated and interlocking lines that create a polyphonic texture reminiscent of counterpoint in classical music.

In the late 1950s and early 1960s, Hall also worked with numerous leading players such as Bill Evans (Chapter 13, 1st Chorus), saxophonist Paul Desmond (Chapter 11, 1st Chorus), Sonny Rollins, trombonist Bob Brookmeyer, and trumpeter-flugelhornist Art Farmer. After moving to New York City, Hall gained great visibility while playing in the house band for the popular television variety show *The Merv Griffin Show*. As his career progressed, Hall became more of a featured artist, recording extensively as a bandleader in duo and trio settings, as well as with larger groups, with a wide variety of musicians. Later in his career he worked with a number of younger musicians including Bill Frisell, John Scofield, and Pat Metheny, three of the top guitarists to follow in his footsteps, as well as saxophonist Chris Potter (all discussed in Chapter 15). Hall also became much more involved with composition and arranging, developing a style that included influences from classical composition.

Bassist Milt Hinton (1910–2000) has been the harmonic and rhythmic foundation of an almost incomprehensibly long list of players and bands, making him one of the most recorded musicians in history as well as being considered "the dean" of jazz bassists. Playing with early stars such as cornetist Freddie Keppard (Chapter 3, 1st Chorus) and performing with Cab Calloway's big band for 15 years (Chapter 5, 2nd Chorus), as well as with the big bands of Benny Carter (Chapter 5, 2nd Chorus), Benny Goodman (Chapter 7, 1st Chorus), and Lionel Hampton (Chapter 7, 1st Chorus), pianists Art Tatum (Chapter 5, 4th Chorus) and Teddy Wilson, trumpeter Louis Armstrong (Chapter 3, 5th Chorus), and vocalist Billie Holiday (Chapter 9, 1st Chorus), among many, many others, made Hinton a walking encyclopedia of jazz.

Hinton was the ultimate professional and, consequently, continually busy as a studio musician playing many types of music on over 600 recordings, including numerous pop hits such as "Under the Boardwalk" (originally by The Drifters), for which he created a classic bass introduction, as well as recordings by Frank Sinatra (Chapter 9, 2nd Chorus), Paul McCartney, and Barbara Streisand. In fact, he was one of the first African Americans to integrate the New York studio scene, paving the way for many other jazz musicians. Hinton also gained visibility through his work as bassist for *The Dick Cavett Show*, a late-night talk show in the late 1960s to early 1970s. Late in his career he also worked with many of the younger jazz stars such as saxophonist Branford Marsalis (this chorus) and trumpeter Terence Blanchard (Chapter 15, 2nd Chorus).

Hinton, nicknamed "The Judge," spoke of the bass as a "service instrument" in an interview with Peter Keepnews: "The word base means support, foundation. If you put up a building, the foundation must be steady and strong. I must identify the chord for everyone, and only after that can I play the other notes. You learn to have a lot of humility. You must be content in the background, knowing you're holding the whole thing together." On the blues "Look Out Jack," from *Bassically with Blue* (1976), Hinton's powerful walking bass dominates the recording, including his solo (0:59–1:29). Hinton also spent his career documenting the world of jazz through his photography and created an invaluable collection of over 60,000 photos that has been published in book form and shown in numerous exhibitions.

Building on the playing of drummers Tony Williams (this chapter, 1st Chorus) and Elvin Jones (Chapter 13, 2nd Chorus), Jack DeJohnette (b. 1942) is one of the most versatile and creative drummers in jazz. Along with leading a wide variety of bands, he has played with the top artists in jazz in mainstream, avant-garde, and jazz fusion settings. From Chicago, DeJohnette was playing drums and piano professionally as a teenager and was involved with the AACM in its early days, including performing with Muhal Richard Abrams (Chapter 12, 3rd Chorus). After moving to New York City, DeJohnette gained early recognition in the mid-1960s when playing with the Charles Lloyd Quartet, where he also began his long musical association with pianist Keith Jarrett (both discussed in this chapter, 1st Chorus). During this period he also played with vocalists Betty Carter and Abbey Lincoln and alto saxophonist Jackie McLean, as well as being a member of the Bill Evans Trio (Chapter 13, 1st Chorus). Beginning in 1968 DeJohnette replaced Tony Williams in Miles Davis's group at the height of its experimentation with fusion. DeJohnette appeared on *Bitches Brew*, *Live-Evil*, *Jack Johnson*, *On the Corner*, as well as several live albums, all seminal records from the period that demonstrated his ability to bring together jazz, rock, and funk influences in an individual manner.

DeJohnette, while continuing to work with numerous artists and groups, began to lead his own bands. During the mid-1970s he worked in less mainstream contexts with guitarist John Abercrombie and bassists Dave Holland and Eddie Gomez, as well as players more associated with the avant-garde. In the 1980s he joined with pianist Keith Jarrett and bassist Gary Peacock to create the Standards Trio, which still plays and records. In the 1990s he joined with Herbie Hancock (Chapter 13, 4th Chorus), guitarist Pat Metheny (this chapter, 1st Chorus), and bassist Dave Holland to tour and record. On his own record label, Golden Beams, he showed further versatility and musical curiosity through a duet recording with the Gambian kora player Foday Musa Sosa as well as new-age records for meditation, one of which, *Peace Time* (2008), won a Grammy Award. DeJohnette continues his many projects and, among many others, has recently worked with guitarists Bill Frisell and John Scofield (Chapter 15, 2nd Chorus), South African singer Sibongile Khumalo, bassist Ron Carter, saxophonist Wayne Shorter (this chapter, 1st Chorus), a trio with bassist John Pattitucci and pianist Danilo Pérez (Chapter 15, introduction), and the Spring Quartet with saxophonist Joe Lovano (Chapter 15, 2nd Chorus), bassist Esperanza Spalding (Chapter 15, 1st Chorus), and Argentinean pianist Leo Genovese. His playing on "The Mean Time," from Michael Brecker's last album, shows DeJohnette driving the band powerfully and subtly, perfectly blending fusion and mainstream styles.

4th Chorus The Downtown Scene

WHAT IS THE DOWNTOWN SCENE, AND WHAT ROLE HAS IT PLAYED IN JAZZ MUSIC?

In the arts, the terms "uptown" and "downtown" are used as descriptions of aesthetic orientation. Very loosely, in music, **uptown** tends to imply a more academic and studied approach, generally with a connection to Western classical music. **Downtown** indicates experimental and out of the classical music mainstream and is often improvisational. The terms have been around since the 1960s and are derived from the idea that uptown art and music will more likely be displayed or performed in established galleries or concert halls in New York City and downtown art and music will be performed in more alternative spaces and clubs in lower Manhattan. Though the terms refer to the cultural geography of New York City, the references to uptown and downtown apply generally to aesthetics in the arts regardless of location.

A downtown music scene began in the late 1950s and lasted through the mid-1970s with performances of the works of experimental composers such as John Cage, La Monte Young, Steve Reich, Terry Riley, and Philip Glass, followed by rock bands such as the Velvet Underground, Sonic Youth, and DNA. Another downtown scene, this time with more jazz influences, emerged in the late 1970s. It involved a loose aggregation of composers and performers, many of them working in each other's bands, so it maintained the feel of a small scene. As mentioned earlier, however, music not originating from downtown New York City that comes from the same basic aesthetic sense can also be referred to by this term.

Many of the downtown musicians are well versed in jazz styles yet do not necessarily think of themselves as jazz players. They are also often interested in moving past traditional expectations of the jazz scene, even though much of their music is rooted in mainstream or avant-garde jazz. Their music frequently has connections to numerous popular music styles, music from around the world, and classical music without showing a particular predilection for one over the other. In addition, though improvisation is frequently an important element of their performances, these improvisations are not necessarily, though they may be, in a mainstream or avant-garde jazz style. The scene tends to emphasize an intense eclecticism, or openness to numerous influences, which can be expressed through a pastiche compositional style—moving through a variety of styles in one piece—or through involvement in a variety of projects that each may be in a very different style. The most prominent name and influence in this period of downtown music has been saxophonist-composer John Zorn.

John Zorn

John Zorn (b. 1953) is an experimental composer, alto saxophonist, and entrepreneur and has been the prime mover of the downtown music scene on the Lower East Side of Manhattan since the mid-1970s. Zorn's interests are wildly broad, and it is his eclecticism that most characterizes him and the downtown music world in general. Through his entrepreneurship, Zorn has remained independent from the mainstream media, major recording companies, and concert promoters, and through his record label, Tzadik, Zorn has prolifically recorded and released a massive amount of music, impressive in its sheer volume. In addition, the label—through its various series, each focusing on a different style of music—has provided an outlet for hundreds of composers and performers who are outside of any mainstream, including important downtown performer-composers such as saxophonists Marty Ehrlich and Ned Rothenberg, guitarist Elliott Sharp, trumpeter Steven Bernstein, bassist Mark Dresser, and drummers Bobby Previte and Gerry Hemingway. Zorn also opened and supports an alternative artist-run storefront concert space on the Lower East Side of Manhattan, The Stone, inviting various other musicians to act as curators to choose the performers. Between his label and concert space, Zorn is essentially supporting an entire network of composers and performers in an extremely wide variety of styles, much of which is jazz or jazz-related. Consequently, examining his career to date allows us to get a picture of the scene and a few of the important musicians in it.

Zorn takes the position of an outsider, not limiting himself stylistically to a particular genre. Partially because of its outsider quality, Zorn's work has also been controversial for a variety of reasons. For example, some refer to Zorn's work

Experimental composer-alto saxophonist-entrepreneur John Zorn on stage in 2003. He is among the leaders of the downtown scene in New York.
© ZUMA Press, Inc./Alamy.

as jazz, while others feel strongly that it is not. Zorn himself rejects this label, but a jazz influence is clear in much of his music. For example, an early release, *Spy vs. Spy: The Music of Ornette Coleman* (1989) that featured another downtown fixture, saxophonist Tim Berne, blends the compositions of Coleman, an icon of avant-garde jazz, with Zorn's interests in hard core punk, grind core, and thrash music, styles never before associated with jazz. For some this was a liberating concept, while for others it was heresy. Yet, like it or not, the record is a fascinating combination of these various genres. "Chronology" is a 1-minute version of the composition from Coleman's *The Shape of Jazz to Come* (Chapter 11, 4th Chorus). It is intense and chaotic from start to finish and is taken at breakneck speed.

Another album, *More News For Lulu* (1992), contained compositions by the jazz stalwarts trumpeter Kenny Dorham and saxophonist Hank Mobley. This record featured guitarist Bill Frisell (Chapter 15, 1st Chorus), who is wildly eclectic as well, and trombonist-composer George Lewis, who is closely associated with the jazz avant-garde and the AACM (Chapter 12, 3rd Chorus), contemporary classical music, and computer-based music, while also being a leading jazz scholar and cultural critic.

Zorn made an early splash with *The Big Gundown: John Zorn Plays the Music of Ennio Morricone* (1985), which featured his interpretations of the compositions by this well-known Italian film score composer, leading Zorn into extensive scoring for independent experimental films. His next release, *Spillane* (1987), featured the leading blues guitarist Albert Collins and the Kronos Quartet, a classical string quartet that, like Zorn, boasts an eclectic repertoire. In the late 1980s Zorn put together his group Naked City to continue to explore his interests in hard core punk and grind core, as well as jazz and other forms of popular music. The group often quickly juxtaposed these styles in an almost frantic manner. The band consisted of the downtown stars guitarists Bill Frisell and Fred Frith (here on bass), keyboardist Wayne Horvitz, and the versatile and ubiquitous drummer Joey Baron. Zorn further examined these styles with his groups Painkiller, which included the bassist-producer Bill Laswell, and the Moonchild Trio.

In the early 1990s Zorn began to explore his Jewish heritage through music and created hundreds of compositions, which were performed and recorded by various groups, including Masada, featuring Zorn and trumpeter Dave Douglas (Chapter 15, 2nd Chorus); the Masada String Trio, featuring violinist Mark Feldman and cellist Erik Friedlander (both discussed in Chapter 15, 4th Chorus); and an expanded version of the string trio that added, among others, the ever-present downtown guitarist-activist Marc Ribot. Others in the downtown scene, such as trumpeter Frank London, coleader of the Klezmatics, have explored the use of klezmer traditions, as well as other types of music from around the world, in combination with other genres, including jazz.

Zorn has also composed many works for classical chamber and orchestral ensembles, and this aspect of his work has recently brought him much wider recognition and acclaim. In 2013, Zorn's 60th birthday was celebrated internationally by a series of concerts at both downtown concert spaces and uptown venues such as Lincoln Center's Alice Tully Hall, the Metropolitan Museum of Art, and the Guggenheim Museum. Despite an increasing appreciation of his works and continuous awards and commissions, including a MacArthur "genius" grant, Zorn remains purposely and steadfastly outside the mainstream, prodigiously producing his own work as well as supporting the work of countless other artists.

CODA Chapter Summary

What Is Jazz Fusion Music, and Why Is It Controversial Among Jazz Fans?

- Jazz fusion combines elements of jazz, rock, funk, and R&B music.
- The music includes the use of electronic instruments such as electric pianos and synthesizers, electric guitars in a rock style, electric basses, as well as instruments from around the world.
- Fusion appeals to varied audiences and is played in both jazz clubs and more rock-oriented venues.
- Leading fusion proponents included guitarists John McLaughlin and Pat Metheny, the group Weather Report, and pianists Chick Corea and Keith Jarrett.

How Did the Avant-Garde Movement of the 1960s Continue to Develop over the Following Decades?

- Cecil Taylor was one of the innovators of "the new thing" of the 1950s and has continued to compose and perform over the last five decades. He has created his own unique combination of highly improvised and highly structured compositions.
- Members of Chicago's AACM spread beyond the city to take their music across the country, notably saxophonist-composer Anthony Braxton.
- Carla Bley has combined avant-garde and big-band techniques in a unique musical style that is rigorous and often humorous.

Who Were the Neo-Traditionalists, and What Impact Did They Have on Jazz in the 1980s–1990s?

- The neo-traditionalists rose in reaction to the growth of both jazz fusion and the jazz avant-garde.
- They sought a return to jazz roots, including the music of Louis Armstrong and Duke Ellington, along with an emphasis on its African American heritage as expressed through the blues.
- The best-known member of the movement has been Wynton Marsalis, who is an important performer, composer, and educator.

How Did Mainstream Jazz Continue to Flourish and Grow in This Period?

- Mainstream jazz performers continued to record and perform through this period, including trumpeters Freddie Hubbard and Woody Shaw, saxophone players Sonny Rollins and Michael Brecker, and rhythm section players such as pianist Tommy Flanagan, guitarist Jim Hall, bassist Milt Hinton, and drummer Jack DeJohnette.

What Is the Downtown Scene, and What Role Has It Played in Jazz Music?

- Associated with downtown New York, downtown music is experimental, freely crossing genres and styles, and performed in small clubs by musicians who collaborate on various projects together.
- Saxophonist-composer-entrepreneur John Zorn has been a leader of the downtown movement since the mid-1970s.

Talkin' Jazz (Key Terms)

Downtown	"Neo-classical" or	Smooth jazz
Jazz–rock fusion	"Neo-traditional"	Strolling
or Jazz Fusion	Reverb	Uptown

Key People

John McLaughlin	Anthony Braxton	Tommy Flanagan
Mahavishnu Orchestra	Carla Bley	Jim Hall
Weather Report	Wynton Marsalis	Milt Hinton
Chick Corea	Freddie Hubbard	Jack DeJohnette
Keith Jarrett	Woody Shaw	John Zorn
Pat Metheny	Sonny Rollins	
Cecil Taylor	Michael Brecker	

Think About This (For Further Discussion and Study)

1. Why was jazz fusion controversial? Does it seem controversial to you? Why or why not?
2. Can you relate jazz fusion to any of the styles of music that you listen to?
3. Describe your experience listening to the music of Cecil Taylor. Discuss its relationship to other music we have listened to so far.
4. When considering the neo-traditionalists and their desire to reestablish connections to classic jazz of the past, can you find a parallel to your feelings about a style of music that you are familiar with?
5. Discuss the similarities and differences that you hear between trumpeters Freddie Hubbard and Woody Shaw.
6. Discuss the similarities and differences that you hear between tenor saxophonists Sonny Rollins and Michael Brecker.
7. When considering "Rhythm Section Players Under the Radar," can you compare their roles to musicians in styles of music that you are familiar with?

Look It Up (Key Resources)

Beal, Amy C. *Carla Bley*. Urbana: University of Illinois Press, 2011.

Brackett, John Lowell. *John Zorn: Tradition and Transgression*. Bloomington: Indiana University Press, 2008.

Carr, Ian. *Keith Jarrett: The Man and His Music*. Boston: Da Capo Press, 1992.

Coryell, Julie, and Laura Friedman. *Jazz–Rock Fusion: The People, the Music*. Milwaukee, WI: Hal Leonard, 2000.

Fellezs, Kevin. *Birds of Fire: Jazz Rock, Funk, and the Creation of Fusion*. Durham, NC: Duke University Press, 2011.

Freeman, Phil. *Running the Voodoo Down: The Electric Music of Miles Davis*. San Francisco: Backbeat, 2005.

Lock, Graham. *Forces in Motion: The Music and Thoughts of Anthony Braxton*. Boston: Da Capo Press, 1988.

Mandel, Howard. *Miles, Ornette, Cecil: Jazz Beyond Jazz*. New York: Routledge, 2008.

Marsalis, Wynton, and Frank Stewart. *Sweet Swing Blues on the Road*. New York: W.W. Norton, 1994.

Mercer, Michelle. *Footprints: The Life and Works of Wayne Shorter*. New York: Tarcher, 2004.

Milkowski, Bill, *Jaco: The Extraordinary and Tragic Life of Jaco Pastorius*. San Francisco: Backbeat, 1995.

Nicholson, Stuart. *Jazz–Rock: A History*. New York: Schirmer Books, 1998.

Nisenson, Eric. *Open Sky: Sonny Rollins and His World of Improvisation*. New York: Da Capo Press, 2000.

Piekut, Benjamin. *Experimentalism Otherwise: The New York Avant-Garde and Its Limits*. Berkeley and Los Angeles: University of California Press, 2011.

Pond, Steven. *Head Hunters: The Making of Jazz's First Platinum Album*. Ann Arbor: University of Michigan Press, 2005.

Tingen, Paul. *Miles Beyond: The Electric Explorations of Miles Davis, 1967–1991*. New York: Billboard, 2001.

JAZZ TODAY

15

Throughout this book, we have examined the history and evolution of jazz while also learning to appreciate and understand its various styles. In each chapter, I have chosen specific musicians—out of the many I could have profiled—because of their importance in the history of jazz. In this chapter we will be looking at numerous contemporary artists in an attempt to give a concise picture of today's jazz scene. These present-day artists are, of course, influenced by new technologies as they have easy access to unlimited styles of music from around the world as well as nontraditional ways of distributing and promoting their music. There is so much going on and there are so many wonderful players, groups, and composers creating terrific music that it is, of course, impossible to cover them all or to choose who is most important. I have grouped musicians and bands in several ways here, primarily by instrument, and provided short descriptions of recordings by selected artists in order to give you a feel for the variety in jazz today.

Defining Contemporary Jazz

WHAT DISTINGUISHES TODAY'S JAZZ FROM THAT OF EARLIER PERIODS?

While generalizations are impossible to make about today's music, there are some traits that distinguish it from jazz in earlier periods.

Rhythm

Beginning with jazz fusion (Chapter 14, 1st Chorus), there has been a trend toward using a much wider variety of time signatures and approaches to rhythm. Contemporary jazz players are almost required to be fluent in what are sometimes referred to as **odd time signatures**—time signatures that have an odd number of beats with asymmetrical groupings within them such as 5/4, 7/8, 9/4, and even those with 11 or 13 beats to a measure. In addition, compositions may change meter regularly.

Instrumental Roles

While the roles of horn players have not changed much—they are generally responsible for playing melodies and solos—the role of the rhythm section instruments has opened up.

Photo: © Scott London/Alamy.

In this chapter, we'll answer these questions:

- ● What Distinguishes Today's Jazz from That of Earlier Periods?
- ● How Has the Role of the Rhythm Section Changed in Contemporary Jazz?
- ● How Have the Changes in the Jazz Scene Impacted Horn Players?
- ● How Have Vocalists Extended Their Technique to Suit Their Work in Contemporary Jazz?
- ● How Does the Popularity of Strings in Jazz Today Reflect a New Interest in More Varied Instrumentation?
- ● How Have Small Groups and Bands—From Musicians' Collectives to Big Bands—Shaped the New Jazz Landscape?

- Keyboardists now have electronic keyboards and a wide variety of synthesizers at their disposal. They use them to create textures that can range from simple background pads of sound to textures that can rival the power of a big band.
- Guitarists took center stage as the popularity of rock infused jazz with a new aesthetic. Beyond playing chords and melody lines, special effects can be added so that the guitarist also can provide texture and atmosphere to any performance.
- Bass players have become equal partners in the texture of the music as opposed to being primarily responsible for timekeeping and providing an underpinning for the chord progressions. Their lines are often quite rhythmically and even melodically complex, while still managing to provide a solid foundation for the rest of the band.
- Drummers are called on to bring together various styles from American popular music as well as music from around the world to add new color to the music. Their role in handling complicated meters and forms is crucial to today's jazz.

Instrumental Groupings

Another trait in contemporary jazz is the use of unusual combinations of instruments. Many bandleaders lead several different groups simultaneously to perform in different styles, choosing the instrumentation to complement their music. Drummer-composer-bandleader John Hollenbeck leads and participates in several groups, working closely with numerous musicians, resulting in a large, varied, and difficult-to-categorize output that exemplifies the range of contemporary jazz. Among the groups he leads is his Large Ensemble, a big band that has an uncanny ability to smoothly navigate a multitude of styles and features many of the top players in New York City. Hollenbeck is also a member of the Refuge Trio, along with vocalist Theo Bleckmann and pianist Gary Versace, and the Claudia Quintet, which features a woodwind player on sax and clarinet, vibraphone, accordion, bass, and Hollenbeck's drums. All of Hollenbeck's work finds a compelling balance between composition and improvisation, another common trait in contemporary jazz.

Trumpeter Dave Douglas (2nd Chorus) is another artist who leads various groups, such as Keystone—with a lineup of trumpet, tenor sax, Fender Rhodes keyboard, electric bass, drums, and turntables—and Brass Ecstasy, which has four brass and a drummer. Bassist Christian McBride (this chapter, 1st Chorus) also leads several groups with different instrumentation.

Virtuosity and Versatility

While jazz has always had tremendous instrumentalists, the overall level of instrumental ability has continued to increase. (As a side note, that does not imply that instrumentalists who have more technical prowess make better music.) In addition, contemporary players are often, even at an early stage in their career, fluent with a wide variety of musical styles and move fluidly from one approach to another. For example, in the past trumpet players often specialized and would work either as a lead player, a section player, or a soloist. Some could do it all, of course; but now the ability to handle any role has become more commonplace. Today's saxophone players are often multi-instrumentalists, "doubling" on several instruments, such as clarinet and flute, or even double reeds such as the oboe and bassoon. Again, while there were some famous players who mastered several different wind instruments in the past, it has become a far more common requirement for today's musicians.

"Freedom Dance" (2012) by Lionel Loueke

INSTRUMENTATION: Guitar, vocals, bandleader: Lionel Loueke; **Bass:** Derrick Hodge; **Drums:** Mark Guiliana.

LISTENING HIGHLIGHT, STYLE: While Loueke's earlier work has at times emphasized an acoustic approach, on his album *Heritage* (2012) he uses a variety of electronic textures. Produced by Robert Glasper (this chapter, 1st Chorus), this album consciously celebrates the relationship between Loueke's various influences. "Freedom Dance" is a loose, groove-oriented tune with Loueke singing and playing the melody. As he solos, Loueke radically but gradually alters his tone using effects pedals. He also at times sings along with his solo, in a way similar to Kurt Rosenwinkel, adding yet another color to his sound. There is a gentle and relaxed quality to Loueke's playing initially that then increases in intensity during the course of his solo. The powerful drum groove has elements of an Afro-pop feel and a funk–jazz vibe reminiscent of Herbie Hancock's "Absolute Truth" (Chapter 13, 1st Chorus). Hodge's bass playing (this chapter, 1st Chorus) is an excellent example of the new approach taken by contemporary bassists as he plays lines that are quite complex and syncopated, as well as being prominent in the texture.

The Role of Composition

While improvisation is still the lifeblood of jazz, composition is playing a crucial role in contemporary jazz. Composers, instrumentalists, and bandleaders are challenging themselves through the creation of new improvisational forms and unique sonic environments. Drummer Tyshawn Sorey's composition "40," from the 2011 album *Oblique–I*, brings together contemporary classical techniques with jazz in a personal manner, making his composition and playing difficult to categorize. European composers and performers, such as Ronan Guilfoyle, have been bringing a unique compositional dimension to jazz for many years; and big-band writing is thriving internationally.

Influence of World Music

Increasingly, jazz composers and performers are bringing their own musical heritages to bear on their work or consciously borrowing from other musical traditions. There are still many composer-performers such as Robert Glasper (this chapter, 1st Chorus) and Nicholas Payton (this chapter, 2nd Chorus) who display the influence of various styles of black popular music. However, others draw on more diverse traditions. Guitarist-composer Lionel Loueke's *Heritage* shows him merging his jazz and African roots. From the West African country Benin, Loueke studied in Ivory Coast and Paris, then Berklee College of Music and the selective and prestigious Thelonious Monk Institute of Jazz. He has worked with, among many others, the bands of Herbie Hancock (Chapter 13, 4th Chorus) and trumpeter Terence Blanchard (this chapter, 2nd Chorus) and has recorded with numerous artists such as Esperanza Spalding (1st Chorus), pianist Kenny Barron, and vocalist Gretchen Parlato. Loueke has also worked regularly as a leader with his trio Gilfema.

South Asian musical instruments and musical styles have been heard in jazz music since the 1960s on occasion, becoming more prominent in the work of jazz fusion players like John McLaughlin (see Chapter 14, 1st Chorus). Vijay Iyer (this chapter, 1st Chorus) and Rudresh Mahanthappa have been tapping into their South Asian heritage very effectively. Although born outside of the South Asian tradition, drummer Dan Weiss became fascinated with the rhythmic approaches found in South Asian music. His studies on tabla, an important South Asian percussion instrument, have greatly influenced his playing and are integrated into his playing in a natural manner. His drumming and tabla playing can be heard on alto saxophonist Rudresh Mahanthappa's Indo-Pak Coalition album *Apti*. The fact that Weiss also has played in the doom-metal band Bloody Panda and incorporates twentieth-century classical music in his compositions makes him an individual voice.

The powerful influence of Latino/Latina musicians upon jazz continues in the music of Miguel Zenón (this chapter, 2nd Chorus), Dafnis Prieto, and Panamanian pianist-composer-bandleader Danilo Pérez. Originally from Cuba, drummer-composer-bandleader Prieto is a master of Afro-Cuban rhythms and techniques including traditional, religious, and contemporary styles, blending these with jazz techniques to create a personal style. While Prieto's technique shines through at times, he is also quite reserved in his playing, allowing the music to dictate what he plays as opposed to imposing his style on the music. The album *Dafnis Prieto Proverb Trio* features keyboardist Jason Lindner and vocalist Kokayi in compositions that fuse pop and jazz seamlessly in tunes such as "You and Me." Pérez studied classical piano at the National Conservatory in Panama and then jazz composition at the Berklee College of Music. His albums, such as *Motherland* (2000) and *Providencia*, including "Bridge of Life, Pt. 1" (2010), feature his compositions and improvisations that deftly merge jazz, Latin, and classical techniques and sensibilities. Pérez's ability to merge his compositional work with his improvisations makes these records shine.

Eclecticism

Many contemporary jazz artists go beyond absorbing one tradition in their performing, recording, and composing to create music that truly transcends easy

---

IN PERFORMANCE
A New Training Ground

Many, if not most, contemporary jazz players have gone to college or music conservatory to study music, often attaining advanced degrees. This is a relatively new trend and is largely replacing the more old-school apprenticeships of the past, such as playing with bands on the road. Also, many of these players—along with their busy playing careers—are teaching in universities and conservatories and conducting clinics and master classes. While most of these players make a living through their performing, it is still a difficult lifestyle with lots of touring and an uncertain future in a fickle marketplace. Consequently, a college teaching job is a welcome relief from the uncertain economic realities of the music business, while also providing education and mentorship to young musicians. In addition, while high-level jazz players such as these can, and do, work steadily, there is generally less work now for the mid-level player, so training in colleges, universities, and jazz conservatories, as well as jazz programs in high schools, has taken on greater importance for young musicians.

categorization. Bassist-composer-bandleader Ben Allison's work crosses handily over genre boundaries, allowing him to express himself in different ways. "Dr. Zaius," from *The Stars Look Very Different Today* (2013), exemplifies Allison's cross-genre approach as it incorporates elements of pop, rock, jazz, and trance music. The inclusion of banjo (an unusual instrument in modern jazz), along with guitar, bass, and drums, is another example of the use of unique instrumentations in contemporary music. On this recording, Allison and his group also employ nontraditional tonalities and playing techniques that go well beyond the traditional jazz timbres.

1st Chorus The Contemporary Rhythm Section

HOW HAS THE ROLE OF THE RHYTHM SECTION CHANGED IN CONTEMPORARY JAZZ?

Drums and Bass Step Forward

There is a semistandard order that most people follow when naming instrumentalists in a band: vocalists, horn players, piano, guitar, bass, and drums. This hierarchy reflects the incorrect notion that the "lead" instruments are more important than those that provide accompaniment. Since the roles of drummers and bass players have gone through the largest evolution in contemporary jazz, we will turn this trend around and begin with a discussion of them.

The role that drummers play in jazz has evolved over the decades. For example, in our study of bebop we noted how drummers became less restricted to playing the role of timekeeper. This liberated them to play a more prominent part in creating the overall texture of a piece, something that has only continued to grow today. In addition, more drummers are becoming bandleaders and composers. Interestingly, in their compositional work they often create subtle environments that don't call for them to show off their always considerable drumming technique. Contemporary jazz compositions are often quite complex, both formally and metrically; abrupt shifts in meter are increasingly common. It is frequently the drummer who holds all of this together by demarking the forms and the meter. In addition, an important feature of contemporary jazz is the increasing incorporation of music from around the world. Many drummers and percussionists seamlessly incorporate contemporary popular music styles as well as Latin, African, Middle East, and South Asian rhythms and rhythmic concepts into jazz.

As is true for a number of jazz drummers today, Chris Dave (b. 1968) is equally comfortable in a jazz, hip-hop, or R&B setting. He has played with top jazz stars such as alto saxophonist Kenny Garrett and trumpeter Terence Blanchard (both discussed in the 2nd Chorus) and plays with pop, hip-hop, and R&B artists such as D'Angelo, Adele, Beyoncé, and Maxwell. His playing combines hip-hop and R&B grooves with a jazz sensibility. Dave has the ability to play any type of odd meter thrown at him, making him an extremely versatile and unique player. He has collaborated with pianist-composer-producer Robert Glasper as well as with guitarist-composer Lionel Loueke. These collaborations have put him in the forefront of music that incorporates the most contemporary forms of R&B with jazz.

Terri Lyne Carrington (b. 1965) has been a leading drummer since she was a child. By the age of 11 she had already received a full scholarship to Berklee College of Music, one of the leading jazz and pop music conservatories in the world. She has been a busy side musician with a wide cross section of artists such as jazz

listening focus

"Rubylou's Lullaby" (2008) by Brian Blade & the Fellowship Band

DOWNLOAD
Track Number 36

INSTRUMENTATION: Drummer, composer, coleader: Brian Blade; **Keyboard, coleader:** Jon Cowherd; **Tenor sax:** Melvin Butler; **Alto sax, bass clarinet:** Myron Walden; **Guitar:** Kurt Rosenwinkel; **Bass:** Chris Thomas.

LISTENING HIGHLIGHT, TEXTURE: From their album *Season of Changes*, "Rubylou's Lullaby" combines a jazz, pop, and rock anthem sensibility. Guitarist Kurt Rosenwinkel (discussed further in this chorus) employs a timbre that is typical in jazz guitar work at the piece's beginning but then changes to a more distorted sound often heard in rock. The combination of tenor sax and bass clarinet playing the simple, almost folk-like melody over Blade's rock beat further complicates the textures in this composition, as does the fact that there are no improvised solos. The abrupt change in the later third of the piece from an all-out rock accompaniment to a softer, more contemplative section also adds to the piece's texture.

Esperanza Spalding, 2009. Thanks to her surprise Grammy win in 2011 as Best New Artist, bassist-vocalist-bandleader Spalding has brought new attention to jazz.
© Scott London/Alamy.

stars Herbie Hancock and Wayne Shorter, crossover guitarist Carlos Santana, avant-garde trumpeter Lester Bowie, saxophonist Pharoah Sanders, and pop–jazz saxophonist David Sanborn; her powerful and highly eclectic playing moves between these various styles in a dizzying manner. Carrington displays a range of styles on her Grammy Award–winning 2012 album *The Mosaic Project*. This record features a lineup of leading female players and vocalists including pianist Gerri Allen and bassist-vocalist Esperanza Spalding, both discussed later in this chorus.

Like many other contemporary drummers, Brian Blade (b. 1970) has made his mark in many different musical settings: he has one of the more prominent gigs in jazz as the longtime drummer for the Wayne Shorter Quartet; he is an in-demand side musician with jazz artists and folk performers such as Joni Mitchell and Bob Dylan; and he works as a singer-songwriter, collaborating with multi-instrumentalist and producer Daniel Lanois (whose credits include platinum albums for the rock group U2). Blade is also a coleader of the Fellowship Band, and his work there reflects this range as well.

Jazz bass playing, like drumming, has evolved a great deal, particularly in recent years. In most of the recordings we have heard so far the bass has had two main roles: to provide a harmonic foundation by emphasizing the root, or main note, of the chord and, along with the drummer, to be a timekeeper by playing either in 4 (playing on all 4 beats of a 4-beat measure) or in 2 (playing only on beats 1 and 3). Like drummers, however, bassists are now much freer and play a larger and more varied role in ensembles. Contemporary bass players are often extremely technically fluent on both acoustic and electric basses. Their lines can be complex, in both melodic and rhythmic content, making them more like equal partners in the texture, as opposed to playing a primarily supportive role. Bass players are also now more frequently seen as composers and leaders in contemporary jazz, which, with the exception of Charles Mingus (Chapter 13, 3rd Chorus), was unusual in the past. As just one example, Ben

listening focus

"Little Fly" (2010) by Esperanza Spalding

INSTRUMENTATION: Bass, leader, composer, coarranger: Esperanza Spalding; **Violin:** Entcho Todorov; **Viola:** Lois Martin; **Cello:** David Eggar; **Coarranger:** Gil Goldstein.

LISTENING HIGHLIGHT, FORM: In "Little Fly," from *Chamber Music Society* (2010), Spalding sets the William Blake poem "The Fly" to music. She plays the bass and sings the poem in her high, light voice, accompanied by a string trio consisting of violin, viola, and cello.

After a brief introduction, this mellow, meditative composition primarily consists of a 16-measure form divided into two somewhat contrasting 8-measure phrases. Since the music repeats exactly while only the lyrics change, the first part of this piece has a **strophic form**.

The first 8-measure phrase has a repeated bass line during which Spalding also strums the bass strings playing chords. After two **strophes**, or verses, there is a brief string trio interlude, and then the first phrase repeats loosely. Spalding finishes the recording with a bass solo, first over **pizzicato strings**—the strings are plucked with the fingers instead of bowed—and then bowed strings. The tempo throughout is somewhat rubato, giving the rhythm a flexible and loose feeling. The string arrangement is also cleverly written, in that it is carefully controlled yet has an improvised feel to it. It combines the style of a classical string trio with the looseness of a jazz performance.

Allison has almost as much fame for his compositions and bandleading as for his bass playing, showing just how far out of the shadows bass players have come.

No one has done more lately than bassist-vocalist-bandleader Esperanza Spalding (b. 1984) to bring the bass literally to the forefront. While bassists are generally placed in the back of the bandstand next to the drums, Spalding stands up front when she plays with her band. She is the star, and her performances are quite striking for the ease with which she plays and sings (in English, Spanish, and Portuguese). She exudes the lightness and fun of a pop singer while playing and singing complicated and involved music in the jazz tradition. Spalding also was the first jazz musician to have won a Grammy Award for Best New Artist in a surprise win over pop star, Justin Bieber, in 2011. Her debut solo album was a hit, and Spalding was immediately in rarefied territory for a jazz musician, garnering wide media coverage. She has two primary vehicles for her work, Chamber Music Society—a chamber group with rhythm section, string trio, and vocalists—and Radio Music Society—featuring a jazz band with hip-hop and R&B vocalists. Her album *Radio Music Society* (2012) won two Grammy Awards. Spalding also works with numerous other groups as bassist and vocalist, including with saxophonist Joe Lovano, one of her early mentors (this chapter, 2nd Chorus).

Bassist-composer-bandleader Christian McBride (b. 1972) has moved smoothly from his role as a young prodigy to become an established and experienced bandleader. His virtuosic playing and preternatural musical maturity made him a first-call side musician as a teenager. McBride has played with an endless string of jazz greats, including trumpeter Freddie Hubbard, Herbie Hancock,

McCoy Tyner, John McLaughlin, and saxophonist Joe Henderson, as well as with popular music stars and groups such as Queen Latifah, Sting, the turntablist DJ Logic, and the Roots. After his long side musician apprenticeship he became a bandleader and has released a dozen albums under his own name. McBride's experience; his material, ranging from acoustic jazz to fusion; and his various groups, ranging from a trio to an eighteen-piece big band, have made him an elder statesperson while only in his early 40s. His current quintet, Inside Straight, features saxophonist Steve Wilson and vibraphonist Warren Wolf. "New Hope's Angel," from their album *People Music* (2013), is a lovely medium-tempo ballad that combines acoustic jazz with a light jazz fusion feel.

Piano and Guitar

While the pianist's role in today's jazz has not gone through as great an evolution as the roles of bass and drums have, the pianist's tools of the trade have certainly expanded. While some pianists play only acoustic piano, most play a variety of electric keyboards and synthesizers and, therefore, also tend to be comfortable working with music technology in general. Consequently, their accompanist's role has expanded beyond comping, as we heard with Joe Zawinul on Weather Report's "Birdland" (Chapter 13, 1st Chorus). At times they are creating aural landscapes or **pads** for the music to rest upon. Pianists still are frequently leaders of piano trios, but the medium of the piano trio has also continued to evolve and expand.

Pianist-composer-bandleader Jason Moran (b. 1975) is one of the very top artists in jazz, both as a leader and in collaboration with other artists. Like drummer Dafnis Prieto, in 2010 Moran was named a MacArthur Fellow (the so-called genius grant). Moran came to jazz by hearing bits and pieces of jazz recordings through samples used on rap recordings, inspiring him to find the original versions. His initial experience when hearing pianist Thelonious Monk (Chapter 10, 2nd Chorus) was also crucial to his development. In 2000, after a stint in saxophonist Greg Osby's band that gave him visibility and led to a recording contract, Moran began to work with what is now his long-standing cooperative trio, the Bandwagon, that features bassist Tarus Mateen and drummer Nasheet Waits. This is his primary working group, although he is regularly involved in numerous projects with a wide range of artists such as jazz saxophonists Charles Lloyd, Steve Coleman, and Ravi Coltrane and the singer-songwriter-rapper-bassist Me'Shell Ndegéocello. Moran, like so many musicians in jazz, works hard to not be pigeonholed by the label "jazz" by creating many different styles of music while working with musicians from diverse backgrounds.

Pianist-composer-bandleader Brad Mehldau (b. 1970) also creates a wide variety of music and, like Moran, works regularly with his longtime trio, which now features bassist Larry Grenadier and drummer Jeff Ballard—both also busy freelance side musicians. Mehldau works with a variety of musicians and bands, including the Joshua Redman Quartet (this chapter, 2nd Chorus), and has a close relationship with guitarist Pat Metheny (Chapter 14, 1st Chorus). Along with his powerful jazz roots, Mehldau's music also reflects a background in rock and pop as well as classical music. He has created his own versions of numerous pop and rock tunes with his trio, and his interest in classical music is reflected in, among other works, several long compositions and commissions for important classical singers. Mehldau is also remarkably adept at playing in odd time signatures and often uses this technique when he plays standard tunes, somehow making them sound as natural as when played in their original time signatures. His musical expansiveness and curiosity are also seen in a duo with drummer Mark Guiliana that

listening focus

"Feedback, Pt. 2" (2010) by Jason Moran

INSTRUMENTATION: Piano, composer, bandleader: Jason Moran; **Bass:** Tarus Mateen; **Drums:** Nasheet Waits.

LISTENING HIGHLIGHT, TIMBRE: "Feedback, Pt. 2," from the album *Ten* (2010), was commissioned by the legendary Monterey Jazz Festival. For it, Moran sampled rock guitarist Jimi Hendrix's guitar **feedback**—loud electronic sounds created by a guitar being held close to an amplifier that is turned up very loud—from a 1967 recording of Hendrix performing live at the Monterey Pop Festival (a particularly famous concert, immortalized in the movie *Monterey Pop*). Interestingly, Moran's compositional concept dramatically alters the feedback samples and counterintuitively electronically transforms them into a subdued yet otherworldly and somewhat ambiguous sound. Moran then created an understated and contemplative ballad—played rubato—around them. He wrote a composition that brings together a sober and soft medium—a ballad—with feedback, a symbol of the cacophony and loud volume that characterizes rock music yet here transformed and reconceived in a radical and surprising manner. Moran's combination of a traditional jazz trio performance with the avant-garde element of sampled and transformed sounds combines jazz and contemporary experimental music approaches.

features Mehldau on electric keyboard and synthesizers. Mehldau also has taken time to write extensively, thoughtfully, and at times analytically about music in various ways, referencing, for example, philosophy and literature.

Mehldau's two-CD album *Highway Rider* (2010) is an example of his wide-ranging musical interests as well as his use of extramusical concepts, such as the notion of order that he expresses here through the use of a primary musical idea to create a sense of unity throughout the recording. As such, it is a concept album with fifteen original compositions that is intended to be taken as a whole, as opposed to individual tracks. "John Boy," the opening composition, sets the mellow tone of the album. It features a lovely melody that slips back and forth between uplifting and wistful. There is no improvising, and the melody is performed by a variety of instrumentations by his group and a small chamber orchestra. A light, rolling percussion keeps this tune moving through its various permutations. The rest of the record goes on to meld composition and improvisation in a fascinating manner while also creating a looseness reminiscent of a live performance.

Canadian pianist-composer-bandleader Renee Rosnes (b. 1962) has found a compelling balance of a traditional straight-ahead approach with a more modern sound. She works in the relatively straightforward medium of the piano trio or jazz quartet as a bandleader and performs piano duets with her husband, the excellent pianist Bill Charlap. Rosnes worked with such leading artists as saxophonists Joe Henderson, Wayne Shorter, and James Moody; vibraphonist Bobby Hutcherson; and trombonist J. J. Johnson. She was an original member of the all-star band SFJAZZ Collective as well as a member of Out of the Blue (OTB), a group formed by Blue Note records to showcase young talent and that included saxophonists Kenny Garrett (this chapter, 2nd Chorus) and Steve Wilson. Rosnes

read all about it
"Explaining the Art of a Trio" by Brad Mehldau

Walser, **Keeping Time,** *Chapter 65*
Mehldau explains his working musical philosophy as well as setting his approach apart from earlier styles.

read all about it

"Exploding the Narrative"
by Vijay Iyer

Walser, **Keeping Time**, *Chapter 67*

Iyer explores alternatives to "telling a story" in jazz improvisation to suggest new ways for musicians to express meaning through their work.

has recorded extensively under her name and with numerous other artists. Many bands play Rosnes's compositions, and she also writes about jazz and hosts a radio show, among other musical endeavors.

Vijay Iyer (b. 1971) has flown to the top of the international jazz world with an exciting mixture of projects that span an incredibly wide range of musical and extra-musical perspectives. Iyer received a PhD in the cognitive science of music and is an extensively published scholar in a variety of areas. Just as his musical works incorporate composition and improvisation, he blends his various areas of interest into a seamless creative whole. He has become known for his incorporation of South Asian music as he examines his cultural heritage as part of his creative palette. His CD *Holding It Down: The Veteran's Dreams Project* (2013) is a fascinating example of his incorporation of social, political, and creative interests beyond music. It is a collaboration with poet Mike Ladd that is based upon dreams of veterans of color who have fought in recent wars. Iyer has participated in numerous other projects, both acoustic and electronic, with a variety of collaborators, including drummer Tyshawn Sorey and saxophonist Rudresh Mahanthappa, as well as accepting commissions from classically oriented ensembles. Now only in his early 40s, he has already released seventeen albums as a leader and has worked with an endless list of major musicians as a side musician and collaborator. Similar to Mehldau and Moran, Iyer has led a long-standing trio that has worked together for 10 years, allowing them to build an exciting rapport. "Accelerando" (2013), from the album of the same name, exhibits his trio's ability to manipulate rhythm, both by using a complicated metrical structure and by continually accelerating the tempo throughout the performance.

From Detroit, pianist-composer-bandleader Geri Allen (b. 1957) studied jazz and classical music in college, as well as **ethnomusicology**—a scholarly field that examines music from a variety of perspectives, including anthropology and sociology. Early influential experiences were her involvement with saxophonist-composer Steve Coleman's (this chapter, 2nd Chorus) M-Base Coalition as well as the Black Rock Coalition, an organization dedicated to opening areas of creative expression often denied to African Americans as well as toward gaining economic parity for black artists. Allen has worked as a pianist, composer, and bandleader as well as a performer with other groups, including those of Terri Lyne Carrington and Esperanza Spalding. She has 19 albums as a leader to her credit. Her work has an openness to it as her blues, gospel, and R&B influences are all clearly present; and she manages to convey them through a modern and very personal take on a traditional jazz approach. Additionally, she is now the director of Jazz Studies at her alma mater, the University of Pittsburgh.

Allen's *Grand River Crossings: Motown and Motor City Inspirations* (2013) explores her Detroit roots. Her solo piano version of Motown artist Smokey Robinson's "Tears of a Clown" is a lovely reflection on Robinson's version, and her extension of his classic introduction to the tune is fascinating. Allen's solo album *Flying Toward the Sound: A Solo Piano Excursion Inspired by Cecil Taylor, McCoy Tyner and Herbie Hancock* (2010) and its eight-part suite *Refractions* beautifully reflect her varied influences, including jazz, contemporary classical music, and **impressionism**—a style of early twentieth-century classical music influenced by the impressionistic painters.

Pianist-composer-bandleader-producer Robert Glasper (b. 1978) has accomplished an extremely unusual feat as a top jazz and R&B artist. Originally from Houston, he attended the same performing arts high school as Jason Moran and a number of other successful jazz players. Glasper worked as a side musician

Robert Glasper, on stage in 2013. His group, the Robert Glasper Experiment, weds elements of hip-hop, R&B, and jazz.
© MS Photos/Alamy.

"Afro Blue" (2012) by the Robert Glasper Experiment

INSTRUMENTATION: Keyboards, bandleader, producer: Robert Glasper; **Bass:** Derrick Hodge; **Drums:** Chris Dave; **Saxophone, flute, synthesizer, vocoder:** Casey Benjamin; **Turntables:** Jahi Sundance.

LISTENING HIGHLIGHT, STYLE: From the album *Black Radio*, "Afro Blue," composed by Mongo Santamaria (Chapter 12, 2nd Chorus) with lyrics by the wonderful vocalist-lyricist Oscar Brown, Jr., features the R&B vocal star Erykah Badu. While paying homage to both Santamaria's and John Coltrane's versions, Glasper clearly makes this tune his own here and illustrates the various influences that he brings together in an organic manner. The use of a repetitive flute line calls to mind the use of samples in hip-hop, while Chris Dave on drums and Derrick Hodge on bass create a light but funky R&B/hip–hop groove. Glasper, on both electric and acoustic piano, adds touches of jazz throughout with his fills behind Badu's slippery smooth, evocative vocal, while also playing in a style that combines jazz and a cool R&B feel. Glasper also combines a simple melodic approach—grooving on a simple vamp—with a more sophisticated harmonic progression on an occasional short bridge section. Glasper's use of sophisticated production techniques more often associated with popular styles than jazz also makes this album stand out.

with many of the younger jazz stars, such as Christian McBride (discussed this chorus), saxophonist Kenny Garrett (this chapter, 2nd Chorus), and trumpet players Nicholas Payton (this chapter, 2nd Chorus), Roy Hargrove, and Terence Blanchard (this chapter, 2nd Chorus). He has gone on to lead his own acoustic trio as well as his electrically oriented band the Robert Glasper Experiment and has combined the two bands for performances and recordings. *Black Radio* (2012), by the Robert Glasper Experiment, won a Grammy Award for Best R&B Album and featured his band along with an impressive list of hip-hop, rap, and R&B vocalists such as Erykah Badu, Lalah Hathaway, Bilal, and Yasiin Bey (formerly known as Mos Def).

While guitarists have always been important in jazz, jazz fusion, with its relationship to rock and other forms of popular music, has brought the guitar and guitarists to the forefront as performers and bandleaders. Their ability to bridge the gaps between all of these styles has been important to their development, as has the guitarist's prominent place in rock and popular music.

Guitarist-composer-bandleader Bill Frisell (b. 1951) might cross more musical boundaries in a more fluid manner than just about any musician in this book. He has played with jazz stars such as saxophonist Joe Lovano (this chapter, 2nd Chorus) and drummer Paul Motian (these three musicians had a collaborative trio), the avant-garde saxophonist Julius Hemphill, saxophonist John Zorn (Chapter 14, 4th Chorus), many others on the New York downtown scene, singer-songwriters like Van Dyke Parks and Loudon Wainwright III, and rock artists such as Elvis Costello and drummer Ginger Baker, as well as performing with the Los Angeles Philharmonic. Consequently, much of Frisell's work would certainly not normally be identified as jazz, yet he brings the spirit of improvisation to all of his work while also using it as a means to tie together various styles of American music, such as jazz, rock, folk, bluegrass, and country, in an extremely effective and evocative manner.

Like so many contemporary players discussed here, Frisell keeps numerous projects going at the same time while also participating in his musical colleagues' projects. His playing is always different depending on the context, yet he also has a consistent voice. In general, his style is quite lyrical and does not tend to emphasize or display his considerable technique. In fact, there is often a kind of understatement and a thoughtfulness about his work that makes you listen more carefully than you normally might. This can be heard in his trio work with Joe Lovano and Paul Motian on their album *Time and Time Again* (2007). The composition "Wednesday" shows a contemplative and lyrical side to all three players, and Motian's drumming here is the epitome of subtle.

Guitarist-composer-bandleader Kurt Rosenwinkel (b. 1970) is one of today's top jazz guitar players. He is a leading voice for a generation of young jazz players as he seems to naturally embody a variety of influences while remaining solidly a dedicated jazz player. Rosenwinkel plays with a round, dark tone that is associated with jazz guitar players, as opposed to the edgy, sharp sound heard in more rock-oriented playing. He does, at times, push the tone to distortion, showing the influence of both styles, and uses a wide variety of effects pedals in an extremely creative and effective manner. A particularly distinctive element of his style, however, is his use of a lapel microphone that captures his voice as he sings along with his guitar, creating a unique and personal sound. Rosenwinkel attended Berklee College of Music but left to go on the road with vibraphonist Gary Burton. After moving to New York City, he began to work with, among others, drummer Paul Motian and the veteran saxophonist Joe Henderson. He currently works and collaborates with saxophonist Mark Turner, with Brian Blade's Fellowship Band, and with Brad Mehldau, as well as with rap star Q-Tip. Rosenwinkel has recorded ten albums as a leader.

While never seeming to emphasize his technique, Rosenwinkel plays in a virtuosic and extremely fluid manner akin to a horn player. He is known for his harmonically rich compositions as well as his ability to bring a unique approach to jazz standards. We can hear his tone fluctuate but remain stylistically consistent in "Rubylou's Lullaby" with the eclectic Fellowship Band, discussed earlier in this chorus. "Ana Maria," from Rosenwinkel's album *Reflections* (2009), performed by his Standards Trio that features bassist Eric Revis and drummer Eric Harland, is his rendition of a Wayne Shorter tune. Played as a bossa nova, Rosenwinkel's version is calm and understated and demonstrates his more traditional jazz style along with his ability to play fluidly and lyrically within a complicated harmonic structure.

Guitarist-composer-bandleader John Scofield's (b. 1951) work is emblematic of contemporary jazz musicians as it has spanned an impressively wide stylistic range. As a result, Scofield's work in jazz and jazz fusion, as well as more R&B-influenced music, has made him a model for the younger generation of guitarists. Like so many of the musicians discussed in this chapter, Scofield attended Berklee College of Music. Early experiences include working with traditional jazz artists such as Gerry Mulligan and Chet Baker (Chapter 11, 1st Chorus), fusion-oriented bands such as the Billy Cobham–George Duke band, as well as playing with Charles Mingus. He quickly began to record as a leader and coleader, eventually recording over forty albums in these capacities as well as countless records as a side musician. His over 3 years of work with Miles Davis (Chapter 13, 1st Chorus) late in Davis's career thrust Scofield further into the spotlight. After leaving Davis, he continued to record as a solo artist as well as playing with other groups, including teaming up

QUESTIONS AND CONTROVERSIES
What Should We Call It?

Many of the musicians who play improvised music that is jazz or avant-garde jazz have difficulty with using the term "jazz" in relation to their music. Perhaps due to the controversies that arose during the 1980s and 1990s that pitted the neo-traditionalists against contemporary players (see Chapter 14, 3rd Chorus), they are wary of being classified as "jazz" musicians lest their music be critiqued for being not in line with more traditional forms. Plus, they want listeners to come to their work without any prejudices about what they might hear. Consequently, a number of these players refer to their music, for want of a better term, simply as "new music" or "improvised music." Some of these musicians are identified with the downtown scene of New York City (see Chapter 14, 4th Chorus) as well as the Brooklyn jazz and improvised music scene. To make matters more complicated, there are also international jazz-related styles that are difficult to categorize as jazz and classical musicians who improvise in a non-jazz style and also use the term "new music" to describe their work.

with guitarists Bill Frisell and Pat Metheny at various times. Scofield has moved back and forth freely between a more straight-ahead jazz approach and a funky soul jazz style, while playing with most of the top artists of the day, as well as collaborating with the eclectic contemporary classical composer Mark-Anthony Turnage.

The pretty and relaxed "Honest I Do," from *Grace Under Pressure* (1992), is a classic Scofield recording that pairs him with guitarist Bill Frisell. "Camelus," from Scofield's CD *Überjam Deux* (2013), shows Scofield in a very different mode, almost in a jam band context. The medium-tempo groove is funky and loose, and Scofield's playing shows his eclecticism as it mixes rock, funk, and jazz influences into his signature style.

2nd Chorus Horn Players

HOW HAVE THE CHANGES IN THE JAZZ SCENE IMPACTED HORN PLAYERS?

The role of horn players has changed very little: their primary role continues to be playing the melody and soloing, as well as playing additional background lines and harmonies. Stylistically, however, jazz continues to evolve and the array of approaches to playing increases, as do musicians' approaches to both business and self-promotion. This chorus briefly looks at some of today's horn stars, grouped by the type of instrument they play.

Saxophone and Clarinet

Alto saxophonist-composer-bandleader Steve Coleman (b. 1956) helped set the tone for the variety of jazz styles we see today. His early embrace of forms of African American popular music styles within a jazz context combined with his open and curious attitude about composition, improvisation, rhythm, and form have made him and his music an important part of the scene for many years. From Chicago, an early influence upon Coleman was the leading Chicago sax player Von

"Beba" (2010) by Steve Coleman and Five Elements

INSTRUMENTATION: Alto saxophone: Steve Coleman; **Trumpet:** Jonathan Finlayson; **Trombone:** Tim Albright; **Vocal:** Jen Shyu; **Bass:** Thomas Morgan; **Drums:** Tyshawn Sorey.

LISTENING HIGHLIGHT, RHYTHM: This is a head–solos–head arrangement with many interesting twists as the solos overlap and weave in and out of each other in a variety of ways. A dominant feature of this piano-less tune, however, is the interaction of the bass and drums as well as the overall approach they take. Morgan's bass line is syncopated throughout (he never walks), reminiscent of a funk bass line such as can be heard in "Cold Sweat" by funk–R&B vocalist-bandleader James Brown, an important influence on Coleman's music. Sorey's drumming also has a strong funk flavor. The effectiveness of their funk-influenced playing is even more remarkable considering that the tune is in an irregular meter yet sounds natural and funky. After an intro, the band plays an angular unison melody (including Shyu's wordless vocal texture). Coleman solos (1:16), and trombonist Albright gradually enters over him with pieces of the melody (1:42) before taking over the solo spot. Trumpeter Finlayson enters over Albright (2:56), and the others begin to chip in, creating a shifting polyphonic texture comprised of group improvisation. Sorey gets a drum solo (4:00) with the band playing small pieces of the melody behind him, while Morgan continues his bass line in support. The melody returns (5:12), this time with the original introduction superimposed over it (5:24).

Freeman, as well as Charlie Parker (Chapter 10, 1st Chorus). His main group has been Steve Coleman and Five Elements. In addition, along with vocalist Cassandra Wilson and saxophonist Greg Osby, Coleman was a cofounder of the M-Base Collective, a group of musicians dedicated to experimentation with improvisation and form, in any style, beyond the boundaries of what is accepted as the norm and that has neatly fused popular styles with avant-garde concepts. This can be heard on Coleman's "Beba," from *Harvesting Semblances and Affinities* (2010).

Coleman's career trajectory is interesting in that while he was fortunate to land early jobs with important bands such as the Thad Jones–Mel Lewis Big Band, he also spent a number of years playing for tips on the street to help make ends meet, a not uncommon source of revenue for musicians. Coleman has been prolific as a leader and a side musician, but he has also spent extensive time traveling and researching cultural and societal aspects of the African Diaspora with travels to, among numerous other places, Ghana, Senegal, and Cuba. Coleman is an outspoken and important spokesperson for underappreciated musicians as well as promoting experimentation. His extensive and well-documented thoughts on musical issues have made him an important music theorist, and he regularly teaches and runs workshops at a wide variety of schools and festivals. Coleman has an informative website on which he also offers much of his music for free download (www.m-base.com). Coleman was named a 2014 MacArthur Foundation Fellow.

Alto saxophonist-composer-bandleader Kenny Garrett (b. 1960) has taken a different, and more traditional, career path from other contemporary players within

Miguel Zenón in 2007. Saxophonist Zenón has championed Puerto Rican folkloric traditions, using them as the basis for contemporary compositions. Photo by Ulrich Fuchs.

© imageBROKER/Alamy.

the jazz field. An early experience with the Duke Ellington Orchestra (under the direction of Duke's son Mercer) set the tone for Garrett's embrace of the mainstream tradition in jazz as well as his desire to expand upon it, while Garrett's 5-year stint with Miles Davis during his electric period gave him extremely wide recognition. Garrett has recorded as a leader since 1984 while also working as a side musician with many top players and bands, including Art Blakey and trumpeters Freddie Hubbard and Woody Shaw. He has received a Grammy Award for his work with the Five Peace Band and Grammy nominations for his own records, including two nominations for *Seeds from the Underground* (2012). "J. Mac" from that album shows Garrett as a standard-bearer for the mainstream of jazz with its straight-ahead approach, intense extended solos, and nod to the style of the John Coltrane Quartet.

The Puerto Rican alto saxophonist-composer-bandleader Miguel Zenón (b. 1976), another jazz musician to have been named a MacArthur Fellow, has his own fascinating approach to tradition as well as to innovation. With albums such as *Jibaro* (2005) and *Esta Plena* (2010), Zenón has championed the rich Puerto Rican folkloric traditions while also using them as the basis for contemporary compositions. Zenón studied classical saxophone in Puerto Rico, graduated from Berklee College of Music, received a master's degree at the Manhattan School of Music, and has taught at countless schools and workshops. He was an original member of the all-star group SFJAZZ Collective, where he is currently co–artistic director, and has received numerous commissions for compositions. Zenón also founded Caravana Cultural, an organization dedicated to bringing high-level jazz and jazz workshops to rural Puerto Rico.

Tenor and soprano saxophonist Joe Lovano (b. 1952) is the veteran of this group and has been a leading saxophonist since the 1980s. His output, like that of his musical colleague guitarist Bill Frisell, is extremely varied, although in a different way because his playing primarily ties together numerous jazz styles. After attending Berklee College of Music, where he now teaches, Lovano established

"Silencio" (2011) by Miguel Zenón

INSTRUMENTATION: Alto saxophone, leader: Miguel Zenón; **Piano:** Luis Perdomo; **Bass:** Claus Glawischnig; **Drums:** Henry Cole; **Conductor, orchestrator:** Guillermo Klein. (A large woodwind ensemble augments his quartet for this recording.)

LISTENING HIGHLIGHT, STYLE: On "Silencio" the complex and demanding harmonies, forms, meters, and rhythmic approaches show the virtuosity of Zenón's long-standing quartet. It appears on the album *Alma Adentro* (2011), which celebrates the compositions of five important Puerto Rican composers, including Rafael Hernández, the composer of this work. As with his drawing on traditional material, Zenón uses the composers' works as the basis for further compositional and improvisational investigation, including altering the metrical structure and form of the compositions. The arrangement begins and ends with a repeated melodic line and, as is typical of Zenón's music, extensively uses unison vamps by the bass and piano. While he captures the romantic quality of the melody with a warm sound, Zenón's tone typically has a bright and edgy sound, which he moves to as his solo progresses. He often pushes the tempo with an aggressive rhythmic approach that is right on top of the beat.

solid jazz credentials through his work as a side musician, beginning with organ trios, John Scofield's band, and the Woody Herman and Mel Lewis (formerly Thad Jones–Mel Lewis) big bands. Lovano has helped to set the stage for today's players with his interest and ability in moving smoothly from avant-garde, such as his work with Bill Frisell and Paul Motian (this chapter, 1st Chorus, "Wednesday" from *Time and Time Again*) to his understated chamber jazz album *Celebrating Sinatra* (1996) to a free-wheeling, contemporary straight-ahead style with *Cross Culture* (2013) by his versatile group Us Five. *Cross Culture* features bassist Esperanza Spalding and guitarist Lionel Loueke (both discussed in the 1st Chorus). "Blessings in May" from that album is an excellent example of Lovano's intriguing combination of precision and looseness on two different types of saxophones. Along with this, he has a very personal tone that is round and dark with an air of both burliness and gentleness.

Tenor and soprano saxophonist Joshua Redman (b. 1969) is a product of the Berkeley (California) High School jazz program and the son of the well-known avant-garde saxophonist Dewey Redman. After graduating from Harvard, Redman won the prestigious Thelonious Monk Jazz Saxophone competition in 1991, which led to a recording contract, setting him on his path to becoming one of the important saxophonists of his generation. While establishing himself as a leader early in his career, he has also worked as a side musician and collaborator with his contemporaries, such as Brad Mehldau (this chapter, 1st Chorus), Brian Blade (this chapter, 1st Chorus), trumpeter Roy Hargrove, and Christian McBride (this chapter, 1st Chorus). Redman also helped found the all-star group SFJAZZ Collective and acted as artistic director for it. Redman's album of ballads *Walking Shadows* (2013) features pianist Mehldau, who also produced the record;

listening focus

DOWNLOAD
Track Number 37

"The Folks Who Live on the Hill" (2013) by Joshua Redman

INSTRUMENTATION: Tenor saxophone, leader: Joshua Redman; **Piano:** Brad Mehldau; **Bass:** Larry Grenadier; **Drums:** Brian Blade: **Conductor, orchestrator:** Dan Coleman.

LISTENING HIGHLIGHT, STYLE: In this lovely standard ballad, we hear Redman with his quartet and string orchestra. Redman's tone is full and rich, and his playing here is a classic example of how soloists handle ballad material, such as we heard with Coleman Hawkins on "Body and Soul" (Chapter 5, 3rd Chorus). After an extended string introduction with Redman playing fills, Redman plays the first A (0:51) in a straightforward, simple rendition to let us hear the melody. For the second A (1:37) we still hear the melody, but it is now in a different octave; and he adds fills between his own phrases and elaborates on the melody. At the bridge (2:24) he again gives us a simple reading. The last A (2:51) sees him combining a clear melodic presentation with ornamentation and fills between phrases, while the energy and intensity are raised to take the tune out. The quartet plays simply and in an understated fashion, and the lush string arrangement provides a warm chordal pad to accompany Redman throughout as he largely lets this pretty tune and gorgeous arrangement speak for itself.

drummer Brian Blade; and bassist Larry Grenadier. The lovely standard "The Folks Who Live on the Hill" presents Redman as a lyrical soloist with his quartet and a string section.

Tenor, alto, and soprano saxophonist Chris Potter (b. 1971) has blazed from being a saxophone prodigy to holding a leading position in jazz. He has perhaps the most impressive "chops" on his instrument today, following the lead of saxophonist Michael Brecker (Chapter 14, 2nd Chorus). In New York City, Potter attended the New School for Jazz and Contemporary Music and the Manhattan School of Music. Potter is most known for his work in an acoustic setting but also plays in more electronically oriented bands. Besides his fifteen albums as a leader, Potter's versatility and ability have led him to record countless records as a side musician with a wide variety of artists, such as drummer Paul Motian, pianist Joanne Brackeen (he was nominated for a Grammy for his playing on her *Pink Elephant Magic* album), trumpeter Dave Douglas, bassist Dave Holland, and the pop–jazz group Steely Dan.

Potter displays a phenomenal technical ability that, mixed with his sensitive musicality, makes for a muscly, intense, and expressive style. His playing on "Breakdealer," from Pat Metheny's *Unity Band*, shows this virtuosity and fluidity all over his horn in a very impressive and hard-driving manner. *Sirens* (2013) is a concept album of his own compositions inspired by Homer's *Odyssey*. Besides his sax playing, the album features his work on bass clarinet.

The clarinet has always been an important part of the jazz tradition, but after the swing era its popularity among musicians, at least as a primary instrument, seemed to wane somewhat. The clarinet recently has seen an increased place in jazz, in both traditional and more avant-garde surroundings.

read all about it

"The Jazz Left" by Herman S. Gray

Walser, **Keeping Time,** *Chapter 68*

In this essay, Gray suggests that musicians like Don Byron and Greg Osby offer an alternate approach to jazz performance and composition from the neo-classicism of Wynton Marsalis and others.

From Tel Aviv, Israel, clarinetist-saxophonist-bandleader Anat Cohen (b. 1975) exudes joy as she seems to play the clarinet effortlessly and with a graceful swing, regardless of the musical context. Since moving to the United States in 1996, Cohen has quickly risen to the top of the jazz world as one of its premier clarinetists. Cohen attended the Berklee College of Music, where, along with her jazz studies, she became acquainted with musical styles of Latin America. After moving to New York City, she played in numerous bands in various styles, including an all-woman big band (the Diva Jazz Orchestra), the Choro Ensemble (a group specializing in that Brazilian style led by cavaquinho player Pedro Ramos), and Duduka Da Fonseca's Samba Jazz Quintet. Her album *Claroscuro* (2012), recorded with her touring band consisting of pianist Jason Lindner, bassist Joe Martin, and drummer Daniel Freedman, also features guest artists such as the Cuban clarinetist-saxophonist-composer Paquito D'Rivera and trombonist Wycliffe Gordon. In addition to clarinet, Cohen plays tenor sax, soprano sax, and bass clarinet on the record; and the album exhibits a wide range of material with jazz, Afro-Cuban, and Brazilian influences. Cohen also works with her two brothers, trumpeter Avishai and saxophonist Yuval, performing as the 3 Cohens Sextet.

The clarinetist-composer-bandleader Don Byron (b. 1958) celebrates his eclecticism with an always surprising stream of projects. His albums and many performing projects have examined the **klezmer music** of Mickey Katz, Byron's Afro-Caribbean heritage, the swing music of swing-band leaders Raymond Scott and John Kirby, and funk and hip-hop. His compositions have blurred the lines between Western classical art songs and popular songs. *Love, Peace, and Soul* (2012) introduced Byron's group, the New Gospel Quintet, which celebrates the gospel music of Thomas A. Dorsey and Sister Rosetta Thorpe. Byron has written music for classical ensembles as well; his *7 Etudes for Piano* was a finalist for the Pulitzer Prize. He has been a professor at the State University of New York–Albany as well as the Massachusetts Institute of Technology and has led numerous clinics and residencies.

Trumpet

It is hard to imagine a more productive musician than trumpeter-composer-bandleader-entrepreneur Dave Douglas (b. 1963). He first gained attention as a side musician working with Horace Silver (Chapter 11, 2nd Chorus), and his early work with John Zorn (Chapter 14, 4th Chorus) also brought him wide recognition. Since the mid-1980s, he has recorded and released many records as a leader in an almost stream-of-consciousness manner, allowing us to see him grow and evolve as a player and composer. Douglas is a model for the notion of creating different types of groups to present a rich variety of creative projects. Many of his projects have different instrumentations, as well as different inspirations that might draw from a novelist's work, poetry, the work of a particular musician or musical style, or the desire to explore new timbres. His composing and playing, however, no matter what the context, always sound personal and are immediately recognizable as his work.

Douglas seems to compose quickly and tirelessly, and the range of musical and cultural influences he draws from is vast. He works in both acoustic and electronic mediums. His group Keystone mixes both styles with trumpet, sax, and drums on the acoustic side and Fender Rhodes electric piano, an upright electric bass, and the well-known turntablist DJ Olive representing the electronic side. "Spark of

Being" from *Spark of Being: Expand* (2010) is the result of a multimedia collaboration with experimental filmmaker Bill Morrison; it is a contemplative soundscape mixed with a languorous melody and free improvisations.

Along with this, Douglas is in the forefront of creating new models for the presentation and dissemination of his work, as well as the work of other musicians, through his independent web-based music company Greenleaf Music. He uses a variety of interesting methods to bring listeners to his music such as streaming concerts free of charge, posting quickly created musical projects only intended for streaming, and hosting contests such as creating mash-ups of his music, as well as more traditional models of selling CDs and downloads of his work and that of other artists on his label.

Trumpeter-composer-bandleader Nicholas Payton (b. 1973) is both enigmatic and an open book. His music is unpredictable, ranging from straight-ahead to R&B; and he blogs straightforwardly, to say the least, about controversial subjects ranging from music to race to sex, seemingly without concern for reception. Payton has coined a term, "BAM"—for black American music—as a preferable term for much of African American music, including jazz. His blog post "On Why Jazz Isn't Cool Anymore" set off a great deal of interesting, and at times acrimonious, public debate.

From a musical family in New Orleans, Payton had early experiences in the New Orleans brass-band tradition, which led to work with New Orleans legends such as guitarist Danny Barker, pianist-producer Allen Toussaint, and Dr. John. Payton went on to work as a side musician with numerous top jazz artists as well as the SFJAZZ collective and has released to date twelve albums as a leader. His albums reflect his eclectic approach: a collaboration with the legendary trumpet player Doc Cheatham that won a Grammy award; *Bitches* (2011), an R&B-oriented album on which Payton plays all of the instruments and sings; and a recreation of the classic Miles Davis–Gil Evans collaboration *Sketches of Spain* (2013). "The Crimson Touch," a pretty, long-lined, and rhythmically surprising tune from *Into the Blue* (2008), brings together jazz and a funk feel in a natural manner, exemplifying this generation's increasing interest in fully accepting and incorporating all of their musical roots.

Trumpeter-composer-bandleader Terence Blanchard (b. 1962) is also from New Orleans. After studying at Rutgers University, Blanchard came to the public's attention in 1982 when he replaced Wynton Marsalis (Chapter 14, 3rd Chorus) in Art Blakey's Jazz Messengers (Chapter 11, 2nd Chorus). He then co-led a successful quintet with his Blakey band mate, saxophonist Donald Harrison, for several years; and they were among a group of young musicians who fueled an interest in straight-ahead jazz in the 1980s. Blanchard's career took another turn when he began to write film scores for Spike Lee, beginning with *Jungle Fever*; and he has composed scores for Lee's films since then, as well as for other directors.

Blanchard has continued to perform and record prolifically with his own band, which has carried on the tradition of Art Blakey as an incubator for young talent. He was the artistic director of the Thelonious Monk Institute of Jazz at the University of Southern California for 10 years and is currently the artistic director for Jazz at the Mancini Institute at the University of Miami Frost School of Music. Blanchard has won five Grammy Awards in various categories. His opera, *Champion*, was premiered in 2013; and he has composed music for Broadway musical productions.

listening focus

"Child's Play" (2005) by Terence Blanchard

INSTRUMENTATION: Trumpet, leader: Terence Blanchard; **Saxophone, composer:** Brice Winston; **Piano:** Aaron Parks; **Bass:** Derrick Hodge; **Drums:** Kendrick Scott; **Vocals:** Gretchen Parlato.

LISTENING HIGHLIGHT, STYLE: "Child's Play" is from the album *Flow* (2005), which was produced by Herbie Hancock and featured Blanchard's working group at the time that included Derrick Hodge (this chapter, 1st Chorus) as well as guest Lionel Loueke (this chapter, introduction). While Blanchard is generally associated with a throwback traditionalism, his music has taken on numerous new dimensions, at times propelled by the young musicians in his band. "Child's Play" has a lovely melody that includes wordless vocals by Gretchen Parlato used as an instrumental timbre. Blanchard and Parks's solos have a straight-ahead sensibility that is deconstructed in character as the rhythm section freely breaks the time up throughout. The piece begins and ends with the rhythm section playing a long and abstract melodic line.

3rd Chorus Vocalists

HOW HAVE VOCALISTS EXTENDED THEIR TECHNIQUE TO SUIT THEIR WORK IN CONTEMPORARY JAZZ?

Vocalists have always been an integral part of jazz. This tradition continues with vocalists being an exciting and important part of today's scene. As is true with instrumentalists, jazz singers are investigating a wide variety of musical material including the extensive use of wordless vocals—transforming the singers into instrumentalists—as well as working in styles ranging from jazz to popular genres while also effectively combining them. Each vocalist discussed here represents a different strain of the jazz world.

The Canadian vocalist-pianist-bandleader Diana Krall (b. 1964) carries on a long tradition of female pianist-vocalists such as Carmen McCrae, Nina Simone, and Shirley Horn. Krall has been able to appeal to a wide audience, making her one of the very top-selling artists in the jazz field. Krall is so popular that on her tours she frequently plays large theaters, festivals, and concert venues, as opposed to clubs. She is an excellent jazz pianist and was hired to play on and bring extra credibility to Paul McCartney's album of standards, *Kisses at the Bottom* (2012).

The Girl in the Other Room (2004) is a collaboration with her husband, the eclectic British guitarist-composer Elvis Costello. It examines Krall's emotional state as she deals with the death of her mother. While Krall is primarily known for her performance of jazz standards, her "I'm Coming Through" from this album shows her in a very different musical environment that blends jazz and a pop sensibility seamlessly. The twists and turns in the song's melody are reminiscent of Costello's wry pop sensibility, along with the melancholic edge to the lyrics. Her smooth vocals are in a relatively low range and generally have a quiet, intimate feel with a relaxed swing.

Vocalist-composer-bandleader Cassandra Wilson (b. 1955) has been an important musician on the jazz scene for many years. She has won two Grammy awards, including Best Jazz Vocal Album for *Loverly* (2008), an album of standards and blues, and has released over twenty albums as a leader. Along with her early and continued work with Steve Coleman and the M-Base Collective, Wilson has performed on countless records for other leaders, including many we've studied, such as Wynton Marsalis (his Pulitzer Prize–winning *Blood on the Fields* featured Wilson), Terence Blanchard, Bill Frisell, and Terri Lyne Carrington. Her vocal style is very personal and idiosyncratic with an instrumental quality, including her use of scat singing, in the vein of vocalists Betty Carter, Nina Simone, and Abbey Lincoln. Wilson is comfortable in a straight-ahead or avant-garde context. As her career has progressed, she has continually expanded her stylistic range to include pop, blues, and country music, while bringing them all together into a stylistic whole that makes her sound unmistakable.

From Chicago, vocalist-lyricist-composer-bandleader Kurt Elling (b. 1967) represents a traditional approach to jazz singing, while he is also known for effectively transforming material from other styles of music to a jazz idiom. He also carries the mantle of the tradition of creating lyrics to the solos of jazz instrumentalists, a medium referred to as **vocalese**, originally perfected by vocalists such as Eddie Jefferson, King Pleasure, and Jon Hendricks. Elling's career had a different trajectory from most artists we have seen. He built a following in Chicago with weekly gigs at a popular jazz club, the Green Mill; and a demo recording landed him a major contract with Blue Note Records. Since then he has released ten albums as a leader and won a Grammy Award for Best Jazz Vocal Album for *Dedicated to You: Kurt Elling Sings the Music of Coltrane and Hartman.* Elling's voice can extend well beyond his normal baritone range, and he has a masculine sound that is almost rough-hewn at times while also being gentle and

Cassandra Wilson, 2009. Wilson is one of the best of the new generation of jazz vocalists.
© Daniel Vrabec/Alamy.

listening focus

"Blackbird" (2010) by Cassandra Wilson

INSTRUMENTATION: Vocalist, leader: Cassandra Wilson; **Piano:** Jonathan Batiste; **Guitar:** Marvin Sewell; **Bass:** Reginald Veal; **Drums:** Herlin Riley; **Percussion:** Lekan Babalola.

LISTENING HIGHLIGHT, STYLE: Wilson's version of the Beatles' "Blackbird" on *Silver Pony* (2010) is an excellent example of the use of pop material in a contemporary jazz context. Wilson and the band transform the song so significantly that it cannot be referred to as a "cover." Not only do they give it a different character and rhythmic treatment but they also change the song slightly and add a vamp section at times for solos. Most significantly, they have a series of solos, giving this pop tune the feel of a jazz tune. Over a light, rolling Latin percussion groove, the texture is dominated by Marvin Sewell's electric guitar, with first a repeated figure and then a bluesy solo. After a piano solo, Wilson plays with the words and phrases, turning them into an understated jazz solo. Wilson's rich, smoky voice here is gentle and fluid; and her rhythmic phrasing is loose, floating over the band as it creates a sparkly pop–jazz environment to accompany her.

emotional. On "She's Funny That Way," from *This Time It's Love* (1998), Elling, after beginning the recording with the verse of the song (1:09), sings a vocalese rendition of saxophonist Lester Young's (Chapter 6, 4th Chorus) well-known solo; Elling wrote additional lyrics for both the tune and Young's solo. On *The Gate* (2011), Elling created a swinging version of pop–rock star Joe Jackson's tune "Steppin' Out."

The German-born vocalist-composer-bandleader Theo Bleckmann (b. 1966) represents a different part of the music spectrum, so much so that identifying him as a jazz singer almost does not seem appropriate given the range of material that he performs and records. He does, however, represent an important trend of musicians who might better be referred to simply as "improvisers" since their range of activities extends well beyond the jazz realm. For example, Bleckmann has sung backup with performance artist–pop singer Laurie Anderson; recorded an album of German art songs (in German); performed with a number of drummer John Hollenbeck's groups (this chapter, introduction), singing standards or as a wordless instrumental texture; sung Las Vegas lounge songs with a string quartet; tackled art songs by the American classical composer Charles Ives with the improvisational jazz–funk group Kneebody (this chapter, 5th Chorus); performed poems and songs solo in a monastery in the Swiss Alps; and interpreted the songs of pop star Kate Bush. In fact, there is no telling what he might do next. Numerous composers have written for Bleckmann's light and flexible voice, which he often uses without vibrato. "Hymenium," from Bleckmann's duet album *At Night* (2007) with his frequent collaborator, the experimental jazz guitarist Ben Monder, features a lovely wordless vocal over beautiful and intense shifting guitar harmonies.

4th Chorus Strings

HOW DOES THE POPULARITY OF STRINGS IN JAZZ TODAY REFLECT A NEW INTEREST IN MORE VARIED INSTRUMENTATION?

In contemporary jazz there is room for any instrument, and band instrumentations are becoming more varied all the time. The expanded use of strings is one example of this. While it has been present in jazz throughout its history, the violin has stayed largely on the margins, with only a few instrumentalists able to use it successfully in a jazz context. Stéphane Grapelli, Stuff Smith, Ray Nance, Joe Venuti, Jean-Luc Ponty, and Leroy Jenkins are a few who have excelled. And aside from bassists such as Ron Carter, Ray Brown, Oscar Pettiford, Charles Mingus (who doubled on cello), and the cellist Fred Katz (who performed with the Chico Hamilton Quintet, a popular West Coast band in the late 1950s), there is little precedent for the cello in jazz as a solo instrument.

Violinist Regina Carter (b. 1966), another MacArthur Fellow, began classical violin studies as a child, including master classes with Itzhak Perlman and Yehudi Menuhin. While attending the New England Conservatory of Music, one of the country's most prestigious conservatories, Carter's interest shifted to jazz. As a freelance violinist she worked with a range of performers such as soul and R&B artists Aretha Franklin and Mary J. Blige and the String Trio of New York, an avant-garde jazz chamber group, while also beginning a solo career during which she has released numerous albums as a leader. In addition, like Cassandra Wilson, she gained recognition performing Wynton Marsalis's work *Blood on the Fields*. Her album *Reverse Thread* (2010) consists of interpretations of African folk melodies and has an unusual instrumentation consisting of violin, kora (a traditional West African string instrument), guitar, accordion, bass, drums, and percussion.

Regina Carter in 2001. Violinist Carter is a leader in contemporary jazz performance and composition.
© Craig Lovell/Eagle Visions Photography/Alamy.

"Full Time" (2010) by Regina Carter

INSTRUMENTATION: Violin: Regina Carter; **Accordion:** Gary Versace; **Bass:** Mamadou Ba; **Drums:** Alvester Garnett; **Kora:** Yacouba Sissoko.

LISTENING HIGHLIGHT, STYLE: Carter begins with a unique instrumentation, using accordion in her rhythm section instead of piano or guitar. For this tune she adds a traditional African 21-stringed instrument, the kora, to the mix as she examines a fusion of jazz, traditional African music, and Afro-pop, a contemporary African pop style, creating a fascinating international blend of styles. The piece is in a funky 6/8, initially driven by drummer Garnett and Senegalese bass player Ba with help from Sissoko, who plays a repetitive montuno-like vamp on the kora. The melody is essentially a long series of riffs that repeat until Carter's solo (2:08). Her solo is jazzy but also digs into the rhythmic style of the rhythm section. After a unison break by the whole band (2:55), the feel changes and mellows out for Sissoko's kora solo. It's in time, but the rhythm section plays sparingly and gently behind him. Carter sneaks in over a Sissoko vamp (4:11) and solos again over the mellower groove before taking the tune out with a gradual building up of intensity (5:08).

Mark Feldman (b. 1955) is a violinist and composer who has been performing and recording internationally with jazz and new music groups on a steady basis for many years. Feldman has released numerous albums as a leader; has worked and recorded extensively with saxophonist John Zorn (Chapter 14, 4th Chorus), trumpeter Dave Douglas (this chapter, 2nd Chorus), and guitarist John Abercrombie; and has been a featured soloist with classical orchestras as well as the WDR Jazz Orchestra from Germany. He is a regular presence on jazz and new music recordings as a side musician and early in his career was a performer and session violinist in Nashville, performing with Loretta Lynn and Ray Price while also recording with the likes of Johnny Cash and Willie Nelson. While his *White Exit* (2006) is clearly a jazz quartet album, Feldman doesn't shy away from displaying violin technique or a chamber music aesthetic that borrow from traditional and contemporary classical music. For example, "Ink Pin" has elements of a classical violin sonata with its virtuosic solo violin cadenzas, careful counterpoint, and blazingly fast solo and unison lines played by piano and violin; but it also features sections with elements of both mainstream and free jazz, creating a fascinating and natural-sounding fusion of styles.

Erik Friedlander (b. 1960) has carved out a niche for himself as a top improvising cellist across several genres, including jazz, and is a fixture on the New York downtown scene (see Chapter 14, 4th Chorus). Like Feldman, his stylistic range and ability to handle seemingly any musical context have made him a constant presence in certain areas of the jazz world. Friedlander has numerous albums as a leader to his credit and has been a frequent collaborator of Mark Feldman and John Zorn. His solo album *Block Ice & Propane* (2007) expresses his impressions of America through a musical investigation of his family's road trips. *Bonebridge* (2011) features Friedlander with a quartet that includes slide guitar and interprets music of the American South. Both albums give us a picture of his inventiveness as a composer and instrumentalist working across genre boundaries.

5th Chorus Small Groups and Big Bands

HOW HAVE SMALL GROUPS AND BANDS—FROM MUSICIANS' COLLECTIVES TO BIG BANDS—SHAPED THE NEW JAZZ LANDSCAPE?

A growing trend in contemporary jazz is the collective, groups that have no leader. Some have traditional instrumentations, while others have unique combinations of instruments. The collective Kneebody has the traditional instrumentation of a jazz quintet—trumpeter Shane Endsley, saxophonist Ben Wendel, keyboardist Adam Benjamin, electric bassist Kaveh Rastegar, and drummer Nate Wood—but uses electronics to create new timbres. Kneebody draws from straight-ahead jazz, avant-garde jazz, rock, and funk. As an example, "Never Remember," from *Kneebody* (2005), deftly combines numerous elements that could seem disparate, such as jazz horn lines, a rock-like vamp, and pop–funk horn lines and accompaniment, into a cohesive whole.

Saxophonist-composer-bandleader Henry Threadgill (b. 1944) has been a powerful presence on the avant-garde scene since the 1970s and was one of the early members of the Association for the Advancement of Creative Musicians (Chapter 12, 3rd Chorus). Threadgill was a member of the popular avant-garde trio Air and has consistently continued his cross-genre explorations through his long and extremely productive career. He has led a variety of bands with different instrumentations, such as his seven-piece Very Very Circus and the twenty-piece Society Situation Band. His recent group, Zooid, features an interesting lineup of Threadgill on saxophone and flute, cellist Christopher Hoffman, tuba player Jose Davila, Liberty Ellman on guitar, Stomy Takeishi on bass guitar, and drummer Elliot Humberto Kavee. From the album *Tomorrow Sunny/The Revelry, Spp* (2012), "Tomorrow Sunny" is an example of the balance Threadgill finds between freedom (improvisation) and organization (composition), a trait that has made him one of the more successful composers of the avant-garde. The piece has many elements including free jazz along with melodies that call to mind contemporary classical music, all over hints of a funk beat.

While big bands have not been as popular or present as in the swing era, there has been a relatively recent resurgence of interest in the medium, largely through the influence of trombonist-composer-educator Bob Brookmeyer (1929–2011). Following in the footsteps of Gil Evans's colorful writing, Brookmeyer, along with composer-arrangers such as Jim McNeeley, have expanded the possibilities of big-band composing through their own writing and their influence as composition teachers. Building on the riff tradition of jazz, much of Brookmeyer's focus was on the use of musical motives—bits of musical material—to create extended compositions.

Composer-bandleader Darcy James Argue (b. 1975) is an example of today's younger big-band composers who concentrate on tightly controlled, extended composition and ensemble playing. These composers are in essence creating a new big-band tradition based on the old but with distinctly new values, such as the extensive use of odd and shifting meters. The release of *Infernal Machines* (2009) by his big band, Darcy James Argue's Secret Society, brought him to the public's attention. His band has been generating excitement through performances and their involvement in numerous projects, and Argue is receiving commissions from other ensembles while also commissioning work by other composers for his band. *Brooklyn Babylon* (2013), originally conceived as a multimedia collaboration, is an extended suite that, through music, considers the changes in Brooklyn through the process of gentrification. "Builders" creates a varied sonic environment, including an electronically enhanced extended trumpet solo, portraying the fraught growth process of the New York City borough.

Composer-arranger-bandleader Maria Schneider (b. 1960) has led a large ensemble since the early 1990s. Her primary early influence was the arranger Gil Evans, for whom she worked in the 1980s; and the coloristic and environmental aspect of her work reflects this. Schneider has a master's degree from the Eastman School of Music and studied extensively with Bob Brookmeyer.

Schneider won the Best Instrumental Composition Grammy Award in 2007 for her extended work "Cerulean Skies" from the album *Sky Blue* (2007). From that album, "Sky Blue" exemplifies her extremely lyrical sensibility, which gives her work a gentle quality that envelops the listener in her pieces, as well as her ability to weave the band's soloists in and out of the texture in a very effective manner. Her work continues to expand in scope, including commissions from numerous classical ensembles as well as the classical and crossover vocalist Dawn Upshaw, resulting in the album *Winter Morning Walks* (2013) that won three Grammy Awards, cementing Schneider's status as a composer across genres. Schneider is also an early adopter of alternate methods of commercial distribution through her participation in ArtistShare, an organization that elicits funding through fan participation in the compositional and production process. *Concert in the Garden* (2004) was the first album solely distributed through the Internet to win a Grammy Award.

Conclusion

Throughout this chapter we have explored many musicians, groups, and styles in an attempt to give a broad picture of the exciting state of jazz today. Ideally, along with a solid foundation in the history of jazz and its various styles, you also have an appreciation and understanding of how it has evolved to the open and broad musical genre that it is today. Hopefully, you are also inspired to adopt an open attitude not only to jazz but to all styles of music as you continue your own musical journey.

CODA Chapter Summary

What Distinguishes Today's Jazz from That of Earlier Periods?
Among contemporary jazz's distinguishing features are the following:
- *Rhythm*: There is more use of varying meters within a single piece as well as the use of odd meters.
- *Instrumental Roles*: Accompanying instruments are treated more equally with the lead instruments.
- *Instrumental Groupings*: There is a more varied and eclectic use of instruments in different ensembles. Leaders often form different groups with lineups to suit the music that they wish to perform.

- *Virtuosity and versatility:* Instrumentalists have excellent training and are able to play in a wider variety of styles than in the past.
- *The Role of Composition:* Although still emphasizing improvisation, composition is coming to the fore as a means of structuring performances.
- *Influence of World Music:* Composers and performers are bringing their own heritages to bear on their work or consciously borrowing from other musical traditions.
- *Eclecticism:* Many contemporary jazz artists draw on various musical traditions to create music that transcends easy categorization.

How Has the Role of the Rhythm Section Changed in Contemporary Jazz?

- Bass, guitar, piano, and drums are taking a more prominent role in contemporary jazz.
- Drummers handle more varied rhythms and many more performance styles than in the past.
- Bass players have to be technically fluent on both acoustic and electric basses. Their melody lines can be complex, in both melodic and rhythmic content, making them equal partners in the texture.
- Pianists are expected to master electric keyboards and synthesizers. They often are called on to provide a basic texture or sound "pad" for the melody instruments.
- Guitarists generally are able to play in rock, funk, and jazz styles. They make greater use of electronic effects (such as reverb, distortion, and feedback) than traditional jazz guitarists.

How Have the Changes in the Jazz Scene Impacted Horn Players?

- Horn players continue to take their traditional role as the primary lead soloists in most ensembles.
- However, they have also been influenced by the increased emphasis on creating new forms, mastering eclectic styles (including rock and funk), and working with electronics and alternate timbres.

How Have Vocalists Extended Their Technique to Suit Their Work in Contemporary Jazz?

- Vocalists have drawn on a variety of traditions, including rock and popular styles, to extend the range of jazz vocal technique.
- Vocalists have built on traditions like the use of scat and vocalese to make the voice an equal to the other melody instruments.
- Vocalists have also experimented with different textures to add to the overall sound of a piece.

How Does the Popularity of Strings in Jazz Today Reflect a New Interest in More Varied Instrumentation?

- Unlike in the past when there were only a few string players on the jazz scene, today numerous players from classical and jazz backgrounds have been able to establish themselves as composers and performers.
- Going beyond the traditional violin, cello players have also made their mark in jazz.

How Have Small Groups and Bands—From Musicians'
Collectives to Big Bands—Shaped the New Jazz Landscape?

- Musicians are increasingly forming leaderless collectives to explore different styles of music.
- The big band tradition has been re-energized, giving new life to larger ensembles.

Talkin' Jazz (Key Terms)

Ethnomusicology	Odd time signatures	Strophic form
Feedback	Pads	Vocalese
Impressionism	Pizzicato strings	
Klezmer music	Strophe	

Key People

Lionel Loueke	Geri Allen	Nicholas Payton
Dafnis Prieto	Robert Glasper	Terence Blanchard
Danilo Pérez	Bill Frisell	Diana Krall
Ben Allison	Kurt Rosenwinkel	Cassandra Wilson
Chris Dave	John Scofield	Kurt Elling
Terri Lyne Carrington	Steve Coleman	Theo Bleckmann
Brian Blade	Miguel Zenón	Regina Carter
Esperanza Spalding	Joe Lovano	Mark Feldman
Christian McBride	Joshua Redman	Erik Friedlander
Jason Moran	Chris Potter	Kneebody
Brad Mehldau	Anat Cohen	Darcy James Argue
Renee Rosnes	Don Byron	Maria Schneider
Vijay Iyer	Dave Douglas	

Think About This (For Further Discussion and Study)

1. What do you notice that's different about today's jazz and jazz musicians?
2. Now that you have heard so much music, what characterizations can you make regarding the jazz of today in relation to the jazz of the past? Pick three artists and compare them with artists from earlier periods.
3. Discuss the ascendency of the rhythm section in relation to the jazz of today.
4. What differences and similarities do you see between today's vocalists and the singers we listened to earlier?
5. Compare big-band music of today with big-band music from earlier periods.
6. What kinds of relationships do you hear between the jazz of today and the music that you are familiar with?

GLOSSARY

A

"ALL-GIRL" BANDS: Bands staffed by women that were popular during the swing era

ALTERNATE CHANGES: Alternate chord progressions. *See also* **changes**

ARPEGGIATING: Singing or playing the individual notes of a chord sequentially as an **arpeggio**

ARPEGGIO: Breaking a chord into its individual notes that are played sequentially rather than simultaneously

ARRANGING: Assigning specific instrumental parts for the performance of a musical composition

ARTICULATION: How musicians attack, sustain, and release a note

AVANT-GARDE: Literally the "front line"; artists who are interested in freeing themselves and their art from accepted traditions. *See also* **free jazz**

B

BACKBEAT: The accents on beats 2 and 4 in 4/4 time

BANJO: A stringed instrument with a drum-like body and a long, fretted neck

BASS: A low-pitched stringed instrument similar to either a large violin or large guitar

BATTLE OF THE BANDS: Contest in which two bands compete with each other to see which can produce the most driving, danceable music

BEAT: Division of musical time into regular repeating units

BIG BAND: A flexible term for a large band that can indicate anywhere from approximately 10 to 40 pieces

"BLACK AND TAN" CLUBS: Integrated nightclubs that allowed both whites and blacks in their audiences

BLOCK-CHORD STYLE: A two-handed approach to playing the piano that involves playing a harmonized melody with both hands moving parallel and held in an almost locked position

BLUE NOTE: A slightly flattened scale note, usually the 3rd and 5th note in the scale

BLUES: A song style that developed in the mid-to-late nineteenth century that often expressed sad or melancholy feelings and features a standard 12-bar structure. *See also* **classic blues**, **country or folk blues**, **12-bar blues**, **urban or electric blues**

BOOGALOO: A Latin popular dance/music style that combines a chachachá groove with a backbeat on 2 and 4

BOOGIE-WOOGIE: A rocking and exciting blues piano style that features a constant and aggressively hard-driving, rolling, repeated left-hand figure, which gained popularity among musicians in Kansas City

BOSSA NOVA: Literally, "new flair"; bossa nova combined elements of **samba** with jazz to create a sophisticated, highly melodic music

BREAK: A rhythmic or melodic figure either played by a soloist as the band stops playing or that the band plays together

C

CABARET CARD: Under New York City law, all musicians had to have a license to perform in nightclubs where liquor was served. The cabaret card had to be renewed every 2 years, and any felony (such as an arrest for drug use) could lead to the card being withdrawn. Without a card, a musician could not make a living performing in New York. The law was finally repealed in 1967.

CADENZA: A written or improvised solo passage that highlights one particular player's virtuosity

CHACHACHÁ: A medium-tempo Latin dance style

CHANGES: The chord (or harmonic) progression of a musical composition

CHARANGA: A Latin music ensemble that features flute and violin

CHARTS: Parts and arrangements for a jazz band

CHOPS: Musical skills or prowess

CHORD PROGRESSION: A sequence of chords that creates the harmonic accompaniment to a melody and solos

CLARINET: An instrument that is generally made of hard wood, is part of the woodwind family, and is played with a reed attached to a mouthpiece in the same manner as the saxophone

CLASSIC BLUES: Popular form of the **blues** performed primarily by female singers in traveling shows and on the vaudeville stage

CLAVE: A repeated 2-bar rhythmic pattern upon which Afro-Cuban music is based

COLLECTIVE IMPROVISATION: A style of performance in which band members improvise their individual parts to create a loosely structured arrangement

COMBO: A small instrumental group

COMP: Short for "accompanies"; refers to a pianist or guitarist playing the chord progression in support of a soloist

COMPOSING (OR ARRANGING): The creation of a musical work

COMPOSITION: A musical work created by a single individual or composer

CONCEPT ALBUM: A record album on which the songs are selected to reflect a single theme or idea

CONGUERO: A player of the conga drums

CONTRAPUNTAL WRITING: Composing featuring two or more distinct melodies played simultaneously in **counterpoint**

COOL JAZZ: As a reaction to the high energy of bebop, cool jazz developed, taking a more relaxed, laid-back approach, with performers and arrangers drawing on classical influences to create smoother melodies played with less vibrato, contrapuntal lines, and harmonically dense accompaniments

CORNET: A member of the trumpet family that appears smaller than a trumpet and has a more veiled, warmer tone and that does not have the cutting quality of a trumpet

COUNTERLINE/COUNTERMELODY: A second, contrasting melody played to accompany the main melodic line of a composition

COUNTERPOINT: Playing two or more contrasting melodies simultaneously

COUNTRY OR FOLK BLUES: Blues songs typically performed by a solo musician playing guitar and singing

CREOLE: A person of mixed racial descent including African, Afro-Caribbean, and European ancestors

CRESCENDO: Gradually get louder

CUBOP: A fusion of Afro-Cuban music and bebop pioneered by trumpeters Dizzy Gillespie and Mario Bauzá

CUP MUTE: A cardboard mute placed in the bell of a brass instrument to alter the sound

CUTTING CONTEST: An informal contest among musicians in which each tries to outplay the other

D–E

DECRESCENDO: Gradually get softer

DOUBLE: The ability to play more than one instrument

DOWNTOWN: Musical compositions and performances that are experimental, out of the music mainstream, and often improvisational

DROPPING BOMBS: In bebop, a loud, hard accent on the bass drum

DRUM: A percussion instrument consisting of a membrane stretched over a hollow body

DRUM KIT: A set of drums and cymbals typically consisting of bass, snare, and tom-tom drums and hi-hat, crash, and ride cymbals

DYNAMICS: The loudness or softness of a section of a piece of music

ELISION: The blurring of the division of phrases or sections in a musical work so that they appear to overlap

ELLINGTON EFFECT: Unique arranging style pioneered by Duke Ellington that emphasized interesting and unique combinations of instruments, as well as writing for these instruments to play in unusual parts of their range

ETHNOMUSICOLOGY: A scholarly field that examines music from a variety of perspectives, including anthropology, sociology, and traditional musical analysis

F

FEEDBACK: Literally the interference of two electrical signals that results in an unintended sound. In rock music, feedback can be created when a guitarist intentionally holds an instrument in front of its amplifier to create often loud, intense electronic sounds.

FENDER RHODES: An electric piano. Instead of strings, it features metal coils (called *tines*) that the hammers strike to produce each tone; the sound is then electrically amplified. The instrument was popular among jazz and pop players during the late 1960s and 1970s.

FILL: A short melodic phrase used to "fill" a gap in the main melody

FLUGELHORN: A member of the trumpet family that is larger than a trumpet and quite dark and mellow, with a full, rich tone

FORM: The shape of a piece of music

FREE JAZZ: Jazz movement of the late 1950s and early 1960s that sought to break free of the harmonic, melodic, and improvisation rules of earlier jazz styles

FUSION: The combination of elements of rock, popular music, and funk with jazz, particularly the incorporation of electric instruments, synthesizers, and pop rhythms

G

GHOST BAND: A band that continues to perform under the same name after the death of its original leader

GIGS: Musicians' slang for jobs

GROUP OR FREE IMPROVISATION: Freely created music by the performers themselves, at times without a pre-arranged or agreed-on structure; this style is particularly found in **free jazz**.

GUITAR: A stringed instrument with either a hollow or a solid body and a long, fretted neck

GUTBUCKET: A bluesy style associated with early New Orleans bands along with the early bands led by Duke Ellington, particularly in the growling trumpet style of Bubber Miley

H–I

HARD BOP: A style of jazz that featured a blues and R&B influence, with a hard and urban edge, generally associated with East Coast musicians

HARLEM STRIDE PIANO: An early virtuosic piano style with roots in Harlem

HARMOLODICS: A theory developed by Ornette Coleman in which melody, harmony, and rhythm are treated equally in performance

HARMON MUTE: A metal mute that constricts the sound of the trumpet and gives it an intense, buzzy quality

HARMONY: The simultaneous combining of notes to create chords

HEAD: The first melody in a jazz composition

HEAD ARRANGEMENTS: Unwritten arrangements that generally are developed on the bandstand as the band plays

HORN: A wind instrument

HOT JAZZ: Jazz that emphasizes its swinging, syncopated nature over the melodies; music that is meant for dancing

IMPRESSIONISM: A style of early twentieth-century classical music influenced by the impressionistic painters that featured slow-moving melodies and lush chords

IMPROVISATION: The spontaneous composition of music

INDIVIDUAL EXPRESSION: A personal tone and a unique vocabulary that distinguishes one jazz musician from others

J–K–L

JAM SESSION: An informal gathering in which musicians get the opportunity to experiment with new musical ideas

JAZZ–ROCK FUSION. *See also* **fusion**

JUNGLE STYLE: Associated with Duke Ellington's early bands, the jungle style described the lead instruments' use of mutes, "growling," and other "animal" sounds to enhance the "exotic" nature of the music

KEYBOARD: A term used to refer to both electronic and acoustic pianos and synthesizers

KLEZMER MUSIC: A popular form of music that combines influences of eastern European Jewish melodies and harmony with 1920s- to 1930s-era jazz

LEAD ALTO: The lead alto saxophonist heads the saxophone section, setting the phrasing and style, and along with the lead trumpet is crucial to a band's sound

LEAD SHEET: A compact notation system that notates the most important elements of a piece

LEGATO: Smoothly played; each note is connected to each other; *contrast* **staccato**

M

MAINSTREAM JAZZ: Since the 1960s, a term used to describe the music created by a core group of artists who most jazz fans universally accept as definitive interpreters of the style

MAMBO: A Cuban dance and musical style popularized in the late 1940s and early 1950s. Also, instrumental interludes within a composition that include new written material.

MELODY The combining of pitches and rhythm to create a musical line

METER: The organization of beats into recurring patterns

MODAL JAZZ: A style of jazz associated with Miles Davis's album *Kind of Blue*, where the melody and harmonies are based on modes rather than modern major and minor scales

MONTUNO: A repeated figure that is a common formal element in Latin music and Latin jazz

MOTIVIC WRITING: A form of musical composition in which musical motives, or ideas, are used many times in a varied manner

N–O

NEO-CLASSICAL OR NEO-TRADITIONAL: Looking to the classic jazz of the past to confirm important values for contemporary jazz. The neo-traditional movement pointed to the recordings of Louis Armstrong and Duke Ellington as ideals for jazz performance, along with emphasizing jazz's African American roots, particularly in the blues.

ODD TIME SIGNATURES: Time signatures that have an odd number of beats with asymmetrical groupings within them such as 5/4 or 7/8

OFFBEAT: The weaker beats in a 4/4 measure, or beats 2 and 4

OSTINATO: A repeated melodic or rhythmic figure that is usually performed by the accompanying instruments as the base for the soloist's work

OUT-CHORUS: The last chorus or partial chorus of a tune when everyone plays forcefully for climactic effect

P–Q

PAD: An aural landscape or sound field that is created usually by a synthesizer or electric keyboard player to support the melody instruments

PHRASE: A section of the melody that expresses a musical thought

PHRASING: How musicians take breaths and articulate a melody, usually to outline a musical phrase

PIANO: A musical instrument that is played using a keyboard

PIANO TRIO: A small jazz group, most often consisting of piano, bass, and drums

PIZZICATO STRINGS: The strings are plucked with the fingers instead of bowed

PLAYING IN 2: A term for the bass playing beats 1 and 3 in 4/4 time

PLAYING IN 4: A term for the bass playing all four beats in 4/4 time. Also called **walking bass**

POLYPHONY: The simultaneous performance of two or more melodies

POLYRHYTHM: Two or more rhythmic patterns played simultaneously

PROGRESSIVE JAZZ: A style of jazz popularized in the late 1940s and 1950s characterized by the use of compositional resources more often associated with classical music, such as extended forms and the use of varied orchestral instruments

R

"RAGGING" (A MELODY): Taking a popular melody and adding **syncopated** rhythms to it to give it a more danceable feeling

RAGTIME: A multisection musical composition that features **syncopated** rhythms

RENT PARTIES: Informal gatherings in which neighbors were charged a small admission fee to enjoy food, liquor, and music as a means of raising money to pay the rent

REVERB: An electronic effect that adds a slight echo to a sound, giving it a richer flavor

RHYTHM: The patterns of sound durations in music

RHYTHM CHANGES: A chord progression based upon the George Gershwin song "I Got Rhythm"

RHYTHM SECTION: The part of a band that provides a rhythmic and harmonic accompaniment for the tunes' melodies and soloists

RIDE CYMBAL: A cymbal used to maintain the regular pulse of the music, as opposed to those used to provide an accent or "crash." It is usually placed on the far right-hand side of the drum set.

RIFF: A short, catchy melodic phrase

RUBATO: Playing with a flexible rhythmic sense; loosely following the tempo to give the music a relaxed feeling

RUMBA: Cuban dance style popularized in the United States during the 1930s by Latin bands

S

SALSA: Latin dance style based on the Cuban **son** that was developed in Latino communities in America during the early 1970s

SAMBA: A quick, yet relaxed Brazilian dance music that combines African and European march-like elements

SAXOPHONE: A metallic member of the woodwind family that comes in a wide variety of sizes, including baritone sax, tenor sax, alto sax, and soprano sax

SCAT SINGING: Wordless improvised vocal line often imitating the sound of a musical instrument

SCHILLINGER SYSTEM: A twentieth-century theory of composition and performance developed by theorist Joseph Schillinger that has been embraced by some jazz composers and performers

SHEETS OF SOUND: A term used to describe John Coltrane's solo style, including rapidly played arpeggios and scales that moved from the lowest to the highest ranges of the instrument

SHOUT CHORUS: A climactic ensemble statement that embellishes the tune in some way during the final chorus (or part of the final chorus)

SHUFFLE: A lightly swinging rhythm found in blues, soul, and R&B music

SIGHT-READ: The ability to play a piece of music directly from the written part without previous practice

SLAP-TONGUE: Saxophone technique in which the player would pop the reed with his or her tongue to create a percussive effect

SMOOTH JAZZ: A jazz style popularized by artists like Kenny G that emphasizes pleasing melodies with a light jazz rhythm accompaniment

SON: Traditional Cuban instrumental style that influenced the development of **salsa** music in the United States

SONG PLUGGER: A musician (often a singer-pianist) hired by a music publisher to promote its latest songs so that other performers will record or play them

SOUL JAZZ: A subgenre of **hard bop** that incorporates blues, gospel, soul, and R&B influences into jazz

SOUNDIES: Short films featuring popular singers and bands that were originally played on special jukeboxes, somewhat equivalent to modern music videos

SPEAKEASY: Illegal bar serving alcoholic beverages and often featuring musical performers during the Prohibition era (1918–1932)

STACCATO: The articulation of short, detached notes; *contrast* **legato**

STOCK ARRANGEMENT: An arrangement for large ensemble, usually with flexible instrumentation, made available to the public by a publisher, often arranged by staff arrangers

STRAIGHT MUTE: A hollow metal cone that fits into the bell of a trumpet (or other brass instrument) to dampen its "brassy" sound, creating a more nasal effect

STROLLING: A soloist accompanied just by bass and drums (removing the usual piano or guitar) to create a different texture in performance

STROPHE: Verse

STROPHIC FORM: Musical form in which the lyrics change but the accompanying melody repeats unchanged

STYLIST: An instrumentalist, composer, or arranger with a recognizable sound, playing style, compositional approach, and perhaps even arranging technique

SWEET JAZZ: Less syncopated and less swinging music, emphasizing the melodies of popular tunes of the day

SWING: The propulsive rhythm, or "groove," of jazz music

SYMPHONIC JAZZ: A melding of jazz, music for the theater, popular music, music for movies, and classical music that includes introducing jazz instrumentation, rhythms, and solo styles into a more conventional orchestral setting

SYNCOPATED RHYTHMS/SYNCOPATION: Accenting the weak or **offbeats** in a measure

T

TAILGATE TROMBONE/TAILGATING: Exaggerated sliding notes played on a trombone that create a unique sonic and rhythmic effect

TERRITORY BANDS: Bands that had an area they were known for touring regularly; only rarely did they achieve national celebrity

TEXTURE: The number of instrumental voices sounding simultaneously

THIRD STREAM: A term created by composer-conductor-scholar Gunther Schuller to describe works that deliberately fused classical and jazz composition

THROUGH COMPOSED: Used to describe a composition that is written without formal repetitions

TIMBALERO: A player of the **timbales**

TIMBALES: A pair of single-headed, high-pitched drums used in Latin dance music

TIMBRE: The "color" or character of sound

TÍPICO: Literally "typical"; used to describe a typical style of a Latin instrumental soloist or a Latin-flavored dance band, including its use of **polyrhythms**

TRADE 4S: Two soloists exchange 4-bar melodies in succession

TRANSCRIBED/TRANSCRIPTION: Writing down in musical notation a musical performance; generally improvised solos were not part of a musical score, so they had to be transcribed off of recordings or from live performances

TREMOLO: A fast alternation of two notes

TROMBONE: A member of the brass family with a lower register that can cover parts of the ranges of bass, baritone, and tenor vocalists

TRUMPET: A member of the brass instrument family and in the range of an alto or soprano voice

TURNAROUND: A series of chords that lead to a new section of a composition.

12-BAR BLUES: Common blues form that features three 4-measure phrases with the lyrics (or melody) repeating for the first 2 phrases and a third phrase that responds, creating a compact AAB form

U–V

UPTOWN: In music, implies a more academic and studied approach, generally with a connection to Western classical music

URBAN OR ELECTRIC BLUES: Country blues adapted by urban musicians and performed in small groups, often consisting of electric guitar, bass, piano, harmonica, and drums

VAMP: A repeated rhythmic or melodic figure

VIBRATO: An intentionally controlled waver in pitch of a player's tone

VOCALESE: Creating lyrics for well-known jazz solos

W–X–Y–Z

WALKING BASS: *See* **playing in 4**

INDEX